Guide to Criminal Procedure
for Florida

Glenn S. Coffey

University of North Florida

THOMSON

WADSWORTH

Australia • Canada • Mexico • Singapore • Spain • United Kingdom • United States

Executive Editor: Sabra Horne
Development Editor: Julie Sakaue
Assistant Editor: Jana Davis
Editorial Assistant: Elise Smith
Marketing Manager: Terra Schultz
Marketing Assistant: Annabelle Yang

Project Manager, Editorial Production: Megan E. Hansen
Print Buyer: Rebecca Cross
Permissions Editor: Kiely Sexton
Cover Designer: Yvo Riezebos
Cover Image: Donovan Reese/Getty Images
Text and Cover Printer: Thomson West

Printed in the United States of America
1 2 3 4 5 6 7   08 07 06 05 04

For more information about our products,
contact us at:
Thomson Learning Academic Resource Center
1-800-423-0563

For permission to use material from this text or product,
submit a request online at
http://www.thomsonrights.com.

Any additional questions about permissions
can be submitted by email to
thomsonrights@thomson.com.

Library of Congress Control Number: 2004110841

ISBN: 0-534-64345-0

Thomson Wadsworth
10 Davis Drive
Belmont, CA 94002-3098
USA

Asia
Thomson Learning
5 Shenton Way #01-01
UIC Building
Singapore 068808

Australia/New Zealand
Thomson Learning
102 Dodds Street
Southbank, Victoria 3006
Australia

Canada
Nelson
1120 Birchmount Road
Toronto, Ontario M1K 5G4
Canada

Europe/Middle East/South Africa
Thomson Learning
High Holborn House
50/51 Bedford Row
London WC1R 4LR
United Kingdom

Latin America
Thomson Learning
Seneca, 53
Colonia Polanco
11560 Mexico D.F.
Mexico

Spain/Portugal
Paraninfo
Calle/Magallanes, 25
28015 Madrid, Spain

<u>Acknowledgements</u>

I would like to express my sincere appreciation to Dr. Lisa Anne Zilney, Southern Illinois University – Carbondale, for her invaluable contribution to this manuscript. Her efforts were truly essential to the completion of this project.

I would also like to thank *Fastcase* [www.fastcase.com] and Lisa Bruno [North Florida Representative] for providing a most efficient and affordable legal search engine to assist in this process.

Table of Contents

Introduction

OVERVIEW

This guide elaborates criminal procedure in the state of Florida. As such, this guide provides:

(1)   Detailed examination of the Florida Constitution;

(2)   An elaboration of the *Florida Rules of Criminal Procedure*; and

(3)   Florida cases to develop further an understanding of criminal procedures and its applications.

CONCEPTUAL FRAMEWORK OF THIS TEXT

Each chapter in this guide is organized in the same format and is designed to parallel issues examined in your text. This guide assumes that you have read materials on criminal procedure and understand the basic principles. Each chapter is organized into sections and each section comprises the following:

(1)   An overview of the main issues addressed in this particular area of criminal procedure. This overview will include relevant sections of the Florida Constitution as well as a delineation of the applicable *Florida Rules of Criminal Procedure*; and

(2)   One or two cases from the Florida courts that address specifically the main issues of each section. Each case is prefaced by a brief introduction to alert you to the main criminal procedure addressed by the court. Following each case are several reading comprehension questions to assess your basic knowledge of the case and the facts presented, as well as critical thinking questions designed to further develop your comprehensive of the procedures and their application.

This guide should prove a useful supplement to general criminal procedure and provide you with a more in-depth understanding of the workings of criminal procedure in Florida.

Chapter One

Criminal Procedure: The Big Picture

In a constitutional democracy such as the United States, crime control is a balance between the search for truth and a commitment to fairness that limits governmental power. This power is limited by the U.S. Constitution and state constitutions and is interpreted by the U.S. Supreme Court. Historically and presently, balancing result and process creates tension as individual liberties sometimes interfere with community security. Thus, there is a continual shift between government power and individual rights, process and result. What results is a shift in balance between formal and informal criminal procedures, and so long as the general principles put forth in the U.S. Constitution are maintained, the Florida Constitution may act to expand these individual freedoms. In the quest for truth and fairness, procedure is continually reinterpreted in the state and federal court system.

Because we address here the larger picture, rather than a view from the state level, we will focus primarily on the role of the Constitution. This chapter will review:

(1)   The balance between order and liberty; and

(2)   Laws, discretion, due process, and precedent.

SECTION 1: THE BALANCE

OVERVIEW

In our critical examination of criminal procedure and the government's power over crime control, we must keep in mind that the United States is a constitutional democracy wherein neither a single individual nor a majority of the citizens have power over us as individuals. A balance must continually be struck between community security, which ensures the safety of all community members, and individual autonomy, where individuals have the right of control over themselves and their actions so long as these actions do not compromise the security of the larger community. The balance between government power and individual control is one that is very flexible, changes over time and with historical circumstance, and one that falls within a zone as opposed to a point on a continuum. Thus, the courts move within this balance between order and liberty.

In a constitutional democracy, crime control also depends on the balance between result and process. The result side of this balance involves a search for the truth, consisting of the apprehension, conviction, and punishment of guilty individuals, and the freeing of innocent people caught in the criminal justice system. The process side of the balance involves a commitment to fairness that limits the power of the government and is outlined in the U.S. Constitution and in every state constitution. The Constitution acts as a set of general principles that are interpreted in the final analysis by the U.S. Supreme Court.

Balancing result and process has historically and continues to create tension as individual liberties may interfere with the protection of community security. Thus, on occasion a guilty party will go free in order to ensure that government control stays within its bounds. In a constitutional democracy however, the priority is not crime control, but fair process, except in situations involving extreme emergencies such as war wherein the Bill of Rights can be disregarded. This was evident and continues to be evident during the government's war on drugs and the current war on terrorism which we be discussed later. The foundation of ensuring fairness in procedure is the exclusionary rule which forces the court to throw out evidence of a defendant's guilt if the methods by which the evidence were obtained were in violation of the U.S. or state Constitutions. The exclusionary rule is used only in the United States and while it is at the root of criminal procedure as will be seen in many cases, it is also extremely controversial. No system, historically or currently, has succeeded in balancing perfectly the tension between government power and individual rights.

In the United States, the Constitution became an infamous effort to embed in law a balance between government power and individual liberty. Anti-Federalists however, feared relying on such a general protection, and thus added the Bill of Rights as an amendment to further protect the liberty of individuals against the potential abuses of government power. Each state's Bill of Rights has similar or identical provisions to those in the U.S. Bill of Rights, and it is the role of the state courts to interpret and apply these constitutional provisions as will be illustrated through the examination of cases throughout this guide.

Enhanced government power prior to the 1960s eventually led to the due process revolution which moved the balance back to process and individual rights. Critics argued this created a criminal justice system that was soft on crime and the pendulum began to swing back to result in the early 1970s nationwide. One cannot simply explain the movement between process and result as occurring from the personal beliefs of individual judges. Instead, judges are to defer to the will of the citizenry as expressed by elected officials in a historic principle called judicial restraint. Increasingly judges have accomplished this by deferring to elected branches of government.

CASE

The *Keen* case gives you an example of the balance between process and result in Florida. Little has been edited from the case and thus it is very factually detailed. When you read the case, consider the balance the previous courts were trying to strike and the opinion of the Supreme Court of Florida.

KEEN V. STATE OF FLORIDA
Supreme Court of Florida
775 So.2d 263 (Fla. 2000)

We have on appeal the judgment and sentence of the trial court imposing the death penalty upon appellant Michael Scott Keen (Keen). We have jurisdiction. Art. V, 3(b)(1), Fla. Const. For the reasons expressed below, we reverse Keen's first-degree murder conviction, vacate his sentence of death and remand for further proceedings consistent with this opinion.

This is the third time this case has been before us. Keen was originally indicted in 1984 and charged with first-degree murder in the death of his wife, Anita Lopez Keen. After Keen was convicted and sentenced to death, we reversed both the conviction and sentence on appeal and remanded for a new trial based on prosecutorial misconduct. On remand, Keen was again convicted of first-degree murder and sentenced to death. As in the first appeal, we again reversed and remanded for a new trial based on the presence of unauthorized materials in the jury room, and the trial court's failure to conduct an in-camera inspection of the grand jury testimony of the State's star witness. In the second retrial, Keen was once again convicted and the jury recommended a sentence of life imprisonment without possibility of parole for twenty-five years. The trial judge held a sentencing hearing and imposed a sentence of death, overriding the jury's advisory sentence of life imprisonment.

The evidence against Keen adduced at trial was primarily based on the testimony of Ken Shapiro. When Shapiro first moved to Florida in 1978 he was hired by Keen. Shortly thereafter Keen invited Shapiro to become his roommate, which continued, with one brief interruption, until at least the end of 1981. According to Shapiro, some time in 1980 Keen informed him that he wished to retire before the age of forty and the easiest way to accomplish this would be to find an unsuspecting girl, marry her, insure her life, murder her and then invest the proceeds. Keen met the victim, Anita Lopez, in late summer of 1980. Lopez was then twenty-one years old, Cuban born and worked in a tractor factory. After Keen began seeing Lopez regularly, he told Shapiro, "I feel Anita is the girl." Shortly thereafter, Lopez moved in with Keen and Shapiro at their Ft. Lauderdale home. By early 1981 Keen began to discuss with Shapiro the actual manner in which his plan could be accomplished. Keen's first suggestion was to push the victim off a high building, but eventually drowning was decided upon. In June 1981, two separate insurance policies were taken out each insuring Anita Lopez's life for $50,000. Both policies contained double indemnity provisions in case Lopez met an accidental death and both policies named Keen as the primary beneficiary.

Keen and Lopez were married on August 1, 1981. Shortly thereafter it was discovered that Lopez was pregnant which, according to Shapiro's testimony, forced Keen to accelerate the plan. Shapiro testified that Keen threatened to kill him or his grandparents if he went to the authorities. In late October or early November of 1981 Keen informed Shapiro that if Sunday November 15 was a nice day, he would proceed with the plan. Sometime in the late morning or early afternoon of the 15th, Keen and the victim left their canal-front home and traveled in Keen's boat through the inter-coastal waterway, and stopped at a waterfront bar. Shortly thereafter, Shapiro arrived at the bar. After some time, the three boarded the boat and headed out into the ocean. When the boat was approximately fifteen to eighteen miles out, Keen, who had been driving, put the boat in neutral, walked to where the victim was standing and pushed her from behind into the ocean. Keen kept the boat out of the victim's range. According to Shapiro, the plan was to actually watch the victim drown so that her body could be recovered and Keen could then collect the insurance proceeds, however darkness set in and they lost sight of the victim. They returned to Keen's backyard dock whereupon Shapiro called the Coast Guard and the Broward County Sheriff's office. Keen gave statements to the authorities that at some point the victim, who was four to five months pregnant at the time, went down into the cabin below to rest and that when they returned home, she was not there. A week later Shapiro gave a sworn statement to the sheriff's office corroborating Keen's version of an unexplained accident. Shapiro also repeated the story to an attorney hired by Keen to initiate the insurance claims process.

The next time Shapiro gave a statement concerning these events was in August 1984 when he related the same version of events that he later testified to at trial. Following Shapiro's August 1984 statement Broward County Detectives Scheff and Amabile arrested Keen who was living under an assumed name in Seminole County.

The Broward County Sheriff's Office began an investigation in August 1984 because they "received information from two insurance companies that they had received information that the case was not a missing persons case, but a murder." During questioning, Keen provided several versions of what had transpired on the boat, beginning with his 1981 statement that Anita was not found upon return to the dock. His second version of the events described Anita and him standing on the side of the boat when they were shoved into the ocean. Keen then allegedly stated that he swam back to the boat, assumed the controls of the vessel from Shapiro who was "frozen like a zombie at the controls," returned to the area where they had been pushed overboard, and began searching for Anita. They returned home only after an hour of fruitless searching. Keen maintained that what transpired at sea was an accident.

Michael Moran, a convicted felon, testified that Keen asked him to kill Shapiro. Moran expected to be released soon from a prior sentence and he allegedly was to confront Shapiro, make him write a confession and a suicide note, and then hang him. Moran also related that he was to receive $20,000 for his services. The State placed in evidence an envelope that Moran claimed contained his handwriting as well as that of Keen. Moran's Broward County armed robbery charge was ultimately dropped after he testified against Keen. He is currently serving a life sentence without possibility of parole in Michigan for first-degree murder.

At trial, the defense presented no testimony, Keen chose not to testify after being advised of his constitutional rights by the trial judge. The State presented no evidence during the penalty phase. The defense read the testimony of Keen's mother into evidence. The defense also introduced official Department of Corrections' records showing that Keen had only one minor disciplinary infraction since his incarceration in the state prison system in 1985. The State presented no rebuttal evidence. During appeal, Keen raises claims of error, several of which we resolve summarily. We address the remaining issues in turn.

Motion for Mistrial after Introduction of Hearsay

The State argues that the subject matter of the testimony challenged was not hearsay because it was not elicited to prove the truth of the matter asserted, but only to show a sequence of events. We reject such contention. First, this Court clearly instructed that an alleged sequence of events leading to an investigation and an arrest is not a material issue in this type of case. Therefore, there is no relevancy for such testimony to prove or establish such a non-issue. When the only possible relevance of an out-of-court statement is directed to the truth of the matters stated by a declarant, the subject matter is classic hearsay even though the proponent of such evidence seeks to clothe such hearsay under a non-hearsay label.

Second, facts concerning the purported determination by insurance companies after investigation that this case involved a murder, not an accident, were used by the State during closing argument for substantive support not "sequence of events" purposes. Thus, regardless of the purpose for which the State now claims the testimony to have been directed, the evidence was in fact used to prove the truth of the content rendering the content of the statement hearsay.

Next, with the predicate of this Court having previously announced on numerous occasions that the admission of this type of evidence is inherently prejudicial, it must be determined if this issue has been properly preserved for review and the standard of review applicable for proper determination. Initially, although the sequence of events in the investigation leading to an arrest was not a material issue in this case, the preliminary question directed to Detective Amabile as to why an investigation was revived was not facially objectionable upon the basis of clearly calling for hearsay testimony. Had the detective simply referred to the event (phone call or tip), without blurting out the hearsay content (insurance company investigation determined that a murder had occurred), a hearsay objection would not have been appropriate. If the relevance was only directed to a sequence of events, the officer could state no more than the existence of a "tip" or generally that information had been received.

The misdirection of the issue did not terminate with the detective's initial statement, but the State then immediately proceeded to connect the inadmissible accusatory information to Keen's brother and then immediately to Shapiro and then to Keen. As soon as the State proceeded to create a nexus between Keen's brother and the insurance investigation which had concluded that a "murder" had occurred, an objection was voiced and a request for mistrial was submitted and denied. This Court has repeatedly admonished that the admission of this type of evidence is inherently prejudicial. In the present case, the inadmissible matter was injected by the State through volunteered testimony of an experienced detective. The nature of the inadmissible materials here consisting of very harmful hearsay evidence indicating that the defendant was guilty of the crime charged is far more egregious and harmful than the admission of material directed to an unrelated collateral wrong. We conclude that the State's position would create an unacceptable approach which would permit the State to receive the benefit of volunteered hearsay testimony directed to the guilt of the defendant of the crime charged. This type of evidence simply should not have been permitted, and when the motion for mistrial was made after such evidence came before the jury, a mistrial should have been granted. For these reasons, the State's analysis of the hearsay issue cannot be accepted under these circumstances.

In this case, the jury could have legitimately relied on Shapiro's extensive testimony, the circumstantial evidence of the two insurance policies on Anita Keen, and Michael Moran's testimony. However, we should not ignore the direct relationship between the erroneous introduction of the out-of-court statements and Shapiro's devastating testimony, especially where the credibility of the two principals to the crime was the key issue in the case. The out-of-court statements produced by the State provided a strong foundation that bolstered and supported Shapiro's detailed account of the planning and execution of Anita's murder. In essence, the State was able to present three witnesses for the price of one, with the bonus that only Shapiro testified and was subject to cross-examination. Patrick Keen never took the stand, nor did the insurance company representatives who forwarded the information that this was not a missing persons case, but a "murder."

The State repeatedly reminded the jury during closing argument that claims for life insurance benefits were pending against the insurance companies with Keen having filed a petition to have Anita presumed dead to collect benefits. This line of argument, of necessity, inherently flowed from the State's theory of this case which was predicated upon a homicide to obtain life insurance proceeds. In the concluding moments of the State's rebuttal argument, the jury's attention was again directed to the investigating detective being advised by the insurance company that Anita Keen's disappearance was a homicide, not an accident. The closing argument was certainly less detailed than Detective Amabile's testimony, but the jury was again informed of the out-of-court statement that Keen had engaged in the criminal activity for which he was being prosecuted. The closing argument, however brief, related the same highly prejudicial elements placed before the jury by Amabile's testimony, i.e., the insurance companies obtained information that Anita's death was a "murder" not an accident. Although it was unstated during the closing argument that the information came from Patrick Keen, that point had been unambiguously made during Amabile's testimony. This was highly prejudicial with no countervailing probative value. Thus, this evidence was hearsay, it was not relevant, and its probative value was far surpassed by its prejudicial impact. These factors all lead to the inescapable conclusion that the conviction must be reversed and the case remanded to the trial court.

Penalty Phase – Jury Override

The trial judge overrode the jury's life recommendation. Keen argues that this was error because there were several reasonable bases for the jury's recommendation. Although two juries previously recommended imposition of a death sentence, the very rigid standard established by this Court requires that we agree with Keen's position. The appropriate standard in analyzing a jury override is well-known: "To sustain a jury override, this Court must conclude that the facts suggesting a sentence of death are 'so clear and convincing that virtually no reasonable person could differ.'" San Martin v. State, 717 So. 2d 462, 471 (Fla. 1998). In other words, we must reverse the override if there is a reasonable basis in the record to support the jury's recommendation of life." In that manner, the narrow inquiry to which we are bound honors the underlying principle that this jury's advisory sentence reflected the "conscience of the community" at the time of this trial. The trial judge's sentencing order is thoughtful and well written; he obviously considered his decision in a very deliberative, serious manner. Reasonable arguments can certainly be presented to support his order. However, we find that the standards for weighing aggravators and mitigators in a death recommendation case have been transposed with those applicable to consideration of a jury recommendation of life imprisonment. The following passage from the sentencing order illustrates the trial judge's reasoning: The Court finds the evidence in mitigation is minimal compared to the magnitude of the crime that has been committed by the defendant. In the final analysis, the mitigating circumstances found to exist have no relationship to the crime committed to such a degree that the jury could reasonably conclude life is a proper penalty.

Furthermore, the jury's decision during the guilt phase of this proceeding essentially disregards any theory that the death of Anita Keen was accidental. If the jury believed that the victim's death was the result of premeditated murder, then the cold and calculated plan to kill her must necessarily outweigh the mitigating circumstances presented by the defense. This Court can only conclude that the jury's hasty recommendation of life indicates that it was based on something other than the sound reasoned judgment required in such cases. Had the jury considered the aggravating and mitigating circumstances, the facts suggesting a sentence of death are so clear and convincing that virtually no reasonable person could differ. The mitigating evidence is wholly insufficient to outweigh the aggravating circumstances in support of a life sentence.

The last line emphasized above indicates that the wrong standard was ultimately applied in consideration of the jury's life recommendation. The singular focus of a Tedder inquiry is whether there is "a reasonable basis in the record to support the jury's recommendation of life," rather than the weighing process which a judge conducts after a death recommendation. Here, we reject the implicit determination that no reasonable juror could find that Shapiro's disparate treatment militated in favor of a life sentence for Keen. To begin, Keen notes that the trial judge cited Campbell v. State, 571 So. 2d 415 (Fla. 1990), a death recommendation case, for the proposition that "disparate treatment of an equally culpable accomplice is a non-statutory mitigating factor which can serve as a basis for a jury's recommendation of life." He argues, and we agree, that this proposition of law was then used to erroneously narrow the definition of what a juror can reasonably consider as disparate treatment. From that faulty premise, the conclusion was then reached that based upon the court's view of the facts, disparate treatment could not be a reasonable basis for a life recommendation because Shapiro was neither "a willing or equally culpable accomplice," citing Colina v. State, 634 So. 2d 1077 (Fla. 1994), another death recommendation case.

Consequently, the focus of the analysis was not upon finding support for the jury's recommendation, i.e., determining if a reasonable basis existed for the jury's decision, but rather toward proving that the jury got it wrong and lacked any reasonable basis to recommend life. In other words, the trial judge disagreed with their recommendation based on his view of the mix of aggravators and mitigators, rather than through the prism of a Tedder analysis. This was error, because just as a Tedder inquiry has no place in a death recommendation case, Franqui v. State, 699 So. 2d 1312, 1327 (Fla. 1997) (rejecting reliance on jury override cases in death recommendation case because such cases "entail a wholly different legal principle and analysis"); Watts v. State, 593 So. 2d 198, 204 (Fla. 1992), the reciprocal holds true when a jury life recommendation is independently analyzed by the trial court and independently reviewed by this Court. In other words, the jury's life recommendation changes the analytical dynamic and magnifies the ultimate effect of mitigation on the defendant's sentence.

In full recognition that Keen was almost certainly the more blameworthy of the two principals, we cannot ignore the fact that Shapiro's participation was an essential element of the planned crime. That is, without Shapiro, Keen's plan to push his wife overboard, allow her to drown, and recover her body as "evidence" of an accident for double indemnity purposes would have never proceeded to the ultimate act. Shapiro testified that the plan was that he would be a witness to Anita's "accidental" death to support Keen in his subsequent insurance claim. The jury could have also seized on Shapiro's admission that he drove the boat away from Anita after Keen pushed her into the water, thus directly injecting himself into the murderous episode and leaving Anita to her fate.

In addition, a reasonable juror could have thought that Shapiro had numerous opportunities to report Keen's plan to the police, but did not because he saw Keen's scheme as a way to absolve his own indebtedness. The end result was that Shapiro colluded with Keen's plan, Anita Keen died in the open sea, and Shapiro walked free and clear of criminal prosecution. Therefore, in light of these undisputed facts presented during the co-perpetrator's own testimony, the decision to downplay the disparate treatment mitigating factor as having "no relationship to the crime committed" seems, at best, a very dubious proposition. Moreover, it ignores our well-settled definition of a mitigating factor as being proffered matters "relevant to the defendant's character or record, or to the circumstances of the offense."

Shapiro's credibility problems could have also served to mitigate Keen's crime, as he was an admitted perjurer who had changed his version of events over time. We have previously found this to be a reasonable basis for a life recommendation. Likewise, a reasonable jury could have believed that Keen evidenced a good potential for rehabilitation based on his largely productive life and good prison record. Such a determination could only have been further bolstered by the fact that the State presented nothing to rebut the evidence that Keen had lived a successful, productive, and law-abiding life prior to Anita's murder.

In the final analysis, there are several reasonable bases upon which a reasonable juror could rely to support the life recommendation. While any of us might or might not have come to the same conclusion with regard to the imposition of a death sentence based upon the evidence presented in this case had we been jurors, that is not the legal standard by which we must evaluate the override of the jury's recommendation. To be sure, the "vast mitigation" found in other cases, is not present here, but certainly enough mitigation exists upon which a reasonable juror could rely to warrant reversal under Tedder. Thus, we find that the trial court erred in overriding the jury's life recommendation.

In conjunction with our reversal for a new trial on the hearsay claim, our reversal on this issue precludes the State from again seeking the death penalty against Keen for this crime. Monge v. California, 524 U.S. 721 (1998) (reaffirming Eighth Amendment prohibition against seeking death penalty on retrial where original sentencer imposed a life sentence). We so direct because "[w]hen it is determined on appeal that the trial court should have accepted a jury's recommendation of life imprisonment pursuant to Tedder, the defendant must be deemed acquitted of the death penalty for double jeopardy purposes" Wright v. State, 586 So. 2d 1024, 1032 (Fla. 1991). Consequently, if Keen is retried for Anita's murder, he may not again be subjected to the death penalty.

Conclusion

Based upon the foregoing reasoning, we reverse the first-degree murder conviction, vacate the sentence of death, and remand further proceedings consistent with this opinion. It is so ordered.

SHAW, HARDING, ANSTEAD, PARIENTE and LEWIS, JJ., concur. WELLS, C.J., concurs in part and dissents in part with an opinion, in which QUINCE, J., concurs.

REVIEW SECTION

READING COMPREHENSION

Articulate the claims of error that Keen raised during appeal and how each was addressed by the Court.

What reasoning was employed by the Supreme Court of Florida to reverse the first-degree murder conviction, vacate the sentence of death, and remand further proceedings?

THINKING CRITICALLY

Do you believe the Supreme Court of Florida leaned more toward process or result in deciding this case? Articulate your position.

SECTION 2: LAWS, DISCRETION, DUE PROCESS, AND PRECEDENT

OVERVIEW

As the balance shifts between process and result, so does the balance between formal and informal criminal procedures. Formal criminal procedure is concerned with the rules as written in the Constitution, laws, judicial precedents, and other written sources. Conversely, informal criminal procedure or discretionary decision making is concerned with unwritten rules made by professionals based on training and experience. Informal criminal procedure is how the system works on a day-to-day basis with each step creating a decision for a professional in the criminal justice system. The only limit to discretionary decision making is that it cannot violate the general principles put forth in the U.S. Constitution.

Discretionary decision making is extremely important in softening written rules, yet fairness and predictability require the certainty and protection provided by such rules. In essence, informal criminal procedures are used to counter balance actions that technically violate a written rule but were not intended by the legislature to be illegal. It is impossible to predict the myriad of ramifications of each statute enacted. Thus, discretion and written law work together to promote a balance between process and result intended to capture the spirit of legislation.

Discretion however, is not entirely discretionary. The objective basis requirement ensures that the government employ facts to support each restraint on individual liberty. In addition, as the limit to be imposed on individuals increases, so does the fact basis required for support. The law may only deprive an individual of life, liberty, privacy, and property according to fair procedures, known as hearing before condemnation. Such judicial review, or review by the court of the actions of other branches of government to ensure such actions comply with the

Constitution, is essential to the legal system. This review occurs at all stages of the criminal justice system and is known as due process.

According to Section Nine of the Florida Constitution, due process entails:

> No person shall be deprived of life, liberty or property without due process of law, or be twice put in jeopardy for the same offense, or be compelled in any criminal matter to be a witness against oneself.

In order to maximize fairness and predictability, judges are bound by *stare decisis*. This requires judges to adhere to the precedent of either their own court or superior courts within their jurisdiction. While courts do alter precedent they do so reluctantly and by indicating that a prior decision does not apply to the facts of the case in question. Once a lower court has determined a finding, the defendant can appeal a conviction by requesting a higher court to review the action. Most requests to review decisions of lower courts made to the U.S. Supreme Court are based on writs of certiorari which involves review of a case with important constitutional issues. These Constitutional issues are of main concern in a Supreme Court review, rather than individual guilt or innocence.

CASE

The *Glosson et al* case addresses the issue of due process as examined by the Supreme Court of Florida. While issues of entrapment and prosecutorial discretion are raised in this case, pay special attention to the issue of due process as related to the material addressed in this chapter.

STATE OF FLORIDA V. GLOSSON ET AL
Supreme Court of Florida
462 So.2d 1082 (1985)

This case is before us to review State v. Glosson, 441 So.2d 1178 (Fla. 1st DCA 1983), which expressly construes a constitutional provision. We have jurisdiction. Art. V, § 3(b)(3), Fla. Const. The issue on review is whether the district court properly affirmed the dismissal of criminal charges because the payment of a contingent fee to an informant conditioned on his cooperation and testimony in criminal prosecutions violated the respondents' constitutional due process right. For the reasons expressed below, we approve the district court's decision.

The state charged Boyce E. Glosson and the five other respondents with trafficking in over 100 but less than 2,000 pounds of cannabis and with conspiring to traffic in over 100 pounds of cannabis. These charges resulted from a "reverse-sting" operation run by the Levy County Sheriff's Department through a paid informant, Norwood Lee Wilson. Wilson traveled to Dade County, where he agreed to sell several hundred pounds of cannabis to the respondents in Levy County. The respondents came to Levy County, took possession of the cannabis controlled by the sheriff, and were arrested soon afterward. As a result of the arrests, the sheriff seized several vehicles and over $80,000 in cash subject to civil forfeiture under sections 932.701-.704, Florida Statutes (1983).

The respondents filed motions to dismiss the information because of entrapment and prosecutorial misconduct. These motions relied primarily upon the agreement between the sheriff and Wilson whereby Wilson would receive ten percent of all civil forfeitures arising out of successful criminal investigations he completed in Levy County. The trial court held hearings on this issue and denied the motions to dismiss. The respondents filed further motions to dismiss which alleged that specific unethical conduct by the prosecutor had deprived them of their due process right. These charges included permitting the payment of a contingent fee to Wilson, a vital witness in a criminal prosecution, and failing to supervise Wilson properly after sending him out to make cases using government-controlled cannabis. A further hearing on these motions resulted in a stipulated set of facts for the trial court to dispose of the due process issue on a Florida Rule of Criminal Procedure 3.190(c)(4) motion to dismiss rather than go to the expense of a trial and possibly have a directed judgment of acquittal on the same facts. The parties stipulated that each defendant had asserted an entrapment defense; that Wilson had an oral agreement with the sheriff, which agreement the state attorney's office knew about and even supervised Wilson's investigations; that Wilson would receive ten percent of all civil forfeiture proceedings resulting from the criminal investigations initiated and participated in by him; that the contingent fee would be paid out of civil forfeitures received by the sheriff; that Wilson must testify and cooperate in criminal prosecutions resulting from his investigations in order to collect the contingent fee; that this is one of those criminal prosecutions; and that Wilson must testify and cooperate in this case for there to be a successful prosecution. The trial court dismissed the information after finding that prosecutorial misconduct in this case had deprived the respondents of their right to due process.

The district court affirmed the dismissal, finding the constitutional due process issue to be a question of law for the trial court and holding that the contingent fee arrangement with Wilson violated the respondents' due process right. The district court relied on Williamson v. United States, 311 F.2d 441 (5th Cir.1962), in holding the respondents had been denied due process because Wilson's contingent arrangement seemed to manufacture, rather than detect, crime. The district court recognized that United States v. Joseph, 533 F.2d 282 (5th Cir.1976), cert. denied, 431 U.S. 905, 97 S.Ct. 1698, 52 L.Ed.2d 389 (1977), limited Williamson to those cases where contingent fees are paid for evidence against particular persons. Nevertheless, the district court found that the pervasive informant activity in this case came closer to the facts in Williamson than to the limited informant activity approved in Joseph. The state contends that the district court erred in affirming the trial court's order dismissing the information. The state argues that the respondents' due process defense is both procedurally and substantively inapplicable in this case. We disagree with both arguments.

Two reasons require us to reject the state's argument that the due process defense in this case presents a credibility issue for the jury rather than a question of law which the trial court may decide on a rule 3.190(c)(4) motion to dismiss. The due process defense based upon governmental misconduct is an objective question of law for the trial court, as opposed to the subjective predisposition question submitted to the jury in the usual entrapment defense. The trial court had sufficient undisputed facts in the stipulation to determine as a matter of law that

Wilson's contingent fee arrangement with the sheriff violated the respondents' due process right, compelling the dismissal of the information. The state's argument must also fail because the prosecutor agreed to the pretrial disposition of the due process issue to avoid a possible adverse ruling during a lengthy trial. The state may not now claim procedural error in a ruling it invited the trial court to make.

The state further contends that the district court should not have affirmed the application of the due process defense in this case, which did not involve acts or threats of violence by government agents. We disagree and hold that the agreement in this case to pay an informant a contingent fee conditioned on his cooperation and testimony in criminal prosecutions violates constitutional due process.

The United States Supreme Court first recognized the entrapment defense, with its emphasis on the predisposition of the defendant to commit a crime in Sorrells v. United States, 287 U.S. 435, 53 S.Ct. 210, 77 L.Ed. 413 (1932). In dicta from United States v. Russell, 411 U.S. 423, 93 S.Ct. 1637, 36 L.Ed.2d 366 (1973), the Court appeared to recognize the due process defense, regardless of the defendant's predisposition, where "the conduct of law enforcement agents is so outrageous that due process principles would absolutely bar the government from invoking judicial processes to obtain a conviction." Only three justices agreed with the later plurality opinion Hampton v. United States, 425 U.S. 484, 96 S.Ct. 1646, 48 L.Ed.2d 113 (1976), holding that the due process defense is unavailable to a predisposed defendant.

We cannot agree with the state's position that Hampton forecloses the due process defense from admittedly predisposed defendants. However, it appears that since Hampton the due process defense has been raised successfully in only one federal circuit court. Indeed, a recent federal circuit court stated that nothing short of "the infliction of pain or physical or psychological coercion" will establish the due process defense. United States v. Kelly, 707 F.2d 1460, 1477 (D.C.Cir.).

The due process defense appears to fare better when used by predisposed defendants in state court proceedings. Courts in two states have recognized and relied upon the due process defense to overturn criminal convictions. We reject the narrow application of the due process defense found in the federal cases. Based upon the due process provision of article I, section 9 of the Florida Constitution, we agree with Hohensee and Isaacson that governmental misconduct which violates the constitutional due process right of a defendant, regardless of that defendant's predisposition, requires the dismissal of criminal charges.

Our examination of this case convinces us that the contingent fee agreement with the informant and vital state witness, Wilson, violated the respondents' due process right under our state constitution. According to the stipulated facts, the state attorney's office knew about Wilson's contingent fee agreement and supervised his criminal investigations. Wilson had to testify and cooperate in criminal prosecutions in order to receive his contingent fee from the connected civil forfeitures, and criminal convictions could not be obtained in this case without his testimony. We can imagine few situations with more potential for abuse of a defendant's due process right. The informant here had an enormous financial incentive not only to make criminal cases, but also to color his testimony or even commit perjury in pursuit of the contingent fee. The due process

12

rights of all citizens require us to forbid criminal prosecutions based upon the testimony of vital state witnesses who have what amounts to a financial stake in criminal convictions.

Accordingly, we hold that a trial court may properly dismiss criminal charges for constitutional due process violations in cases where an informant stands to gain a contingent fee conditioned on cooperation and testimony in the criminal prosecution when that testimony is critical to a successful prosecution. We approve the district court decision under review. It is so ordered.

BOYD, C.J., and ADKINS, OVERTON, EHRLICH and SHAW, JJ., concur. ALDERMAN, J., dissents.

REVIEW SECTION

READING COMPREHENSION

How did prosecutorial misconduct deprive the respondents of their right to due process?

According to the Supreme Court of Florida, how were the respondents' due process rights violated under the Florida constitution?

THINKING CRITICALLY

Is prosecutorial misconduct a deprivation of one's right to due process? Elaborate your position.

Articulate why you believe the due process defense should be unavailable to a predisposed defendant?

CONCLUSION

Crime control is the balance struck between the search for truth and a commitment to fairness which serves to limit governmental power through the U.S. and state's constitutions as interpreted by the U.S. Supreme Court. To maximize both individual liberties and community security, there must be a balance between process and result. What occurs is a balancing of formal and informal criminal procedures, designed to maintain the general principles of the U.S. Constitution and the Florida Constitution. While sections of the Florida Constitution will be elaborated throughout this guide, Article I, The Declaration of Rights is provided in full text in the appendix. This chapter addressed the balance between order and liberty, as well as laws, discretion, due process, and precedent. The reinterpretation of how truth and fairness are guaranteed rests in the hands of the court system.

Chapter Two

The Constitution and Criminal Procedure

Criminal procedure comes from a variety of sources and is continually reinterpreted in court decisions. As there is a balance between process and result, there also exists a balance between laws which are specifics passed by legislatures, and constitutions which are principles to guide the populace. A main source of criminal procedure provisions is the Bill of Rights which provides rights to individuals at the local, state, and federal levels. This chapter details the exchange between the U.S. Constitution and the U.S. Supreme Court, with specific emphasis on due process and equal protection of laws. As such, the focus of this chapter remains at the federal level to elaborate the importance of the Constitution. Elements therein will be elaborated with specific reference to Florida throughout the remainder of this guide.

This chapter will review:

(1)   The sources of criminal procedure;

(2)   Due process; and

(3)   Equal protection of the law.

SECTION 1: SOURCES OF CRIMINAL PROCEDURE

OVERVIEW

In examining the differences between laws and constitutions, it should be noted that laws are detailed and changing rules passed by state or federal legislatures, and constitutions are general and involve a relatively permanent set of principles. Constitutions are the highest forms of law and are vested with political authority. Theoretically, the Florida Constitution, reflects the will and values of the people of the state and can only be changed by the people, thereby binding the government. The rules or criminal procedures that must be followed at all stages of the criminal justice system can be found in constitutions, court decisions, statutes, and administrative rules.

Most criminal procedure provisions are found in the Bill of Rights. Indeed, of the 28 provisions in the Bill of Rights, 12 are guarantees to individuals suspected, charged, or convicted of crimes. Since the 1960s, these guarantees have been applied to state and local, as well as federal governments. Within the Constitution there are two criminal procedure provisions: habeas corpus and guarantee of a trial by jury.

Habeas corpus is intended to review the constitutionality of the petitioner's imprisonment and is a noncriminal or civil proceeding. According to Section Thirteen of the Florida Constitution:

The writ of habeas corpus shall be grantable of right, freely and
without cost. It shall be returnable without delay, and shall never
be suspended unless, in case of rebellion or invasion, suspension is
essential to the public safety.

The second criminal procedure guaranteed by Section Twenty-Two of the Florida Constitution is
trial by jury:

The right of trial by jury shall be secure to all and remain inviolate.
The qualifications and the number of jurors, not fewer than six,
shall be fixed by law.

According to the supremacy clause, Article VI of the U.S. Constitution, this is the final authority
that binds criminal procedure. The courts however have established the principle of judicial
review which gives the U.S. Supreme Court, as opposed to the Congress or the President, final
responsibility for interpretation of the meaning of the Constitution. While all levels of the court
system can interpret the Constitution, the Supreme Court makes final interpretations that bind
lower courts, executives, legislatures, and all criminal justice officials. This power is somewhat
limited by two factors. First, on a day-to-day basis local courts and police administer the
interpretations as the Supreme Court is at the top of a very large criminal justice system pyramid.
Second, because very few cases ever reach the Supreme Court, much interpretation is conducted
at the level of the U.S. Court of Appeals, U.S. District Courts, and state courts.

You want to keep in mind that because of supervisory power to manage lower federal courts, the
control of the U.S. Supreme Court is stronger over federal courts than state courts. The U.S.
Supreme Court can control criminal procedures at the state level only if such actions are in
violation of the U.S. Constitution. In Florida for example, the Supreme Court has jurisdiction
over cases wherein the death penalty is imposed, cases that pass upon the validity of a state or
federal statute or construe a provision of the state or federal constitution, and in district court
cases wherein there is conflict with another court, writs or orders by a district court of appeal that
require immediate resolution.

As mentioned previously, state constitutions guarantee parallel rights to those outlined in the
U.S. Constitution and Bill of Rights, as well as guarantee rights that may not be guaranteed in
these other provisions. While the U.S. Constitution sets the minimum standards required by the
states, each state in their Constitution is free to raise this minimum. The final authority in cases
based on the Florida Constitution are the Florida state courts, as the U.S. Supreme Court cannot
interpret state constitutions and statutes so long as it complies with the U.S. Constitution.

Remember that criminal procedures can be found not only in constitutions, court decisions, and
statutes, but also in administrative rules. During the beginning of the 20th century in response to
dissatisfaction with justice administration, the *Federal Rules of Criminal Procedure* was created.
This set of rules was authorized by Congress and involved practitioners and scholars detailing
rules to put the spirit of the U.S. Constitution into daily criminal justice system procedure. At the
state level, the rules that put the spirit of the Florida Constitution into daily criminal justice
system procedure are elaborated in the *Florida Rules of Criminal Procedure*, published by the

Continuing Legal Education Publications and The Florida Bar in Tallahassee. Because these rules do not elaborate the period prior to arrest, the *Model Code of Pre-Arraignment Procedure* was established in the 1970s. Although this document is not law, it is frequently cited by the courts in decisions.

SECTION 2: DUE PROCESS

OVERVIEW

When the Confederacy was defeated during the Civil war and slavery was abolished, guarantees of state's rights and equal protection became extremely important. The Fourteenth Amendment guarantees:

> No state shall . . . deprive any citizen of life, liberty, or property
> without due process of law.

This sentiment is mirrored in Section Nine of the Florida Constitution as provided in the first chapter. Remember that the 1960s due process revolution resulted in the expansion of individual rights. This was accomplished as more individuals were included in constitutional protections and states and the federal government became compelled to extend these guarantees to the most vulnerable classes. The concept of due process is vague and thus subject to varied interpretations by the U.S. Supreme Court, though at minimum guarantees fair procedures when deciding cases.

While the underlying goal was to protect individuals from excessive government power, the U.S. Supreme Court was unwilling to apply the Fourteenth Amendment to state criminal proceedings until the 1930s, arguing it was a local matter and should not be in the hands of the federal government. Once the First World War began however, suspicions of excessive and arbitrary government were reinvigorated and the U.S. Supreme Court applied for the first time the due process clause of the Fourteenth Amendment to state criminal procedures in *Brown v. Mississippi* (297 U.S. 278 1936). The due process clause requires that "state action, whether through one agency or another, shall be consistent with the fundamental principles of liberty and justice which lie at the base of all our civil and political institutions."

Brown v. Mississippi (297 U.S. 278 1936) and *Powell v. Alabama* (287 U.S. 45 1932) were paramount in establishing the fundamental fairness doctrine of due process. This doctrine provides that due process commands states to notify defendants of charges, and provide a full fact hearing prior to conviction and punishment. In Rule 3.140(1)(b) of the *Florida Rules of Criminal Procedure*, this is elaborated as "the indictment or information on which the defendant is to be tried shall be a plain, concise, and definite written statement of the essential facts constituting the offense charged."

In sum, the fundamental fairness doctrine commands the states to provide a fair trial. This doctrine focused on general fairness defined at the state level, and while due process may include some specific guarantees of the Bill of Rights, this is neither a requirement nor intentional. From the 1930s until the 1950s, majority of the court continued to reject the notion that the Bill of

Rights applied to criminal procedure at the state level, though came to recognize during the latter part of this period that the Bill of Rights does impose limits at this level. The controversy was: what are these limits?

The court began to reject the fundamental fairness doctrine in favor of interpreting the Fourteenth Amendment using the incorporation doctrine. The incorporation doctrine applied the provisions of the Bill of Rights to state criminal procedures, and this was the position of majority of the court by the 1960s. The incorporation doctrine focused on specific procedures as outlined in the Bill of Rights and applied at the state level. When the Court adopted this doctrine, contention remained regarding whether all or a select portion of the provisions of the Fourteenth Amendment should be included in due process. In cases decided by the Courts in the 1960s, all provisions of the Fourteenth Amendment were included except indictment by grand jury. The U.S. Supreme Court suggested that these rights were to apply at the state level exactly as in federal proceedings. The result was not only a shift in reasoning for intervention at the state level, but also an expanded role in the ways in which day-to-day criminal justice is implemented. Nevertheless, much local experimentation is still permitted as is highlighted in case example.

CASE

Chandler v. Florida addresses the impact of radio, television, and still photographic coverage of a criminal trial on the rights of the accused to a fair trial as guaranteed by the Sixth and Fourteenth Amendments. This is one example of local experimentation, and as you read this case, think about the role of the media in today's society and the impact this may have on securing a fair trial.

CHANDLER V. FLORIDA
U.S. Supreme Court, Appeal from the Supreme Court of Florida
449 U.S. 560 (1981)

The Florida Supreme Court, following a pilot program for televising judicial proceedings in the State, promulgated a revised Canon 3A (7) of the Florida Code of Judicial Conduct. The Canon permits electronic media and still photography coverage of judicial proceedings, subject to the control of the presiding judge and to implementing guidelines placing on trial judges obligations to protect the fundamental right of the accused in a criminal case to a fair trial. Appellants, who were charged with a crime that attracted media attention, were convicted after a jury trial in a Florida trial court over objections that the televising and broadcast of parts of their trial denied them a fair and impartial trial. The Florida District Court of Appeal affirmed, finding no evidence that the presence of a television camera hampered appellants in presenting their case, deprived them of an impartial jury, or impaired the fairness of the trial. The Florida Supreme Court denied review.

Held: The Constitution does not prohibit a state from experimenting with a program such as is authorized by Florida's Canon 3A (7).

(a) This Court has no supervisory jurisdiction over state courts, and, in reviewing a state-court judgment, is confined to evaluating it in relation to the Federal Constitution.

(b) There was no constitutional rule that all photographic, radio, and television coverage of criminal trials is inherently a denial of due process. It does not stand as an absolute ban on state experimentation with an evolving technology.

(c) An absolute constitutional ban on broadcast coverage of trials cannot be justified simply because there is a danger that, in some cases, conduct of the broadcasting process or prejudicial broadcast accounts of pretrial and trial events may impair the ability of jurors to decide the issue of guilt or innocence uninfluenced by extraneous matter. The appropriate safeguard against juror prejudice is the defendant's right [449 U.S. 560, 561] to demonstrate that the media's coverage of his case - be it printed or broadcast - compromised the ability of the particular jury that heard the case to adjudicate fairly.

(d) Whatever may be the "mischievous potentialities [of broadcast coverage] for intruding upon the detached atmosphere which should always surround the judicial process," Estes v. Texas, supra, at 587, at present no one has presented empirical data sufficient to establish that the mere presence of the broadcast media in the courtroom inherently has an adverse effect on that process under all circumstances. Here, appellants have offered nothing to demonstrate that their trial was subtly tainted by broadcast coverage - let alone that all broadcast trials would be so tainted.

(e) Nor have appellants shown either that the media's coverage of their trial - printed or broadcast - compromised the jury's ability to judge them fairly or that the broadcast coverage of their particular trial had an adverse impact on the trial participants sufficient to constitute a denial of due process.

(f) Absent a showing of prejudice of constitutional dimensions to these appellants, there is no reason for this Court either to endorse or to invalidate Florida's experiment.

CHIEF JUSTICE BURGER delivered the opinion of the Court. The question presented on this appeal is whether, consistent with constitutional guarantees, a state may provide for radio, television, and still photographic coverage of a criminal trial for public broadcast, notwithstanding the objection of the accused.

Background. Over the past 50 years, some criminal cases characterized as "sensational" have been subjected to extensive coverage by news media, sometimes seriously interfering with the conduct of the proceedings and creating a setting wholly inappropriate for the administration of justice. Judges, lawyers, and others soon became concerned, and in 1937, after study, the American Bar Association House of Delegates [449 U.S. 560, 563] adopted Judicial Canon 35, declaring that all photographic and broadcast coverage of courtroom proceedings should be prohibited. In 1952, the House of Delegates amended Canon 35 to proscribe television coverage as well. The Canon's proscription was reaffirmed in 1972 when the Code of Judicial Conduct replaced the Canons of Judicial Ethics and Canon 3A (7) superseded Canon 35. A majority of the states, including Florida, adopted the substance of the ABA provision and its amendments. In Florida, the rule was embodied in Canon 3A (7) of the Florida Code of Judicial Conduct.

In February 1978, the American Bar Association Committee on Fair Trial-Free Press proposed revised standards. These [449 U.S. 560, 564] included a provision permitting courtroom coverage by the electronic media under conditions to be established by local rule and under the control of the trial judge, but only if such coverage was carried out unobtrusively and without affecting the conduct of the trial. The revision was endorsed by the ABA's Standing Committee on Standards for Criminal Justice and by its Committee on Criminal Justice and the Media, but it was rejected by the House of Delegates on February 12, 1979. In 1978, based upon its own study of the matter, the Conference of State Chief Justices, by a vote of 44 to 1, approved a resolution to allow the highest court of each state to promulgate standards and guidelines regulating radio, television, and other photographic coverage of court proceedings.

The Florida Program. In January 1975, while these developments were unfolding, the Post-Newsweek Stations of Florida petitioned the Supreme Court of Florida urging a change in Florida's Canon 3A (7). In April 1975, the court invited presentations in the nature of a rulemaking proceeding, and, in January 1976, announced an experimental program for televising one civil and one criminal trial under specific guidelines. These initial guidelines required the consent of all parties. It developed, however, that in practice such consent could not be obtained. The Florida Supreme Court then supplemented its order and established a new 1-year pilot program [449 U.S. 560, 565] during which the electronic media were permitted to cover all judicial proceedings in Florida without reference to the consent of participants, subject to detailed standards with respect to technology and the conduct of operators. The experiment began in July 1977 and continued through June 1978.

When the pilot program ended, the Florida Supreme Court received and reviewed briefs, reports, letters of comment, and studies. It conducted its own survey of attorneys, witnesses, jurors, and court personnel through the Office of the State Court Coordinator. A separate survey was taken of judges by the Florida Conference of Circuit Judges. The court also studied the experience of 6 States that had, by 1979, adopted rules relating to electronic coverage of trials, as well as that of the 10 other States that, like Florida, were experimenting with such coverage.

Following its review of this material, the Florida Supreme Court concluded "that on balance there [was] more to be gained than lost by permitting electronic media coverage of judicial proceedings subject to standards for such coverage." The Florida court was of the view that because of the significant effect of the courts on the day-to-day lives of the citizenry, it was essential that the people have confidence in the process. It felt that broadcast coverage of trials would contribute to wider public acceptance and understanding of decisions. Consequently, after revising the 1977 guidelines to reflect its evaluation of the pilot program, the Florida Supreme Court promulgated a revised Canon 3A (7). The Canon provides:

> Subject at all times to the authority of the presiding judge to (i)
> control the conduct of proceedings before the court, (ii) ensure
> decorum and prevent distractions, and (iii) ensure the fair
> administration of justice in the pending cause, electronic media and
> still photography coverage of public judicial proceedings in the
> appellate and trial courts of this state shall be allowed in

accordance with standards of conduct and technology promulgated
by the Supreme Court of Florida.

The implementing guidelines specify in detail the kind of electronic equipment to be used and the manner of its use. For example, no more than one television camera and only one camera technician are allowed. Existing recording systems used by court reporters are used by broadcasters for audio pickup. Where more than one broadcast news organization seeks to cover a trial, the media must pool coverage. No artificial lighting is allowed. The equipment is positioned in a fixed location, and it may not be moved during trial. Videotaping equipment must be remote from the courtroom. Film, videotape, and lenses may not be changed while the court is in session. No audio recording of conferences between lawyers, between parties and counsel, or at the bench is permitted. The judge has sole and plenary discretion to exclude coverage of certain witnesses, and the jury may not be filmed. The judge has discretionary power to forbid coverage whenever satisfied that coverage may have a deleterious effect on the paramount right of the defendant to a fair trial. The Florida Supreme Court has the right to revise these rules as experience dictates, or indeed to bar all broadcast coverage or photography in courtrooms.

In July 1977, appellants were charged with conspiracy to commit burglary, grand larceny, and possession of burglary tools. The counts covered breaking and entering a well-known Miami Beach restaurant. The details of the alleged criminal conduct are not relevant to the issue before us, but several aspects of the case distinguish it from a routine burglary. At the time of their arrest, appellants were Miami Beach policemen. The State's principal witness was John Sion, an amateur radio operator who, by sheer chance, had overheard and recorded conversations between the appellants over their police walkie-talkie radios during the burglary. Not surprisingly, these novel factors attracted the attention of the media.

By pretrial motion, counsel for the appellants sought to have experimental Canon 3A (7) declared unconstitutional on its face and as applied. The trial court denied relief but certified the issue to the Florida Supreme Court. However, the Supreme Court declined to rule on the question, on the ground that it was not directly relevant to the criminal charges against the appellants. After several additional fruitless attempts by the appellants to prevent electronic coverage of the trial, the jury was selected. At *voir dire*, the appellants' counsel asked each prospective juror whether he or she would be able to be "fair and impartial" despite the presence of a television camera during some, or all, of the trial. Each juror selected responded that such coverage would not affect his or her consideration in any way. A television camera recorded the *voir dire*.

A defense motion to sequester the jury because of the television coverage was denied by the trial judge. However, the court instructed the jury not to watch or read anything about the case in the media and suggested that jurors "avoid the local news and watch only the national news on television." Subsequently, defense counsel requested that the witnesses be instructed not to watch any television accounts of testimony presented at trial. The trial court declined to give such an instruction, for "no witness' testimony was [being] reported or televised [on the evening news] in any way."

A television camera was in place for one entire afternoon, during which the State presented the testimony of Sion, its chief witness. No camera was present for the presentation of any part of the case for the defense. The camera returned to cover closing arguments. Only 2 minutes and 55 seconds of the trial below were broadcast - and those depicted only the prosecution's side of the case. The jury returned a guilty verdict on all counts. Appellants moved for a new trial, claiming that because of the television coverage, they had been denied a fair and impartial trial. No evidence of specific prejudice was tendered.

The Florida District Court of Appeal affirmed the convictions. It declined to discuss the facial validity of Canon 3A (7); it reasoned that the Florida Supreme Court, having decided to permit television coverage of criminal trials on an experimental basis, had implicitly determined that such coverage did not violate the Federal or State Constitutions. Nonetheless, the District Court of Appeal did agree to certify the question of the facial constitutionality of Canon 3A (7) to the Florida Supreme Court. The District Court of Appeal found no evidence in the trial record to indicate that the presence of a television camera had hampered appellants in presenting their case or had deprived them of an impartial jury. The Florida Supreme Court denied review, holding that the appeal was moot.

At the outset, it is important to note that in promulgating the revised Canon 3A (7), the Florida Supreme Court pointedly rejected any state or federal constitutional right of access on the part of photographers or the broadcast media to televise or electronically record and thereafter disseminate court proceedings. It carefully framed its holding as follows: "While we have concluded that the due process clause does not prohibit electronic media coverage of judicial proceedings per se, by the same token we reject the argument of the [Post-Newsweek stations] that the first and sixth amendments to the United States Constitution mandate entry of the electronic media into judicial proceedings." The Florida court relied on our holding in Nixon v. Warner Communications, Inc., 435 U.S. 589 (1978), where we said: "In the first place, . . . there is no constitutional right to have [live witness] testimony recorded and broadcast. Second, while the guarantee of a public trial, in the words of Mr. Justice Black, is `a safeguard against any attempt to employ our courts as instruments of persecution,' it confers no special benefit on the press. Nor does the Sixth Amendment require that the trial - or any part of it - be broadcast live or on tape to the public. The requirement of a public trial is satisfied by the opportunity of members of the public and the press to attend the trial and to report what they have observed."

The Florida Supreme Court predicated the revised Canon 3A (7) upon its supervisory authority over the Florida courts and not upon any constitutional imperative. Hence, we have before us only the limited question of the Florida Supreme Court's authority to promulgate the Canon for the trial of cases in Florida courts. This Court has no supervisory jurisdiction over state courts, and, in reviewing a state-court judgment, we are confined to evaluating it in relation to the Federal Constitution.

It is not necessary either to ignore or to discount the potential danger to the fairness of a trial in a particular case in order to conclude that Florida may permit the electronic media to cover trials in its state courts. Dangers lurk in this, as in most experiments, but unless we were to conclude that television coverage under all conditions is prohibited by the Constitution, the states must be free to experiment. We are not empowered by the Constitution to oversee or harness state procedural experimentation; only when the state action infringes fundamental guarantees are we authorized to intervene. We must assume state courts will be alert to any factors that impair the fundamental rights of the accused.

The Florida program is inherently evolutional in nature; the initial project has provided guidance for the new canons which can be changed at will, and application of which is subject to control by the trial judge. The risk of prejudice to particular defendants is ever present and must be examined carefully as cases arise. Nothing of the "Roman circus" or "Yankee Stadium" atmosphere, as in Estes, prevailed here, however, nor have appellants attempted to show that the unsequestered jury was exposed to "sensational" coverage. Absent a showing of prejudice of constitutional dimensions to these defendants, there is no reason for this Court either to endorse or to invalidate Florida's experiment.

In this setting, because this Court has no supervisory authority over state courts, our review is confined to whether there is a constitutional violation. We hold that the Constitution does not prohibit a state from experimenting with the program authorized by revised Canon 3A (7).

Affirmed. JUSTICE STEVENS took no part in the decision of this case.

REVIEW SECTION

READING COMPREHENSION

Detail the constitutional issues addressed in this case.

What facts contributed to this case being heard by the U.S. Supreme Court?

THINKING CRITICALLY

Does allowing radio, television, and still photographic coverage of a criminal trial for public broadcast violate rights of the accused to a fair trial as guaranteed by the Sixth and Fourteenth Amendments?

Should the U.S. Supreme Court play a greater role in regulating activity at the state level that is not in violation of the U.S. Constitution?

SECTION 3: EQUAL PROTECTION OF THE LAW

OVERVIEW

Equality before the law is deeply embedded in a constitutional democracy and has been since 1868 in the Fourteenth Amendment. In Florida, equality before the law is guaranteed in Section Two of the Florida Constitution:

All natural persons, female and male alike, are equal before the
law and have inalienable rights, among which are the right to enjoy
and defend life and liberty, to pursue happiness, to be rewarded for
industry, and to acquire, possess and protect property . . . No
person shall be deprived of any right because of race, religion,
national origin, or physical disability.

While this does not translate to equal treatment for each individual by criminal justice officials, it does mean that investigation, apprehension, conviction, and punishment cannot occur for reasons that are considered unacceptable. In bringing a claim that equal protection was denied, claimants must prove discriminatory effect, and discriminatory purpose which means that specific officials intended to discriminate based on illegal criteria against the claimant in question. If discriminatory effect and discriminatory purpose are proved, the claimant must also disprove the presumption of regularity. Thus, the claimant must disprove the presumption that actions by the government are lawful in the absence of clear evidence to indicate otherwise. As you can imagine, this is extremely difficult to accomplish.

CASE

State of Florida v. Cox addresses the denial by the Florida Statute for homosexuals to adopt children. This case involves issues of privacy as outlined in Section Twenty-Three of the Florida Constitution which states:

Every natural person has the right to be let alone and free from
governmental intrusion into the person's private life.

On summary judgment the trial court was convinced that the Florida statute is unconstitutional, however the District Court of Appeal of Florida reversed the decision. The rationale was that the debate over homosexuality should be dealt with in the legislature rather than the court system, so long as decisions are within the confines of the Constitution. As you read this case, think about where moral decisions facing the citizenry of the United States should be decided.

STATE OF FLORIDA V. COX
District Court of Appeal of Florida, Second District
627 So.2d 1210, 62 USLW 2436, 18 Fla. L. Weekly D2551, 18 Fla. L. Weekly D2668

The plaintiffs, Mr. Cox and Mr. Jackman, voluntarily disclosed to the Department of Health and Rehabilitative Services (HRS) that they are homosexual. Each has been denied the opportunity to apply to adopt a child because section 63.042(3), Florida Statutes (1991), prohibits adoptions by homosexuals. At summary judgment, they convinced the trial court that this statute is unconstitutional for several reasons. We reverse because the plaintiffs failed to establish that the legislature lacked the constitutional power to make this public policy decision. The debate over the nature of homosexuality and the wisdom of the strictures that our society has historically placed upon homosexual activity cannot and should not be resolved today in this court. For purposes of governance, the legislature is the proper forum in which to conduct this debate so long as its decisions are permitted by the state and federal constitutions.

The factual record in this case is very limited. It is undisputed that Mr. Cox attempted to sign up for HRS parenting classes in Sarasota, Florida, on March 22, 1991. At that time, he voluntarily disclosed that he is homosexual. Mr. Jackman took the same steps on April 3, 1991. HRS became aware that the two men lived at the same address and sent them a letter in late April advising them that HRS would not accept an application for the adoption of a child from either man in light of section 63.042(3). 1 That statute, enacted in 1977, provides: "No person eligible to adopt under this statute may adopt if that person is a homosexual." After receiving the letter, the two men filed this action to declare section 63.042(3) unconstitutional on its face and as applied to them. They based their complaint on the right of privacy, substantive due process, and equal protection. Both sides filed motions for summary judgment, and the trial court decided to determine the facial validity of the statute based on the above-described facts and any information the parties wished to provide to the court.

The trial court, relying heavily upon an unappealed circuit court opinion in Seebol v. Farie, 16 Fla.L.Weekly C52 (16th Cir.Ct.1991), held that section 63.042(3) is void for vagueness and that it violates homosexuals' rights of privacy and equal protection. HRS filed this appeal. Section 63.042(3) does not define "homosexual." Despite the fact that the statute has been in effect since 1977, there are no reported cases in which a litigant has ever alleged that the term "homosexual" in section 63.042(3) is unconstitutionally vague. We have not been provided with any legislative history suggesting that anyone has ever attempted to amend this statute because of any perceived ambiguity. Mr. Cox and Mr. Jackman have admitted that they are homosexual and have never alleged that they found the term to be unconstitutionally vague. Thus, we are troubled by the trial court's unilateral amendment of the plaintiffs' complaint to add a constitutional due process theory that the parties had not chosen to litigate. The plaintiffs have not established that this statute is unconstitutionally vague.

The only other state that has enacted a similar statute is New Hampshire. That statute has withstood constitutional scrutiny. In upholding its statute, the New Hampshire Supreme Court limited its definition to persons voluntarily engaging in homosexual activity reasonably close in time to the filing of the adoption application. HRS argues that the Florida statute can be reasonably interpreted to include the same concepts as those employed in the New Hampshire definition. HRS does not claim that the statute applies to persons who merely have some degree of homosexual orientation or to people who have experimented with homosexual activity in the past. HRS does not intend to bar adoption based on homosexual orientation, but only when it knows of current, voluntary homosexual activity by an applicant.

We recognize that a definition of "homosexual," limited to applicants who are known to engage in current, voluntary homosexual activity, draws a distinction between homosexual orientation and homosexual activity. We understand that some people have concluded that it is unreasonable or unfair to distinguish homosexual orientation from homosexual activity. They believe that the activity is nothing more than an inevitable expression of the orientation. From this perspective, a rule which discriminates against the activity is no different than a rule which discriminates against the orientation. At this time, the orientation/activity question is simply a matter upon which reasonable persons can and do disagree--as a matter of scientific fact and as a matter of moral, religious, and legal opinion. Certainly, the record presented to the trial court and to this court does not end the debate. Under these circumstances, the legislature is constitutionally permitted to reach its own conclusions on the validity of the distinction between homosexual orientation and activity without any mandate from this court.

The trial court determined that section 63.042(3) violates the Florida constitutional right of privacy under article I, section 23. In so doing, it was strongly influenced by the earlier trial court decision in Seebol. Both decisions focus on a perceived right of privacy concerning sexual orientation. Neither decision evaluates the statute if the definition of "homosexual" is limited to current voluntary sexual conduct. In our opinion, neither decision gives sufficient consideration to the fact that the statute does not establish a governmental intrusion into a person's private life; it bars the statutory privilege to adopt a child when it is known that the applicant is homosexual. We reverse this holding in the summary judgment and rule that HRS is entitled to summary judgment on these issues.

These plaintiffs presented a narrow privacy issue. Mr. Cox and Mr. Jackman voluntarily admitted that they are homosexual. They cannot claim an expectation of privacy concerning a fact that they have willingly disclosed. Moreover, they do not object to revealing their homosexuality on an adoption application. Further, they agree that HRS may make this inquiry. They simply believe that Florida should treat information concerning their current sexual activity as one of the many factors involved in the decision to approve an application. They argue that many other states take this approach. The right to privacy is a fundamental right. Section 63.042(3) denies one group of natural persons the opportunity to adopt based upon their known sexual activities. It does not require public disclosure of personal matters. Indeed, chapter 63 makes the files and the proceedings concerning adoptions confidential. This statute does not compel unwarranted inquiry concerning private matters. In fact, this statute does not mandate any specific inquiry concerning an applicant's background. In this case, the state did not demand secret information; the plaintiffs voluntarily provided the information. "[B]efore the right of privacy is attached and the delineated standard applied, a reasonable expectation of privacy must exist."

Moreover, adoption is simply not a private matter. As the trial court recognized, adoption is not a right; it is a statutory privilege. Thus, adopting a child is not the same as choosing to have a natural family. To make decisions that accord with the best interests of children, government agencies and courts are clearly entitled to conduct extensive examinations into the background of prospective parents. These plaintiffs have not argued that such investigations violate the right of privacy. Even if the right of privacy had been invoked concerning such an investigation, it is clear that the best interests of a child can create a very substantial state interest.

The trial court has not directly ruled upon the plaintiffs' substantive due process claim. It did, however, extensively rely upon the decision in Seebol, which expressly held the statute unconstitutional under a substantive due process analysis. Moreover, an analysis of fundamental rights under due process is necessary to determine whether strict scrutiny applies under the right to equal protection. Accordingly, we conclude that a brief consideration of due process is appropriate. Both the United States Constitution and the Florida Constitution limit the application of due process to deprivations of "life, liberty or property." The plaintiffs do not seriously argue that the statutory privilege of adoption invokes an interest in life or in property. They argue that the statute invokes an interest in liberty.

From the usage of "liberty" in everyday language, a person might think that adoption was a "liberty" in a free society. However, for the purpose of explaining due process as a matter of constitutional law, "liberty" must be carefully defined. The courts have been cautious in extending the concept of liberty beyond a person's physical freedom. A broad definition of "liberty" for due process analysis would substantially change the balance of powers between the federal government and those of the states, and between the judicial and legislative branches of government. Accordingly, liberty interests that do not involve physical freedom must be "fundamental liberties" before they are protected by due process. Such liberties must be "implicit in the concept of ordered liberty." They are freedoms "deeply rooted in this Nation's history and tradition." We agree with the New Hampshire Supreme Court that the opportunity to adopt an unrelated child is not a fundamental liberty. Similarly, the United States Supreme Court has held that the decision to engage in homosexual activity is not a fundamental right.

The Due Process Clause in the United States Constitution and the similar clauses in the state constitutions, however, have a shared and overlapping history. We conclude that it is not appropriate for this court, as a matter of state constitutional law, to depart from a recent United States Supreme Court ruling under a virtually identical federal constitutional clause unless we are convinced that aspects of Florida's constitution, law, or announced public policies clearly justify such a departure. We have considered Florida's right of privacy under article I, section 23, and the basic rights described in article I, section 2. We are not convinced that these aspects of the Florida Constitution expand the concept of liberty under article I, section 9, so that homosexuality is a fundamental right. The plaintiffs have not clearly established a valid legal justification for this court to depart from the rule announced in Bowers.

Adopting the analysis in Seebol, the trial court held that section 63.042(3) violates equal protection under either the strict scrutiny or the rational basis standard. We conclude that the plaintiffs have established no right to strict scrutiny and have not established that the statute fails the rational basis test. There are two long-established standards applicable to equal protection review: strict scrutiny and rational basis. Equal protection analysis requires strict scrutiny by the judiciary only in cases involving fundamental rights or a suspect class. As discussed in the preceding section, neither the statutory privilege to adopt nor the choice to engage in homosexual activity involves a fundamental right. Thus, strict scrutiny can apply in this case only if homosexual activity creates a suspect classification.

The state clearly has a legitimate governmental purpose in seeking to provide for the best interests of children in need of adoption. HRS argues that the legislature can rationally decide that this governmental purpose is promoted by a total prohibition of adoptions by homosexuals. Perhaps the simplest argument in support of this position can be summarized as follows: whatever causes a person to become a homosexual, it is clear that the state cannot know the sexual preferences that a child will exhibit as an adult. Statistically, the state does know that a very high percentage of children available for adoption will develop heterosexual preferences. The state has not yet had any obligation to provide evidence to support the reasonably conceivable state of facts that supply an initial rational basis for its classification. It may be that the legislature should revisit this issue in light of the research that has taken place in the last fifteen years, but we cannot say that the limited research reflected in this record compels the judiciary to override the legislature's reasoning.

Reversed and remanded.

REVIEW SECTION

READING COMPREHENSION

What is the role of privacy in this case?

On what grounds did Cox challenge the decision of the Department of Health and Rehabilitative Services?

THINKING CRITICALLY

Should the court system or the legislature lead morality in the United States?

How are the "best interests of the child" constrained or enhanced by current legislation and precedent?

CONCLUSION

State law provides the specifics passed by legislatures, and the Florida Constitution is the principle used to guide citizens. This chapter outlined the difficulty of leading moral crusades in this country, through an elaboration of the sources of criminal procedure. It is the role of the courts to, in an attempt to balance process and result, interpret and reinterpret criminal procedure. Where however, should issues of morality such as homosexual adoption be decided – in the courts or in the legislature? This chapter detailed the exchange between the U.S. Constitution and the U.S. Supreme Court, with specific emphasis on due process and equal protection of laws.

Chapter Three

Searches and Seizures

As a guiding principle, Section Twelve of the Florida Constitution reads as follows regarding searches and seizures:

> The right of the people to be secure in their persons, houses, papers and effects against unreasonable searches and seizures, and against the unreasonable interception of private communications by any means, shall not be violated. No warrant shall be issued except upon probable cause, supported by affidavit, particularly describing the place or places to be searched, the person or persons, thing or things to be seized, the communication to be intercepted, and the nature of evidence to be obtained. This right shall be construed in conformity with the 4th Amendment to the United States Constitution, as interpreted by the United States Supreme Court. Articles or information obtained in violation of this right shall not be admissible in evidence if such articles or information would be inadmissible under decisions of the United States Supreme Court construing the 4th Amendment to the United States Constitution.

This is premised on the notion that while crime control depends on police gathering of information, this information frequently results from reluctant sources, and authorities must use only legal methods to obtain facts. To control crime, government officials rely on searches and seizures, interrogation, and identification procedures, all of which are involuntary. Thus, the state has created guidelines to ensure both the rights of individuals and fact-finding by police officials.

This chapter will review:

(1)   Searches and seizures;

(2)   The "expectation of privacy;"

(3)   Plain view, hearing, smell, and touch; and

(4)   Unprotected places.

SECTION 1: SEARCHES AND SEIZURES

OVERVIEW

Section Twelve of the Florida Constitution comprises the main elements of the Fourth Amendment which was created to ensure the government follow the law in obtaining evidence. Initially warrants were used against seditious libels to control criticism of the government, and agents had the power to search anyone, at anytime, in any location. Opposition to the blanket power of such a general warrant was written into the Constitution in the Fourth Amendment. A reasonableness limit was established to protect one's liberty or right of movement, and one's privacy from government intrusion.

To determine whether or not the government has complied with the Fourth Amendment involves analysis of three questions that will be elaborated over several chapters:

(1)   Was the action by the government a search or a seizure?

(2)   If considered a search or a seizure, was it an unreasonable search or seizure?

(3)   If considered an unreasonable search or seizure, should the evidence obtained during the unreasonable search be excluded from consideration?

Further, actions taken by the government that may be considered Fourth Amendment searches or seizures take place in three stages that will also be elaborated over several chapters:

(1)   Encounters between citizens and government officials in public places;

(2)   Encounters between citizens and government officials after transportation to the police station; and

(3)   Encounters occurring after conviction between prisoners and jail/prison officials.

Not all encounters by government officials are considered searches and/or seizures, though keep in mind that as the level of government intrusion increases, the objective basis or facts and circumstances required to justify the action also increase.

CASE

In *Sands v. State of Florida* the question at issue is whether a warrantless search is considered unreasonable and thus in violation of rights guaranteed by the Fourth and Fourteenth Amendments to the U.S. Constitution and Article I, Section 12 of the Florida Constitution. Approached in an airport, a method of profiling, in conjunction with a statement believed by the majority to be a confession are used to conclude that the search and seizure of the defendant was conducted incident to a valid arrest and therefore, did not constitute a violation of rights. The dissenting opinion presents alternative considerations for your review.

The central question presented by this appeal is whether the warrantless search of the defendant's person by the police in this case constituted an unreasonable search and seizure in violation of the defendant's rights guaranteed by the Fourth and Fourteenth Amendments to the United States Constitution and Article I, Section 12 of the Florida Constitution. For the reasons which follow, we conclude that the subject search and seizure was conducted incident to a valid arrest of the defendant and, therefore, did not constitute a violation of the defendant's search and seizure rights. We, accordingly, affirm the judgment of conviction and sentence appealed from, as the trial court was eminently correct in denying the defendant's motion to suppress the fruits of the subject search and seizure.

The facts relevant to the above search and seizure issue are based entirely on the testimony of Officer William Johnson--the only witness who testified below at the hearing on the defendant's motion to suppress. These facts are as follows. On September 19, 1979, Officer Johnson was working at the Miami International Airport as part of the airport narcotics unit with his partner Officer Pearson. Officer Johnson had worked in this unit for a period of two years and received extensive training and experience with reference to the arrest of drug suspects; in particular, Officer Johnson was familiar and had worked extensively with the so-called "drug courier profile" with reference to the spotting and arresting of narcotic drug suspects.

On the above-stated date at approximately 4:40 p. m., Officer Johnson observed the defendant Barry Sands exiting a taxicab in front of the airport with one Gerald Russell. The defendant Sands was carrying a brown leather suit bag and a brown purse; his companion Russell carried a brown leather totebag. The two men entered the terminal and walked to the ticket counter, both men appeared to be peering anxiously at all the persons around them. Russell approached the counter first, took out a large amount of cash from his pants pocket and requested tickets to Houston, Texas. No bags were checked.

Both men proceeded toward the concourse with Officers Johnson and Pearson following. Officer Pearson approached Russell, displayed his badge and identified himself as a police officer. At that point the defendant Sands, who was a foot ahead of Russell, turned in the direction of the two and walked rapidly away, still looking back at Officer Pearson and Russell. At that point, Officer Johnson approached the defendant, identified himself as a police officer and "asked him if he had a minute to talk." Sands replied, "yes, of course." Officer Johnson asked the defendant for identification and he produced a Houston driver's license which remained in Officer Johnson's possession during the following questioning.

Officer Johnson asked the defendant if he was flying that day; the defendant said, "no." Officer Johnson then pointed out Russell to the defendant and asked the defendant if he knew him; the defendant again said, "no." Officer Johnson then indicated that he had seen the two exit the same taxicab and make a ticket purchase together. The defendant Sands immediately changed his story and began to tremble visibly and to sweat. Officer Johnson advised that he was concerned with narcotics passing through the airport, requested permission to search the defendant's suit bag, and advised that the defendant had a right to refuse the search; the defendant agreed to the search.

Officer Johnson also asked for and received permission to search the defendant's purse. Prior to conducting any of these searches, however, Officer Johnson suggested that the two walk over some ten yards to where Officer Pearson and Mr. Russell were standing.

Officer Johnson thereupon proceeded to search the defendant Sands' suit bag and purse, but found nothing incriminating. Officer Johnson then asked Mr. Sands for permission to check his ankles because it is a very popular place to carry reasonably large quantities of contraband. Mr. Sands said "really, well let's go somewhere where it's more private." Officer Johnson suggested the men's room that was a few feet away. Upon standing, Mr. Sands turned around and said, "well, you might as well take me downtown and file your complaint." Officer Johnson took that to be an admission of contraband on his ankle. Officer Johnson immediately thereafter directed the defendant to go into the men's room where he frisked the defendant and discovered a quantity of cocaine being carried in a malleable lump on each one of the defendant Sands' ankles.

The defendant was subsequently charged by information with trafficking in a controlled substance, and possession of a controlled substance with intent to sell in the Circuit Court for the Eleventh Judicial Circuit of Florida based on the above seizure of cocaine. The defendant moved pretrial to suppress the fruits of the subject search on the ground that said search was conducted in violation of the defendant's search and seizure rights guaranteed by the state and federal constitutions. The trial court heard and denied the motion to suppress. Thereafter the defendant entered a plea of nolo contendere to both charges, specifically reserving for appeal the denial of his motion to suppress. The defendant was thereupon adjudged guilty as charged and was sentenced to two five-year concurrent sentences in the state penitentiary. The defendant appeals this judgment of conviction and sentence; we have jurisdiction to entertain this appeal.

The law is well-settled that a search and seizure conducted by state officials is presumptively unreasonable under the Fourth and Fourteenth Amendments to the United States Constitution and Article I, Section 12 of the Florida Constitution when conducted without a search warrant, subject only to certain specifically established and well-delineated exceptions justified by absolute necessity. The state has the burden of proving that such an exception applies in a given case. One of the well-recognized exceptions to the search warrant requirement rule is that the police may conduct a warrantless search incident to effecting a lawful arrest of a person. Gustafson v. Florida, 414 U.S. 260, 94 S.Ct. 488, 38 L.Ed.2d 456 (1973). Two requirements must necessarily be met before this exception is applicable in a given case: (1) the arrest of the said person must be lawful, and (2) the search must be properly incident to effecting that arrest. We turn now to a brief discussion of each of these two requirements.

The substance of all the definitions' of probable cause is a reasonable ground for belief of guilt. Probable cause exists where the facts and circumstances within their (the officers') knowledge, and of which they had reasonably trustworthy information, (are) sufficient in themselves to warrant a man of reasonable caution in the belief that an offense has been or is being committed. These long prevailing standards seek to safeguard citizens from rash and unreasonable interferences with privacy and from unfounded charges of crime. They also seek to give fair leeway for enforcing the law in the community's protection. Because many situations which confront officers in the course of executing their duties are more or less ambiguous, room must be allowed for some mistakes on their part. But the mistakes must be those of reasonable men, acting on facts leading sensibly to their conclusions of probability. Requiring more would unduly hamper law enforcement. To allow less would be to leave law abiding citizens at the mercy of the officers' whim or caprice.

Given a valid arrest, a police officer is authorized to conduct a search incident to effecting that arrest. This means that subsequent to such an arrest, "the police have an automatic right, without any further evidentiary showing, to conduct a full-blown search of the person arrested and the physical area into which he might reach in order to grab a weapon or destroy evidentiary items." State v. Ramos, 378 So.2d 1294, 1297 (Fla. 3d DCA 1979). "It is the fact of the lawful arrest which establishes the authority to search, and we hold that in the case of a lawful custodial arrest a full search of the person is not only an exception to the warrant requirement of the Fourth Amendment, but is also a 'reasonable' search under that Amendment." United States v. Robinson, 414 U.S. 218, 235, 94 S.Ct. 467, 477, 38 L.Ed.2d 427 (1973).

Turning to the instant case, we have no trouble in concluding that the state established that the "search incident" exception was applicable to the warrantless search conducted herein. The arrest, when effected, was plainly based on probable cause and the search of the defendant's person was clearly incident to effecting that arrest. The arrest, in this case, took place when the defendant was, in effect, ordered into the men's room by Officer Johnson after the defendant had stated, "Well, you might as well take me downtown and file your complaint." Prior thereto, the defendant's liberty was in no way restrained by the police. True, the defendant did give his plane ticket and driver's license to Officer Johnson, but both items were returned to the defendant so that his liberty cannot be said to have been restrained on that account. The arrest, in turn, of the defendant, when effected, was clearly a lawful one based on all the facts and circumstances of the case. We turn now to a review of those incriminating facts and circumstances.

First, the defendant's behavior prior to Officer Johnson's approach to the defendant in the airport fit, in part, a "drug courier profile" developed for use at major metropolitan airports by law enforcement agencies; indeed, this is what initially attracted Officer Johnson's attention to the defendant. This behavior, briefly stated, was that the defendant: (a) arrived at the airport just before flight time and was extremely rushed, (b) appeared to be very nervous and was looking into the faces of everyone around him as he entered and moved through the airport, (c) was carrying light carry-on luggage, (d) purchased his place ticket in cash, rather than by check or credit card, (e) purchased a one-way plane ticket to Houston, Texas, a "target" city used by couriers for drug deliveries, and most importantly, (f) disassociated himself and his companion Russell when Officer Pearson began speaking to Russell and thereafter attempted to leave the airport. Although this informal "drug courier profile" behavior did not and could not constitute probable cause, in itself, for the defendant's arrest, it was, when considered in totality, certainly suspicious behavior which warranted further scrutiny.

Secondly, the defendant's conduct during his conversation with Officer Johnson prior to arrest was equally suspicious and in our view, reasonably corroborated Officer Johnson's suspicion that he was dealing with a drug courier. Indeed, we are of the view that at this point there was a founded suspicion that the defendant was carrying contraband drugs which would have justified a temporary detention of the defendant, although such detention was not, in fact, effected in this case.

Finally, the defendant's statement to Officer Johnson which precipitated the arrest in this case was, without doubt, incriminating in nature. Sands stated, "Well you might as well take me downtown and file your complaint." By this statement, the defendant was surely indicating, albeit indirectly, that he had contraband drugs on his ankles which Officer Johnson was about to discover, and that he was submitting to an arrest which he knew would inevitably follow; indeed, Officer Johnson, as well as the trial judge, interpreted the statement to mean, in effect, "You've got me." That inference, in our view, seems irresistible given the context in which it was made. Moreover, we have no doubt that under the law the defendant's statement here was properly used against him. It was plainly a free and voluntary statement--indeed, a volunteered statement-- made at a time when the defendant was entirely free to go his way with his airline ticket and luggage in hand. It was in no sense the product of illegal police coercion, threats, promises, or intimidation. Indeed, the entire subject of a possible arrest did not even come up in the conversation until the defendant mentioned it. Agreed, the defendant was, in fact, frightened during his encounter with Officer Johnson and no doubt believed that an arrest was imminent when he made his statement, but that was entirely due to his own consciousness of guilt and was in no way prompted by anything improper done by Officer Johnson.

Nor can the statement be excluded as being a crude assertion of constitutional rights for which, concededly, no incriminating inference could be drawn. The defendant by this statement was not daring Officer Johnson to arrest him or leave him alone, he was not refusing his consent to a police search of his person, he was not asserting any rights at all. Plainly and simply, he was acquiescing in an arrest which he saw as inevitable solely because of his own consciousness of guilt. As such, the statement was not an assertion of constitutional rights or a defiance to authority, crudely expressed, but an incriminating statement which Officer Johnson had a right to consider in determining whether to arrest the defendant.

Putting together, then the sum total of all of the above facts and circumstances presented to Officer Johnson at the point of arrest, we have no trouble in concluding that a reasonable man, having the specialized training of a police officer, would have concluded that the defendant was carrying contraband drugs; the subsequent arrest was, therefore, based on probable cause. The defendant fit, in part, the law enforcement "drug courier profile," displaying a total of six such characteristics of the profile; the defendant lied to Officer Johnson concerning his travel plans and association with his companion while visibly shaking and sweating; and, finally, the defendant made a highly suspicious statement to Officer Johnson pointing toward his present possession of contraband drugs. These facts, when considered as a whole, and not in isolation, gave Officer Johnson probable cause to arrest the defendant; indeed, we think the defendant's suspicious statement made just prior to the arrest tipped the scales from founded suspicion to probable cause and fully justified Officer Johnson's belief that the defendant was carrying contraband drugs.

Given a valid arrest of the defendant herein, we have no trouble in further concluding that the subsequent search of his person--which revealed the contraband cocaine--was clearly incident to effecting that arrest. As previously noted, searches of an arrestee's person, are, without exception, considered properly incident to effecting the arrest; indeed, the defendant has raised no contention to the contrary in either the trial court or this court. Accordingly, the subject search was plainly a reasonable one under the appropriate state and federal constitutional provisions as the search was conducted incident to effecting a valid arrest of the defendant.

For the above stated reasons, the trial court was eminently correct in denying the defendant's motion to suppress in this cause. The judgment of conviction and sentence under review is, accordingly, Affirmed.

DANIEL S. PEARSON, Judge, dissenting.

While I realize that, in some quarters, it is forcefully argued that telling a police officer that he cannot enter your home without a warrant is a circumstance which gives rise to a suspicion that the sought-after evidence is within, I believed, until today, that no court would announce that such a statement or, here, its counterpart, either by itself or when added to other "suspicious" circumstances, provides probable cause to search. I thought that the courts of this country were in complete agreement that because the lawful exercise of constitutional rights in the face of police authority comes from both the righteous and the wicked, that such exercise proves nothing at all.

Sands' words, "Well you might as well take me downtown and file your complaint," are quite simply the functional equivalent of "arrest me," or in other settings, "get a warrant," "get lost," or even more provocative challenges to authority. If these words are to be interpreted, as the majority says, "given the context," then I suggest that the context will nearly always be one in which the statement can be construed as evincing consciousness of guilt. Thus, the most unequivocal statement, "You cannot search my person," in the context of a previous consent to a search of luggage, could quite clearly be construed as indicating excessive and particular concern that a search of the person will turn up incriminating evidence and be, therefore, a circumstance to be viewed with suspicion. The context then will nearly always supply the ambiguity, and words which ostensibly rebuff a perceived unauthorized intrusion can nearly always be said to be an admission of guilt.

By affirming the trial court, the majority approves a rule of law that a constitutionally sanctioned challenge to authority, or, as the majority seems to prefer, acquiescence to arrest in the face of authority, given the proper (and, I suggest, not unusual) context, is an incriminating admission. Here, despite the majority's omniscient hindsight, the statement by Sands no more clearly signified Sands' guilt than it signified the exercise of his constitutional right to be searched incident to a lawful arrest. In my view, the correct rule of law is that only a clear and unequivocal incriminating statement--looking to the words alone--can be a circumstance used in determining the existence of probable cause.

I have a still greater concern about the majority opinion. The majority implicitly concedes that the search was conducted without the defendant's voluntary consent. They do this quite obviously because the defendant's "ambiguous" statement did not provide the necessary clear and convincing evidence of consent. But the majority takes that very same statement and uses it as the last straw for probable cause. By this process of converting non-consent into a factor for probable cause, the majority obviates the need for the defendant's consent to search where probable cause is lacking. If refusal to consent--unequivocal or ambiguous--is, viewed in context, suspicious and can provide probable cause, then an officer who has less than probable cause need only ask for permission to search, and no matter what the answer, proceed to search. Although likely unintended, this is the pernicious outcome of the majority opinion. I dissent.

REVIEW SECTION

READING COMPREHENSION

Detail the actions of Sands and Officer Johnson leading up to and including the search in the men's restroom.

What factors contributed to Officer Johnson's assertion of probable cause?

THINKING CRITICALLY

The dissenting Judge states: "If refusal to consent--unequivocal or ambiguous--is, viewed in context, suspicious and can provide probable cause, then an officer who has less than probable cause need only ask for permission to search, and no matter what the answer, proceed to search. Although likely unintended, this is the pernicious outcome of the majority opinion." Do you agree or disagree with this potentially slippery slope statement? Articulate your reasons.

Using both the arguments of the majority and the dissenting Judge, outline why or why not you believe there was probable cause to search. That is, justify your finding in this case.

SECTION 2: EXPECTATION OF PRIVACY

OVERVIEW

Until 1967 the trespass doctrine was implemented by the U.S. Supreme Court to define searches. This doctrine deemed a 'search' by officers any physical invasion of a 'constitutionally protected area,' which included persons, houses, papers, and effects as named in the Fourth Amendment. In 1967 in *Katz v. United States*, the privacy doctrine became law. This doctrine interpreted the Fourth Amendment to protect persons as opposed to places, whenever a citizen has an expectation of privacy recognized by the larger society. Section Twenty-Three of the Florida Constitution elaborates a citizen's right of privacy:

> SECTION 23. **Right of privacy.**--Every natural person has the
> right to be let alone and free from governmental intrusion into the
> person's private life except as otherwise provided herein. This
> section shall not be construed to limit the public's right of access to
> public records and meetings as provided by law.

What was not so clearly elaborated was when an individual has a reasonable expectation of privacy, and what constitutes a plain-view search by government officials. While in theory the privacy doctrine shifted the balance in favor of the citizenry, courts almost always weigh the balance in favor of the government.

Established by the privacy doctrine was a test to determine whether a government action can be considered a search. First, the subjective privacy prong addresses whether the citizen had an actual individual expectation of privacy. Second, the objective privacy prong addresses whether the subjective expectation of privacy is one that would be considered reasonable by society.

CASE

In *State of Florida v. Sarantopoulos* the state appeals a trial court order which permitted suppression of marijuana and diazepam seized in the backyard of Sarantopoulos pursuant to a search warrant. The Court of Appeals reverses the decision on the grounds that although there was a subjective expectation of privacy in the defendant's backyard, society at large would not recognize this expectation as reasonable. The Court concludes that the marijuana and diazepam were seized during a lawful search.

STATE OF FLORIDA V. SARANTOPOULOS
604 So.2d 551 (Fla. App. 2 Dist., 1992)

The State of Florida appeals a trial court order which granted a motion to suppress marijuana and diazepam seized pursuant to a search warrant. We reverse, concluding that although James Sarantopoulos manifested a subjective expectation of privacy in the curtilage of his home, society is not prepared to recognize his expectation as reasonable. Thus the officers seized the contraband during a lawful search.

The parties provided the following evidence to the trial court at the hearing on the motion to suppress. A detective for the Largo Police Department testified that he received information from a fellow officer that an unidentified individual had contacted the police and informed the police that marijuana was inside James Sarantopoulos's home and marijuana plants were growing in the backyard. The officers went to the residence to verify the information. The residence had a backyard surrounded by a six-foot wooden board-on-board fence; the front yard did not have a fence. The officers walked through an adjoining neighbor's unfenced yard without seeking the neighbor's permission. The officers could not see through the fence into Sarantopoulos's backyard but from the neighbor's yard, a detective stood on his tip toes and saw several marijuana plants growing. The officers used no other devices to view the property nor did they trespass onto Sarantopoulos's property. Based upon their observations and the anonymous tip, the officers obtained a search warrant to search the residence and the backyard.

The trial court, however, suppressed the evidence seized pursuant to this search warrant. In its order granting the motion to suppress the evidence, the trial court made the following findings: The photographs of the location, the testimony of the officer and the testimony of the defendant regarding the construction, maintenance and location of the fence and the adjacent structures make it clear that Sarantopoulos had a reasonable expectation of privacy in the subject location. The Court finds law enforcement engaged in "extraordinary efforts" to overcome the defendant's reasonable attempts to maintain the privacy of his curtilage. Since the only other information contained in the affidavit for the search warrant was from an unnamed tipster, the trial court concluded that the search warrant must fail. We recognize that the area of Sarantopoulos's fenced backyard is clearly within the curtilage of his home and warrants fourth amendment protection.

A fourth amendment analysis must begin with the two-part inquiry to determine whether a person has a constitutionally protected reasonable expectation of privacy. First, has the individual manifested a subjective expectation of privacy in the object of the challenged search? Second, is society prepared to recognize that expectation as reasonable? Clearly, Sarantopoulos with his solid six-foot fence has manifested a subjective expectation of privacy in his backyard. Thus he meets the first prong of the inquiry. This court, however, must consider the second prong of the inquiry and determine whether society is prepared to recognize his expectation as reasonable. The way society views the actions of Sarantopoulos defines the zone of privacy he may create for protection from searches under the fourth amendment. We conclude that society is not prepared to honor Sarantopoulos's expectation of privacy and that his expectation of privacy, viewed objectively, is unreasonable.

First, Sarantopoulos, by building a solid six-foot fence, has created his zone of privacy from persons in adjoining yards attempting to peer into his yard from six feet or lower. Sarantopoulos has not created a zone of privacy from a neighbor's observations over the fence if that neighbor is seven feet tall. A property owner reasonably should foresee that neighbors or other persons on the adjoining land may use devices which place those persons in a position to view over a six-foot fence. Further, as Sarantopoulos acknowledges, the Supreme Court has recognized that it would not be an unlawful search for law enforcement to fly over his property and view the backyard, so long as law enforcement does not violate any laws or Federal Aviation Administration (FAA) regulations.

Second, Sarantopoulos had no legitimate expectation of privacy in his neighbor's property, and his fourth amendment rights were not violated by the detective's presence on that property. Sarantopoulos cannot create his zone of privacy in his backyard upon the premise that his adjoining neighbors will not permit police officers or others to enter the neighbor's backyard and use means to peer over a six-foot fence. Such a reliance is unrealistic. Most neighbors who were not suspects of a criminal violation likely would permit a police officer to enter his or her backyard to gain evidence concerning a crime occurring nearby.

Finally, since the zone of privacy Sarantopoulos has created by his fence is at best a limited zone of privacy, the observations of the detective cannot be an illegal search unless the detective's entry into the neighbor's yard, without permission, is a factor which makes the detective's actions an illegal search. We conclude that the police officer's entry into the neighbor's yard, without permission, to look over the fence into Sarantopoulos's backyard, did not violate Sarantopoulos's constitutionally protected right to privacy in violation of the fourth amendment. Therefore, in this case the officers' civil trespass on adjoining land to look into the curtilage of Sarantopoulos's home should not make the search illegal.

We believe our Supreme Court has answered this question <u>State v. Rickard, 420 So.2d 303 (Fla.1982)</u> when it inferred that officers may make observations, without permission, from private property which is adjacent to the defendant's property without intruding into a protected area. We reverse the trial court's order suppressing the evidence seized by search warrant and remand for further proceedings consistent with this opinion.

Reversed and remanded. PATTERSON and BLUE, JJ., concur.

REVIEW SECTION

READING COMPREHENSION

Under what circumstances did the police pursue a warrant to search the home of the defendant?

THINKING CRITICALLY

Elaborate why you agree or disagree with the court's opinion that there was no reasonable expectation of privacy in this case.

SECTION 3: PLAIN VIEW, HEARING, SMELL, AND TOUCH

OVERVIEW

When government officials discover evidence using their ordinary senses (seeing, touching, smelling and hearing), these are not considered Fourth Amendment searches. Three conditions must be met however in order to comply with the plain-view doctrine:

(1)   Officers are in a location in which they have a legal right to occupy;

(2)   Officers do not use the assistance of advanced technology to improve upon ordinary senses; and

(3)   The discovery of the evidence by the office is by chance.

The difficulty in applying the plain-view doctrine surrounds the issue of what is considered advanced technology.

CASE

In *Minter-Smith v. Florida* police entered the defendant's home under the belief that illegal dog fighting was occurring in the back yard. With no warrant, officers conducted a search that resulted in the seizure of dog fighting paraphernalia, drug paraphernalia, a firearm and cannabis residue. The State argues two exceptions to the warrant requirement in this case and the Florida Court of Appeals disagrees with both arguments and reverses the finding.

SHOMARI N. MINTER-SMITH V. STATE OF FLORIDA
1D02-4045 (Fla. App. 1 Dist., 2003)

Police entered the defendant's home upon their belief that illegal dog fighting was occurring in the back yard. After entering the home, a protective sweep and subsequent search resulted in the seizure of dog fighting paraphernalia, drug paraphernalia, a firearm and cannabis residue. Since no warrant was obtained before police entered the home, an exception to the warrant requirement must exist before the items obtained can be introduced as evidence. The State argues two exceptions to the warrant requirement: (1) the officers obtained valid consent to search the defendant's home; and alternatively, (2) the dog fighting paraphernalia was in plain view during the initial protective sweep, thus the police would have been able to obtain a search warrant and, consequently, the other evidence would have been inevitably discovered. We disagree with both arguments and reverse.

Fort Walton Beach Police were dispatched to the defendant's home in response to a complaint that dogs were fighting, and male voices were heard encouraging the dogs to continue fighting. As officers arrived at the scene, they positioned themselves at various locations around the home. While looking over a fence, one officer, although observing no illegal activity, heard noises she interpreted as consistent with people conducting a dog fight in the backyard. After several patrol cars responded to the scene, officers entered through the unlocked front door of the home without permission, and one officer entered the backyard by going over the fence.

Once inside, the officers handcuffed the defendant and four other individuals. Officers performed a protective sweep where they observed a broomstick with bite marks and an exacto knife with a heavily taped handle. The officers testified they were not able to identify these items as dog fighting paraphernalia until assistance was received from a non-police officer advisor. It is interesting to note that not only were the broomstick and exacto knife not immediately recognizable as evidence, but no other evidence of dog fighting was discovered, even after a full search of the home. The officer who testified she looked over the fence did not even report seeing any illegal activity.

While the suspects were being removed, a young woman arrived who the police believed lived at the home. The State maintains the woman consented to a search of the home after she was told "we need to treat the house as a crime scene and we need to look in the house for evidence." This statement does not request consent. Rather it is a statement that police planned to "look in the house for evidence." A consent to search is valid when the consent is freely and voluntarily given and the search is conducted within the scope of the consent. Here, the young woman's response to the officer's statement is no more than acquiescence to authority, not consent. Because no consent to search was given, this exception to the warrant requirement fails.

The State alternatively argues, using two exceptions to the warrant requirement in tandem, that all of the evidence is admissible. The State maintains the plain view doctrine allowed them to seize the dog fighting paraphernalia, and that paraphernalia would have provided them with the requisite probable cause to obtain a search warrant. Had they obtained a warrant, the additional evidence would have been inevitably discovered and thus admissible. The plain view doctrine allows police to seize contraband in plain view when (1) the seizing officer is in a location he has a legal right to be, (2) the incriminating character of the evidence is immediately apparent, and (3) the seizing officer has a lawful right of access to the object. In examining whether the seizing officer was where he had a right to be, we note all of the alleged illegal activity was taking place in the back yard. One officer even entered the backyard by going over the fence. Thus, entry into the home appears unnecessary to respond to the alleged dog fighting.

However, even assuming the police had a right to be in the home, the State cannot meet the second prong of the plain view doctrine. It is well settled that when closer examination of an item observed in plain view is necessary to confirm its incriminating nature, its nature is not considered "immediately apparent." Here, because they were later informed of the items' significance by "someone else's expertise," the nature of the broomstick and the exacto knife were not "immediately apparent" to the police. Thus, the officers were precluded from lawfully seizing these items.

The next step of the State's argument is that the drug paraphernalia, firearm, and cannabis residue would be admissible under the doctrine of inevitable discovery. The inevitable discovery doctrine allows evidence obtained as a result of an unconstitutional police search to be admitted if the evidence would ultimately have been discovered by legal means. To apply this doctrine, there must be only a reasonable probability of discovery, not an absolute certainty. This doctrine can provide relief to the State only if the plain view exception applies. Since the plain view exception fails, the State had no evidence to establish probable cause to obtain a search warrant. Since they could not have obtained a warrant, no lawful search would have taken place. Therefore, the drug paraphernalia, firearm, and cannabis residue would not have been inevitably discovered. Accordingly, the trial court's denial of the defendant's motion to suppress is REVERSED, the defendant's sentence VACATED, and the cause REMANDED.

REVIEW SECTION

READING COMPREHENSION

Detail the events precipitating the search of the defendant's home.

Elaborate why the plain-view doctrine was rejected by the court in this case.

THINKING CRITICALLY

How was the plain-view doctrine applied differently in *Florida v. Sarantopoulos* and *Minter-Smith v. Florida*?

What were the main distinctions in *Florida v. Sarantopoulos* and *Minter-Smith v. Florida* that resulted in different judgments?

SECTION 4: UNPROTECTED PLACES

OVERVIEW

Fourth Amendment protection extends to persons, houses, papers, and effects, however places considered unprotected such as open fields, public places, and abandoned property are not guaranteed. What are the guidelines however in defining an unprotected place? With regard to open fields, included are privately owned lands that are not within the area immediately surrounding one's home. To determine this, the court considers the distance from the home, the presence/absence of a fence, the purpose of the area in question, and the measures taken by a citizen to protect this area from public view. A public place is considered publicly owned areas and private places that are open to the public. Abandoned property includes both physical abandonment as well as an intention to surrender the expectation of privacy. The court has adopted a totality-of-circumstance test to differentiate a place with an expectation of privacy from a place considered unprotected and thus not addressed by the Fourth Amendment.

CASE

State of Florida v. Anderson reviews Anderson v. State, 576 So.2d 319 (Fla. 2d DCA 1991). The main issue in question is: Can an abandonment of property after an illegal police stop but not pursuant to a search be considered involuntary? That is, if you are illegally stopped by the police and abandon incriminating evidence, can this be used against you at trial?

STATE OF FLORIDA V. ANDERSON
591 So.2d 611 (Fla., 1992)

We review Anderson v. State, 576 So.2d 319 (Fla. 2d DCA 1991), on the basis of the following question certified by the district court of appeal as one of great public importance: Can an abandonment of property after an illegal police stop but not pursuant to a search be considered involuntary?

The relevant facts of this case are as follows. Shortly after midnight, police officers conducting an undercover surveillance observed an unknown black male engage in several hand transactions with others that appeared to be distributing items. Some of the transactions occurred with persons on foot and some with persons in vehicles. The man conducted a transaction with Anderson. Anderson then walked to the front porch of his house. An officer drove by the house

41

in a marked patrol car. When Anderson saw the police unit, he threw an object from his hand into a nearby planter. After the cruiser passed, Anderson removed something from the planter and put it in his shoe. An officer detained Anderson, placed him in the police cruiser, and ran a warrants check on him. No outstanding warrants were found, and Anderson was released. When Anderson got out of the police car, an officer checked the back seat and found a cocaine pipe. Officers searched Anderson and found one gram of marijuana and a one-dollar bill containing powdered cocaine in his shoe. Anderson was arrested for possession of cocaine, possession of drug paraphernalia, and possession of marijuana.

The trial judge denied Anderson's motion to suppress. The district court of appeal found that the officers lacked a founded suspicion of criminal activity and therefore Anderson was illegally detained. The court found that Anderson abandoned the cocaine pipe as a result of the illegal detention, and thus the pipe and other evidence should have been suppressed.

We address first the legality of Anderson's detention. Police officers may temporarily detain a person upon circumstances which reasonably indicate that the person has committed, is committing, or is about to commit a crime. The state argues that under the totality of the circumstances, the officers had a founded suspicion that Anderson had engaged in a narcotics transaction. We agree.

Officers had observed the man with whom Anderson conducted business engage in several similar transactions. The transactions occurred in the late evening hours. Officers observed Anderson's furtive, suspicious actions upon the approach and passing of the police car. We find these facts sufficient to lead the officers reasonably to conclude, in light of their experience, that Anderson had engaged in criminal activity.

Although we have determined that the detention at issue here was valid, the certified question presumes an illegal stop. "While it is true that a criminal defendant's voluntary abandonment of evidence can remove the taint of an illegal stop or arrest, it is equally true that for this to occur the abandonment must be truly voluntary and not merely the product of police misconduct." United States v. Beck, 602 F.2d 726, 729-30 (5th Cir.1979). Where there is a nexus between illegal police conduct and abandonment of the challenged evidence, and the nexus has not become attenuated so as to dissipate the taint, the evidence should be suppressed.

Accordingly, we answer the certified question in the affirmative. An abandonment which is the product of an illegal stop is involuntary, and the abandoned property must be suppressed. However, in the instant case, because we have determined that the detention was valid, the subsequent abandonment of the cocaine pipe in the police car was not the fruit of police misconduct. Thus, there is no basis for its suppression. Accordingly, Anderson is not entitled to relief. We answer the certified question in the affirmative and quash the decision below. It is so ordered.

REVIEW SECTION

READING COMPREHENSION

Detail the circumstances under which police approached the defendant.

Elaborate the totality-of-circumstance test that the court employed in rendering its decision.

THINKING CRITICALLY

Did officers have reasonable grounds, in your opinion, to detain the defendant and thus benefit from abandonment of property?

CONCLUSION

The Fourth Amendment of the U.S. Constitution and Section Twelve of the Florida Constitution are designed to ensure that government officials conform to the law when obtaining evidence. While crime control obviously depends on police gathering of information from often reluctant sources, authorities are bound by law when obtaining evidence. To control crime and balance the rights of individuals, the state has created guidelines as outlined in constitutions and interpreted by the courts. This chapter reviewed searches and seizures; the "expectation of privacy;" plain view, hearing, smell, and touch; and unprotected places. These are a few of the issues that deal directly with placing a reasonable limit on government officials and establishing the protection of liberty and privacy from government intrusion of the citizenry.

Chapter Four

Stop and Frisk

According to the Fourth Amendment to the U.S. Constitution and Section Twelve of the Florida Constitution, a seizure occurs when a government official removes an individual's right to leave or stay in a specific location. As outlined in *Florida v. Royer 1982*, officers do not violate the Fourth Amendment when they approach individuals in a public place and request responses to questions, or request to search an individual. "Stop and frisk" was brought to the American colonies by the English and was not challenged in the U.S. until the 1960s.

As outlined by §901.151 of the Florida Statutes, "Florida Stop and Frisk Law" involves the following:

> (2) Whenever any law enforcement officer of this state encounters any person under circumstances which reasonably indicate that such person has committed, is committing, or is about to commit a violation of the criminal laws of this state of the criminal ordinances of any municipality or county, the officer may temporarily detain such person for the purpose of ascertaining the identity of the person temporarily detained and the circumstances surrounding the person's presence abroad which led the officer to believe that the person had committed, was committing, or was about to commit a criminal offense.
>
> (3) No person shall be temporarily detained under the provisions of subsection (2) longer than is reasonably necessary to effect the purposes of that subsection. Such temporary detention shall not extend beyond the place where it was first effected or the immediate vicinity thereof.
>
> (6) No evidence seized by a law enforcement officer in any search under this section shall be admissible against any person in any court of this state or political subdivision thereof unless the search which disclosed its existence was authorized by and conducted in compliance with the provisions of subsections (2)-(5).

This chapter will review:

(1)   Stops, frisks, and the Fourth Amendment;

(2)   Stops and the Fourth Amendment;

(3)   Special situation stops; and

(4)   Frisks and the Fourth Amendment.

SECTION 1: STOPS, FRISKS, AND THE FOURTH AMENDMENT

OVERVIEW

There are two types of Fourth Amendment seizures, frequently referred to as stops. First, an actual-seizure stop occurs when government officials physically grab a suspect with the intention of preventing departure. Second, a show-of-authority stop occurs when officers demonstrate a show of authority wherein a reasonable individual would not feel free to terminate the encounter. Examples would include a roadblock, the presence of several officers, drawing a weapon, or surrounding an individual's automobile, to name only a few.

In sum, a Fourth Amendment stop involves a brief detention for the purposes of investigation by law enforcement. A Four Amendment frisk involves a once-over-lightly pat-down of a suspect to protect officers from potential harm. As discussed earlier, the greater the invasion upon the individual, the greater the objective basis required for support on the part of government officials. Indeed, officers need relatively few suspicious facts to support a stop and frisk as it represent the beginning of the criminal justice process and is thus considered more visible, but less intrusive than other measures. What is important to consider as you read this chapter is the visibility of stop and frisks. Because a stop and frisk occurs where many other individuals can view its occurrence, this transparency of police control has an impact on public perception of police power. Most individuals have probably witnessed a stop and frisk of another individual, if you have not been subjected to one yourself. Recall this experience and reflect on how this incident shaped your perception of police power in this community. Reflect on how this perception may be intensified if you reside in a low-income or minority neighborhood where police presence is greater, thus increasing the transparency of police power even further.

To determine whether or not the government has complied with the Fourth Amendment involves analysis of three questions that we began discussion of in Chapter Three:

(1)   Was the action by the government a stop and frisk?

(2)   If considered a stop and frisk, was it unreasonable?

(3)   If considered an unreasonable stop and frisk, should the evidence obtained be excluded from consideration?

As in the case of search and seizure outlined in the previous chapter, if the action can not be considered a stop and frisk, the Fourth Amendment and Section Twelve of the Florida Constitution do not apply.

There are two clauses in both the Fourth Amendment of the U.S. Constitution and Section Twelve of the Florida Constitution that are included in this analysis. The first is the reasonableness clause which in Section Twelve of the Florida Constitution reads:

> The right of the people to be secure in their persons, houses, papers and effects against unreasonable searches and seizures, and against

the unreasonable interception of private communications by any means, shall not be violated.

The second is the warrant clause which in Section Twelve of the Florida Constitution reads:

No warrant shall be issued except upon probable cause, supported by affidavit, particularly describing the place or places to be searched, the person or persons, thing or things to be seized, the communication to be intercepted, and the nature of evidence to be obtained.

Prior to the 1960s, the U.S. Supreme Court viewed the warrant and reasonableness clauses and firmly connected in what was called the conventional Fourth Amendment approach. After 1960, the court shifted to a reasonableness Fourth Amendment approach which suggested that the two clauses are separate. What this meant in practice was that searches and seizures that occur without a warrant can still be considered reasonable by the courts. In light of this, when does Section Twelve of the Florida Constitution require warrants? And, what does 'unreasonable' really mean?

While a search and seizure can be based on warrants and probable cause, most must pass the reasonableness test. The government must prove to the court that the need to either search or seize outweighed any invasion of liberty and privacy of the individual. In addition, the government must prove that there were enough facts to support the search or seizure. To answer the reasonableness question, the courts use a totality of circumstances approach to analyze each case individually. Needless to say, in creating law enforcement strategies this complicates things immeasurably. Because the courts have been attempting to sort out what is and is not reasonable since the 1960s, and still are not entirely clear, it should come as no surprise that this chapter is extensive in both case example and discussion. The lack of clarity from the courts extends to all lower courts which are bound to follow these decisions, as well as to state legislatures who attempt to incorporate court decisions into criminal procedure guidelines. In each case what remains the same is that the need to control crime must outweigh the invasion that occurs of individual rights.

CASE

In *McNeil v. Florida,* the court examines an appeal from the Circuit Court in which McNeil appeals the denial of his motion to suppress cocaine. The Circuit Court ruled that the officer in this case had a legal basis to expand the instant seizure and search beyond the boundaries of a Terry stop and frisk. This court reversed. When reading this case, keep in mind both the difference between a Terry stop and frisk and a search and seizure, as well as the reasonableness approach adopted by the courts.

MCNEIL V. FLORIDA
746 So.2d 547 (Fla. App. 5 Dist., 1999)

In February 1998, McNeil was adjudicated guilty of possession of cocaine and tampering with physical evidence. The court placed him on probation for 30 months. In April 1998, he was arrested and charged with possession of cocaine and resisting arrest without violence. He was further charged with violating his probation in the earlier case based on the cocaine possession and the uncharged crime of tampering with evidence.

McNeil filed a motion to suppress arguing the cocaine was found as a result of an illegal investigatory detention. At the suppression hearing, the arresting officer testified that while on patrol he observed McNeil coming from behind a shopping plaza at approximately 3:00 a.m. Since the businesses were closed at that time, the officer viewed McNeil's activity as suspicious. He also observed what appeared to be a quart bottle of beer in McNeil's back pants pocket. The officer called McNeil over and, although directed by the officer to keep his hands out of his pockets, as McNeil approached he put his left hand into his front pants pocket three times. Concerned for his own safety, the officer repeatedly told McNeil to remove and keep his hand from the pocket. Finally, he ordered McNeil to put his hands on the rear of the patrol car "to get his hand out of his pocket." McNeil obeyed.

As the officer prepared to perform a pat down, he noticed a wadded piece of brown paper in McNeil's left fist. The officer testified his training and experience told him McNeil "was trying to conceal something within the paper" but he never testified that he thought McNeil had a weapon or drugs. The officer attempted to wrest the paper from McNeil, but McNeil resisted and put the paper in his mouth. The officer tried unsuccessfully to pull McNeil's arm away from his mouth. However, during the scuffle, a white, rock-like substance fell from the paper. Field testing determined the substance was cocaine.

The trial court found the officer's actions reasonable under the circumstances and denied the motion to suppress. McNeil thereafter pled nolo contendere to possession of cocaine, resisting arrest without violence and violation of probation, reserving his right to appeal the denial of his motion. The trial court erred in denying the motion. McNeil was seized when the officer ordered him to place his hands on the back of the patrol car. The first issue for this court is whether the officer had a founded suspicion to stop McNeil. We think there was. To effect a lawful investigatory stop, an officer must have a founded suspicion, or a reasonable articulable suspicion, that the person detained has committed, is committing or is about to commit a crime.

Considering the totality of the circumstances before us, the officer formed a founded suspicion that McNeil was involved in some form of criminal activity and that he was in possession of a weapon. McNeil's presence at the shopping center at 3:00 a.m. and his failure to obey a command to keep his hands out of his pocket and in plain view were sufficient to give the officer a founded suspicion of criminal activity and that McNeil was in possession of a weapon. Accordingly, an investigatory stop and a frisk for weapons was proper. However, these facts did not establish a legal basis to expand the limitation of the Terry stop and frisk. Florida's Stop and Frisk Law allowed the officer to pat down McNeil for weapons. During the suppression hearing, the officer testified that before he commenced the frisk of McNeil for weapons, based on his training and experience as a street officer, he believed McNeil was trying to conceal "something" within a piece of paper in his hand. The officer did not testify that he believed that the "something" was a weapon. The officer also did not state that the "something" appeared to be contraband. As a result, the record does not support the trial court's ruling that the officer had a legal basis to expand the instant seizure and search beyond the boundaries of a Terry stop and frisk.

The motion to suppress was dispositive of the cocaine possession and probation violation charges. In addition, McNeil was entitled to resist the unlawful search without violence. Accordingly, those convictions and sentences are reversed.

REVIEW SECTION

READING COMPREHENSION

Detail the events that lead to the officer's suspicion and subsequent stop of the defendant.

What is the difference between a 'stop and frisk' and a 'search and seizure?'

THINKING CRITICALLY

What was the rationale in the court determining that "an investigatory stop and a frisk for weapons was proper" but the "facts did not establish a legal basis to expand the limitation of the Terry stop and frisk?"

Do you believe that an analysis of the totality of the circumstances revealed a reasonableness on the part of the officer? Articulate why you agree or disagree with the court's finding.

SECTION 2: STOPS AND THE FOURTH AMENDMENT

OVERVIEW

When examining encounters between individuals and police, there are three types:

(1)   Voluntary encounters are those not involving any sort of police force or coercion and thus the Fourth Amendment does not apply;

(2)   Stops are brief but involuntary seizures that occur in public places, and which require reasonable suspicion according to the Fourth Amendment; and

(3)   Arrests are involuntary detentions that usually occur in a police station, last an extended period of time, and require probable cause according to the Fourth Amendment.

As we discuss stops in this section, keep in mind that a 'reasonable' stop must include an objective basis that adds up to reasonable suspicion by the officer, and that the scope of the stop must be both short and occur at the initial scene. What is reasonable suspicion as required in a stop and how does it differ from probable cause as required in an arrest? Reasonable suspicion involves examination of the totality of the facts that lead an officer to suspect a crime may be occurring. To build reasonable suspicion, government officials may rely on either direct information or hearsay information. In fact in *Florida v. J.L. 2000* the Florida Supreme Court found that hearsay information can form the basis for reasonable suspicion, but only if accompanied by some specific sense of reliability. In contrast, probable cause involves an examination of the totality of the facts that lead an officer to believe that a crime is occurring. These distinctions are extremely important to keep in mind as you read the cases in this and the following chapter. The question that should remain in the forefront of your mind is: Did the officer suspect or believe that a crime may be or is occurring.

CASE

The below case, *Florida v. Royer* was addressed briefly in your textbook in the discussion of *Illinois v. Wardlow*. In the case below, the court determined that if an officer approaches an individual without either reasonable suspicion or probable cause, that individual has the right to terminate contact with the police and proceed with their activity. This case is provided with minimal editing due to its significance in later cases. As well, a dissenting opinion is provided for your review.

FLORIDA V. ROYER
460 U.S. 491, 103 S.Ct. 1319, 75 L.Ed.2d 229 (1983)

After purchasing a one-way airline ticket to New York City at Miami International Airport under an assumed name and checking his two suitcases bearing identification tags with the same assumed name, respondent went to the concourse leading to the airline boarding area, where he was approached by two detectives, who previously had observed him and believed that his characteristics fit the so-called "drug courier profile." Upon request, but without oral consent, respondent produced his airline ticket and driver's license, which carried his correct name. When the detectives asked about the discrepancy in names, respondent explained that a friend had made the ticket reservation in the assumed name. The detectives then informed respondent that they were narcotics investigators and that they had reason to suspect him of transporting narcotics, and, without returning his airline ticket or driver's license, asked him to accompany them to a small room adjacent to the concourse. Without respondent's consent, one of the detectives retrieved respondent's luggage from the airline and brought it to the room. While he did not respond to the detectives' request that he consent to a search of the luggage, respondent produced a key and unlocked one of the suitcases in which marihuana was found. When respondent said he did not know the combination to the lock on the second suitcase but did not object to its being opened, the officers pried it open and found more marihuana. Respondent was then told he was under arrest.

We are required in this case to determine whether the Court of Appeal of Florida, Third District, properly applied the precepts of the Fourth Amendment in holding that respondent Royer was

49

being illegally detained at the time of his purported consent to a search of his luggage. Prior to his trial for felony possession of marihuana, Royer made a motion to suppress the evidence obtained in the search of the suitcases. The trial court found that Royer's consent to the search was "freely and voluntarily given," and that, regardless of the consent, the warrantless search was reasonable because "the officer doesn't have the time to run out and get a search warrant because the plane is going to take off." Following the denial of the motion to suppress, Royer changed his plea from "not guilty" to "nolo contendere," specifically reserving the right to appeal the denial of the motion to suppress. Royer was convicted.

The District Court of Appeal, sitting en banc, reversed Royer's conviction. The court held that Royer had been involuntarily confined within the small room without probable cause; that the involuntary detention had exceeded limited restraint permitted at the time his consent to the search was obtained; and that the consent to search was therefore invalid because tainted by the unlawful confinement. Several factors led the court to conclude that respondent's confinement was tantamount to arrest. Royer had "found himself in a small enclosed area being confronted by two police officers—a situation which presents an almost classic definition of imprisonment." 389 So.2d 1007, 1018 (Fla.App.1980). The detectives' statement to Royer that he was suspected of transporting narcotics also bolstered the finding that Royer was "in custody" at the time the consent to search was given. In addition, the detectives' possession of Royer's airline ticket and their retrieval and possession of his luggage made it clear, in the District Court of Appeal's view, that Royer was not free to leave.

At the suppression hearing Royer testified that he was under the impression that he was not free to leave the officers' presence. The Florida Court of Appeal found that this apprehension "was much more than a well-justified subjective belief," for the State had conceded at oral argument before that court that "the officers would not have permitted Royer to leave the room even if [Royer] had erroneously thought he could." Detective Johnson, who conducted the search, had specifically stated at the suppression hearing that he did not have probable cause to arrest Royer until the suitcases were opened and their contents revealed. In the absence of probable cause, the court concluded, Royer's consent to search, given only after he had been unlawfully confined, was ineffective to justify the search and thus invalid as a matter of law. We granted the State's petition for certiorari, 454 U.S. 1079, 102 S.Ct. 631, 70 L.Ed.2d 612 (1981), and now affirm.

Some preliminary observations are in order. First, it is unquestioned that without a warrant to search Royer's luggage and in the absence of probable cause and exigent circumstances, the validity of the search depended on Royer's purported consent. Neither is it disputed that where the validity of a search rests on consent, the State has the burden of proving that the necessary consent was obtained and that it was freely and voluntarily given, a burden that is not satisfied by showing a mere submission to a claim of lawful authority.

Second, law enforcement officers do not violate the Fourth Amendment by merely approaching an individual on the street or in another public place, by asking him if he is willing to answer some questions, by putting questions to him if the person is willing to listen, or by offering in evidence in a criminal prosecution his voluntary answers to such questions. Nor would the fact that the officer identifies himself as a police officer, without more, convert the encounter into a seizure requiring some level of objective justification. The person approached, however, need not answer any question put to him; indeed, he may decline to listen to the questions at all and may go on his way. He may not be detained even momentarily without reasonable, objective grounds for doing so; and his refusal to listen or answer does not, without more, furnish those grounds.

Third, it is also clear that not all seizures of the person must be justified by probable cause to arrest for a crime.

Fourth, there are only limited exceptions to the general rule that seizures of the person require probable cause to arrest. The reasonableness requirement of the Fourth Amendment requires no less when the police action is a seizure permitted on less than probable cause because of legitimate law enforcement interests. The scope of the detention must be carefully tailored to its underlying justification.

Fifth, statements given during a period of illegal detention are inadmissible even though voluntarily given if they are the product of the illegal detention and not the result of an independent act of free will.

Sixth, if the events in this case amounted to no more than a permissible police encounter in a public place or a justifiable detention, Royer's consent, if voluntary, would have been effective to legalize the search of his two suitcases. The Florida Court of Appeal in the case before us, however, concluded not only that Royer had been seized when he gave his consent to search his luggage but also that the bounds of an investigative stop had been exceeded, thus Royer's statement was tainted by the illegality, a conclusion that required reversal in the absence of probable cause to arrest. The question before us is whether the record warrants that conclusion. We think that it does.

The State proffers three reasons for holding that when Royer consented to the search of his luggage, he was not being illegally detained. First, it is submitted that the entire encounter was consensual and hence Royer was not being held against his will at all. We find this submission untenable. Asking for and examining Royer's ticket and his driver's license were no doubt permissible in themselves, but when the officers identified themselves as narcotics agents, told Royer that he was suspected of transporting narcotics, and asked him to accompany them to the police room, while retaining his ticket and driver's license and without indicating in any way that he was free to depart, Royer was effectively seized for the purposes of the Fourth Amendment. These circumstances surely amount to a show of official authority such that "a reasonable person would have believed he was not free to leave."

Second, the State submits that if Royer was seized, there existed reasonable, articulable suspicion to justify a temporary detention and that the limits of a *Terry*-type stop were never exceeded. We agree with the State that when the officers discovered that Royer was traveling under an assumed name, this fact, and the facts already known to the officers—paying cash for a one-way ticket, the mode of checking the two bags, and Royer's appearance and conduct in general—were adequate grounds for suspecting Royer of carrying drugs and for temporarily detaining him and his luggage while they attempted to verify or dispel their suspicions in a manner that did not exceed the limits of an investigative detention. We also agree that had Royer voluntarily consented to the search of his luggage while he was justifiably being detained on reasonable suspicion, the products of the search would be admissible against him. We have concluded, however, that at the time Royer produced the key to his suitcase, the detention to which he was then subjected was a more serious intrusion on his personal liberty than is allowable on mere suspicion of criminal activity. Royer was never informed that he was free to board his plane if he so chose, and he reasonably believed that he was being detained. At least as of that moment, any consensual aspects of the encounter had evaporated, and we cannot fault the Florida Court of Appeal for concluding that the restraint to which Royer was then subjected was not justified. As a practical matter, Royer was under arrest.

We also think that the officers' conduct was more intrusive than necessary to effectuate an investigative detention otherwise authorized by the *Terry* line of cases. First, by returning his ticket and driver's license, and informing him that he was free to go if he so desired, the officers may have obviated any claim that the encounter was anything but a consensual matter from start to finish. Second, there are undoubtedly reasons of safety and security that would justify moving a suspect from one location to another during an investigatory detention, such as from an airport concourse to a more private area. There is no indication in this case that such reasons prompted the officers to transfer the site of the encounter from the concourse to the interrogation room. It appears, rather, that the primary interest of the officers was not in having an extended conversation with Royer but in the contents of his luggage, a matter which the officers did not pursue orally with Royer until after the encounter was relocated to the police room. As we have noted, had Royer consented to a search on the spot, the search could have been conducted with Royer present in the area where the bags were retrieved by Officer Johnson and any evidence recovered would have been admissible against him.

Third, the State has not touched on the question whether it would have been feasible to investigate the contents of Royer's bags in a more expeditious way. The courts are not strangers to the use of trained dogs to detect the presence of controlled substances in luggage. There is no indication here that this means was not feasible and available. If it had been used, Royer and his luggage could have been momentarily detained while this investigative procedure was carried out. Indeed, it may be that no detention at all would have been necessary. A negative result would have freed Royer in short order; a positive result would have resulted in his justifiable arrest on probable cause.

The State's third and final argument is that Royer was not being illegally held when he gave his consent because there was probable cause to arrest him at that time. We agree with the Florida Court of Appeal that probable cause to arrest Royer did not exist at the time he consented to the search of his luggage. Because we affirm the Florida Court of Appeal's conclusion that Royer was being illegally detained when he consented to the search of his luggage, we agree that the consent was tainted by the illegality and was ineffective to justify the search. The judgment of the Florida Court of Appeal is accordingly AFFIRMED.

Justice REHNQUIST, with whom THE CHIEF JUSTICE and Justice O'CONNOR join, dissenting.

The plurality's meandering opinion contains in it a little something for everyone, and although it affirms the reversal of a judgment of conviction, it can scarcely be said to bespeak a total indifference to the legitimate needs of law enforcement agents seeking to curb trafficking in dangerous drugs. The opinion nonetheless, in my view, betrays a mind-set more useful to those who officiate at shuffleboard games, primarily concerned with which particular square the disc has landed on, than to those who are seeking to administer a system of justice whose twin purposes are the conviction of the guilty and the vindication of the innocent. The plurality loses sight of the very language of the Amendment which it purports to interpret. Analyzed simply in terms of its "reasonableness" as that term is used in the Fourth Amendment, the conduct of the investigating officers toward Royer would pass muster with virtually all thoughtful, civilized persons not overly steeped in the mysteries of this Court's Fourth Amendment jurisprudence. Analyzed even in terms of the most meticulous regard for our often conflicting cases, it seems to me to pass muster equally well.

The plurality inferentially concedes, as of course it must, that at the time the suitcases were opened and 65 pounds of marijuana were disclosed, the officers had probable cause to arrest and detain Royer. But working backward through this very brief encounter, the plurality manages to sufficiently fault the officers' conduct so as to require that Royer's conviction for smuggling drugs be set aside. Analyzed in terms of the "reasonableness" which must attend any search and seizure under the requirements of the Fourth Amendment, I find it impossible to conclude that any step in the officers' efforts to apprehend Royer fails to meet that test. The point at which I part company with the plurality's opinion is in the assessment of the reasonableness of the officers' conduct following their initial conversation with Royer.

The plurality focuses on the transfer of the place of the interview from the main concourse of the airport to the room off the concourse. The quoted language is intended to convey stern disapproval of the described conduct of the officers, yet to my mind, it merits no such disapproval and was eminently reasonable. Would it have been more "reasonable" to interrogate Royer about the contents of his suitcases, and to seek his permission to open the suitcases when they were retrieved, in the busy main concourse of the airport, rather than to find a room off the concourse where the confrontation would surely be less embarrassing to Royer? If the room had been large and spacious, rather than small, if it had possessed three chairs rather than two, would the officers' conduct have been made reasonable by these facts? The plurality's answers to these questions, to the extent that it attempts any, are scarcely satisfying. The officers might have taken different steps than they did to investigate Royer, but the same may be said of virtually every investigative encounter that has more than one step to it.

The question we must decide is what was *unreasonable* about the steps which *these officers* took with respect to *this* suspect on this particular day. But since even the plurality concedes that there was articulable suspicion warranting an investigatory detention, the fact that the inquiry had become an "investigatory procedure in a police interrogation room" would seem to have little bearing on the proper disposition of a claim that the officers violated the Fourth Amendment.

53

Does the plurality intimate that if the Florida Court of Appeal had reached the opposite conclusion with respect to the holdings of *Terry* and the cases which follow it, it would affirm that holding? If the plurality's opinion were to be judged by standards appropriate to Impressionist paintings, it would perhaps receive a high grade, but the same cannot be said if it is to be judged by the standards of a judicial opinion.

Since the plurality concedes the existence of "articulable suspicion" at least after the initial conversation with Royer, the only remaining question is whether the detention of Royer during that period of time was permissible. Although *Terry* itself involved only a protective pat down for weapons, subsequent cases have expanded the permissible scope of such a "seizure." The reasonableness of the officers' activity in this case did not depend on Royer's consent to the investigation. Nevertheless, the presence of consent further justifies the action taken. The plurality does not seem to dispute that Royer consented to go to the room in the first instance. Certainly that conclusion is warranted by the totality of the circumstances. The plurality concludes that somewhere between the beginning of the 40 foot journey and the resumption of conversation in the room the investigation became so intrusive that Royer's consent "evaporated" leaving him "[a]s a practical matter . . . under arrest." But if Royer was legally approached in the first instance and consented to accompany the detectives to the room, it does not follow that his consent went up in smoke and he was "arrested" upon entering the room. Absent any evidence of objective indicia of coercion, and even absent any claim of such indicia by Royer, the size of the room itself does not transform a voluntary consent to search into a coerced consent. For any of these several reasons, I would reverse the judgment of the Florida District Court of Appeal.

REVIEW SECTION

READING COMPREHENSION

Detail the scenario in which Royer was approached by officers and drugs were eventually seized.

Elaborate the reasons of this court for affirming the judgment of the Florida Court of Appeals.

THINKING CRITICALLY

Keeping in mind the elements involved in a reasonable stop, did officers meet the objective basis and scope of the stop requirements?

At what point, if any, did the voluntary encounter between Royer and officers become involuntary?

Do you agree with the plurality or the dissenting opinion? Elaborate your response using the stop or search and seizure requirements discussed in the text and the relevance to the Fourth Amendment of the U.S. Constitution and Section Twelve of the Florida Constitution.

CASE

In *Hayes v. Florida* the issue is whether the Fourth Amendment to the Constitution of the United States, and Section Twelve of the Florida Constitution was properly applied by the District Court of Appeal of Florida, Second District. In this case police transported a suspect to the station for fingerprinting, without his consent and without probable cause or prior judicial authorization. As you read this case, look for similarities and differences in how the Fourth Amendment was applied as compared to its application in *Florida v. Royer*.

HAYES V. FLORIDA
470 U.S. 811 (1985)

When the police, without probable cause or a warrant, forcibly remove a person from his home and transport him to the station, where he is detained, although briefly, for investigative purposes, such a seizure, at least where not under judicial supervision, is sufficiently like an arrest to invoke the traditional rule that arrests may constitutionally be made only on probable cause. Thus, 439 So.2d 896, reversed.

A series of burglary-rapes occurred in Punta Gorda, Florida, in 1980. Police found latent fingerprints on the doorknob of the bedroom of one of the victims, fingerprints they believed belonged to the assailant. The police also found a herringbone pattern tennis shoe print near the victim's front porch. Although they had little specific information to tie petitioner Hayes to the crime, after police interviewed him along with 30 to 40 other men who generally fit the description of the assailant, the investigators came to consider petitioner a principal suspect. They decided to visit petitioner's home to obtain his fingerprints or, if he was uncooperative, to arrest him. They did not seek a warrant authorizing this procedure.

Arriving at petitioner's house, the officers spoke to petitioner on his front porch. When he expressed reluctance voluntarily to accompany them to the station for fingerprinting, one of the investigators explained that they would therefore arrest him. Petitioner, in the words of the investigator, then "blurted out" that he would rather go with the officers to the station than be arrested. While the officers were on the front porch, they also seized a pair of herringbone pattern tennis shoes in plain view. Petitioner was then taken to the station house, where he was fingerprinted. When police determined that his prints matched those left at the scene of the crime, petitioner was placed under formal arrest.

Before trial, petitioner moved to suppress the fingerprint evidence, claiming it was the fruit of an illegal detention. The trial court denied the motion and admitted the evidence without expressing a reason. Petitioner was convicted of the burglary and sexual battery committed at the scene where the latent fingerprints were found. The District Court of Appeal of Florida, Second District, affirmed the conviction. 439 So.2d 896 (1983). The court declined to find consent, reasoning that in view of the threatened arrest it was, "at best, highly questionable" that Hayes voluntarily accompanied the officers to the station. The court also expressly found that the officers did not have probable cause to arrest petitioner until after they obtained his fingerprints. Nevertheless, although finding neither consent nor probable cause, the court held that the officers

55

could transport petitioner to the station house and take his fingerprints on the basis of their reasonable suspicion that he was involved in the crime.

The Florida Supreme Court denied review by a four-to-three decision, 447 So.2d 886 (1983). We granted certiorari to review this application and we now reverse. We agree with petitioner that Davis v. Mississippi, 394 U.S. 721 (1969), requires reversal of the judgment below. In Davis, in the course of investigating a rape, police officers brought petitioner Davis to police headquarters on December 3, 1965. He was fingerprinted and briefly questioned before being released. He was later charged and convicted of the rape. An issue there was whether the fingerprints taken on December 3 were the inadmissible fruits of an illegal detention. Concededly, the police at that time were without probable cause for an arrest, there was no warrant, and Davis had not consented to being taken to the station house. The State nevertheless contended that the Fourth Amendment did not forbid an investigative detention for the purpose of fingerprinting, even in the absence of probable cause or a warrant. We rejected that submission, holding that Davis' detention for the purpose of fingerprinting was subject to the constraints of the Fourth Amendment and exceeded the permissible limits of temporary seizures. This was so even though fingerprinting, because it involves neither repeated harassment nor any of the probing into private life and thoughts that often marks interrogation and search, represents a much less serious intrusion upon personal security than other types of searches and detentions. Nor was it a sufficient answer to the Fourth Amendment issue to recognize that fingerprinting is an inherently more reliable and effective crime-solving mechanism than other types of evidence such as lineups and confessions. The Court indicated that perhaps under narrowly confined circumstances, a detention for fingerprinting on less than probable cause might comply with the Fourth Amendment, but found it unnecessary to decide that question since no effort was made to employ the procedures necessary to satisfy the Fourth Amendment. Rather, Davis had been detained at police headquarters without probable cause to arrest and without authorization by a judicial officer.

Here, as in Davis, there was no probable cause to arrest, no consent to the journey to the police station, and no judicial authorization for such a detention for fingerprinting purposes. Unless later cases have undermined Davis we now disavow that decision, the judgment below must be reversed.

None of our later cases have undercut the holding in Davis that transportation to and investigative detention at the station house without probable cause or judicial authorization together violate the Fourth Amendment. There is no doubt that at some point in the investigative process, police procedures can qualitatively and quantitatively be so intrusive with respect to a suspect's freedom of movement and privacy interests as to trigger the full protection of the Fourth and Fourteenth Amendments. And our view continues to be that the line is crossed when the police, without probable cause or a warrant, forcibly remove a person from his home or other place in which he is entitled to be and transport him to the police station, where he is detained, although briefly, for investigative purposes. We adhere to the view that such seizures, at least where not under judicial supervision, are sufficiently like arrests to invoke the traditional rule that arrests may constitutionally be made only on probable cause.

None of the foregoing implies that a brief detention in the field for the purpose of fingerprinting, where there is only reasonable suspicion not amounting to probable cause, is necessarily impermissible under the Fourth Amendment. There is support in our cases for the view that the Fourth Amendment would permit seizures for the purpose of fingerprinting, if there is reasonable suspicion that the suspect has committed a criminal act, if there is a reasonable basis for believing that fingerprinting will establish or negate the suspect's connection with that crime, and if the procedure is carried out with dispatch. Of course, neither reasonable suspicion nor probable cause would suffice to permit the officers to make a warrantless entry into a person's house for the purpose of obtaining fingerprint identification.

We also do not abandon the suggestion in Davis that under circumscribed procedures, the Fourth Amendment might permit the judiciary to authorize the seizure of a person on less than probable cause and his removal to the police station for the purpose of fingerprinting. We do not, of course, have such a case before us. We do note, however, that some States, in reliance on the suggestion in Davis, have enacted procedures for judicially authorized seizures for the purpose of fingerprinting. The state courts are not in accord on the validity of these efforts to insulate investigative seizures from Fourth Amendment invalidation. As we have said, absent probable cause and a warrant, Davis v. Mississippi, 394 U.S. 721 (1969), requires the reversal of the judgment of the Florida District Court of Appeal. It is so ordered.

REVIEW SECTION

READING COMPREHENSION

Detail the scenario in which Hayes ended up at the police station being fingerprinted.

Elaborate the reasons of this court for reversing the judgment of the Florida District Court of Appeal.

THINKING CRITICALLY

The court determined that the removal of Hayes to the station was involuntary and thus required the suppression of the fingerprint evidence. Had Hayes been approached by officers at his house and consented to providing fingerprints, describe how the outcome would be altered. What if Hayes felt coerced by officers at his home to provide fingerprints?

Discuss the differences between reasonable suspicion and probable cause as related to the facts of this case.

SECTION 3: SPECIAL SITUATION STOPS

OVERVIEW

We know already that reasonable suspicion is required for a stop, and probable cause is required for arrest, and that voluntary encounters are indeed just that and therefore not addressed by the Fourth Amendment or Section Twelve of the Florida Constitution. The lines begin to blur however in the discussion of special situation stops. The courts have delineated that under some special situations it is reasonable to move or detain individuals based on no articulable facts at all. These circumstances include but are not limited to: the movement of passengers out of stopped vehicles for the safety of the officer; detention of individuals entering the United States by way of an international border; and detaining a number of individuals in a particular place such as in a roadblock. Is it constitutional to, based on no individualized suspicion at all, move or detain individuals?

CASE

Jones v. State of Florida is an extremely interesting case as it occurred in 1984 and was the first case of this kind in Florida. The case involves the constitutionality of an arrest made at a police roadblock maintained for the purpose of stopping motorists to ascertain and apprehend those to be charged with driving while under the influence of alcohol. At issue is whether the Fourth Amendment exclusionary rule should be applied to evidence obtained at the roadblock. You may think you already know the result of this case from your reading, however let us look in detail at the decision and rationale employed by the court in Florida.

JONES V. STATE OF FLORIDA
459 So.2d 1068 (Fla.App. 2 Dist., 1984)

Petitioner was arrested for driving while under the influence of alcoholic beverages (DUI), a violation of section 316.193, Florida Statutes (1983). He filed a pretrial motion to suppress all evidence obtained as a result of what he contends was an illegal seizure. The county court denied the motion. Petitioner then pleaded nolo contendere, reserving the right to appeal the denial of the motion to suppress. He appealed to the circuit court, which affirmed. He has petitioned this court to issue a writ of certiorari. We grant the petition, quash the circuit court's affirmance, and reverse the judgment of conviction. We hold that the police roadblock at which petitioner was apprehended and on the basis of which evidence against him was obtained was an unconstitutional invasion of his rights under the Fourth Amendment to the United States Constitution proscribing unreasonable searches and seizures.

On July 4, 1982, at about 2:30 a.m., the City of Tampa Police Department established a roadblock, the undisputed purpose of which was to apprehend DUI drivers. The three northbound lanes were blocked off to form a "funnel" requiring all traffic to travel in one lane and to pass by a police officer stationed on the roadway. That officer was instructed to stop every fifth automobile when traffic was heavy and to stop every third automobile when traffic was light. The stopped cars were directed off the roadway into an otherwise unused parking lot.

58

Waiting in the parking lot were five police officers who were to determine if the drivers were DUI. The only specific instruction given to those officers was to request the driver's licenses of the drivers of cars diverted into the parking lot. Each officer was left to his own method to determine whether he believed a driver was DUI.

Petitioner was the driver of a car that was diverted into the parking lot. The arresting officer requested petitioner's driver's license and began his investigation of petitioner's sobriety. The officer decided petitioner was DUI and arrested him.

We summarize our conclusions as follows:

(1) We hold that the arrest of petitioner at the roadblock was an improper seizure in violation of the Fourth Amendment.

(2) Our principal concern is not only with petitioner but with the rights of the vast bulk of those innocent citizens who may in the future be stopped at roadblocks like that involved in this case with the resulting loss of their Fourth Amendment rights to security and privacy.

(3) The subject of the validity of roadblocks, and roadblock arrests, is extremely difficult. The governing test--balancing the public interest in apprehending DUI violators against motorists' rights to security and privacy--may produce legitimate arguments either way.

(4) In arriving at our holding we follow guidelines which we believe have been set forth by the U.S. Supreme Court, although there is no controlling U.S. Supreme Court or Florida Supreme Court holding which is in point as to the precise issue of this case.

(5) Of the five cases in point in the courts of other states involving DUI roadblocks of varying descriptions, three (Massachusetts, with one dissent, South Dakota and Arizona) have held such roadblocks to be violative of the Fourth Amendment, and two (Kansas, with one dissent, and New Jersey) have held them to be proper. None of the five courts disagreed that the state has the burden of proof to show that a roadblock arrest is constitutional. Due to the scarcity of evidence in the record in the case before us, we believe that even the approaches taken by the New Jersey and Kansas courts would produce a holding that petitioner's arrest in this case was unconstitutional.

(6) Although our principal task is only to decide this case, we undertake in this opinion to provide at least general guidance to law enforcement authorities as to what types of DUI roadblocks may and may not produce valid arrests.

At the outset we should emphasize that our holding does not mean the petitioner's conduct is condoned. The issue is not to decide from hindsight whether or not the petitioner in this case was drunk and deserving of constitutional safeguards. That type of erroneous approach to the issue would misconceive constitutional ramifications of cases of this kind. Since views seem to be espoused by some persons that to set free one person who has obviously committed a crime is wrong under any circumstances, we take pains at the outset of this opinion to point out what the fundamental issue does involve.

The fundamental issue here involves those motorists who are stopped by law enforcement authorities and who are driving while not under the influence of alcohol. Those motorists comprise the vast bulk of those who have been subjected to roadblocks of this kind in the past and who would be subjected to them in the future if we were to approve the roadblock in question here. Our holding is not keyed to any special concern for petitioner's individual sensibilities. He is the fortuitous vehicle for our consideration of the liberties of others--although also of his liberties in this case and in the future hopefully under circumstances potentially less adverse to him. We have substantial concern for the vast numbers of innocent motorists. The issue here is whether the Fourth Amendment permits officers to stop and question persons whose conduct is innocent, unremarkable and free from suspicion.

At the same time we do not question the good faith of the police officers involved in this case nor their doubtless commendable motivations. We do not doubt their desire to do their jobs in the best ways they can. In their dealings with matters involving this area of the law they have not had the benefit of clear-cut guidance in all respects from the case law as to the proper parameters of their conduct. We undertake in this opinion to provide some measure of additional guidance and thus must use as the parameters of our authority interpretations placed upon the Fourth Amendment by the United States Supreme Court. We are aware of no case in which the issue here has been presented to the Florida Supreme Court.

The precise issue presented in this case--whether a warrantless police roadblock to apprehend DUI drivers by stopping cars without any articulable suspicion of illegal activity is constitutional under the Fourth Amendment--has not been widely addressed by American courts. We have found only the above-referenced opinions of five other state courts dealing with it. A stop of an automobile is a "seizure" under the Fourth and Fourteenth Amendments. The constitutionality of a particular seizure is judged by balancing the degree of its intrusion on the individual's Fourth Amendment interests in privacy and personal security against the seizure's promotion of legitimate governmental interests.

The U.S. Supreme Court has held unconstitutional the "roving patrol" type of warrantless stop, where an officer stops cars on the road at random with no probable cause to perceive criminal activity and even without meeting the "reasonable suspicion" standard. In contrast, the Supreme Court approved of a border patrol "checkpoint" type of permanent roadblock which was for the purpose of apprehending illegal aliens and which stopped all vehicles for brief questioning of occupants. In State v. Olgaard, 248 N.W.2d 392 (S.D.1976), a roadblock was found by the South Dakota Supreme Court to cause constitutional violations, therefore evidence obtained was found to be inadmissible, and the conviction of defendant was reversed. This case concerned a roadblock conducted in connection with South Dakota's Alcohol Safety Action Program, concededly for the primary purpose of investigating alcohol-related offenses. Conversely, in State v. Coccomo, 177 N.J.Super. 575, 427 A.2d 131 (N.J.Super.Ct.Law.Div.1980), the constitutionality of evidence obtained and arrests made at a roadblock was upheld by a New Jersey appellate court. The New Jersey court recognized the state's vital interest in promoting public safety by detecting drunk drivers. Balancing that interest against a motorist's interest in his expectation of privacy, the court found the roadblock procedure to be a reasonable and valid infringement on the expectation of privacy. The court described the intrusion on privacy as "minimal."

We have no quarrel with the self-evident truth that there may be surprise from a temporary roadblock, and the more surprise from a roadblock, the more effective the roadblock may be for the legitimate and important governmental purpose of reducing alcohol-related accidents. But we believe there is also substantial merit in that it is a Fourth Amendment violation. No matter how bad the crime may be which law enforcement officers are trying to stop, they may not abandon Fourth Amendment concerns in their efforts, however commendable in purpose, to stop all citizens, including the vast bulk of them who are innocent, in order to sift out and apprehend violators. We would be inclined to think that advance publicity may well provide a meaningful substitute for the type of permanency, and therefore advance knowledge by motorists. Advance publicity would seem to lessen questions as to whether a roadblock constitutes an unwarranted intrusion upon innocent motorists who would, with such publicity, anticipate and understand the circumstances. While, admittedly, advance notice would reduce chances of catching some criminals, it might well at the same time have some tendency to dissuade motorists from driving while drinking without unduly violating the interests of the vast majority of innocent drivers. A basic key to previous cases is whether the governmental interest in curtailing drunk driving by the use of roadblocks is actually so overwhelming as to justify serious intrusions into the security and privacy of innocent citizens who constitute the overwhelming majority of those stopped at these types of roadblocks. In answering that question, we must take into account the ramifications of approving these types of intrusions upon innocent citizens in law enforcement efforts to apprehend suspected violators of a broad range of other criminal laws.

The issue involved is extremely difficult. In this opinion we are indicating some agreement or disagreement with various views expressed in other states. But we have no doubt of the closeness of the balance of the arguments on one side or the other. Again, the basic balancing challenge is does the public interest in a DUI roadblock outweigh the individual's right to be free from intrusion on his or her right of privacy? However, we would again clarify and expand upon the foregoing statement by stressing that "the individual's right to be free" refers also to the rights of individuals whose conduct is innocent and is not centered on the rights of the individual DUI arrestee alone.

In the final analysis we are inclined to agree with the unconstitutionality of the roadblock stops. The point is not whether drunk drivers are a danger and a serious threat to public safety. That must be conceded by any reasonable person of good faith. The point is that the public interest in apprehending drunk drivers does not justify the use of any indiscriminate law enforcement methods of investigation and apprehension. As an admittedly extreme example for the purpose of illustrating that point, no reasonable person of good faith would disagree that house to house searches of arbitrarily selected neighborhoods to discover which citizens are drunk and are about to drive or might drive, which would terrorize the citizenry in the process, would be wrong. That that example is absurd in this country today may serve to emphasize what the Fourth

Amendment has accomplished relative to the disregard for individual rights which had existed under British colonial rule not long before the Bill of Rights was adopted.

The roadblock did not meet the types of criteria which we believe to be important. In our view, on the record before us the roadblock involved in this case would not even have passed muster under the less rigorous New Jersey and Kansas criteria. The state either introduced no evidence at all as to, or presented insufficient evidence to meet, the relevant criteria which might support a roadblock. To further explain why we believe those criteria were not met, and in an effort to provide more specific future guidance, we refer to what we view as the most important of the criteria as follows:

First, was the roadblock conducted pursuant to a plan set up by supervisory personnel and was little or no discretion in the method of operation and selection of vehicles left to the officers conducting the roadblock? We have before us no evidence as to what level of law enforcement personnel made the decision to set up the roadblock or made the decisions regarding location and method of operation. The record does show that the officers who were to participate in the roadblock were briefed by a sergeant. The officers in the parking lot were told to ask for driver's licenses but were given no further instructions. At deposition, the officer who made the arrest in this case stated that he received no instructions as to what to look for, saying, "[T]hat's my discretion."

Second, was the safety of motorists assured by proper means, including adequate lighting, warning signs or signals, and clearly uniformed or otherwise identifiable police officers? Although the record shows barricades and traffic cones channeling traffic from three lanes to two lanes to one lane, the record contains no evidence as to any safety features, such as flares, flashing lights or signs. Whether we should assume that the city police officers at the scene were in uniform we need not decide. The record does not say.

Third, was the degree of intrusion upon motorists and the length of detention of each motorist minimized? Although the record shows that five officers were in the parking lot, the record does not indicate whether or not this was a sufficient number to handle expeditiously the volume of vehicles or how long the average motorist waited. The record does not indicate further whether the number of officers on the road was actually adequate to expeditiously maintain the traffic flow with minimum intrusion upon motorists who were not stopped.

Fourth, was that roadblock procedure for apprehending criminal law violators significantly more effective to combat an egregious law enforcement problem of very serious proportions than other available less intrusive means? The question of whether some of these aspects may be established by judicial notice or must be shown by evidence at trial has not been presented or argued to us. The procedural requirements at trial for both methods of proof are well established. The arresting officer testified that between 100 and 200 cars were stopped and 5 or 6 DUI arrests were made. There is no evidence as to how this figure compares with the number of DUI arrests which can be anticipated from using the same number of officers to conduct another type of operation, such as roving patrols acting upon reasonable suspicion, to combat the DUI problem.

Also, the record indicates that the roadblock was temporary but contains no evidence as to whether or not there was advance warning or notice to the public. To the greater extent that factors surrounding a particular roadblock reduce surprise, fear and inconvenience, the greater tendency there will be for a roadblock to not have Fourth Amendment problems. Just as in this case of first impression the lack of a more descriptive record may be understandable, we trust the need for a more complete record is clear. Even a valid roadblock within the foregoing criteria should be employed with reasonable circumspection. Our democratic form of free government continues to exist because our laws do not permit restraints of that kind upon our freedoms. As is sometimes also attributed to Thomas Jefferson, "Eternal vigilance is the price of liberty."

We do not have before us for decision the application of the Fourth Amendment to other types of police roadblocks, e.g., those to apprehend fleeing felons believed to be in the vicinity. We should add that if a roadblock is established in a constitutionally permissible way, arrests of individual motorists ensuing therefrom should nonetheless be based upon probable cause. Only if an officer, based upon his observations following a proper stop of a vehicle, has probable cause to believe that the driver is DUI could the officer conduct a more extensive investigation, such as asking the motorist to exit the car for a roadside sobriety test.

The petition for writ of certiorari is granted, the decision of the circuit court is quashed, and the judgment of conviction by the county court is reversed. Petitioner shall be discharged.

We have recognized that the subject of this opinion is susceptible to legitimate debate. There is no doubt that the subject is of substantial importance to the public and to law enforcement authorities. We feel confident of the correctness of our holding and our opinion as providing proper guidelines, however general, for the trial courts of this state as well as law enforcement authorities. Nonetheless, we feel it would be consistent with the constitutional provisions establishing district courts of appeal and with the tenet that the Florida Supreme Court is the paramount policy-making Florida court that the Florida Supreme Court pass upon this matter which is so important and which has not previously been addressed in Florida, whether on review of this case or in another DUI temporary roadblock case. Whether the state will seek Florida Supreme Court review in this particular case we will not speculate. In any event, we certify to the Florida Supreme Court as a matter of great public importance the following question: Can a warrantless temporary roadblock which is established to apprehend persons driving while under the influence of alcohol and which stops automobiles without any articulable suspicion of illegal activity produce constitutionally permissible arrests?

REVIEW SECTION

READING COMPREHENSION

What did the court attempt to delineate in this case?

Elaborate why this case was less about Jones as an individual and more about Fourth Amendment protection?

THINKING CRITICALLY

The court in the above judgment noted: "The subject of the validity of roadblocks, and roadblock arrests, is extremely difficult. The governing test--balancing the public interest in apprehending DUI violators against motorists' rights to security and privacy--may produce legitimate arguments either way." In light of the debate about balancing public interest in crime control and individual rights, articulate your position on this controversial issue.

CASE

Jones v. State of Florida 1986 is the Florida Supreme Court ruling on the case you just read. As you are aware, the Second District Court of Appeal indicated the following question was one of great public importance: Can a warrantless temporary roadblock which is established to apprehend persons driving while under the influence of alcohol and which stops automobiles without any articulable suspicion of illegal activity produce constitutionally permissible arrests? The Second District Court noted that the Florida Supreme Court is the paramount policy-making Florida court and therefore did not want to speculate, but inferred that perhaps the Florida Supreme Court may end up reviewing this case. The Supreme Court of Florida finding is below without the repetition of case facts.

STATE V. JONES
483 So.2d 433, 11 Fla. L. Weekly 67 (Fla., 1986)

On certiorari the Second District Court of Appeal quashed the circuit court's affirmance and reversed the conviction. The district court ruled that the roadblock violated Jones' fourth amendment rights against unreasonable search and seizure. The state subsequently filed both a motion to stay mandate and a motion for rehearing, en banc. The district court denied both motions. This Court has likewise declined to review the order denying the stay.

Unquestionably, stopping an automobile and detaining its occupant constitutes a seizure within the meaning of the fourth amendment to the United States Constitution. As with all warrantless searches and seizures, courts determine the constitutionality of DUI roadblocks by balancing the legitimate government interests involved against the degree of intrustion on the individual's fourth amendment rights. This balancing test involves three considerations: (1) the gravity of the public concern that the seizure serves; (2) the degree to which the seizure advances the public interest; and (3) the severity of the interference with individual liberty. While the United States Supreme Court has never directly addressed the issue before this Court, several decisions of our nation's highest court provide some guidance in our attempt to apply fourth amendment principles to the case at bar.

We note at the beginning of our analysis that, while the instant case deals with an issue of first impression in Florida, an increasing number of our sister states has dealt with the constitutionality of DUI roadblocks. According to the district court, when that court rendered its opinion only five states had directly addressed the constitutionality of DUI roadblocks of varying descriptions. Today a survey of other jurisdictions indicates that we can add at least nine more states to this list. As with the previous five states, these courts have reached a variety of results.

These cases have considered numerous conditions and factors in determining whether a given roadblock passes constitutional muster. Indeed, the recent proliferation of DUI roadblock cases decided across the country indicates little uniformity in the approaches taken in analyzing these stops. Different courts have assigned different weights to the various factors involved in the fourth amendment balancing test. Certain considerations, however, have been consistently stressed, albeit with varying results.

In the case at bar the district court assimilated a number of these cases and formulated a set of criteria for use in determining whether a given roadblock satisfies the constitution. The district court embraced the criteria adopted State v. Deskins, 234 Kan. 529, 673 P.2d 1174 (1983), a Kansas case and in this respect the district court appears to have fallen into line with a growing number of courts from other states which are utilizing the Deskins criteria as a helpful framework for analyzing the constitutional viability of specific DUI roadblocks. These criteria include: (a) degree of discretion left to field officers; (b) location, time and duration of the roadblock; (c) standards set by superior officers; (d) advance notice to public; (e) warning to approaching motorists; (f) degree of fear or anxiety caused; (g) length of detention of each motorist; (h) safety conditions; (i) physical factors of the method of operation; (j) availability of less intrusive methods for combating the problem; (k) effectiveness of the procedure; (l) any other relevant circumstances.

In the case at bar the district court, attempting to offer some guidance through this amorphous area, specified which of these criteria it considered most important. The critical considerations included: (1) whether the law enforcement agency conducted the roadblock pursuant to a plan which supervisory personnel formulated and which substantially restricted the discretion of field officers as to both operating procedures and the selection of vehicles; (2) whether the roadblock procedures assured the safety of motorists through the use of proper means such as adequate lighting, warning signs or signals, and clearly identifiable police officers; (3) the degree of intrusion upon motorists and the length of the detention of each motorist; and (4) whether the roadblock procedures proved significantly more effective in combating an egregious law enforcement problem than other available less intrusive means. The court also indicated that where a roadblock was temporary courts should require some sort of advance notice to the public in order to reduce the fear and surprise involved when law enforcement officers suddenly stop a passing motorist. Clearly, not all of these factors must favor the state in order to validate a sobriety checkpoint. On the other hand, some factors can prove fatal to a roadblock regardless of the existence of other favorable conditions. Before we apply the balancing test to the case at bar, we will proceed to examine the criteria which the district court stressed.

Paramount among all other considerations, the fourth amendment requires that all seizures be based on either: (1) specific evidence of an existing violation; (2) a showing that reasonable legislative or administrative inspection standards are met; or (3) a showing that officers carry out the search pursuant to a plan embodying specific neutral criteria which limit the conduct of the individual officers. Because DUI roadblocks involve seizures made without any articulable suspicion of illegal activity, most states examining this issue have ruled that such roadblocks stand or fall based on some set of neutral criteria governing the officers in the field. Courts requiring such a neutral plan do so out of a fear that unbridled discretion in the field invites abuse. We agree and find that it is essential that a written set of uniform guidelines be issued before a roadblock can be utilized.

Law enforcement officials must conduct sobriety checkpoints so as to minimize the discretion of field officers, thereby restricting the potential intrusion into the public's constitutional liberties. Written guidelines should cover in detail the procedures which field officers are to follow at the roadblock. Ideally, these guidelines should set out with reasonable specificity procedures regarding the selection of vehicles, detention techniques, duty assignments, and the disposition of vehicles. Of course, if the guidelines fail to cover each of these matters they need not necessarily fail. Rather, courts should view each set of guidelines as a whole when determining the plan's sufficiency.

Moreover, in our view roadblocks need not stop every car in order to avoid running afoul. While a roadblock stopping every third or fifth automobile may not equal a 100 percent roadblock, such a roadblock is nonetheless a long way from a selective vehicle stop denounced. We also agree with the district court that the procedures followed at a given roadblock are extremely important when determining the checkpoint's constitutionality. Police should provide both proper lighting and sufficient warning on the roadway in advance of the stop so as to reduce the threat of startling the driver. Failing to do so would increase the threat of traffic accidents at the roadblock and thereby frustrate the entire goal of the checkpoint. Additionally, law enforcement officers at the checkpoint should be easily identifiable. Visible signs of authority such as police uniforms reduce the potential for frightening motorists who may otherwise fear pulling off the road late at night at the order of strangers. Police should present enough vestiges of authority to allay such fears.

We also agree with the district court that law enforcement officials should keep the degree of intrusion upon motorists and the length of detention of each driver to a minimum. Accordingly, police should use the guidelines discussed above to streamline procedures. The public, however, must keep in mind that the privilege of driving an automobile over public highways does not amount to an absolute organic right. Our government provides the roadways of Florida as a benefit to the public at large. Accordingly, this state retains extensive authority to safeguard the driving public via its police power. If the holder of a driver's license cannot utilize the privilege of driving on our public streets and highways in a careful manner and respect the rights of others to do likewise, that driver becomes a public nuisance and should be either temporarily or permanently excluded from those roads. In order to safeguard Floridians against such drivers, motorists should reasonably accept the minor inconvenience which they may endure at a properly run DUI roadblock.

We do not agree with the district court that it is essential to have prior public dissemination of roadblock information. We do not mean to discourage the police from making nonspecific announcements, if they choose to do so, concerning their intent to establish sobriety check points for the giving of this information would reduce claims of unlawful seizure. Such announcements, however, are unnecessary where the police position signs and lights at the checkpoint giving approaching drivers notice of the roadblock's purpose pursuant to a written plan.

As for the remainder of the factors listed above, their cumulative use would prove helpful in determining the validity of a given DUI roadblock. Therefore, we follow many of our sister states in adopting the bulk of these criteria. We also agree with the district court in stressing the four principal criteria which we discussed above, except for the requirement of advance public notice.

The record in this case requires us to rule that the state failed to prove that the City of Tampa roadblock procedure met the balancing test and therefore violates the requirements of the fourth amendment to the United States Constitution. We stress, however, that, when the record in a given case adequately reflects that a roadblock procedure satisfies the criteria discussed above, such a roadblock would likely pass constitutional muster. The state's compelling interest in protecting the public from drunk drivers outweighs any minimal intrusion into their privacy which a proper roadblock procedure might cause.

We therefore answer the certified question in the affirmative, but approve the result of the district court below. It is so ordered.

REVIEW SECTION

READING COMPREHENSION

What did the Florida Supreme Court attempt to delineate in this case? What were the similarities and differences between this case and *Jones v. State of Florida 1984.*

Elaborate why the Supreme Court hearing of this case remained less about Jones as an individual and more about Fourth Amendment protection?

THINKING CRITICALLY

The Supreme Court delineated several factors that would likely result in a DUI roadblock passing constitutional muster if implemented. In light of the debate about balancing public interest in crime control and individual rights, articulate your position on this controversial issue if these conditions were all met in establishing a roadblock.

In a footnote, the Florida Supreme Court notes the following: "We point out that the parties have failed to present any valid arguments concerning the applicability of article I, section 12 of the Florida Constitution. The state contends that Florida's Constitution has adopted the federal case law interpreting the fourth amendment of the United States Constitution and, therefore, affords identical protection as that of the federal constitution. The state, however, errs in relying on the language of the 1983 amendment to article I, section 12 as authority for that position. The 1983 amendment cannot be applied retroactively. Because Jones was arrested prior to January 1, 1983, the effective date of the amendment, the amended language of article I, section 12 is inapplicable and the pre-1983 language prevails. Neither the parties nor the court below, however, presented any justification for applying different standards under the applicable provisions of the United

States and Florida Constitutions. Because this issue has been neither briefed nor argued in the present petition, the decision in the instant case rests solely on the federal constitution." Discuss what this may mean for interpretation of similar cases in Florida Court.

SECTION 4: FRISKS AND THE FOURTH AMENDMENT

OVERVIEW

While a frisk and a stop are similar, it is important to distinguish between the two. A stop is a seizure of an individual, whereas a frisk is a search. Thus, a lawful stop must occur prior to the occurrence of a frisk. Furthermore, the facts that support a stop do not automatically support a frisk as well. Frisks are considered Fourth Amendment searches by the court and therefore to be lawful must be backed by a stop that involves a reasonable suspicion that a crime may have been underway and/or reasonable suspicion that the individual is armed and therefore an officer can do a once-over-lightly pat-down to detect only weapons to ensure their safety.

CASE

In *State of Florida v. Bostick, a*s part of a drug interdiction effort, Broward County Sheriff's Department officers routinely board buses at scheduled stops and ask passengers for permission to search their luggage. Without articulable suspicion, Bostick was questioned on a bus at a scheduled stop and officers requested consent to search his luggage for drugs, advising him of his right to refuse. Bostick gave his permission, and after finding cocaine the officers arrested him on drug trafficking charges. His motion to suppress the cocaine on the ground that it had been seized in violation of the Fourth Amendment was denied by the trial court. The Florida Court of Appeal affirmed, but certified a question to the State Supreme Court. That court, reasoning that a reasonable passenger would not have felt free to leave the bus to avoid questioning by the police, adopted a per se rule that the sheriff's practice of "working the buses" is unconstitutional.

STATE OF FLORIDA V. BOSTICK
501 U.S. 429 (1991)

The Florida Supreme Court erred in adopting a per se rule that every encounter on a bus is a seizure. The appropriate test is whether, taking into account all of the circumstances surrounding the encounter, a reasonable passenger would feel free to decline the officers' requests or otherwise terminate the encounter. A consensual encounter does not trigger Fourth Amendment scrutiny. Even when officers have no basis for suspecting a particular individual, they may generally ask the individual questions, ask to examine identification, and request consent to search luggage provided they do not convey a message that compliance with their requests is required. Thus, there is no doubt that, if this same encounter had taken place before Bostick boarded the bus or in the bus terminal, it would not be a seizure.

That this encounter took place on a bus is but one relevant factor in determining whether or not it was of a coercive nature. The state court erred in focusing on the "free to leave" language rather than on the principle that those words were intended to capture. This inquiry is not an accurate measure of an encounter's coercive effect when a person is seated on a bus about to depart, has no desire to leave, and would not feel free to leave even if there were no police present. The more appropriate inquiry is whether a reasonable passenger would feel free to decline the officers' request or otherwise terminate the encounter.

This case is remanded for the Florida courts to evaluate the seizure question under the correct legal standard. The trial court made no express findings of fact, and the State Supreme Court rested its decision on a single fact - that the encounter took place on a bus - rather than on the totality of the circumstances. Rejected, however, is Bostick's argument that he must have been seized because no reasonable person would freely consent to a search of luggage containing drugs, since the "reasonable person" test presumes an innocent person.

O'CONNOR, J., delivered the opinion of the Court, in which REHNQUIST, C.J., and WHITE, SCALIA, KENNEDY, and SOUTER, JJ., joined. MARSHALL, J., filed a dissenting opinion, in which BLACKMUN and STEVENS, JJ., joined.

We have held that the Fourth Amendment permits police officers to approach individuals at random in public places to ask them questions and to request consent to search their luggage, so long as a reasonable person would understand that he or she could refuse to cooperate. This case requires us to determine whether the same rule applies to police encounters that take place on a bus. The underlying facts of the search are in dispute, but the Florida Supreme Court, whose decision we review here, stated explicitly the factual premise for its decision: "Two officers, complete with badges, insignia and one of them holding a recognizable zipper pouch, containing a pistol, boarded a bus bound from Miami to Atlanta during a stopover in Fort Lauderdale. Eyeing the passengers, the officers admittedly without articulable suspicion, picked out the defendant passenger and asked to inspect his ticket and identification. The ticket, from Miami to Atlanta, matched the defendant's identification and both were immediately returned to him as unremarkable. However, the two police officers persisted, and explained their presence as narcotics agents on the lookout for illegal drugs. In pursuit of that aim, they then requested the defendant's consent to search his luggage. Needless to say, there is a conflict in the evidence about whether the defendant consented to the search of the second bag in which the contraband was found and as to whether he was informed of his right to refuse consent. However, any conflict must be resolved in favor of the state, it being a question of fact decided by the trial judge."

Two facts are particularly worth noting. First, the police specifically advised Bostick that he had the right to refuse consent. Bostick appears to have disputed the point, but, as the Florida Supreme Court noted explicitly, the trial court resolved this evidentiary conflict in the State's favor. Second, at no time did the officers threaten Bostick with a gun. The Florida Supreme Court indicated that one officer carried a zipper pouch containing a pistol - the equivalent of carrying a gun in a holster - but the court did not suggest that the gun was ever removed from its pouch, pointed at Bostick, or otherwise used in a threatening manner. Bostick was arrested and charged with trafficking in cocaine. He moved to suppress the cocaine on the grounds that it had been seized in violation of his Fourth Amendment rights. The trial court denied the motion, but made no factual findings. Bostick subsequently entered a plea of guilty, but reserved the right to appeal the denial of the motion to suppress.

The Florida District Court of Appeal affirmed, but considered the issue sufficiently important that it certified a question to the Florida Supreme Court which reasoned that Bostick had been seized because a reasonable passenger in his situation would not have felt free to leave the bus to avoid questioning by the police. It ruled categorically that "an impermissible seizure results when police mount a drug search on buses during scheduled stops and question boarded passengers without articulable reasons for doing so, thereby obtaining consent to search the passengers' luggage." The Florida Supreme Court thus adopted a per se rule that the practice of "working the buses" is unconstitutional. The result of this decision is that police in Florida, as elsewhere, may approach persons at random in most public places, ask them questions and seek consent to a search, but they may not engage in the same behavior on a bus. We granted certiorari to determine whether the Florida Supreme Court's per se rule is consistent with our Fourth Amendment jurisprudence.

The sole issue presented for our review is whether a police encounter on a bus of the type described above necessarily constitutes a "seizure" within the meaning of the Fourth Amendment. The State concedes, and we accept for purposes of this decision, that the officers lacked the reasonable suspicion required to justify a seizure and that, if a seizure took place, the drugs found in Bostick's suitcase must be suppressed as tainted fruit. Our cases make it clear that a seizure does not occur simply because a police officer approaches an individual and asks a few questions so long as a reasonable person would feel free "to disregard the police and go about his business." The encounter will not trigger Fourth Amendment scrutiny unless it loses its consensual nature. There is no doubt that, if this same encounter had taken place before Bostick boarded the bus or in the lobby of the bus terminal, it would not rise to the level of a seizure. Bostick insists that this case is different because it took place in the cramped confines of a bus. A police encounter is much more intimidating in this setting, he argues, because police tower over a seated passenger and there is little room to move around. Bostick maintains that a reasonable bus passenger would not have felt free to leave under the circumstances of this case because there is nowhere to go on a bus. Also, the bus was about to depart. Had Bostick disembarked, he would have risked being stranded and losing whatever baggage he had locked away in the luggage compartment.

The Florida Supreme Court found this argument persuasive, so much so that it adopted a per se rule prohibiting the police from randomly boarding buses as a means of drug interdiction. The state court erred, however, in focusing on whether Bostick was "free to leave," rather than on the principle that those words were intended to capture. When a person is seated on a bus and has no desire to leave, the degree to which a reasonable person would feel that s/he could leave is not an accurate measure of the coercive effect of the encounter. Here, for example, the mere fact that Bostick did not feel free to leave the bus does not mean that the police seized him. Bostick was a passenger on a bus that was scheduled to depart. He would not have felt free to leave the bus even if the police had not been present. Bostick's movements were "confined" in a sense, but this was the natural result of his decision to take the bus; it says nothing about whether or not the police conduct at issue was coercive. Thus, Bostick's freedom of movement was restricted by a factor independent of police conduct - i.e., by his being a passenger on a bus. Accordingly, the "free to leave" analysis on which Bostick relies is inapplicable. In such a situation, the appropriate inquiry is whether a reasonable person would feel free to decline the officers' requests or otherwise terminate the encounter. This formulation follows logically from prior cases and breaks no new ground.

The facts of this case, as described by the Florida Supreme Court, leave some doubt whether a seizure occurred. Nevertheless, we refrain from deciding whether or not a seizure occurred in this case. The trial court made no express findings of fact, and the Florida Supreme Court rested its decision on a single fact - that the encounter took place on a bus - rather than on the totality of the circumstances. We remand so that the Florida courts may evaluate the seizure question under the correct legal standard. We do reject, however, Bostick's argument that he must have been seized because no reasonable person would freely consent to a search of luggage that s/he knows contains drugs. This argument cannot prevail because the "reasonable person" test presupposes an innocent person.

This Court, as the dissent correctly observes, is not empowered to suspend constitutional guarantees so that the Government may more effectively wage a "war on drugs." If that war is to be fought, those who fight it must respect the rights of individuals, whether or not those individuals are suspected of having committed a crime. By the same token, this Court is not empowered to forbid law enforcement practices simply because it considers them distasteful. The Fourth Amendment proscribes unreasonable searches and seizures; it does not proscribe voluntary cooperation. The cramped confines of a bus are one relevant factor that should be considered in evaluating whether a passenger's consent is voluntary. We cannot agree, however, with the Florida Supreme Court that this single factor will be dispositive in every case. We adhere to the rule that, in order to determine whether a particular encounter constitutes a seizure, a court must consider all the circumstances surrounding the encounter to determine whether the police conduct would have communicated to a reasonable person that the person was not free to decline the officers' requests or otherwise terminate the encounter. The Florida Supreme Court erred in adopting a per se rule. The judgment of the Florida Supreme Court is reversed, and the case remanded for further proceedings not inconsistent with this opinion. It is so ordered.

JUSTICE MARSHALL, with whom JUSTICE BLACKMUN and JUSTICE STEVENS join, dissenting.

Our Nation, we are told, is engaged in a "war on drugs." No one disputes that it is the job of law enforcement officials to devise effective weapons for fighting this war. But the effectiveness of a law enforcement technique is not proof of its constitutionality. The general warrant, for example, was certainly an effective means of law enforcement. Yet it was one of the primary aims of the Fourth Amendment to protect citizens from the tyranny of being singled out for search and seizure without particularized suspicion notwithstanding the effectiveness of this method. In my view, the law enforcement technique with which we are confronted in this case - the suspicionless police sweep of buses in intrastate or interstate travel - bears all of the indicia of coercion and unjustified intrusion associated with the general warrant. Because I believe that the bus sweep at issue in this case violates the core values of the Fourth Amendment, I dissent.

At issue in this case is a "new and increasingly common tactic in the war on drugs": the suspicionless police sweep of buses in interstate or intrastate travel. Typically under this technique, a group of state or federal officers will board a bus while it is stopped at an intermediate point on its route. Often displaying badges, weapons or other indicia of authority, the officers identify themselves and announce their purpose to intercept drug traffickers. They proceed to approach individual passengers, requesting them to show identification, produce their tickets, and explain the purpose of their travels. Never do the officers advise the passengers that they are free not to speak with the officers. An "interview" of this type ordinarily culminates in a request for consent to search the passenger's luggage.

These sweeps are conducted in "dragnet" style. The police admittedly act without an "articulable suspicion" in deciding which buses to board and which passengers to approach for interviewing. By proceeding systematically in this fashion, the police are able to engage in a tremendously high volume of searches. The percentage of successful drug interdictions is low. To put it mildly, these sweeps "are inconvenient, intrusive, and intimidating," they occur within cramped confines, with officers typically placing themselves in between the passenger selected for an interview and the exit of the bus. Because the bus is only temporarily stationed at a point short of its destination, the passengers are in no position to leave as a means of evading the officers' questioning.

This aspect of the suspicionless sweep has not been lost on many of the lower courts called upon to review the constitutionality of this practice. Remarkably, the courts located at the heart of the "drug war" have been the most adamant in condemning this technique. As one Florida court put it: "The evidence in this cause has evoked images of other days, under other flags, when no man traveled his nation's roads or railways without fear of unwarranted interruption, by individuals who held temporary power in the Government. The spectre of American citizens being asked, by badge-wielding police, for identification, travel papers is foreign to any fair reading of the Constitution, and its guarantee of human liberties. This is not Hitler's Berlin, nor Stalin's Moscow, nor is it white supremacist South Africa. Yet in Broward County, Florida, these police officers approach every person on board buses and trains ("that time permits") and check identification [and] tickets, [and] ask to search luggage - all in the name of "voluntary cooperation" with law enforcement. . . .'" 554 So.2d, at 1158.

The question for this Court, then, is whether the suspicionless, dragnet-style sweep of buses in intrastate and interstate travel is consistent with the Fourth Amendment. The majority suggests that this latest tactic in the drug war is perfectly compatible with the Constitution. I disagree. I have no objection to the manner in which the majority frames the test for determining whether a suspicionless bus sweep amounts to a Fourth Amendment "seizure." I agree that the appropriate question is whether a passenger who is approached during such a sweep "would feel free to decline the officers' requests or otherwise terminate the encounter." What I cannot understand is how the majority can possibly suggest an affirmative answer to this question.

The majority reverses what it characterizes as the Florida Supreme Court's "per se rule" against suspicionless encounters between the police and bus passengers, suggesting only in dictum its "doubt" that a seizure occurred on the facts of this case. However, the notion that the Florida Supreme Court decided this case on the basis of any "per se rule" independent of the facts of this case is wholly a product of the majority's imagination. As the majority acknowledges, the Florida Supreme Court "stated explicitly the factual premise for its decision." This factual premise contained all of the details of the encounter between respondent and the police. The lower court's analysis of whether respondent was seized drew heavily on these facts, and the court repeatedly emphasized that its conclusion was based on "all the circumstances" of this case.

The majority's conclusion that the Florida Supreme Court, contrary to all appearances, ignored these facts is based solely on the failure of the lower court to expressly incorporate all of the facts into its reformulation of the certified question on which respondent took his appeal. The majority never explains the basis of its implausible assumption that the Florida Supreme Court intended its phrasing of the certified question to trump its opinion's careful treatment of the facts in this case. Certainly, when this Court issues an opinion, it does not intend lower courts and parties to treat as irrelevant the analysis of facts that the parties neglected to cram into the question presented in the petition for certiorari. But in any case, because the issue whether a seizure has occurred in any given factual setting is a question of law, nothing prevents this Court from deciding on its own whether a seizure occurred based on all of the facts of this case as they appear in the opinion of the Florida Supreme Court.

These facts exhibit all of the elements of coercion associated with a typical bus sweep. As far as is revealed by facts on which the Florida Supreme Court premised its decision, the officers did not advise respondent that he was free to break off this "interview." Inexplicably, the majority repeatedly stresses the trial court's implicit finding that the police officers advised respondent that he was free to refuse permission to search his travel bag. This aspect of the exchange between respondent and the police is completely irrelevant to the issue before us. For as the State concedes, and as the majority purports to "accept," if respondent was unlawfully seized when the officers approached him and initiated questioning, the resulting search was likewise unlawful no matter how well advised respondent was of his right to refuse it. Consequently, the issue is not whether a passenger in respondent's position would have felt free to deny consent to the search of his bag, but whether such a passenger - without being apprised of his rights - would have felt free to terminate the antecedent encounter with the police.

Unlike the majority, I have no doubt that the answer to this question is no. Apart from trying to accommodate the officers, respondent had only two options. First, he could have remained seated while obstinately refusing to respond to the officers' questioning. But in light of the intimidating show of authority that the officers made upon boarding the bus, respondent reasonably could have believed that such behavior would only arouse the officers' suspicions and intensify their interrogation. Indeed, officers who carry out bus sweeps like the one at issue here frequently admit that this is the effect of a passenger's refusal to cooperate. The majority's observation that a mere refusal to answer questions, "without more," does not give rise to a reasonable basis for seizing a passenger, is utterly beside the point, because a passenger unadvised of his rights and

73

otherwise unversed in constitutional law has no reason to know that the police cannot hold his refusal to cooperate against him.

Second, respondent could have tried to escape the officers' presence by leaving the bus altogether. But because doing so would have required respondent to squeeze past the gun-wielding inquisitor who was blocking the aisle of the bus, this hardly seems like a course that respondent reasonably would have viewed as available to him. Our decisions recognize the obvious point, however, that the choice of the police to "display" their weapons during an encounter exerts significant coercive pressure on the confronted citizen. We have never suggested that the police must go so far as to put a citizen in immediate apprehension of being shot before a court can take account of the intimidating effect of being questioned by an officer with weapon in hand. Even if respondent had perceived that the officers would let him leave the bus, moreover, he could not reasonably have been expected to resort to this means of evading their intrusive questioning. For so far as respondent knew, the bus's departure from the terminal was imminent. Unlike a person approached by the police on the street, a passenger approached by the police at an intermediate point in a long bus journey cannot simply leave the scene and repair to a safe haven to avoid unwanted probing by law enforcement officials. The vulnerability that an intrastate or interstate traveler experiences when confronted by the police outside of his "own familiar territory" surely aggravates the coercive quality of such an encounter.

Rather than requiring the police to justify the coercive tactics employed here, the majority blames respondent for his own sensation of constraint. The majority concedes that respondent "did not feel free to leave the bus" as a means of breaking off the interrogation by the Broward County officers. But this experience of confinement, the majority explains, "was the natural result of his decision to take the bus." Thus, in the majority's view, because respondent's "freedom of movement was restricted by a factor independent of police conduct - i.e., by his being a passenger on a bus," - respondent was not seized for purposes of the Fourth Amendment. This reasoning borders on sophism, and trivializes the values that underlie the Fourth Amendment. Obviously, a person's "voluntary decision" to place himself in a room with only one exit does not authorize the police to force an encounter upon him by placing themselves in front of the exit. It is no more acceptable for the police to force an encounter on a person by exploiting his "voluntary decision" to expose himself to perfectly legitimate personal or social constraints. By consciously deciding to single out persons who have undertaken interstate or intrastate travel, officers who conduct suspicionless, dragnet-style sweeps put passengers to the choice of cooperating or of exiting their buses and possibly being stranded in unfamiliar locations. It is exactly because this "choice" is no "choice" at all that police engage this technique.

In my view, the Fourth Amendment clearly condemns the suspicionless, dragnet-style sweep of intrastate or interstate buses. Withdrawing this particular weapon from the government's drug war arsenal would hardly leave the police without any means of combating the use of buses as instrumentalities of the drug trade. The majority attempts to gloss over the violence that today's decision does to the Fourth Amendment with empty admonitions. "If th[e] [war on drugs] is to be fought," the majority intones, "those who fight it must respect the rights of individuals, whether or not those individuals are suspected of having committed a crime." The majority's actions, however, speak louder than its words. I dissent.

REVIEW SECTION

READING COMPREHENSION

Indicate the rationale used by the majority to determine Bostick's cooperation was voluntary.

Indicate the rationale used by the minority to determine that Bostick's cooperation was involuntary.

THINKING CRITICALLY

In your opinion was Bostick seized or free to conduct his personal business? Elaborate your response. What role did the fact that this suspicionless search occurred on an intrastate bus play in formulation of your response?

How would you decide this case? Articulate your reasoning using both majority and dissenting opinion.

CONCLUSION

This chapter has reviewed stops, frisks, and the Fourth Amendment; stops and the Fourth Amendment; special situation stops; and frisks and the Fourth Amendment. You have become aware that government officials are free to approach individuals in public places to request response to inquiries or to request a search. As well, you know that according to the Fourth Amendment to the U.S. Constitution and Section Twelve of the Florida Constitution, a seizure occurs when a government official removes an individual's right to leave or stay in a specific location. What should have become obvious in review of this chapter is that it is not always clear when an individual feels free to "go about their business" and when the police have created a situation of coercion. The courts attempt to define such scenarios in continually occurring interpretations of the Fourth Amendment.

Chapter Five

Seizures of Persons: Arrest

While we have previously discussed voluntary contact with government officials, stops by officers which must involve reasonable suspicion, we now turn to arrests. Because arrest is more intrusive than either a stop or voluntary contact, arrest involves more factual support by government officials in the form of probable cause. To make an arrest reasonable, the government must demonstrate that is was based on probable cause and the manner in which the arrest was made was reasonable.

Keep in mind the guidelines as set forth in §901.16 Florida Statutes detailing method of arrest by an officer with a warrant which reads:

> A peace officer making an arrest by a warrant shall inform the person to be arrested of the cause of arrest and that a warrant has been issued, except when the person flees or forcibly resists before the officer has an opportunity to inform the person, or when giving the information will imperil the arrest. The officer need not have the warrant in his or her possession at the time of the arrest but on request of the person arrested shall show it to the person as soon as practicable.

Finally, §901.17 of the Florida Statutes details the method of arrest by an officer without a warrant and reads:

> A peace officer making an arrest without a warrant shall inform the person to be arrested of the officer's authority and the cause of arrest except when the person flees or forcibly resists before the officer has an opportunity to inform the person or when giving the information will imperil the arrest.

This chapter will review:

(1)   The definition of arrest;

(2)   Probable cause; and

(3)   The manner of arrest.

SECTION 1: THE DEFININTION OF ARREST

OVERVIEW

By definition, an arrest involves the stop, seizure, or deprivation of one's liberty by virtue of legal authority. All individuals properly accused of a crime or misdeameanor, may be arrested, however by the laws of the United States, ambassadors and other public ministers are exempt from arrest.

Whether a detention was an investigatory stop or a full-blown arrest is a question of law wherein the courts attempt to determine at what point, in view of the totality of the circumstances, a reasonable person would not feel free to leave a situation. This gets a little complicated however, because a person may feel detained by an investigative stop, yet this would not officially constitute an arrest. There is no bright-line test that separates an investigatory stop from an arrest, though the length of time of the detention certainly plays some role. Thus, whether a seizure constitutes an arrest is answered on a case-by-case basis in light of the totality of the circumstances.

The courts consider various factors in making this distinction, such as the number of officers present, the show of authority, and the use of physical restraint, though in the end the courts have indicated that 'common sense' and 'ordinary experience' must prevail in the analysis. Keep in mind that police must not necessarily recite the magic words, 'You are under arrest.' For example in <u>Dunaway v. New York, 442 U.S. 200 (1979)</u>, whether the suspect was told that he was 'under arrest' was irrelevant to determining whether he was, in fact, under arrest. Thus, when officers use restrictive seizure to investigate suspicions of criminal activity, the detention of the suspect is sufficient to constitute an arrest even if the officer did not formally advise the suspect. Thus, you need to think of arrest as a zone, with the common element being the requirement of probable cause in order to be considered reasonable by the Fourth Amendment.

SECTION 2: PROBABLE CAUSE

OVERVIEW

Between reasonable suspicion and proof beyond a reasonable doubt, lies probable cause which is required by officers to make an arrest. This means that officers must have enough facts to reasonably believe that the arrested individual has committed, is committing, or is about to commit a crime. This reasonable belief can be based either on direct information or hearsay. While hearsay cannot be admitted in a court of law, it can be used to establish probable cause for arrest, though an anonymous tip in and of itself is insufficient in this regard. Courts employ the totality of circumstances of informant reliability test to determine whether or not hearsay evidence is reliable. You must keep in mind that when doubts arise as to reasonableness, courts tend to accept the facts as perceived by law enforcement officers.

CASE

In *State of Florida v. Gifford* the Court of Appeals examines a case wherein Gifford became a suspect in a sexual offense case. Using a warrant no longer in force, Gifford was arrested and gave a written confession. At the motion to suppress hearing, the trial court determined that while the continued detention was lawfully based on probable cause, the written statement was inadmissible because it flowed from an initial illegal arrest. The Court of Appeals addresses these concerns.

STATE OF FLORIDA V. GIFFORD
558 So.2d 444 (Fla.App. 4 Dist., 1990)

In the course of a police investigation, appellee became a suspect in a sexual offense case and a police records check revealed an outstanding probation violation warrant in appellee's name. Even though appellee protested repeatedly that the warrant was no longer in force, police officers arrested him and brought him to a jail facility. Further inquiry into the warrant substantiated appellee's claims. When jail authorities informed the investigating officer, who was interviewing the two victims of the sexual offense at the hospital's emergency room, the officer instructed them to continue to detain appellee since the officer had probable cause to arrest. When, approximately four hours later, the detective arrived at the jail, he advised appellee of his Miranda rights and conducted an interview during which appellee gave a written confession. Subsequent to the interview, the detective formally informed appellee that he was under arrest for the sexual offense crime. At the motion to suppress hearing, the trial court determined that while the continued detention was lawfully based on probable cause, the written statement was inadmissible because it flowed from an initial illegal arrest, the taint of which was never dissipated. We reverse.

A void or nonexistent warrant may not be the basis for a legal arrest and search, therefore the fact that the arresting officers did not discover the warrant's invalidity until after the arrest did not transform it into a lawful one. Nor does the "good faith exception" to the exclusionary rule apply and validate the arrest. However, subsequent to the initial unlawful arrest, when the detective ordered appellee's continued detention, appellee was lawfully "arrested" based on probable cause, advised of his Miranda rights and confessed. The record reflects ample support for the trial court's finding of a sufficient showing of independent probable cause for this arrest.

The detective testified that, prior to interviewing appellee, he had probable cause because (a) he had interviewed the victims and witnesses; (b) while with the victims and sexual assault counselors at the medical center, he picked up bits and pieces of information from the road patrol commander; and (c) the vehicle described as an instrumentality of the offense by both victims was found at appellee's residence. This is much more than a mere suspicion lacking articulable facts or a bare conclusion. While it would have been theoretically more pristine for the officer to follow protocol, especially given the illegality of the initial arrest, the sequence of events and totality of the circumstances were such that the officer had no realistic alternative but to order appellee detained rather than released and re-arrested. Detention by one officer at the direction of another is legal.

It is not dispositive that appellee was not informed of the carnal knowledge arrest until after receiving Miranda warnings and giving his confession. The court has stated that application of the fourth amendment's requirement of probable cause does not depend on whether an intrusion of this magnitude is termed an "arrest" under state law. No formal words are required stating that an individual is under arrest. The critical issue is whether probable cause for the arrest exists in light of the facts of each case. In determining whether a statement made subsequent to an illegal arrest is the product of free will, in addition to the giving of Miranda warnings, a fifth amendment threshold requirement, the court must satisfy fourth amendment concerns by examining the "causal connection" between the illegal arrest and the subsequent statement. The court must consider: (1) the temporal proximity of the illegal arrest and the statement; (2) the presence of intervening circumstances; (3) and the purpose and flagrancy of the official misconduct. In the instant case, approximately four hours passed between the illegal arrest and appellee's statement, the elements that supported the detective's probable cause were intervening factors and the official conduct was performed in good faith.

Appellee's claim that his confession was involuntary due to intoxication, being under the influence of narcotics and fear of the detective, was a question of credibility which the trial court resolved adversely to appellee. The officers testified appellee exhibited no signs of fear or intoxication. Appellee's testimony indicates he imbibed no intoxicants for a period of fourteen hours prior to the confession. His testimony of inability to remember the entire interrogation is insufficient to establish intoxication. Nor was there evidence of coercion or threats made against appellee. His belief that the detective harbored ill will towards him was subjective, not caused by the detective's conduct and not grounds for suppression.

Granting the primary illegality of the arrest based on the warrant, appellee's confession, rather than resulting from exploitation of that illegality, was an act of free will sufficiently distinguishable to purge any "primary taint." The trial court's order granting the motion to suppress is reversed.

ESQUIROZ, MARGARITA, Associate Judge, dissents with opinion.

I respectfully dissent. I cannot agree with the majority's holding that the record contains sufficient evidence of independently acquired probable cause to justify Walter Gifford's continued detention after he was admittedly arrested illegally at his home, without probable cause and without a valid warrant.

First, case law suggests that this after-the-fact determination of probable cause is not constitutionally permissible, at least not when the initial detention amounts to a full-scale arrest. This is not a case featuring an initial police contact generated by a reasonable or founded suspicion of criminal activity, which turns sequentially into full-blown probable cause to arrest as events lawfully progress. Even assuming that a reasonable or founded suspicion of criminal activity--based on articulable facts to justify a temporary detention--existed at the time of the initial police contact with Gifford, it is clear that Gifford was not merely "temporarily detained" for investigatory purposes when he was involuntarily taken from his home to the jailhouse for the ostensible purpose of interrogation. In Hayes, the Court cautioned: [T]he line is crossed when the police, without probable cause or a warrant, forcibly remove a person from his home or other place in which he is entitled to be and transport him to the police station, where he is detained, although briefly, for investigative purposes. We adhere to the view that such seizures, at least where not under judicial supervision, are sufficiently like arrests to invoke the traditional rule that arrests may constitutionally be made only on probable cause (Hayes v. Florida, 105 S.Ct.).

Secondly, my review of the record fails to persuade me that it reflects probable cause for Gifford's arrest at any time prior to Gifford's jailhouse confession to Detective Walker. Other than Walker's generalized claim to having acquired probable cause by the time he ordered Gifford's continued detention at the jail, the record's only discernible link between Gifford and the crime is Walker's bare bones statement that the vehicle used in the commission of the offense, as "described" by the victims, was found by other officers "at the residence where Mr. Gifford had been located." During his testimony, Walker did not provide even a general description of the vehicle, even though a description was allegedly given by the victims, nor did he refer to any other basis for the match presumably made with the vehicle parked outside Gifford's residence, which the arresting officers seized contemporaneously with Gifford's arrest. Detective Walker was the state's sole witness at the motion to suppress hearing, since neither the officer allegedly first at the scene, nor the officers who physically arrested Gifford and seized the vehicle, testified.

I must therefore disagree with the majority's conclusion that the trial court was furnished with a sufficient basis to find probable cause from Detective Walker's testimony that, prior to interviewing Gifford, he had probable cause because: (a) he had earlier interviewed the victims and witnesses, (b) he had picked up "bits and pieces" of information from the road patrol commander, while with the victims and sexual assault counselors at the medical center, and (c) the vehicle described as an instrumentality of the offense by both victims was found at Gifford's residence. Walker did not relay what the factual data or "bits and pieces" of information gained from the interviews were. He did not say if the victims or witnesses gave a description of the offender, or if they positively inculpated Gifford in the crime, by name or otherwise. As stated, he also failed to provide any supporting facts for his statement claiming a connection between the "described" vehicle and the vehicle parked outside Gifford's residence. His testimony therefore amounted to no more than naked conclusions, on the basis of which the trial court could do little more than ratify, as opposed to decide, the issue of probable cause. In short, for purposes of probable cause determination, the record is so devoid of factual information that the connection between Gifford and the commission of the offense can only be made by innuendo at best.

It has long been held that a conclusion of probable cause, or a plain belief by the arresting officer that he has probable cause to arrest, without providing supporting facts, is insufficient to establish probable cause. It is well established that at a motion to suppress hearing, once the defendant has initially shown a warrantless search and seizure of his person, house or belongings, the burden shifts to the state to establish that the case falls within an exception to the Fourth Amendment warrant requirement. The burden of showing admissibility of defendant's statement thus rests on the prosecution. Our reviewing function, limited as it is by the record, is similarly crippled by such a failure of proof. The state must come forward with sufficient evidence, on the record, establishing the basis for an arrest based on probable cause.

Finally, one other perspective of Fourth Amendment protection, not addressed by the majority, applies to Gifford's arrest. Even if armed with probable cause, the officers could not lawfully enter Gifford's home to arrest him without a warrant, absent exigent circumstances. Such a warrantless seizure of a person inside his home is presumptively unreasonable and violates the Fourth Amendment. Gifford was arrested at his home on the strength of a probation violation warrant that turned out not to exist, and no exigent circumstances are urged to justify the intrusion. The majority recognizes the principle that a void or nonexistent warrant may not be the basis for a legal arrest and search, and acknowledges that the "good faith exception" to the exclusionary rule does not change the result, even if the arresting officers acted under a good faith belief that the warrant was valid. Indeed, an otherwise illegal arrest is not insulated from challenge by the fact that the arresting officer relies on erroneous information dispatched by a fellow officer or employee. Yet the majority concludes that, given the sequence of events and the totality of the circumstances, Detective Walker had no realistic alternative but to keep Gifford in custody. Based on the contents of this record, I am unable to agree.

When the initial detention is unlawful, however, a subsequent confession may still be admissible as evidence against the defendant. The pertinent inquiry in this regard focuses on whether the causal link between the illegal police conduct and any incriminating statement obtained from the arrestee during the unlawful detention is sufficiently attenuated so as to dissipate the taint of the primary illegality and permit the use of such statement at trial. The majority concludes that Gifford's confession was an act of free will sufficiently distinguishable from the initial illegality to purge the primary taint. For this conclusion, the majority once again relies on the premise that Walker had independently developed probable cause by the time he interviewed Gifford. The majority takes the view that the four-hour span between arrest and statement, the good faith conduct of the officers, and the elements that supported probable cause, constituted intervening factors that broke the causal connection between the illegal arrest and the statement. But I suggest that even if Walker indeed acquired such probable cause, the fact remains that the objective existence of probable cause away from the jailhouse need not necessarily affect the arrestee's exercise of free will while confined. In this instance, Gifford was never informed of any such newly acquired probable cause. His unrebutted testimony was that, except to complain of the warrant's inefficacy and up until the time that he was interviewed by Walker, he did not communicate with anyone else throughout his detention. Gifford was held handcuffed or in a holding cell for approximately four hours, and the purpose of his detention was for interrogation.

In a written order containing extensive findings of fact and conclusions of law, the trial court found that there were no intervening circumstances that served to break the causal link between Gifford's illegal arrest and his subsequent statement. As such, Gifford's statement was not sufficiently an act of free will to purge the primary taint. The trial court's findings are amply supported by the record, and I see no reason to disturb them. I would therefore affirm the trial court's order granting Gifford's motion to suppress the statement.

REVIEW SECTION

READING COMPREHENSION

Elaborate the details leading to the arrest and subsequent confession by Gifford.

Articulate the trial court's logic in determining the written statement was inadmissible.

THINKING CRITICALLY

Did probable cause exist to arrest Gifford for the sexual offense in question?

Using argument from both the majority and dissenting opinions, articulate how you would decide this case.

CASE

In *Porter v. State of Florida,* Porter appeals his conviction and sentence for robbery with a weapon. While four points are raised on appeal, the Court finds none warrant a reversal but address only the point related to the trial court's denial of Porter's motion to suppress. The Court determines that officers who arrested Porter were in "fresh pursuit," and therefore hold that the trial court properly denied Porter's motion to suppress.

PORTER V. STATE
765 So.2d 76 (Fla.App. 4 Dist., 2000)

The ruling of the trial court on a motion to suppress comes to the appellate court clothed with a presumption of correctness and the reviewing court will interpret the evidence and reasonable inferences and deductions derived therefrom in a manner most favorable to sustaining the trial court's ruling. While we are required to accept the trial court's determination of the historical facts leading to the search, a defendant is entitled to a de novo review of whether the application of the law to the historical facts establishes an adequate basis for the trial court's finding of probable cause.

On May 17, 1998, at approximately 10:59 p.m., Pompano Beach police officers received a BOLO that an armed robbery had occurred. The BOLO specified that the perpetrators of the crime were four black males who left the scene in a white, four-door older model Cadillac headed west in the direction of I-95. When the BOLO came over the radio, officers Romb and Fletcher were traveling in close proximity to the crime and to I-95. In response to the BOLO, and based on additional information reported by an off-duty police officer that a white Cadillac was observed getting on I-95 in a southbound direction, Officers Romb and Fletcher immediately drove a short distance and entered I-95 southbound. Officers Romb and Fletcher were unable to see or locate the Cadillac when they first entered I-95 and continued to travel south, pulling over into the left hand emergency lane to wait to see if the Cadillac was in fact southbound on I-95. The officers continued south which put them in an area approximately five to seven miles from the alleged crime scene. The officers drove slowly, watching for any vehicle matching the description. Within three to three and one-half minutes of receiving the BOLO, the officers spotted a white, four-door Cadillac in the far left lane approaching them from behind. As the Cadillac passed the officers, they observed it traveling at a high rate of speed and that it was being driven by a black male. Officers Romb and Fletcher immediately began to follow the white Cadillac as it met the description in the BOLO. As the officers got closer, they were able to ascertain that at least four black males were in the vehicle.

The officers followed the vehicle for approximately one and one-half miles and then put on their flashing lights, signaling the driver to pull over. After the police lights were activated, the vehicle continued to travel at a high rate of speed for approximately another mile and then exited I-95. The officers followed the vehicle as it traveled and pulled into a nearby apartment complex. All four occupants immediately tried to flee from the vehicle. Officers Romb and Fletcher were able to detain the four occupants. Once the occupants were safely secured, the officers approached the Cadillac and saw through the car windows several items that met the descriptions of items taken during the robbery. The four occupants were arrested for robbery and all relevant evidence was seized.

Based upon the foregoing historical facts, the trial court concluded that pursuant to section 901.25, Florida Statutes (1997), the officers were in fresh pursuit and entitled to effectuate a valid arrest outside their jurisdiction which thereafter led to a valid search and seizure. Generally, an officer of a county or municipality has no official power to arrest an offender outside the boundaries of the officer's county or municipality, however, "[t]he fresh pursuit exemption allows officers who attempt to detain or arrest within their territorial jurisdiction, to continue to pursue a fleeing suspect even though the suspect crosses jurisdictional lines. The power to arrest after fresh pursuit presupposes that the officer had legally sufficient grounds to detain or arrest before they left their jurisdiction."

"Fresh pursuit" and "arrest outside the jurisdiction" are defined, in pertinent part, in section 901.25, Florida Statutes (1997), as follows:

(1) The term "fresh pursuit" as used in this act shall include fresh pursuit as defined by the common law and also the pursuit of a person who has committed a felony or who is reasonably suspected of having committed a felony. It shall also include the pursuit of a person suspected of having committed a supposed felony, though no felony has actually been committed, if there is reasonable ground for believing that a felony has been committed. It shall also include the pursuit of a person who has violated a county or municipal ordinance or chapter 316 or has committed a misdemeanor.

(2) Any duly authorized state, county, or municipal arresting officer is authorized to arrest a person outside the officer's jurisdiction when in fresh pursuit. Such officer shall have the same authority to arrest and hold such person in custody outside his or her jurisdiction, subject to the limitations hereafter set forth, as has any authorized arresting state, county, or municipal officer of this state to arrest and hold in custody a person not arrested in fresh pursuit. Under the common law doctrine of fresh pursuit, an officer may pursue a felon or a suspected felon, with or without a warrant, into another jurisdiction and arrest him there.

In arriving at the conclusion that section 901.25 entitled the officers to arrest Porter outside their jurisdiction, the trial court found the following: Although Officers Romb and Fletcher were outside their jurisdiction when they initially observed the defendants and when they effectuated their arrest, such an area is not far in time or distance from where the alleged robbery had occurred. The area in which the officers waited to see if a vehicle matching a description in the BOLO would pass is a logical travel route for the perpetrators to take and in fact, they did take. Once in pursuit of the vehicle due to its match of the description given in the BOLO, the officers were in hot or fresh pursuit.

Porter argues that the officers were not in fresh pursuit and thus the arrest and search and seizure are invalid. There is nothing in section 901.25 to suggest that fresh pursuit is somehow negated by virtue of the fact that the perpetrator and/or his vehicle are located for the first time outside the officers' jurisdiction. Just as the statute does not contain such restrictions, we can find no Florida cases to support these restrictions. One crucial factor is the police must act without unnecessary delay. This criterion is apparent from the statutory language itself. Another factor is that the pursuit must be continuous and uninterrupted, but there need not be continuous surveillance of the suspect or uninterrupted knowledge of his whereabouts. A final consideration, implicit in the statute is the relationship in time between the commission of the offense, the commencement of the pursuit, and the apprehension of the suspect. The greater the length of time, the less likely that the circumstances under which the police acted were sufficiently exigent to justify an extra-jurisdictional arrest.

Thus, fresh pursuit encompasses: 1) that the police act without unnecessary delay; 2) that the pursuit be continuous and uninterrupted; and 3) that there be a close temporal relationship between the commission of the offense and the commencement of the pursuit and apprehension of the suspect. We adopt these criteria for establishing what constitutes fresh pursuit. We believe these factors to be in keeping with the realities of our state with its elaborate intrastate and interstate expressway systems and its ubiquitous municipalities.

Although the trial court in the instant case classified the pursuit as a "fresh pursuit" as beginning once the officers saw the white Cadillac, there is no logical reason why the pursuit should not be deemed a "fresh pursuit" when the officers responded without unnecessary delay to the BOLO and, in continuous and uninterrupted fashion, sought and apprehended the occupants of the white Cadillac within a matter of minutes.

For the above stated reasons we hold that the trial court was correct in finding that the officers were engaged in a fresh pursuit when they made the arrest. Therefore, the trial court was correct in denying the motion to suppress. Thus, we affirm the sentence imposed on Porter. AFFIRMED.

REVIEW SECTION

READING COMPREHENSION

Describe in detail the facts of the case.

What grounds did this court use to affirm the decision of the trial court?

SECTION 3: THE MANNER OF ARREST

OVERVIEW

Aside from probable cause, the Fourth Amendment also includes a reasonable manner of arrest requirement. Chapter 776 Florida Statutes in Section 776.05 has set forth the following laws governing the use of force in making an arrest:

> A law enforcement officer, or any person whom he has summoned or directed to assist him, need not retreat or desist from efforts to make a lawful arrest because of resistance or threatened resistance to the arrest. He is justified in the use of any force: which he reasonably believes to be necessary to defend himself or another from bodily harm while making the arrest; when necessarily committed in arresting felons who have escaped; or when necessarily committed in arresting felons fleeing from justice. However, this subsection shall not constitute a defense in any civil action for damages brought for the wrongful use of deadly force unless the use of deadly force was necessary to prevent the arrest from being defeated by such flight and, when feasible, some warning had been given, and the sworn member reasonably believes that the fleeing felon poses a threat of death or serious physical harm to the officer or others; or the sworn member reasonably believes that the fleeing felon has committed a crime involving the infliction or threatened infliction of serious physical harm to another person.

Further, it is the policy of the Division of Law Enforcement of Florida to comply with the provisions of law concerning the use of control to complete an arrest, to prevent escape, to apprehend a fugitive or to prevent injury/death to its sworn members and to the public. Sworn members may resort to the use of control, including the use of force likely to cause death or great bodily harm, only when authorized by law. According to Florida Statutes Section 776.06, deadline force is:

> That force that is likely to cause death or great bodily harm and includes, but is not limited to: firing a firearm in the direction of the person to be arrested, even though no intent exists to kill or

85

inflict great bodily harm; and firing a firearm at a vehicle or vessel in which the person to be arrested is riding.

Deadly force does not include the discharge of a firearm by a law enforcement officer during and within the scope of their official duties which is loaded with a less-lethal munition which involves a projectile that is designed to stun, temporarily incapacitate, or cause temporary discomfort to a person without penetrating the person's body. Thus, when you consider if the manner of an arrest was reasonable, you must also consider whether the level of force used by law enforcement personnel was reasonable. The courts employ an objective standard of reasonable force, wherein according to the Fourth Amendment, officers are entitled to employ the amount of force necessary to apprehend suspects.

CASE

In *City of Miami v. Sanders* the City appeals a final judgment in favor of Sanders addressing "negligent" use of excessive force for injuries resulting from a lawful arrest. Note that Section 776.05 of the Florida Statutes provided above that ". . . this subsection shall not constitute a defense in any civil action for damages brought . . ." The court must assess the limit of an arresting officer's liability in making a lawful arrest.

CITY OF MIAMI V. SANDERS
672 So.2d 46 (Fla. App. 3 Dist., 1996)
627 So.2d 1210, 62 USLW 2436, 18 Fla. L. Weekly D2551, 18 Fla. L. Weekly D2668

Appellant City of Miami (City), appeals a final judgment in favor of appellee Sanders. We reverse because there is no cause of action for "negligent" use of excessive force for injuries resulting from a lawful arrest.

The facts reveal that Sanders was driving home after dropping her brother off at someone's house. Undercover police officers pulled her car over and told Sanders that her car would be towed because they just arrested her brother. Sanders was upset and asked one detective not to take her car. The detective allowed Sanders to remove her personal belongings from the car and asked her to leave. According to the detective, Sanders refused to move. He then advised her she was under arrest. Sanders, however, turned and started to walk away. The detective then grabbed her by the shoulder and again stated she was under arrest. Sanders turned around, hit the detective, and then continued walking. The detective followed her and grabbed her shoulder again. This time, Sanders spun around and slapped him in the face, causing his glasses to fall and break. He described Sanders as "going nuts," and in an attempt to control her, they both stumbled and the detective fell on her. Sanders' ankle broke at some point during this incident.

Sanders sought damages for "negligent" use of excessive force. The jury found the City negligent in causing Sanders' damage, and found that Sanders was 35% comparatively negligent. The City now appeals, arguing that there is no cause of action for "negligent" use of excessive force.

Traditionally, a presumption of good faith attaches to an officer's use of force in making a lawful arrest and an officer is liable for damages only where the force used is clearly excessive. If excessive force is used in an arrest, the ordinarily protected use of force by a police officer is transformed into a battery. A battery claim for excessive force is analyzed by focusing upon whether the amount of force used was reasonable under the circumstances. Law enforcement officers are provided a complete defense to an excessive use of force claim where an officer "reasonably believes [the force] to be necessary to defend himself or another from bodily harm while making the arrest." § 776.05(1), Fla.Stat. (1995).

The critical factor in this case is that Sanders pleaded a cause of action for "negligent" use of excessive force in making the arrest. The problem with Sanders' legal theory is that a suit for a police officer's use of excessive force necessarily involves the intentional tort of battery. The requisite elements for intentional tort actions are obviously more stringent than the elements for negligence actions. The Restatement (Second) of Torts § 18, states the essential elements of the intentional tort of battery are intent and contact:

(1) An actor is subject to liability to another for battery if (a) he acts intending to cause a harmful or offensive contact with the person of the other or a third person, or an imminent apprehension of such a contact, and (b) an offensive contact with the person of the other directly or indirectly results.

(2) An act which is not done with the intention stated in Subsection (1,a) does not make the actor liable to the other for a mere offensive contact with the other's person although the act involves an unreasonable risk of inflicting it and, therefore, would be negligent or reckless if the risk threatened bodily harm.

A cause of action for battery requires the showing of intentional affirmative conduct and cannot be premised upon an omission or failure to act. Negligence, on the other hand, requires only the showing of a failure to use due care and does not contain the element of intent. As noted McDonald v. Ford, 223 So.2d 553 (Fla. 2d DCA 1969), "An assault and battery is not negligence for such action is intentional, while negligence connotes an unintentional act."

Hence, we come to the inescapable conclusion that it is not possible to have a cause of action for "negligent" use of excessive force because there is no such thing as the "negligent" commission of an "intentional" tort. A contrary determination places a chilling effect on law enforcement efforts, and would render meaningless the defense under Section 776.05(1). Law enforcement officers should not have to worry about being "detectives of perspective" concerning every potential cause of action flowing from discretionary police functions.

We recognize, however, that a separate negligence claim based upon a distinct act of negligence may be brought against a police officer in conjunction with a claim for excessive use of force. Nevertheless, the negligence component must pertain to something other than the actual application of force during the course of the arrest. It cannot serve as the exclusive basis for liability in an excessive force claim.

In conclusion, we hold that the sole basis and limit of an arresting officer's liability in making a lawful arrest is founded on a claim of battery, in that excessive force was involved in making the arrest. The concept of a cause of action for "negligent" excessive force is an oxymoron, and we decline to adopt an argument which would perhaps "make us look like oxen or morons or both." United States v. Lam, 20 F.3d 999, 1004 (9th Cir.1994). Accordingly, we reverse with directions to enter judgment in favor of the City.

REVIEW SECTION

READING COMPREHENSION

Delineate why the elements of an intentional tort of battery were not met in this case.

Differentiate between a cause of action for battery and that of negligence.

THINKING CRITICALLY

In this case the court states: " . . . we come to the inescapable conclusion that it is not possible to have a cause of action for "negligent" use of excessive force because there is no such thing as the "negligent" commission of an "intentional" tort. A contrary determination places a chilling effect on law enforcement efforts, and would render meaningless the defense under Section 776.05(1)." Hypothesize the effects on law enforcement of an alternate court opinion.

Take a position on the following statement of this court: "Law enforcement officers should not have to worry about being "detectives of perspective" concerning every potential cause of action flowing from discretionary police functions."

CONCLUSION

This chapter has established that arrest is more intrusive than either a stop or voluntary contact, and thus involves more factual support by government officials in the form of probable cause. To make an arrest reasonable, the government must demonstrate that is was based on probable cause and the manner in which the arrest was made was reasonable. Further elaborated were the factors considered in determining whether or not law enforcement personnel used excessive force in making an arrest.

Chapter Six

Searches for Evidence

The method of analysis used to examine government action, stop and frisk, and arrest, is also used for searches, whether conducted with or without a warrant. As a reminder, to determine whether or not the government has complied with the Fourth Amendment involves analysis of three questions:

(1)   Was the action by the government a search?

(2)   If considered a search, was it an unreasonable search?

(3)   If considered an unreasonable search, should the evidence obtained during the unreasonable search be excluded from consideration?

This chapter will review these questions in light of:

(1)   Searches with warrants; and

(2)   Searches without warrants.

SECTION 1: SEARCHES WITH WARRANTS

OVERVIEW

As a reminder, Section Twelve of the Florida Constitution reads as follows regarding searches with warrants:

> The right of the people to be secure in their persons, houses, papers and effects against unreasonable searches and seizures, and against the unreasonable interception of private communications by any means, shall not be violated. No warrant shall be issued except upon probable cause, supported by affidavit, particularly describing the place or places to be searched, the person or persons, thing or things to be seized, the communication to be intercepted, and the nature of evidence to be obtained.

More specifically, three elements are required to meet the warrant requirement as outlined by the Fourth Amendment and elaborated in Section Twelve of the Florida Constitution. These three requirements are:

(1)   The particularity requirement which means that the warrant must state the place(s) to be searched, the person(s) or thing(s) to be seized, the communication that will be intercepted, and the nature of the evidence;

(2)   The probable cause affidavit is the document which supports the notion that said information will be found in the location specified; and

(3)   The "knock and announce" rule which requires officers to announce their status and that they have a warrant in hand, prior to entering a location. This rule can be abandoned if officers need to prevent violence, prevent the destruction of evidence, or prevent the escape of a suspect.

As you read through several cases involving searches with warrants, keep in mind the requirements of a warrant and potential exceptions to the "knock and announce" rule.

CASE

Kellom v. State of Florida involves an appeal of the trial court's denial of a motion to suppress contraband discovered in the appellant's residence. Kellom contends that the officers who executed the search warrant violated the "knock and announce" rule.

KELLOM V. STATE OF FLORIDA
Fla. App. 1st Dist., 2003

By information, the State charged appellant with one count of possession of cocaine, one count of possession of less than twenty grams of cannabis, and one count of obstructing a police officer without violence. Appellant subsequently filed a motion to suppress the contraband found within his residence as a result of the officers' execution of the search warrant. Deputy O'Leary testified at the hearing that appellant had been suspected of selling crack cocaine from his single residence. O'Leary further testified that, after securing a search warrant, he and the other officers executed the warrant at approximately 5:30 p.m. that same day.

According to O'Leary, the officers knocked on appellant's back door, announced their presence only once, and, upon receiving no response, waited "several seconds" before forcibly entering appellant's residence. When questioned by the State as to the reason for making such a quick entry on a case such as this, O'Leary replied that on this particular case, the officers were not sure whether weapons were involved or whether evidence would be destroyed. O'Leary stated, "They do get rid of the dope once they know - once we knock, they usually get rid of the dope . . . ." On cross-examination, O'Leary testified that his Affidavit for Search Warrant set forth that the confidential informant observed "a substantial quantity of cocaine," although, according to O'Leary, the informant may have stated that there was a truckload of cocaine in the residence. The affidavit made no mention of possible weapons or of the possibility that the suspected contraband would be destroyed as O'Leary had no knowledge of such at that time either. O'Leary further testified that, prior to their forcible entry, the officers did not hear any noise coming from inside the residence. Nor did the officers know, after knocking and announcing, whether weapons were involved. Upon their forcible entry, the officers found appellant located on his bed attempting to retrieve the contraband that was beside the bed. Smith, another officer, testified that he was last in the group of three officers headed towards the back door of appellant's residence. According to Smith, by the time he made it to the back door, entry was already being made.

The trial court subsequently denied appellant's motion to suppress without stating any grounds in support of its ruling. During appellant's trial, the trial court set forth that appellant retained his right to appeal the court's ruling as to his motion. Following jury deliberations, the jury found appellant guilty as to counts one and two and not guilty as to count three. Thereafter, the trial court sentenced appellant to five years' imprisonment as to count one and one year's imprisonment as to count two with credit for time served, the sentences to run concurrently. This appeal followed.

The Fourth Amendment to the United States Constitution and article I, section 12 of the Florida Constitution guarantee the people of this nation the right to be secure in their homes from unreasonable searches and seizures. The common law knock and announce principle forms a part of the Fourth Amendment reasonableness inquiry. The knock and announce rule has been recognized as a part of the common law of Florida. The Florida Legislature codified the knock and announce rule in section 933.09, which provides as follows: The officer may break open any outer door, inner door or window of a house, or any part of a house or anything therein, to execute the warrant, if after due notice of the officer's authority and purpose he or she is refused admittance to said house or access to anything therein.

Section 933.09 imposes two requirements. First, law enforcement must provide due notice of their authority and purpose. The statute also requires that law enforcement be refused admittance, which can be express or implied. A lack of response is deemed a refusal. Regardless of whether the ultimate refusal will be express or implied, section 933.09 and case law interpreting such require that some quantity of time, sufficient under the particular circumstances, be permitted for an occupant to respond.

Where officers knock, announce their authority and purpose, and then enter with such haste that the occupant does not have a reasonable opportunity to respond, the search violates section 933.09. The trial court's decision on the issue of due notice is a decision of fact that is binding on this Court if it is supported by competent, substantial evidence. In the instant case, Deputy O'Leary testified that several seconds elapsed between the officers' knock and announce and their forcible entry into appellant's residence. During oral argument, the State conceded that it was more likely that some length of time closer to five seconds elapsed between the officers' knock and announce and their forcible entry. Moreover, O'Leary testified on direct examination that he was not sure whether weapons were involved or whether the evidence would be destroyed. On cross-examination, he similarly testified that the officers did not know, after knocking and announcing, whether weapons were involved. O'Leary's affidavit did not mention the possibility of weapons because he had no knowledge of such at that time either.

Based upon these circumstances, we hold that the officers' execution of the search warrant violated the knock and announce rule in section 933.09. While the quantity of time sufficient to provide a suspect with due notice will vary depending upon the particular circumstances at issue, the facts of this case do not establish that the quantity of time between the officers' knock and announce and their hasty entry was sufficient to permit appellant to respond. Because we conclude that the officers in this case violated section 933.09 by failing to provide appellant with due notice before forcibly entering his residence, we must also determine whether any exigent circumstances existed to excuse the officers' actions.

The supreme court has recognized four exceptions to the knock and announce rule: (1) where the person within already knows of the officer's authority and purpose; (2) where the officers are justified in the belief that the persons within are in imminent peril of bodily harm; (3) if the officer's peril would have been increased had he demanded entrance and stated the purpose; or (4) where those within made aware of the presence of someone outside are then engaged in activities which justify the officers in the belief that an escape or destruction of evidence is being attempted. This Court must presume that a search that does not comply with the knock and announce rule is invalid, unless the State proves that the officers' conduct comes within one of these recognized exceptions.

With regard to the destruction of evidence and officer peril exceptions, the two exceptions relied upon by the State, the supreme court has held that an officer's belief of the immediate destruction of evidence must be based upon particular circumstances existing at the time of entry and must be grounded on something more than his or her generalized knowledge as a police officer. In holding such, the supreme court rejected the State's argument that a "blanket approach" should apply as an exception to section 933.09 and should excuse forcible entry if police generally believed that a small quantity of drugs were present in a residence with standard plumbing.

As we previously stated, O'Leary testified that he was not sure whether appellant would destroy the evidence or whether appellant possessed any weapons. As O'Leary's testimony demonstrates, the officers' actions resulted from their generalized belief that individuals in possession of contraband will "usually get rid" of such. However, this generalized belief is not sufficient to excuse the officers' violation of section 933.09. Therefore, because the officers had no particularized belief that appellant was likely to destroy the contraband or that he was likely to be armed, no exigent circumstances existed to excuse the officers' violation of section 933.09. The State also contends on appeal that if the officers' actions violated section 933.09 and were not excused through exigent circumstances, suppression of the contraband would be unnecessary as the evidence would have been inevitably discovered. However, we conclude that the inevitable discovery doctrine is not applicable in cases in which section 933.09 is violated, as the application of the doctrine to evidence seized in violation of the knock and announce rule would render section 933.09 and the policy behind the rule meaningless.

As such, the trial court's order denying appellant's motion to suppress is not supported by competent, substantial evidence. Accordingly, because the officers violated section 933.09 and because no exigent circumstances existed at the time of entry to excuse the violation, we reverse and remand with directions that appellant be discharged. REVERSED and REMANDED with directions.

REVIEW SECTION

READING COMPREHENSION

Elaborate the fact of this case, including why officers deemed it necessary to enter the residence after such a brief wait time after the knock and announce.

What is the rationale behind the knock and announce rule?

THINKING CRITICALLY

Should the inevitable discovery doctrine have applied in this case? Justify your response.

Should a generalized belief on the part of officers regarding disposal of contraband be enough to form a particularized belief?

CASE

Wilson v. State of Florida examines a case in which Wilson appeals the trial court's denial of his motion to suppress. Wilson purports that the search warrant was unlawfully executed since the police did not comply with the knock-and-announce provisions of section 933.09, Florida Statutes (1993). Unlike the previous case however, the court determined that the police had a reasonable basis for an unannounced entry.

WILSON V. STATE OF FLORIDA
673 So.2d 505 (Fla. App. 1 Dist., 1996)

In the instant case, a confidential police informant reported to the police that he had been in Wilson's home, where the informant noticed a "substantial quantity" of off-white rock-like substance on the kitchen table, which the informant recognized as crack cocaine. Within ten days, Detective Koivisto applied for and was granted a search warrant for the residence. The record reflects that, immediately preceding the execution of the search warrant, Detective Koivisto talked to Detective Thurne and discussed the execution of the search warrant. Detective Thurne then said: "Well, you know, that's the same guy's house that we served out on Lee Street." Detective Koivisto testified that he and Detective Thurne had served a warrant on a so-called drug "sales house" of Wilson's on Lee Street in Jacksonville and, when the officers executed the search warrant on the Lee Street house, several handguns were recovered.

Detective Koivisto and several other officers proceeded to the house. Detective Koivisto was wearing street clothes, and a blue vest with a reflector police marking across the chest over his bulletproof vest. According to him, he had a mask sitting on top of his head which was not pulled down, but it could be pulled down once he entered the residence so that those within would be unable to recognize his identity. When the officers arrived, they jumped from their vehicles and immediately began yelling "police, search warrant." Upon reaching the home the officers inserted a large pry bar into the outer burglar bar door and, using a sledge hammer to drive the pry bar, opened the burglar bar door. At the same time, they were yelling "police, search warrant." Detective Koivisto rammed the front door with a battering ram allowing the detectives to enter the home. No one knocked on the door.

In the house, the officers found a trafficking amount of cocaine in a shaving kit in the kitchen. Regina Evans was in a back bedroom watching television. She said she heard banging, and the police ran in wearing ski masks. She testified that she asked the police why they did not knock on the door and that she would have let them in. She also testified that she knew Wilson carried a gun. Wilson was later arrested, in possession of a firearm, and admitted that the cocaine found in the house belonged to him.

Wilson moved to suppress the evidence against him contending, among other things, that the warrant was illegally executed contrary to section 933.09, Florida Statutes (1993), which requires officers to knock and announce their presence before forcibly entering a residence. At the conclusion of the suppression hearing, the trial court orally announced its decision that, although the police officers had not complied with the knock-and-announce provision of the Florida Statutes, exigent circumstances justified a no-knock entry. The trial court stated its reasons, as follows: The officers had reason to believe that the cocaine in question was in the kitchen of the house, and this being a quote, unquote, nice house with standard plumbing, it's certainly reasonable to believe it could have been easily disposed of at that particular location within the house. They also had reasonable suspicions based upon prior knowledge of this defendant that he may be in possession of weapons, and not having any idea whether he was present at the time of the execution of this warrant,--for officers' safety those two exigent circumstances as far as I'm concerned are satisfied....

Reserving his right to appeal the trial court's denial of his motion to suppress, Wilson pled nolo contendere to trafficking in 400 grams or more of cocaine or a mixture containing cocaine contrary to section 893.135(1)(b)1.c., a first degree felony, and was sentenced to a 15-year minimum mandatory and ordered to pay a $250,000 fine.

As most states, Florida has adopted the knock-and-announce requirement by statute. In codifying the knock-and-announce requirement, Florida has also recognized the established exceptions to the common law rule. Recently, the United States Supreme Court has recognized that the common law knock-and-announce rule forms a part of the reasonableness inquiry of the Fourth Amendment to the United States Constitution. Wilson v. Arkansas, 514 U.S. 927, 115 S.Ct. 1914, 131 L.Ed.2d 976 (1995). However, the Court did not require a rigid rule that "every entry must be preceded by announcement," but recognized that "the common-law principle of announcement was never stated as an inflexible rule requiring announcement under all circumstances." Thus, the Court held that "although a search or seizure of a dwelling might be constitutionally defective if police officers enter without prior announcement, law enforcement interests may also establish the reasonableness of an unannounced entry." The supreme court left to the lower courts the task of determining the circumstances under which an unannounced entry is reasonable under the Fourth Amendment. The parties here have not raised, and we do not decide, whether Florida's knock-and-announce rule and its exceptions, as applied here, are reasonable under the Fourth Amendment. Our consideration here is limited to whether the unannounced entry in the instant case is lawful under section 933.09.

Wilson argues that finding that the destruction of evidence exception is not applicable here because "particularized" facts are not present which would lead to a reasonable belief that drugs would be destroyed if the officers knocked and announced their presence before gaining entry. As to the officer-peril exception, Wilson contends that at no time did the state bring forth any testimony regarding the officers' particular knowledge or belief that they, as officers, would be in peril if they followed the knock-and-announce provisions of the statute.

The state first responds that the entry here complies with the knock-and-announce requirements of section 933.09. Alternatively, the state argues that the destruction of evidence exception is supported in the instant case by the fact that the officers had been notified in advance by a reliable informant that Wilson was keeping the cocaine in the kitchen area of his home from which it could be easily destroyed. Next, the state contends that the officer-peril exception was present because Detective Koivisto had participated in an earlier search of a home owned by Wilson in which several firearms were seized.

At the outset, we agree with the trial court's conclusion that the police did not comply with section 933.09. The officers failed to allow any time after their announcement of "police, search warrant" to permit anyone inside to open the door voluntarily before they broke open the door. Thus, in order to sustain the trial court's order in the instant case, the facts of this case must fall within one of the exceptions to the knock-and-announce requirements of section 933.09. Turning to the destruction of evidence exception, we must disagree with the trial court's conclusion that simply having "cocaine ... in the kitchen of ... a nice house with standard plumbing" establishes an adequate basis for a reasonable belief that evidence will be destroyed.

We conclude that the police had reason to believe that Wilson was a dealer with at least one "crack house" dedicated to the sale of drugs in addition to his second residence. Where the police have a reasonable suspicion that a person is dealing in drugs and running a crack house in which weapons are kept, it is reasonable to draw the inference that such a person would have a plan in effect to destroy drug evidence in his home before it can be confiscated, especially where the police are informed that the drugs are placed in the kitchen near a sink or disposal. Similarly, with respect to the officer-peril exception, we conclude that the officers' belief was based on more than generalized knowledge. In the instant case, based on the officers' actual knowledge of Wilson's possession of firearms at his Lee Street drug sales house, it is reasonable for the police to believe that firearms would be present at this house. Further, it is common sense for officers to believe that a person reasonably suspected to be in possession of both firearms and substantial quantities of illegal drugs will use his firearms to protect himself and his holdings and, thus, poses a threat to the safety of police officers attempting to seize the drugs.

In short, we believe that the police in the instant case could reasonably infer that Wilson would be armed and in possession of a large quantity of drugs and would likely pose a threat to their safety when they sought to seize his drugs. Thus, we conclude that this case presents the particularized facts from which the officers could reasonably believe an unannounced entry was necessary to protect their safety and prevent the destruction of evidence. AFFIRMED.

BENTON, J., dissents with written opinion.

"[F]orcible entry is lawful only under exceptional circumstances, where no reasonable alternative is available." State v. Bamber, 630 So.2d 1048, 1055 (Fla.1994). An officer to whom a search warrant is directed "may break open any outer door ... to execute the warrant, if after due notice of his authority and purpose he is refused admittance to said house." § 933.09, Fla.Stat. (1989). But before forcing entry he is obliged to give notice of his authority, make demand for entry, and be refused, except in "an emergency that meets certain narrowly prescribed conditions." Because the evidence adduced at the suppression hearing in the present case does not, in my view, support either the destruction of evidence exception or the officer peril exception, I respectfully dissent.

To the extent the majority opinion approves the forcible, unannounced entry of a private dwelling in order to conduct a search merely on the basis of reason to believe that crack cocaine was in the kitchen, it flouts the clear, core holding in Bamber. The majority opinion also addresses important questions about the scope of the officer peril exception to the "knock and announce" requirement. Although the exception is not a new one, few reported Florida cases have found the exception applicable. Today's majority opinion leaps evidentiary hurdles that should likewise have obviated any need to grapple with "the safety issue" to give, on the merits, a disconcerting answer to what has more than once proven--although fortunately not in the present case--a question of life and death.

The search yielding the evidence which the trial court declined to suppress took place after a search warrant issued "for a single story, single family dwelling" at a specified address. Issuance of the warrant followed a finding that probable cause to search existed, a finding predicated on Detective Koivisto's affidavit that a confidential informant had told him "that said informant has been inside the above described premises within ten (10) days of the application of the Affidavit for Search Warrant and at that time personally observed ... a substantial quantity of off white rocklike substance which the occupant represented to be cocaine (crack)." The "standard search warrant" that issued here did not purport to authorize unannounced, forcible entry into appellant's house, or rest on a finding that any exception to the notice and demand requirement applied. Neither the warrant nor the affidavit mentioned guns or other weapons. At a suppression hearing like the one below, even though a "standard search warrant" authorized a search, the *de novo* question is whether a no-knock search of a residence was lawful based on exigent circumstances. Since Florida does not have "no-knock" warrants, the exception for good faith reliance on warrants, does not pertain to "knock and announce" questions.

On the question of the lawfulness of a forcible, unannounced entry, the prosecution has the burden of proof. "Under the Fourth Amendment, a specific showing must always be made to justify any kind of police action tending to disturb the security of the people in their homes. Unannounced forcible entry is in itself a serious disturbance of that security...." People v. Gastelo, 67 Cal.2d 586, 63 Cal.Rptr. 10, 12, 432 P.2d 706, 708 (1967). Since the test for exigent circumstances is objective, not subjective, the only evidence adduced at the suppression hearing that even suggested officer peril was not competent. It was rightly deemed hearsay: an out-of-court assertion that the house the officers were raiding was associated with the same person with whom another house was associated in which two or three handguns had been found. It is not enough to show that one police officer relied on the word of another police officer. The trial court's implicit finding that Detective Koivisto relied in good faith on what a fellow officer told him does not establish the truth of the fellow officer's assertion or a basis for deeming it reliable. The prosecution did not meet its burden to demonstrate that exigent circumstances actually existed.

The majority opinion fails to acknowledge the difference between an unsupported official claim of exigent circumstances and the particularized evidentiary showing our constitutions require. No basis was proven for any exception to the rule requiring officers serving a search warrant to give notice of their authority and make demand for admission, before using sledge hammer and battering ram to gain entry. I respectfully dissent.

REVIEW SECTION

READING COMPREHENSION

Detail the facts of this case.

Why was entry considered an exception to the knock and announce rule?

THINKING CRITICALLY

Do you believe the state established sufficient particularized facts in this case?

How would you decide this case? Use arguments from both majority and dissenting opinions.

SECTION 2: SEARCHES WITHOUT WARRANTS

OVERVIEW

Perhaps contrary to popular public perception, majority of searches are executed without warrants because the courts interpret broadly the exceptions provided to law enforcement. The U.S. Supreme Court has elaborated five major exceptions to the warrant requirement:

(1)   Searches incident to arrest are reasonable under the Fourth Amendment. In fact, §901.21 of the Florida Statutes elaborates the search of a person arrested:

> (1) When a lawful arrest is effected, a peace officer may search the person arrested and the area within the person's immediate presence for the purpose of: (a) Protecting the officer from attach;

(b) Preventing the person from escaping; or (c) Discovering the fruits of a crime. (2) A peace officer making a lawful search without a warrant may seize all instruments, articles, or things discovered on the person arrested or within the person's immediate control, the seizure of which is reasonably necessary for the purpose of: (a) Protecting the officer from attack; (b) Preventing the escape of the arrested person; or (c) Assuring subsequent lawful custody of the fruits of a crime or of the articles used in the commission of a crime;

(2)   Consent searches must be voluntary are needed when there is no probable cause to search and involve searches wherein an individual gave a law enforcement personnel permission to search belongings or conduct a pat-down;

(3)   Vehicle searches are permitted with probable cause due to a reduced expectation of privacy;

(4)   Container searches are permitted if the container is in a vehicle and an officer has probable cause to search; if there is only reasonable suspicion, an officer may briefly seize a container but must obtain a warrant backed by probable cause in order to search;

(5)   Exigent circumstances searches are based on an officer's reasonable suspicion and can involve a pat-down for weapons, a search if there is reasonable belief that evidence may be destroyed, entrance into a house without a warrant if the officer is in hot pursuit, or a search wherein an officer has probable cause that an individual is of danger to the community.

CASE

Benefield v. State of Florida is a 1964 case that addresses the applicability of the "knock and announce" rule without a search warrant. This case is premised on the interpretation of §901.19(1) Florida Statutes which reads:

> Right of officer to break into building. If a peace officer fails to fain admittance after she or he has announced her or his authority and purpose in order to make an arrest either by warrant or when authorized to make an arrest for a felony without a warrant, the officer may use all necessary and reasonable force to enter any building or property where the person to be arrested is or is reasonably believed to be.

Benefield has appealed his conviction using as support another case wherein the facts were virtually the same, yet the rule of law was applied differentially.

BENEFIELD V. STATE OF FLORIDA
160 So.2d 706 (Fla., 1964)

Petitioner, Benefield was informed against for grand larceny. He was tried by a jury and convicted of attempt to commit grand larceny. On appeal his conviction was affirmed by the District Court of Appeal, Second District. Petitioner now seeks review of the latter judgment by certiorari on the theory that it is in direct conflict with this court's decision in Dickens v. State, Fla.1952, 59 So.2d 775. It is clear from an examination of the opinions in the case at bar and the Dickens case that although both involve substantially the same controlling facts, identical rules of law were applied to each in such a way as to produce opposite results. That is sufficient to activate this court's jurisdiction. If there are those who do not think we have jurisdiction on this theory, certainly we have it on the theory that the decision of the district court of appeal herein has generated confusion and instability among the precedents rendering the law unclear, if not in conflict.

The essential facts in the case are as follows: Petitioner is alleged to have approached Hollander and Rosenthal, operators of a bowling alley and offered to help them secure a liquor license if they would pay him $5,000 in small bills. On April 27, 1961, Hollander and Rosenthal, after notifying the police department and securing certain marked money from their attorney, went to the petitioner's office. The petitioner was not at his office but was at home sick so they proceeded to his home. They were accompanied by two city detectives who waited outside while Hollander and Rosenthal entered the petitioner's home for the purpose of delivering the marked money to him. Upon completion of the transaction with petitioner, Hollander and Rosenthal left the house. One of the police officers, Sgt. Hooper, approached Hollander and Rosenthal just as they left the doorway. The sergeant asked Hollander if the petitioner had the money. Hollander nodded yes. The police officer then 'stepped inside the door,' asked petitioner's wife if the petitioner was home and if he could see him, walked back to the petitioner's bedroom, and after identifying himself to the petitioner, placed the petitioner under arrest. Sgt. Hooper further testified that when he entered the front door it was open, that Hollander was holding it open, and that he stepped inside before he saw petitioner's wife.

Hollander testified that he did not hold the door open for the officers, and petitioner's wife testified that by the time she had reached the hall, Sgt. Hooper had opened the door and was standing inside. The record discloses that the two arresting officers made no announcement of their authority and purpose before entering petitioner's home; in fact, this was not done until the officers entered petitioner's bedroom at the rear of the home. The trial judge himself noted that the officers were not inside the home with the permission of petitioner or his wife.

On May 11, 1961, petitioner made timely motion to suppress the introduction of the marked money on the ground that it was secured by an unlawful search and seizure. Said motion was denied by the trial court on August 17, 1961, after hearing testimony and arguments of counsel. It is clear from the record that the police officers did not have a search warrant or a warrant for petitioner's arrest and that the search for the money took place subsequent to petitioner's arrest.

The district court of appeal held that because the police officers had reasonable grounds to believe that petitioner had committed a felony, his arrest without a warrant was authorized by §901.15, Florida Statutes, F.S.A., and thus valid. Said holding of the district court of appeal might have been a correct interpretation of § 901.15 if the officers had found petitioner out on the commons and were attempting to arrest him. In this case petitioner was in his home and the officers were proceeding under § 901.19(1), Florida Statutes, F.S.A. They were bound by the requirements of that act and what we have said here relates to the execution of it. There was no attempt whatever to comply with § 901.19(1), Florida Statutes, F.S.A., and the two acts relate to a different kind of arrest.

The evidence seized, in order to be admissible at trial, must be the product of a search incident to a lawful arrest, since the officers had no search warrant. The lawfulness of an arrest without warrant, in turn must be based upon probable cause, which exists, where the facts and circumstances within the officer's knowledge and of which he had reasonably trustworthy information are sufficient in themselves to warrant a man of reasonable caution in the belief that an offense has been committed. In the instant case the officers were in possession of the affidavits of Hollander and Rosenthal which described the petitioner's activities prior to the payoff. The officers also were aware that Hollander and Rosenthal had entered the petitioner's house for the purpose of delivering certain marked money to him. Immediately prior to their entry into petitioner's home, Hollander had informed the arresting officer that the money had been delivered. It is, therefore, clear that the officers may have had probable cause to believe a felony had been committed. Nevertheless, the question recurs, was the lawfulness of the arrest, even though based on probable cause, vitiated by the unlawful means in which the home was entered?

The facts reveal that the officers did not make the slightest effort to comply with this Florida statute. Although there is some question as to whether or not Hollander held the door open for Sgt. Hooper, Hollander's testimony, as well as that of Mrs. Benefield, clearly discloses that the officer opened the unlocked screened door and stepped into the house. Such an entry would constitute entry by breaking. It is true that the act is ambiguous and poorly drawn, but a reasonable interpretation of it runs like this: When an officer is authorized to make an arrest in any building, he should first approach the entrance to the building. He should then knock on the door and announce his name and authority, and what his purpose is in being there. If he is admitted and has a warrant, he may proceed to serve it. He is not authorized to be there to make an arrest unless he has a warrant or is authorized to arrest for a felony without a warrant. If he is refused admission and is armed with a warrant or has authority to arrest for a felony without a warrant, he may then break open a door or window to gain admission to the building and make the arrest. If the building happens to be one's home, these requirements should be strictly observed.

Entering one's home without legal authority and neglect to give the occupants notice have been condemned by the law and the common custom of this country from time immemorial. This sentiment has moulded our concept of the home as one's castle as well as the law to protect it. There is nothing more terrifying to the occupants than to be suddenly confronted in the privacy of their home by a police officer decorated with guns and the insignia of his office. This is why the law protects its entrance so rigidly. The law so interpreted is nothing more than another expression of the moral emphasis placed on liberty and the sanctity of the home in a free country.

In this case the officers totally ignored every requirement of the law as above interpreted. They barged into petitioner's home without knocking or giving any notice whatever of their presence; they did not have a search warrant or warrant to arrest anyone; they ransacked petitioner's home without the least semblance of any showing of authority. The petitioner was in bed sick at the time and the officers knew it. For all the record shows, there is no material difference in the entrance here from that in the Dickens case. In that case they entered the back door without permission, while in this case they entered the front door without permission. They were trespassers in both cases. They completely ignored every requirement of § 901.19(1), Florida Statutes, F.S.A., so everything they did inside the home was done as trespassers in total disregard of the responsibility the law imposed. We do not attempt to prescribe what would constitute a reasonable search except to say that what was done here was unreasonable under any standard that would be approved by a free country.

As we interpret the common law authorities in relation to § 901.19(1), Florida Statutes, F.S.A., we conclude that even if probable cause exists for the arrest of a person, our statute is violated by an unannounced intrusion in the form of a breaking and entering any building, including a private home, except (1) where the person within already knows of the officer's authority and purpose; (2) where the officers are justified in the belief that the persons within are in imminent peril of bodily harm; (3) if the officer's peril would have been increased had he demanded entrance and stated the purpose, or (4) where those within made aware of the presence of someone outside are then engaged in activities which justify the officers in the belief that an escape or destruction of evidence is being attempted. Time and experience will no doubt suggest other exceptions, but when the facts of this case are measured against the statutory criteria and its exceptions, it is clear that the unannounced entry of the officers in this case violated the statute and vitiated the arrest made pursuant to probable cause without warrant.

In reaching this conclusion, we have not overlooked the state's argument that the marked money could have easily been disposed of by the classic method of flushing it down the drain. This argument must be rejected in the face of the practical difficulties inherent in disposing of $3,000 in small bills by that method. Under the peculiar facts of this case, we are convinced that §901.19(1), Florida Statutes, F.S.A., was violated and that its violation is not excused by any of the exceptions discussed herein and for this reason the fruits of the search being the product of an unlawful arrest and a search incident thereto, should have been excluded by the trial court upon proper motion.

For the reasons above stated, the decision of the district court of appeal herein is quashed and this cause is remanded to said court for further consideration not inconsistent with the decision herein.

REVIEW SECTION

READING COMPREHENSION

Outline the facts of the case that lead to the entry of officers into Benefield's home.

What statutes did the court apply in making its decision.

THINKING CRITICALLY

Do you believe the lawfulness of the arrest, though based on probable cause, vitiated the unlawful means in which the home was entered?

Using the element of the Florida statute in question, do you agree that the entry into the Benefield home constituted trespassing? Defend your response.

CASE

In *State of Florida v. Wells,* an arrest occurred for driving under the influence of alcohol, followed by the respondent giving the Florida Highway Patrol permission to open the trunk of his impounded car. After the state trial court denied Wells' motion to suppress, he pleaded nolo contendere to a charge of possession of a controlled substance, but retained his right to appeal the denial of the motion to suppress. The intermediate appellate court held that the trial court erred in denying suppression of the marijuana found in the suitcase. The State Supreme Court affirmed.

STATE OF FLORIDA V. WELLS
495 U.S. 1 (1990)

A Florida Highway Patrol trooper stopped respondent Wells for speeding. After smelling alcohol on Wells' breath, the trooper arrested Wells for driving under the influence. Wells then agreed to accompany the trooper to the station to take a breathalyzer test. The trooper informed Wells that the car would be impounded and obtained Wells' permission to open the trunk. At the impoundment facility, an inventory search of the car turned up two marijuana cigarette butts in an ashtray and a locked suitcase in the trunk. Under the trooper's direction, employees of the facility forced open the suitcase and discovered a garbage bag containing a considerable amount of marijuana.

Wells was charged with possession of a controlled substance. His motion to suppress the marijuana on the ground that it was seized in violation of the Fourth Amendment to the United States Constitution was denied by the trial court. He thereupon pleaded nolo contendere to the charge but reserved his right to appeal the denial of the motion to suppress. On appeal, the Florida District Court of Appeal for the Fifth District held, *inter alia*, that the trial court erred in denying suppression of the marijuana found in the suitcase. Over a dissent, the Supreme Court of

Florida affirmed. 539 So.2d 464, 469 (1989). We granted certiorari and now affirm (although we disagree with part of the reasoning of the Supreme Court of Florida).

JUSTICE BRENNAN, with whom JUSTICE MARSHALL joins, concurring in the judgment.

I agree with the Court that the judgment of the Florida Supreme Court should be affirmed because the Florida Highway Patrol had no policy at all with respect to opening closed containers. As the majority recognizes, the search was therefore unconstitutional under any reading of our cases. See Colorado v. Bertine, 479 U.S. 367, 374 (1987). Our cases have required that inventory searches be "sufficiently regulated," so as to avoid the possibility that police will abuse their power to conduct such a search. The facts of this case demonstrate a prime danger of insufficiently regulated inventory searches: police may use the excuse of an "inventory search" as a pretext for broad searches of vehicles and their contents. In this case, there was no evidence that the inventory search was done in accordance with any standardized inventory procedure. Although the State characterized the search as an inventory search in the trial court, it did not point to any standard policy governing inventory searches of vehicles (much less to any policy governing the opening of closed containers) until the case reached the Florida Supreme Court.

At that time, the Florida Highway Patrol entered the case as *amicus curiae* and argued that Chapter 16 of the "Florida Highway Patrol Forms and Procedural Manual" contained the standard policy that guided the conduct of the search in this case. The Florida Supreme Court concluded that the manual did not provide any policy for the opening of closed containers. But it now appears that the Florida Supreme Court may have been under the misapprehension that the manual was in effect at the time of the search in this case. The State conceded at oral argument before this Court that the manual was not in effect at the time of the search in this case, but argued nonetheless that the officer had performed the search according to "standard operating procedures" that were later incorporated into the Highway Patrol Manual. But the State did not offer any evidence at the suppression hearing to support a finding that Trooper Adams performed the inventory according to "standard operating procedures." Trooper Adams testified that he asked his immediate superior whether he should impound and inventory the car but that his superior left it to Adams' discretion, stating that he found nothing suspicious about the car. Trooper Adams testified that he "took it upon himself to go ahead and have the car towed." He also testified that he thought that opening the suitcase was part of a proper inventory but that he did not ask anyone else's opinion until after the search was completed. He testified "Well, I had to take my chances."

In addition, there was no evidence that an inventory was actually done in this case: the State introduced neither an inventory sheet nor any testimony that the officer actually inventoried the items found in respondent's car. Rather, the testimony at the suppression [495 U.S. 1, 7] hearing suggests that the officer used the need to "inventory" as an excuse to search for drugs. The testimony establishes that after arresting respondent for driving under the influence of alcohol and accompanying him to the station house, Trooper Adams returned to the impound lot to conduct the inventory search at 1:30 a. m. Grover Bryan, who assisted the state trooper with the inventory, testified at the hearing that Trooper Adams told him that "he wanted to inventory the car good, he wanted to go through it real good because he felt that there was drugs in it." According to Bryan, Adams' desire to inventory the car stemmed from the fact that there was a

103

large amount of cash lying on the floor of the car when respondent was arrested. Bryan testified that Adams insisted that contraband would be found in the car because "[t]here ain't nobody runs around with that kind of money in the floorboard unless they're dealing drugs or something like that." When they finally found the locked suitcase in the trunk, Bryan testified that Adams "want[ed] in the suitcase" because he "had a strong suspicion there was drugs in that car and it was probably in that suitcase." The men then spent 10 minutes prying open the lock on the suitcase with two knives. Bryan testified that once they opened the suitcase and found a bag of marijuana inside, "[Adams] was quite excited. He said `there it is.'"

The majority finds it unnecessary to recount these facts because it affirms the Florida Supreme Court on the narrow ground that police may not be given total discretion to decide whether to open closed containers found during an inventory search. With this much I agree. Like JUSTICE BLACKMUN however, I cannot join the majority opinion because it [495 U.S. 1, 8] goes on to suggest that a State may adopt an inventory policy that vests individual police officers with some discretion to decide whether to open such containers. This suggestion is pure dictum given the disposition of the case. But as JUSTICE BLACKMUN notes, there is a danger that this dictum will be relied on by lower courts in reviewing the constitutionality of particular inventory searches, or even by local policymakers drafting procedures for police to follow when performing inventories of impounded vehicles. Thus, I write separately to emphasize that the majority's suggestion is inconsistent with the reasoning underlying our inventory search cases and relies on mischaracterization prior findings.

Our cases clearly hold that an inventory search is reasonable under the Fourth Amendment only if it is done in accordance with standard procedures that limit the discretion of the police. Contrary to the majority's assertion today, police may not exercise discretion with respect to the opening of closed containers during an inventory search. Opening a closed container constitutes a great intrusion into the privacy of its owner even when the container is found in an automobile. For this reason, I continue to believe that in the absence of consent or exigency, police may not open a closed container found during an inventory search of an automobile.

REVIEW SECTION

READING COMPREHENSION

Elaborate the facts of the case leading to the discovery of contraband.

Outline the findings of the lower courts in reference to this case.

THINKING CRITICALLY

Discuss the role of Florida Highway Patrol policy in deciding this case.

Should individual officers have some discretion in conducting an inventory search? What are the implications of such a practice?

CASE

State of Florida v. Jimeno involves the dynamics surrounding a consensual search. After being stopped for a traffic infraction, Jimeno consented to a search of his automobile requested based on reasonable suspicion of Officer Trujillo. Cocaine was found and Jimeno was charged with possession with intent to distribute cocaine in violation of Florida law. The state trial court granted his motion to suppress the cocaine on the ground that his consent to search the car did not carry with it specific consent to open the bag the drugs were found in and examine its contents. The Florida District Court of Appeal and Supreme Court affirmed.

STATE OF FLORIDA V. JIMENO
500 U.S. 248 (1991)

REHNQUIST, C.J., delivered the opinion of the Court, in which WHITE, BLACKMUN, O'CONNOR, SCALIA, KENNEDY, and SOUTER, JJ., joined. MARSHALL, J., filed a dissenting opinion, in which STEVENS, J., joined.

In this case, we decide whether a criminal suspect's Fourth Amendment right to be free from unreasonable searches is violated when, after he gives a police officer permission to search his automobile, the officer opens a closed container found within the car that might reasonably hold the object of the search. We find that it is not. The Fourth Amendment is satisfied when, under the circumstances, it is objectively reasonable for the officer to believe that the scope of the suspect's consent permitted him to open a particular container within the automobile.

This case began when a Dade County police officer, Frank Trujillo, overheard respondent, Enio Jimeno, arranging what appeared to be a drug transaction over a public telephone. Believing that respondent might be involved in illegal drug trafficking, Officer Trujillo followed his car. The officer observed respondent make a right turn at a red light without stopping. He then pulled respondent over to the side of the road in order to issue him a traffic citation. Officer Trujillo told respondent that he had been stopped for committing a traffic infraction. The officer went on to say that he had reason to believe that respondent was carrying narcotics in his car, and asked permission to search the car. He explained that respondent did not have to consent to a search of the car. Respondent stated that he had nothing to hide and gave Trujillo [500 U.S. 248, 250] permission to search the automobile. After two passengers stepped out of respondent's car, Officer Trujillo went to the passenger side, opened the door, and saw a folded, brown paper bag on the floorboard. The officer picked up the bag, opened it, and found a kilogram of cocaine inside.

Respondent was charged with possession with intent to distribute cocaine in violation of Florida law. Before trial, he moved to suppress the cocaine found in the bag on the ground that his consent to search the car did not extend to the closed paper bag inside of the car. The trial court granted the motion. It found that, although respondent "could have assumed that the officer would have searched the bag" at the time he gave his consent, his mere consent to search the car did not carry with it specific consent to open the bag and examine its contents.

The Florida District Court of Appeal affirmed the trial court's decision to suppress the evidence of the cocaine. 550 So.2d 1176 (Fla. 3d DCA 1989). In doing so, the court established a per se rule that "consent to a general search for narcotics does not extend to `sealed containers within the general area agreed to by the defendant.'" The Florida Supreme Court affirmed. We granted certiorari to determine whether consent to search a vehicle may extend to closed containers found inside the vehicle. 498 U.S. 997 (1990), and we now reverse the judgment of the Supreme Court of Florida.

The touchstone of the Fourth Amendment is reasonableness. The Fourth Amendment does not proscribe all state-initiated searches and seizures; it merely proscribes those which are unreasonable. Thus, we have long approved consensual searches because it is no doubt reasonable for the police to conduct a search once they have been permitted to do so. The standard for measuring the scope of a suspect's consent under the Fourth Amendment is that of "objective" reasonableness - what would the typical reasonable person have understood by the exchange between the officer and the suspect? The question before us, then, is whether it is reasonable for an officer to consider a suspect's general consent to a search of his car to include consent to examine a paper bag lying on the floor of the car. We think that it is.

The scope of a search is generally defined by its expressed object. In this case, the terms of the search's authorization were simple. Respondent granted Officer Trujillo permission to search his car, and did not place any explicit limitation on the scope of the search. Trujillo had informed respondent that he believed respondent was carrying narcotics, and that he would be looking for narcotics in the car. We think that it was objectively reasonable for the police to conclude that the general consent to search respondent's car included consent to search containers within that car which might bear drugs. A reasonable person may be expected to know that narcotics are generally carried in some form of a container. The authorization to search in this case, therefore, extended beyond the surfaces of the car's interior to the paper bag lying on the car's floor.

Respondent argues, and the Florida trial court agreed with him, that, if the police wish to search closed containers within a car, they must separately request permission to search each container. But we see no basis for adding this sort of superstructure to the Fourth Amendment's basic test of objective reasonableness. A suspect may, of course, delimit as he chooses the scope of the search to which he consents. But if his consent would reasonably be understood to extend to a particular container, the Fourth Amendment provides no grounds for requiring a more explicit authorization.

The judgment of the Supreme Court of Florida is accordingly reversed, and the case remanded for further proceedings not inconsistent with this opinion. It is so ordered.

JUSTICE MARSHALL, with whom JUSTICE STEVENS joins, dissenting.

The question in this case is whether an individual's general consent to a search of the interior of his car for narcotics should reasonably be understood as consent to a search of closed containers inside the car. Nothing in today's opinion dispels my belief that the two are not one and the same from the consenting individual's standpoint. Consequently, an individual's consent to a search of the interior of his car should not be understood to authorize a search of closed containers inside the car. I dissent. In my view, analysis of this question must start by identifying the differing expectations of privacy that attach to cars and closed containers. It is well established that an individual has but a limited expectation of privacy in the interior of his car. In contrast, it is equally well established that an individual has a heightened expectation of privacy in the contents of a closed container.

The distinct privacy expectations that a person has in a car, as opposed to a closed container, do not merge when the individual uses his car to transport the container. In this situation, the individual still retains a heightened expectation of privacy in the container. Nor does an individual's heightened expectation of privacy turn on the type of container in which he stores his possessions. Notwithstanding the majority's suggestion to the contrary, this Court has soundly rejected any distinction between "worthy" containers, like locked briefcases, and "unworthy" containers, like paper bags. Because an individual's expectation of privacy in a container is distinct from, and far greater than, his expectation of privacy in the interior of his car, it follows that an individual's consent to a search of the interior of his car cannot necessarily be understood as extending to containers in the car. At the very least, general consent to search the car is ambiguous with respect to containers found inside the car.

In my view, the independent and divisible nature of the privacy interests in cars and containers mandates that a police officer who wishes to search a suspicious container found during a consensual automobile search obtain additional consent to search the container. If the driver intended to authorize search of the container, he will say so; if not, then he will say no. The only objection that the police could have to such a rule is that it would prevent them from exploiting the ignorance of a citizen who simply did not anticipate that his consent to search the car would be understood to authorize the police to rummage through his packages. According to the majority, it nonetheless is reasonable for a police officer to construe generalized consent to search an automobile for narcotics as extending to closed containers, because "[a] reasonable person may be expected to know that narcotics are generally carried in some form of a container." This is an interesting contention. By the same logic, a person who consents to a search of the car from the driver's seat could also be deemed to consent to a search of his person, or indeed of his body cavities, since a reasonable person may be expected to know that drug couriers frequently store their contraband on their persons or in their body cavities. I suppose (and hope) that even the majority would reject this conclusion, for a person who consents to the search of his car for drugs certainly does not consent to a search of things other than his car for drugs. But this example illustrates that, if there is a reason for not treating a closed container as something "other than" the car in which it sits, the reason cannot be based on intuitions about where people carry drugs. The majority, however, never identifies a reason for conflating the distinct privacy expectations that a person has in a car and in closed containers.

The majority also argues that the police should not be required to secure specific consent to search a closed container, because "`the community has a real interest in encouraging consent.'" I find this rationalization equally unsatisfactory. If anything, a rule that permits the police to construe consent to search more broadly than it may have been intended would discourage individuals from consenting to searches of their cars. Apparently, the majority's real concern is that, if the police were required to ask for additional consent to search a closed container found during the consensual search of an automobile, an individual who did not mean to authorize such additional searching would have an opportunity to say no. In essence, then, the majority is claiming that "the community has a real interest" not in encouraging citizens to consent to investigatory efforts of their law enforcement agents, but rather in encouraging individuals to be duped by them. This is not the community that the Fourth Amendment contemplates. I dissent.

REVIEW SECTION

READING COMPREHENSION

Did the officer meet the requirements of reasonable suspicion?

Detail the fact of the case.

THINKING CRITICALLY

Does an unreasonable search result, ad thus a Fourth Amendment violation, when officers open a closed container? Were the requirements met of a consensual search?

Was it reasonable for Jimeno to assume the officer would not open the bag containing the contraband?

CONCLUSION

As the past several chapters have detailed, the method of analysis used to examine government action, stop and frisk, and arrest, is also used for searches. This involves analysis of whether the action constituted a search, its reasonableness, and the potential of exclusion of evidence if unreasonable. This chapter examined this analysis in greater detail with regard to searches with a warrant and searches without a warrant.

Chapter Seven

Special-Needs Searches

Our discussions up to this point have involved searches and seizures for the purpose of crime control. The U.S. Supreme Court however has applied the Fourth Amendment to a myriad of special needs that go beyond traditional enforcement of criminal laws. These are referred to as "special needs searches" and will be elaborated throughout this chapter including:

(1)   Special needs vs. the expectation of privacy;

(2)   International border searches;

(3)   Custody-related searches;

(4)   Student searches; and

(5)   Employee drug searches.

SECTION 1: SPECIAL NEEDS VS. THE EXPECTATION OF PRIVACY

OVERVIEW

Although there are a variety of types of special needs searches, there are four main characteristics that link such searches:

(1)   The direction is at the populace generally, rather than suspects specifically;

(2)   The result can still be prosecution and conviction;

(3)   There is no requirement of a warrant or probable cause; and

(4)   The reasonableness of such a search depends on the balance of special needs of government and individual privacy.

Thus, while the goal is not crime control per se, special needs searches still have the underlying aim of protection of the citizenry. What you must keep in mind as you read the cases in this chapter is that the special need of the government almost always outweighs an individual's right to privacy, and thus the search is considered reasonable.

SECTION 2: INTERNATIONAL BORDER SEARCHES

OVERVIEW

The border search exception delineated in *U.S. v. Ramsey* (1977) stated that searches at an international border are reasonable without either a warrant or probable cause. The only exception to this rule is body-cavity searches which do require probable cause due to it invasive nature. What is required of an international border search is reasonable suspicion to search for items such as contraband and weapons.

CASE

Backus v. State of Florida details a charge for trafficking in cocaine, 400 or more grams, after law enforcement officers, including United States Customs agents, discovered cocaine on a boat after it had returned to land. A motion was filed to suppress the cocaine as the fruit of an illegal search and seizure, and the State asserted the border search exception of 19 U.S.C. § 482(a) in response. The trial court denied the motion to suppress, finding that the boat was navigated more than three but less than twelve nautical miles from the shore of Boynton Beach and that for purposes of the border search exception the United States sea border is three nautical miles. Backus then pled guilty, reserving his right to appeal the dispositive motion to suppress.

BACKUS V. STATE OF FLORIDA
Case No. 4D02-2803 (Fla. App. 4th Dist., 2003)

The standard of review applicable to a motion to suppress evidence requires that this Court defer to the trial court's factual findings but review legal conclusions *de novo*. Batson v. State, 847 So. 2d 1149, 1150 (Fla. 4th DCA 2003). A border search conducted by a United States Customs officer is not governed by state law, therefore federal law, including the border search exception to the Fourth Amendment, applies.

The border search exception provides: Any of the officers or persons authorized to board or search vessels may stop, search, and examine, as well without as within their respective districts, any vehicle, beast, or person, on which or whom he or they shall suspect there is merchandise which is subject to duty, or shall have been introduced into the United States in any manner contrary to law, whether by the person in possession or charge, or by, in, or upon such vehicle or beast, or otherwise, and to search any trunk or envelope, wherever found, in which he may have a reasonable cause to suspect there is merchandise which was imported contrary to law; and if any such officer or other person so authorized shall find any merchandise on or about any such vehicle, beast, or person, or in any such trunk or envelope, which he shall have reasonable cause to believe is subject to duty, or to have been unlawfully introduced into the United States, whether by the person in possession or charge, or by, in, or upon such vehicle, beast, or otherwise, he shall seize and secure the same for trial.

19 U.S.C. § 482(a). For the exception to apply, "[t]here must at least be some articulable facts from which it is reasonable to infer that there was a recent border crossing." United States v.

Garcia, 598 F. Supp. 533, 535-536 (S.D. Fla. 1984). In the case at bar, the evidence supports the trial court's factual finding that Backus navigated his boat more than three but less than twelve nautical miles from shore. Whether this finding establishes that Backus crossed the border is a matter of whether the trial court correctly set the United States sea border at three nautical miles. Prior to 1988, the uncontested United States territorial sea border was three nautical miles, however, in 1988 President Ronald Reagan issued Presidential Proclamation No. 5928 on the Territorial Sea of the United States. The proclamation extends the territorial sea to twelve nautical miles, based on the international legal trend established by the United Nations Convention on the Law of the Sea, to which the United States is not a party. However, the proclamation also states that the extension of the territorial sea was not intended to extend or alter existing federal or state law.

The impact of the extension and apparent limitation has been the subject of debate by both courts and scholars ever since. Some scholars maintain that the proclamation affected the definition of the territorial sea only for international purposes and not for domestic matters. Others contend that the extension of the territorial sea to twelve nautical miles created United States sovereignty to that distance, and question whether the limitation can have the inconsistent effect of declaring United States ownership and control without applying current federal law. Both federal and state courts have had similar difficulty addressing the impact of the proclamation, where the subject has even been addressed post-1988.

We can locate no post-1988 case that has expressly explored the effect of the proclamation on the border search exception or Fourth Amendment jurisprudence. Because existing federal case law does indicate that the border is at three nautical miles for border search purposes, and controversy surrounds the operation of Presidential Proclamation 5928, we decline, on a matter of federal law, to conclude that the trial court erred by setting the United States sea border at three nautical miles for purposes of the border search exception. As a result, the denial of Backus's motion to suppress the cocaine is AFFIRMED.

REVIEW SECTION

READING COMPREHENSION

Detail and explain if all requirements of the border search exception were fulfilled.

What role does Presidential Proclamation No. 5928 have in the decision of this case.

THINKING CRITICALLY

What are the possible implications of varied interpretations of Presidential Proclamation No. 5928 for international border searches?

SECTION 3: CUSTODY-RELATED SEARCHES

OVERVIEW

If you are a prisoner, a parolee or probationer, a defendant detained before trial, or even a prison visitor, you are subject to a significantly reduced expectation of privacy. While the courts have held that such individuals are not beyond the reach of the Constitution, the need to maintain safety and security outweighs individual privacy. Courts examine the particular circumstances of the case, however have repeatedly accepted that full-body, strip, and body-cavity searches are Fourth Amendment searches, yet are considered reasonable without a warrant or probable cause if overridden by safety concerns. Such searches do require reasonable suspicion as support and violate prisoner rights if conducted when not required to secure safety and discipline.

CASE

In *D.F. v. State of Florida,* a juvenile defendant appeals the denial of his motion to suppress cocaine. The Florida Court of Appeals concludes that the cocaine was obtained as a result of an unlawful strip search and therefore should have been suppressed because the strip search constituted a clear and substantial violation of section 901.211, Florida Statutes (1993), a statute designed to regulate police conduct. Section 901.211 of the Florida Statutes reads as follows:

> (1) As used in this section, the term "strip search" means having an arrested person remove or arrange some or all of his or her clothing so as to permit a visual or manual inspection of the genitals; buttocks; anus; breasts, in the case of a female; or undergarments of such person. (2) No person arrested for a traffic, regulatory, or misdemeanor offense, except in a case which is violent in nature, which involves a weapon, or which involves a controlled substance, shall be strip searched unless: (a) There is probable cause to believe that the individual is concealing a weapon, a controlled substance or stolen property; or (b) A judge at first appearance has found that the person arrested cannot be released either on recognizance or bond and therefore shall be incarcerated in the county jail. (3) Each strip search shall be performed by a person of the same gender as the arrested person and on premises where the search cannot be observed by persons not physically conducting or observing the search pursuant to this section. Any observer shall be of the same gender as the arrested person. (4) Any body cavity search must be performed under sanitary conditions. (5) No law enforcement officer shall order a strip search within the agency or facility without obtaining the written authorization of the supervising officer on duty. (6) Nothing in this section shall be construed as limiting any statutory or common-law

right of any person for purposes of any civil action or injunctive relief.

As you read *D.F. v. State of Florida* take special note of the statutory requirements of a strip search in Florida.

D.F. V. STATE OF FLORIDA
682 So.2d 149 (Fla.App. 4 Dist., 1996)

Defendant, a juvenile, was placed under arrest as a result of three outstanding warrants arising from traffic matters. At the time of arrest, he and his friends were walking on the street in Riviera Beach. The arresting officer knew defendant and his friends who always hung around in the same area, known by the officer to be a high drug area. After seeing defendant earlier in the day, the officer had done a computer check on defendant for warrants. The officer arrested defendant, handcuffed him, and performed a pat-down search for weapons. Not finding any contraband or weapons, the officer felt comfortable placing defendant in the patrol car. The officer transported defendant to the police station to fill out paperwork. With defendant still handcuffed, the officer had him remove his shoes and socks and then did a more thorough pat-down for weapons. Although the officer found no weapons during the pat-down, he noticed what felt like a plastic baggie containing hard objects between defendant's buttocks. He later described the ziploc end of the baggie as rolled up like a cylinder, which, based on his experience, is typical of the way people keep cocaine.

Upon feeling and squeezing the baggie, the officer instructed defendant to "drop his pants." Defendant complied. The officer then saw the tip of a baggie sticking out from between defendant's buttocks. He requested that defendant spread his legs so he could see the baggie, and when defendant did not comply, the officer spread his buttocks. The baggie fell to the ground. The officer did not wear gloves or wash his hands before conducting the strip search. During the strip search, an adult male inmate was also present in a holding cell. The baggie was found to contain five cocaine rocks.

The officer had worked for the City of Riviera Beach for five months and previously as a jailer in New York for five years. As a jailer, he performed both strip searches and body cavity searches. The officer testified that there was a verbal policy in the Riviera Beach police department requiring a supervisor's permission before performing a strip search. However, in the past, his supervisor had told the officers, "if you feel something like that, you can just go get it." The officer was unaware that other inmates should not be present during a strip search. The officer testified that if the cocaine had not been discovered, defendant would have been transported to the sheriff's department to complete the paperwork on the warrant and then he would have been released to his mother.

Defendant claims that the strip search in his case violated subsections (3), (4) and (5) of the statute because the search was conducted in the presence of another inmate; it was not conducted under sanitary conditions; and the officer did not obtain written authorization of his supervisor before the search. Defendant also claims that the strip search constituted an unreasonable search in violation of the Fourth Amendment and violated defendant's rights as a juvenile when he was placed in a holding cell with an adult inmate.

The state concedes that the strip search was done in violation of section 901.211 in that the search was done with another inmate present and the officer did not obtain the prior permission of his supervisor. The state does not agree that 901.211(4) was violated because the officer's strip search did not include penetration of a body cavity. Despite conceding that the search violated portions of section 901.211, the state argues that the exclusionary rule should not be the sanction where the search was undertaken with probable cause under section 901.211(2)(a). Furthermore, the state contends that the failure to follow the statutory requirements should be excused because the search was done "in good faith."

"The purpose of a judicially imposed exclusionary rule is to deter police misconduct resulting in constitutional violations, or its equivalent." Rice v. State, 525 So.2d 509, 511 (Fla. 4th DCA 1988). Because the exclusionary rule was intended to serve as a deterrent to prevent future violations, the United States Supreme Court developed the good faith exception, which the state asserts applies here: Where the officer's conduct is objectively reasonable, "excluding the evidence will not further the ends of the exclusionary rule in any appreciable way; for it is painfully apparent that ... the officer is acting as a reasonable officer would and should act in similar circumstances. Excluding the evidence can in no way affect his future conduct unless it is to make him less willing to do his duty" (Leon, 468 U.S. at 919-20, 104 S.Ct.). However, the police officer's ignorance here of the requirements for a strip search and the supervisor's ignorance and misadvice to the officers do not constitute objective reasons for excusing the statutory violation. Ignorance of the law does not excuse a private citizen; it certainly does not excuse a law enforcement officer from violating a statute designed to regulate police conduct.

While a strip search of a juvenile does not per se violate the Fourth Amendment, a strip search of a juvenile suspect implicates both Fourth Amendment rights against unreasonable searches and seizures and privacy rights protected under the United States Constitution and, more explicitly, under the Florida Constitution Article I Section 23. It is the manner in which the search is conducted in a given case which may violate the Fourth Amendment. As the third district stated Gonzalez v. State, 541 So.2d 1354, 1355-56 (Fla. 3d DCA 1989), a case dealing with the strip search of a prisoner: One of the constitutional rights retained by a prisoner, at least to some minimal extent, is the protection of the Fourth Amendment against unreasonable searches and seizures. With respect to searches of the person of a prisoner, the court balances four factors in determining whether such searches are reasonable under the Fourth Amendment: (1) the scope of the intrusion, (2) the manner in which it was conducted, (3) the justification for initiating it, and (4) the place in which it was conducted. Applying these standards, it seems clear to us that a more substantial showing should be necessary to justify a search of the person [of a prisoner] when it involves a strip search or an intrusion into the body.

Section 901.211 codifies minimum acceptable standards of conduct for law enforcement officers conducting strip searches in Florida. When a strip search is deemed necessary by a supervisor, the statute mandates that the strip search should be performed in the least humiliating and least intrusive manner and only under sanitary conditions. This strip search expressly violated statutory rights afforded defendant by a statute designed to regulate police behavior. The violations were not technical or *de minimis*. The courts of this state have uniformly held test results obtained in violation of statutory directives to be inadmissible.

Here defendant was arrested for outstanding traffic warrants. He was handcuffed and taken to the police station solely for paperwork to be performed before transport to the Sheriff of Palm Beach County. Given both the historical purpose of the exclusionary rule and the substantial statutory violation of the statute, suppression of the cocaine obtained by the unlawful strip search is an appropriate remedy. We therefore do not reach the question of whether the strip search violated the juvenile's constitutional rights against unreasonable searches and rights of privacy guaranteed by the Florida Constitution.

Accordingly we reverse the order denying the motion to suppress and remand with directions to vacate the adjudication of delinquency. REVERSED AND REMANDED.

FARMER, J., dissents with opinion.

I note that, in the only reported case involving this statute, the second district held that the statute did not apply where an individual was arrested on a *capias* warrant for failure to appear. Welch v. Rice, 636 So.2d 172 (Fla. 2d DCA 1994). Welch held that a failure to appear is an indirect criminal contempt of court, which does not constitute "a traffic, regulatory, or misdemeanor offense for which strip searching is prohibited" under section 902.211. The court held, however, that subsection (5), requiring a supervisor's prior written permission, applied to all strip searches. The misdemeanor warrants in our case, as in Welch, were issued upon defendant's failure to appear in court after proper notice. I know of no reason why we should not follow the second district's reasoning, as this too constitutes an indirect criminal contempt of court, to which subsection (2) of the statute does not apply. Hence these law enforcement officers were not prohibited from strip searching the defendant after his arrest on these warrants.

Even if I felt that the statute applied to this search, however, I would still be unable to agree that the remedy for a statutory violation would be to exclude evidence obtained thereby. Section (6) states unequivocally that "nothing in this section shall be construed as limiting any statutory or common-law right of any person for purposes of any civil action or injunctive relief." This indicates that the legislature did not intend to displace common law damages remedies for statutory violations. That makes clear to me that the legislature intended for damages to be the remedy if the statute is ignored. I know of no reason why that would not be true for the violation that occurred here.

The Supreme Court has fashioned the exclusionary rule for constitutional violations, and has never suggested that the exclusionary rule should be applied as a matter of constitutional law when nonconstitutional violations occur in an investigation. Moreover, the Court has recently reaffirmed its adoption of a good-faith exception to the exclusionary rule. I do not believe that judges should fashion a constitutional remedy for good faith statutory violations of the kind involved here. To do so in this case has the associated difficulty of adding a provision to the statute that legislature thought not to include. Judges are not empowered to rewrite statutes under the guise of statutory construction. I would affirm.

REVIEW SECTION

READING COMPREHENSION

Were the requirements met of Section 901.211 of the Florida Statutes?

Detail the facts of this case and the grounds of the strip search.

THINKING CRITICALLY

Did the officer have reasonable suspicion for a strip search given Section 901.211 of the Florida Statutes?

Should the exclusionary rule have been the sanction for the statutory violations?

Elaborate your reasons for siding with the majority or dissenting opinion.

SECTION 4: STUDENT SEARCHES

OVERVIEW

The doctrine of *in loco parentis* means that while in school, administrators act as substitute parents. As such, the court has determined that the Fourth Amendment ban on unreasonable searches does apply to those conducted by school officials who need reasonable suspicion to perform such a search.

In September 1994, the Florida Cabinet passed an administrative rule called "Zero Tolerance" which is a declaration of intent to deal with certain types of improper student behavior in a more severe manner. One element of this rule requires local schools to report all part-one crimes (homicide, sexual battery, armed robbery, aggravated assault, arson, etc.) to local law enforcement authorities. The Zero-Tolerance rule declares that Florida teachers are responsible for classroom safety, and thus without definition, authorizes teachers to use "reasonable force" to defend themselves and others.

Further, Florida Statute established two commissions that have responsibility to develop, monitor, and enforce the professional standards of educators - the Education Standards Commission (ESC) and the Education Practices Commission (EPC). Florida Statute 231.546 defines and delineates the role of the Educational Standards Commission:

The Educational Standards Commission (1) shall have the duty to (a) Recommend to the State board desirable standards. (2) The Commission shall develop through the teaching profession, standards of professional practice including, but not limited to ethical and professional performance. (3) Any apparent violation of these codes and standards so adopted shall be deemed to be sufficient for the bringing of a charge of unprofessional practices, which charge shall be reviewed and acted upon by the Education Practices Commission.

Florida Statute 231.216 defines and delineates the role of the Educational Practices Commission:

(7) The duties and responsibilities of the commission are to (a) Interpret and apply the standards of professional practice established by the State Board of Education, (b) Revoke or suspend a certificate or take other appropriate action . . . (d) Have rule making authority . . . (8)(b) Panels of the commission shall have final agency authority in all cases involving the revocation and suspension of certificates of teachers and school administrators.

Thus, these commissions are to establish, interpret, and enforce State policy in the area of professional standards for educators through making decisions on specific unacceptable behavior. The EPC can interpret and clarify ESC rules in much the same way courts interpret and clarify legislation. Because the commissions are required to meet regularly and cooperate, it is believed they will act in a more coordinated way than the legislature and the judiciary. Even without definitive ESC policy on a particular case, the EPC reflects state policy positions in its decisions. One area of behavior the EPC regularly addresses is excessive force by teachers.

CASE

State of Florida v. J.A. involves an appeal by the State of Florida on an order granting J.A.'s motion to suppress physical evidence discovered during a random weapons search at a public high school.

STATE OF FLORIDA V. J.A.
679 So.2d 316 (Fla. App. 3 Dist., 1996)

Responding to the growing presence of firearms and other weapons in public schools, and the dangerous and deleterious effects of these weapons on the learning environment, the Dade County School Board adopted a policy authorizing random searches of students in high school classrooms with hand-held metal detector wands. To carry out the policy, the Board enacted various guidelines for the search procedures. The searches are designed to deter and curtail the presence of weapons in schools. In analyzing the central issue in this case, we are not unmindful that metal detector searches have become commonplace in everyday living and are deemed constitutional. The central issue in this case is whether a search conducted pursuant to the Board's policy violated J.A.'s Fourth Amendment rights.

To execute the policy, the Board hired an independent security firm to conduct the searches. The firm employees (referred to as a "search team") arrive at a randomly selected secondary school. The search team is accompanied by a school administrator. There are signs posted in the school informing students that these random searches are conducted. When the team enters the selected classroom, a team member informs the students about the search's purpose and procedures. The students are segregated by gender and asked to remove all metal objects from their persons. The students are scanned with the wand by a team member of the same sex. If the wand indicates the presence of metal the student is asked to remove any object in that area which may be triggering the device. If the wand again alerts to the presence of metal, the area is patted down. All coats, bags and other items are also scanned with the wand. If the wand alerts, the team member looks inside the item for weapons. A student may refuse to be searched, but refusal may subject the student to discipline. If the search reveals a school policy violation, the student may suffer disciplinary action. If contraband is discovered, the school notifies the police officers who are routinely assigned to patrol school campuses. The student may be arrested.

On the day J.A. was arrested, the search team selected and entered J.A.'s classroom with the assistant principal. As the team was explaining the search procedure, the assistant principal noticed that a jacket was passed to the back of the room and was placed on a shelf. A team member retrieved the jacket, scanned it, and discovered a gun. J.A. was identified as the jacket's owner. He was taken to an office where he admitted owning the jacket but denied owning the gun, and he asserted that the jacket was behind him, but he did not pass it back.

The State filed a delinquency petition against J.A. for carrying a concealed firearm, possession of a firearm on school property, and possession of a firearm by a minor. J.A. filed a motion to suppress the firearm asserting that the search was unlawful. In the order granting the motion to suppress, the trial judge found that the administrative search was a police search, not based on probable cause and was, therefore, unconstitutional. The court also found that, even if the search only required reasonable suspicion, the policy's search method was not sufficiently effective to outweigh the severe intrusion into the students' privacy interests.

We note that only three jurisdictions (New York, Pennsylvania, and Illinois) have addressed this issue. The courts have upheld, as constitutional, magnetometer searches and hand-held metal detector searches of students. The case before us involves a random, suspicionless, administrative search of public high school students in furtherance of a valid administrative purpose. The legality of this search is governed by the United States Supreme Court's pronouncements in Vernonia School Dist. (47J v. Acton, --- U.S. ----, 115 S.Ct. 2386, 132 L.Ed.2d 564 (1995)), and New Jersey v. T.L.O., (469 U.S. 325, 105 S.Ct. 733, 83 L.Ed.2d 720 (1985)). T.L.O. addressed the propriety of a search based on individualized suspicion that a student had committed a school rule violation. Acton addressed random suspicionless searches of student athletes to detect drug use. In student search cases, the challenge is always how to "strike the balance between the schoolchild's legitimate expectations of privacy and the school's equally legitimate need to maintain an environment in which learning can take place?" (T.L.O., 469 U.S. at 340, 105 S.Ct. at 742). Although T.L.O. applies the Fourth Amendment's prohibition of unreasonable searches and seizures to searches conducted by public school officials, "the legality of a search of a student should depend simply on the reasonableness, under all the circumstances, of the search." (T.L.O., 469 U.S. at 341, 105 S.Ct. at 742).

The ultimate measure of the constitutionality of a governmental search is 'reasonableness.' At least in a case such as this, where there was no clear practice, either approving or disapproving the type of search at issue, at the time the constitutional provision was enacted, whether a particular search meets the reasonableness standard is judged by balancing its intrusion on the individual's Fourth Amendment interests against its promotion of legitimate governmental interests. As the following analysis demonstrates, the search we review today satisfies this reasonableness standard. "The first factor to be considered is the nature of the privacy interest upon which the search here at issue intrudes" (Acton, --- U.S. at ----, 115 S.Ct. at 2391). Without question, students in public schools have an expectation of privacy in their persons and personal belongings (T.L.O., 469 U.S. at 338, 105 S.Ct. at 740-41). However, because of the state's custodial and tutorial authority over the student, public school students are subject to a greater degree of control and administrative supervision than is permitted over a free adult.

The next factor we must weigh is the character of the intrusion at issue. The Board has delineated search parameters in its policy to minimize the intrusion into the student's privacy. As stated above, the individuals are asked to remove all metal objects from their pockets and persons to avoid setting off the wand. If the wand detects the presence of metal the student is requested to remove any object in that area. The area is only patted down if the wand again indicates the presence of metal. The Board's search is no broader than metal detector searches upheld in other jurisdictions. This Court finds that the Board's policy and the guidelines enacted to carry it out delineate a search that involves a minimal intrusion into the students' privacy.

Against the backdrop of a student's privacy interest, and the scope of the search, we must consider the nature and immediacy of the governmental concern at issue here which must be one important enough to justify the search at hand. The incidences of violence in our schools have reached alarming proportions. In the year prior to the Board's implementation of the search policy, Dade County Public Schools reported both homicides and aggravated batteries as well as the confiscation from students of a very high number of weapons, including handguns. The immediacy of the Board's concern for students' safety, and the safety of all school personnel, is certainly well justified. Despite this background of escalating violence, the Board must maintain an environment that fosters learning and growth. In keeping with that obligation, the search policy was effected to deter and curtail the presence of weapons in schools and promote a safe learning environment. The means the Board has selected to address this severe problem is effective. The logical way to keep weapons out of school is to let the students know that they may be searched for weapons and that possession of weapons in a public high school is not permissible and will be seriously sanctioned.

Although there are alternative methods for detecting weapons (such as a magnetometer), these alternatives are attended by substantial difficulties because of Dade County's open-campus high schools. Moreover, these alternative methods are very time consuming and would disrupt an entire school, as opposed to randomly selected classrooms. The Board has chosen the method it felt would best satisfy the needs of its high schools. The Supreme Court has never declared that only the least intrusive search practicable can be reasonable under the Fourth Amendment. Upon balancing the students' privacy interest, the nature of the search, and the severity of the need met by the search, this Court holds that the Board's policy is both reasonable and constitutional.

The administrative search that led to the discovery of the weapon in J.A.'s jacket is constitutional. Therefore, the suppression of the weapon was error. Since the trial court's order departs from the essential requirements of law, we grant certiorari, quash the order under review, and remand the case to the trial court for further proceedings consistent herewith. Certiorari granted; order quashed; cause remanded.

REVIEW SECTION

READING COMPREHENSION

Elaborate the procedures used in school searches in this case.

Is the method employed by the Board effective according to the ruling?

THINKING CRITICALLY

Take a position on whether you believe random searches in schools for guns and drugs are acceptable? Because school violence certainly occurred prior to recent occurrences that have become widely publicized such as Columbine, what do you feel the role of the media is in creating a perception of danger at schools?

SECTION 5: EMPLOYEE DRUG SEARCHES

OVERVIEW

The use of drug testing and search of employee personal effects is one way to reduce public danger when it involves pilots, law enforcement personnel, or others. Conversely, there is an obvious element of invasion of privacy underlying such policies.

CASE

In *City of Palm Bay v. Bauman* the City appeals a final judgment that permanently enjoins it from requiring police officers and fire fighters to give urine specimens at random and unspecified times for the purpose of determining the presence of controlled substances. This holds unless probable cause exists to believe the employee has been using a controlled substance, or except during regularly scheduled periodic physical examinations.

CITY OF PALM BAY V. BAUMAN
475 So.2d 1322, 10 Fla. L. Weekly 2218 (Fla. App. 5 Dist., 1985)

The factual background and legal analysis are succinctly set forth in the trial court's order which is set forth in pertinent part. This action was tried before the Court and on the evidence presented, the Court finds as follows:

POLICE DEPARTMENT: (a) On February 24, 1984, the following notice was addressed "TO: ALL SWORN OFFICERS" and signed by City Manager, ROBERT G. MATTE, and by Chief of Police, CHARLES R. SIMMONS: "The City's Personnel Policies and Procedures prohibit possession, consumption or being under the influence of drugs or intoxicating substances while on duty because sworn police officers are subject to call-out on a twenty-four (24) hour basis. Consumption of non-prescribed drugs or other illegal substance at any time is strictly prohibited. If a police officer has consumed alcohol prior to being called to duty, he/she shall notify the shift supervisor of that fact. The City is actively taking steps to enforce the above policy. Urine samples may be required from police officers on a random basis. Police officers found to have consumed non-prescribed drugs or other illegal substances will be subject to discipline or discharge." (b) All members of the Police Department were then instructed to submit to urine tests to determine if marijuana had been used. The police officers were told that if they refused to submit to urine testing, they would be subject to discipline up to and including termination. In addition, the refuser would be reported to the State Police Standards Commission for refusing to obey a lawful order.

FIRE DEPARTMENT: (a) Prior to June 1983 two fire fighters told David Green, Fire Chief of the City of Palm Bay, that they had used marijuana. These individuals were not terminated, but were ordered to counseling. (b) In June 1983, pursuant to a recommendation made by the City personnel director and implemented by the fire chief, all fire fighters were ordered to take annual physicals. One of the reasons for the physicals was to test urine specimens for evidence of past use of marijuana, although this was not disclosed to the fire fighters (except one was told during the testing). This testing revealed two positives. These individuals were not terminated, but ordered to counseling. (c) On or just before October 18, 1983, the City Manager, ROBERT G. MATTE, addressed the following notice to all City employees: "The City's Personnel Policies and Procedures provide--the possession, consumption or being under the influence of drugs or intoxicating beverage while on duty is considered a major offense. Violations may entail dismissal. The City will strictly apply the disciplinary measures provided. The proviso relating the offense to 'on duty' status must be judiciously evaluated. Those subject to call during off duty hours, which applies to most personnel in the City, are expected to be in a fit condition to respond and effectively perform assigned duties when they are required to report." (e) In February 1984, the City Manager ordered all fire fighters to submit to urine testing. In fact, Chief Green was told by the City Manager to advise the fire fighters (and he did so advise them) that if they did not consent to the testing, they would be terminated. The tests revealed three positives.

POLICY CONSIDERATIONS: (a) Fire fighters must be possessed of all their physical and mental faculties on the job. Their safety and the safety of property, their fellow fire fighters, and the public is at stake. (b) Police officers use weapons, drive vehicles and make instant judgments involving life and death. They, too, must be possessed of all their normal faculties. In addition, they are sworn to enforce the law and must have credibility if public confidence and respect is to be maintained. Known use of illegal substances would undermine that confidence and respect. (c) Public employees are legitimately subject to more regulation of their activities than the general populace. (d) A non-probationary municipal employee has a constitutionally protected property interest in such employment entitling him to protection against unjust and unlawful job deprivation.

CONSTITUTIONAL ISSUES:

(a) Self Incrimination (5th and 14th Amendments to U.S. Constitution and Art. 1, Sec. 9, Fla. Const.). Since this privilege applies only to testimonial communications, it is not a bar to the action complained of here.

(b) Search and Seizure (4th Amendment to U.S. Constitution and Art. 1, Sec. 12, Fla. Const.).

This case does not involve urine testing conducted as a part of annual or other specified physical examination delineated in City policy. Certainly, municipal police officers and fire fighters must expect to meet required minimum standards of physical condition in order to be hired and retained. Physical examinations conducted to insure that those standards are met are to be reasonably expected even though urine testing is a part of those examinations. Likewise, this case does not involve urine testing either alone or as a part of other physical examinations required by virtue of a delineated City policy invoked on evidence of suspected diminished capacity. Here, the City states that all fire fighters and police officers must submit to urine testing or be subject to discipline up to and including discharge.

A citizen has a reasonable expectation of privacy in the discharge and disposition of his urine. At the same time, police officers and fire fighters, because of the nature of their jobs, must reasonably expect their employer to have, and to demonstrate, legitimate concern that their ability to discharge their job responsibilities is not compromised by the use of controlled substances.

The proposed compelled production and surrender of the urine for testing, under the evidence presented here, constitutes a search and seizure within the purview of the law. But, the City argues, by signing the "Notice", consent was given to the search. This argument is without substance for it is abundantly clear from the evidence that such signatures were procured under threat of disciplinary action. Consent cannot be inferred from an act so manifestly coerced.

The next question is whether such testing, considered in the light of its scope, nature, incidence and effect, is unreasonable when the immediate end sought is weighed against the private right affected. Palm Bay's policy does not identify the person, or persons, by name or position, who are authorized to require employees to provide a urine sample. The policy does not articulate any standards for its implementation and no separate written standards have been promulgated. Reasonable suspicion plays no part--the testing is to be all encompassing. Yet, as noted above, the Chief of Police has received no information, and has no independent knowledge, that any member of the Palm Bay Police Department has used marijuana. The incidence of known marijuana use among fire fighters is set forth above. The total known involvement on and off the job, even after urine testing, is less than six people. While not suggesting that this figure is insignificant, it is hardly a legal springboard for the trip the City now seeks to take. Without a scintilla of suspicion directed toward them, many dedicated fire fighters and police officers are told, in effect, to submit to such testing and prove themselves innocent, or suffer disciplinary action. When the immediate end sought is weighed against the private right affected, the proposed search and seizure is constitutionally unreasonable.

The Court finds urine testing not performed as part of physical examinations required annually or at other specified career times by City personnel policy, and designed to determine the presence of controlled substances, may constitutionally be required only on the basis of probable cause

CONCLUSION: The Court therefore, finds that the urine testing required by the City herein constitutes an unreasonable search and seizure, violative of the 4th Amendment to the U.S. Constitution and Art. 1, Sec. 12, Fla. Const. and should be enjoined.

Incorporating these findings, the trial court entered a final judgment which provided:

That except for urine testing performed as a part of physical examinations required by City Personnel Policy for initial employment, or annually, or at other designated career times, the City of Palm Bay is hereby permanently enjoined from requiring Plaintiffs to give urine specimens for the purpose of determining the presence of controlled substances unless probable cause exists.

Upon review of the final judgment we find that it imposes too severe a standard when it requires the City to have "probable cause" to believe that the policeman or fire fighter has been using a controlled substance. The federal courts which have considered this and analagous issues have held that the "reasonable suspicion standard" (something less than probable cause) is the basis upon which this type of search can be justified. The "reasonable suspicion" test requires that to justify this intrusion, officials must point to specific objective facts and rational inferences that they are entitled to draw from these facts in the light of their experience. We see no reason for imposing a stricter standard than that imposed by the federal courts, so we modify the final judgment in that respect.

Additionally, the judgment limits the City's right to require such testing only when it appears that the employee has "been on the job using, or after having recently used" a controlled substance. This is too narrow a restriction. The City has the right to adopt a policy which prohibits police officers and fire fighters from using controlled substances at any time while they are so employed, whether such use is on or off the job. The nature of a police officer's or fire fighter's duties involves so much potential danger to both the employee and to the general public as to give the City legitimate concern that these employees not be users of controlled substances.

Their work requires and the safety of the public demands complete mental and physical functioning of these officers. There is competent, unrebutted evidence in the record that marijuana causes severe long and short term physical, mental and psychological effects; that the length and severity of the effects of that drug cannot be predicted because they depend on the physical make-up of the individual and the potency of the substance. However, while the effects may last for hours or for days, the effects are certain, and can include impairment of physical function, auditory and visual perception changes. Other controlled substances produce similar effects. Moreover, as pointed out by the trial court, police officers who are sworn to enforce the laws lose credibility and public confidence if they violate the very laws they are sworn to enforce. The City therefore has a right to insist that its law enforcers not be law breakers. Therefore, the final judgment is also modified in this respect.

We find no merit in the issues raised by appellees on their cross-appeal. Except as modified herein, the final judgment is AFFIRMED.

REVIEW SECTION

READING COMPREHENSION

What did the notice entail that was distributed to all police officers and fire fighters?

What were the considerations behind a drug testing policy?

THINKING CRITICALLY

Is loss of employment a legitimate response to failure to submit to a drug test at a place of employment? Would your answer differ depending on the place of employment?

Should reasonable suspicion or probable cause be the basis for drug testing at one's place of employment?

CONCLUSION

While most searches and seizures are conducted for the purpose of crime control, the U.S. Supreme Court has applied the Fourth Amendment to a myriad of special needs that are beyond traditional enforcement of criminal laws. Such "special needs searches" include inventory searches, international border searches, airport searches, custody-related searches, student searches, and employee drug searches. What you should have noticed is that "special needs searches" require far less evidence to conduct, and therefore involve a lower expectation of privacy by the citizenry than found in many traditional searches.

Chapter Eight

Police Interrogation and Confessions

Three provisions in the U.S. Constitution, which are mirrored in the Florida Constitution, develop guidelines to oversee police interrogation and confession. The first is the Fifth Amendment, as well as Section Nine of the Florida Constitution in the self-incrimination clause:

> No person shall . . . be compelled in any criminal matter to be a witness against oneself.

The self-incrimination clause is used by the courts to determine if coercion was used before formal charges have been filed. The landmark case was *Miranda v. Arizona* in 1966 where the court implemented this clause to determine the constitutionality of interrogation.

The second is the Fourteenth Amendment, as well as Section Nine of the Florida Constitution is the due process clause:

> No person shall be deprived of life, liberty or property without due process of law.

The due process clause is designed to ensure the voluntary nature of a confession. A coerced confession violates due process not only because it was compelled, but also because the reliability rationale dictates that the admission of unreliable evidence to demonstrate guilt denies individuals the right to their life. Further, the accusatory system rationale suggests that coerced confessions, even if true, undermine the criminal justice system wherein the burden of proving guilt beyond a reasonable doubt is placed on the state. Finally, there is a fundamental fairness rationale behind due process which requires that fundamental fairness in our society be upheld.

The third is the Sixth Amendment right-to-counsel clause:

> In all criminal prosecutions, the accused shall . . . have the assistance of counsel for his defense.

The right-to-counsel clause has been the subject of debate because what does "in all criminal prosecutions" mean? The courts use this clause to determine if coercion was used after formal charges have been filed.

To examine police interrogation and confession, this chapter will elaborate:

(1)   The interrogation and confession setting;

(2)   The Constitution and self-incrimination;

(3)   The application of *Miranda v. Arizona* in Florida case law; and

(4)   The waiver of rights to counsel and to remain silent.

SECTION 1: THE INTERROGATION AND CONFESSION SETTING

OVERVIEW

What has become known as the *Miranda* warning is the subject of much debate and controversy in American culture. While some view it as an integral tool in maintaining the integrity of the judicial system, many see it as a technicality that clever criminals exploit only to cause harm once again to an innocent society. Once we reach the accusatory stage of the criminal justice system the stakes become higher both for those involved as suspects and those who work in law enforcement. The balancing act between crime control and individual liberty and privacy becomes even more precarious. Because interrogation is an act that occurs privately between an officer of the law and an individual suspect, the balance in question is between obtaining a correct result in the specific case in question but also guaranteeing fairness in cases generally.

CASE

In *State of Florida v. Glatzmayer* the court reviews <u>Glatzmayer v. State, 754 So. 2d 71 (Fla. 4th DCA 2000)</u>, wherein the district court asked: When suspects who are considering waiving their Miranda rights ask law enforcement officers if they should invoke the right to counsel, what is required of officers?

STATE OF FLORIDA V. GLATZMAYER
789 So.2d 297 (Fla. 2001)

The relevant facts are set forth in the trial court's order denying Glatzmayer's motion to suppress: In the early morning hours of February 15, 1998, Eric Schunk was shot and killed in the Rainberry Woods Park in Delray Beach, Florida. When the police arrived, the defendant, Brian Glatzmayer, was at the scene and believed to be a witness to what he claimed was a drive-by shooting. After speaking with Glatzmayer the police felt that the physical evidence at the scene was inconsistent with his version of the incident. Through follow up investigation, Glatzmayer and three other individuals became suspects in the murder of Eric Schunk.

On February 16, 1998, Detective Ed Flynn went to the home of a witness to show her a photo lineup. The defendant was present and told Flynn that he wanted to change his statement. He was taken to the police department and Flynn along with Sgt. Robert Brand questioned him. He was advised of his Miranda Warnings from a standard rights card which was signed by the defendant. After a brief statement, a formal taped statement was taken. Pursuant to the agreement of the parties, the Court reviewed that statement prior to the hearing. The defendant confessed to his involvement in the murder of Eric Schunk. Both officers testified that the defendant was not promised or threatened to give a statement, did not appear to be under the influence of any alcohol or drugs, and that he freely and voluntarily spoke with them. After the officers took a statement from him, he was asked if he would put the statement on tape. At that point the defendant asked the officers if "they thought he should get a lawyer?" The officers responded that it was his choice. At that point the defendant, who was eighteen years old, requested to speak with his mother. She was located by the officers and given an opportunity to speak with her son alone for about a half hour. After speaking with his mother, the defendant gave a taped statement. On the tape itself the defendant stated that he understood his rights and that he was not threatened or promised anything. The defense did not present any testimony.

Based on the totality of the testimony presented and the tape recorded statement of the defendant, the Court finds that the statement given by the defendant was done so after he was properly advised of his Miranda Warnings and that it was done so freely and voluntarily. The evidence demonstrates that the defendant did not invoke his right to counsel, that his question was at best an equivocal request for counsel, and that the officers were correct in telling the defendant that whether or not he should get a lawyer was his choice. It was ordered and adjudged that the defendant's motion to suppress is denied.

The taped statement was admitted at trial and Glatzmayer was convicted of first-degree felony murder and attempted robbery without a firearm and was sentenced to concurrent terms of life imprisonment without the possibility of parole and twelve years imprisonment, respectively. The district court reversed the convictions based on this Court's then-recent decision Almeida v. State, 737 So. 2d 520 (Fla. 1999), which was unavailable to the trial court at the time of the suppression hearing. The district court certified the above question.

Suppression issues are extraordinarily rich in diversity and run the gamut from (1) pure questions of fact, to (2) mixed questions of law and fact, to (3) pure questions of law. Reviewing courts must exercise care when examining such issues, for while the issues themselves may be posed in broad legal terms, the actual ruling is often discrete and factual. Appellate courts cannot use their review powers in such cases as a mechanism for reevaluating conflicting testimony and exerting covert control over the factual findings. As with all trial court rulings, a suppression ruling comes to the reviewing court clad in a presumption of correctness as to all fact-based issues, and the proper standard of review depends on the nature of the ruling in each case.

The law in Florida governing custodial utterances has undergone significant change in recent years: This court in Long v. State, 517 So. 2d 664, 667 (Fla. 1987), held that if in the course of custodial interrogation a suspect makes an utterance that may be an attempt to invoke his or her rights, police may "continue questioning for the sole purpose of clarifying the equivocal request." Subsequent to Long, the United States Supreme Court in Davis v. United States, 512 U.S.452 (1994), held that if a suspect initially waives his or her rights, the suspect thereafter must clearly invoke those rights during the ensuing interview. The particular statements at issue Owen v. State, 696 So. 2d 715 (Fla. 1997), were equivocal utterances and the Court concluded that to require police to stop an interview and clarify such statements "places too great an impediment upon society's interest in thwarting crime." The Court followed Davis: Thus, we hold that police in Florida need not ask clarifying questions if a defendant who has received proper Miranda warnings makes only an equivocal or ambiguous request to terminate an interrogation after having validly waived his or her Miranda rights.

Subsequently in Almeida v. State, 737 So. 2d 520 (Fla. 1999), the Court examined the legal interests at stake and concluded that no valid reason exists for not answering such a question: No valid societal interest is served by withholding such information. Indeed, both sides can only benefit from disclosure: Disclosure ensures that any subsequent waiver will be knowing and intelligent, and it reaffirms those qualities in a prior waiver. Nondisclosure, on the other hand, is doubly harmful: It exacerbates the inherently coercive atmosphere of the interrogation session, and it places in doubt the knowing and intelligent nature of any waiver-whether prior or subsequent. Thus the Court ruled: If at any point during custodial interrogation, a suspect asks a clear question concerning his or her rights, the officer must stop the interview and make a good-faith effort to give a simple and straightforward answer. To the extent that officers may be uncertain how to respond to a particular question, they may-where appropriate-readvise the suspect of his or her rights.

Although the trial court below did not have the benefit of Almeida when it decided the suppression issue, this Court generally applies the law as it exists at the time the Court conducts its review. Almeida thus controls the present case. During the suppression hearing, officers Flynn and Brand testified for the State concerning the circumstances surrounding Glatzmayer's utterance.

Flynn testified as follows on direct examination:

A. We were at the end of the interview when we felt that everything had been explained, all the evidence had been explained and he had given a truthful statement. We then asked him to put it on tape.

Q. And what did he say at that time?

A. He had no objections to it. He was ready to comply with it.

Q. Did he ever mention anything as far as an attorney?

A. No. I am sorry, he did ask if we thought he should have an attorney.

Q. And what did you say?

A. And we said, that's not our decision to make, that yours, it's up to you.

Applying the analytical model set forth in Almeida to the above dialogue, we first must determine whether Glatzmayer was in fact referring to his right to counsel. As noted above, Glatzmayer asked the officers if they thought he should have an attorney. That utterance was made under the following conditions: (1) during a respite in the custodial interrogation session; (2) immediately after Glatzmayer had revealed to the officers highly incriminating information about his involvement in the crime; and (3) in direct response to the officers' request to memorialize his incriminating statements on tape. Under these circumstances, it is reasonable to assume that Glatzmayer was concerned about his legal rights and was referring to his right to counsel.

Next, the Court must determine whether the utterance was a bona fide question calling for an answer. The testimony of Officers Flynn and Brand reveals that, based on their perception of the utterance, they believed it to be a question. This Court thus may reasonably conclude that the utterance was a genuine question; it was not a rumination or a rhetorical question. Glatzmayer was seeking a frank answer.

Finally, the Court must determine whether the officers made a good-faith effort to give a simple and straightforward answer. Glatzmayer in effect was soliciting the officers' subjective opinion, and the officers told him that their opinion was beside the point, that he needed to make up his own mind. Their response was simple, reasonable, and true. Unlike the situation in Almeida, the officers did not engage in gamesmanship; they did not try to give an evasive answer, or to skip over the question. None of the policy concerns implicated in Almeida were violated here. By responding frankly, the officers acted to assuage the inherently coercive atmosphere of the interrogation session and to reaffirm the validity of Glatzmayer's prior waiver.

In sum, nothing in Almeida requires that law enforcement officers act as legal advisors or personal counselors for suspects. Such a task is properly left to defense counsel. To require officers to advise and counsel suspects would impinge on the officers' sworn duty to prevent and detect crime and enforce the laws of the state. All that is required of interrogating officers under Almeida is that they be honest and fair when addressing a suspect's constitutional rights: In sum, whenever constitutional rights are in issue, the ultimate bright line in the interrogation room is honesty and common sense.

In the present case, officers Flynn and Brand conducted themselves in an eminently forthright manner in addressing Glatzmayer's rights. This conclusion is consonant with numerous appellate court decisions throughout the nation. The district court below erred in ruling otherwise. Based on the foregoing, we answer the certified question as explained herein and quash the district court decision below. It is so ordered.

REVIEW SECTION

READING COMPREHENSION

What are the facts of this case leading to the taped confession?

Elaborate the relevant case law as discussed in *Almeida v. State* (1999).

THINKING CRITICALLY

Do you believe Glatzmayer intended to invoke his right to counsel? Elaborate your response.

While there is nothing that requires law enforcement officers to act as legal advisors or personal counselors, should officers be required to advise a suspect to seek counsel if he/she indicates their doubt in this manner? Does the age of the suspect have any bearing on your response?

SECTION 2: THE CONSTITUTION AND SELF-INCRIMINATION

OVERVIEW

What does it mean to be considered a witness against yourself? It means that government officials cannot compel you to give testimony against yourself in a court of law. In essence, what this means is that confessions and other incriminating statements must meet the voluntariness test of self-incrimination. The totality circumstances surrounding one's statement must demonstrate that the confession was given voluntarily.

CASE

In Florida, when a suspect is undergoing a custodial interrogation and equivocally indicates that he wishes the interrogation to cease, thus invoking his right to remain silent under Section Nine of the Florida Constitution, the interrogating officer must terminate further questioning except to clarify the suspect's wishes. The appellant in *Kipp v. State of Florida* argues that the only evidence used to convict him of murder and robbery was obtained in violation of his Florida constitutional right.

KIPP V. STATE OF FLORIDA
668 So.2d 214, 21 Fla. L. Weekly D211 (1996)

In December 1992 while police were investigating the murder of James Boyington in Zephyrhills, Florida, suspicion fell on the appellant and a companion who were in Georgia using credit cards issued to Boyington, driving a car registered to Boyington, and staying in a hotel room under the name of Boyington. Georgia authorities took the appellant into custody and began interrogating him. They began their first interrogation at 9:30 p.m. by informing the appellant of his Miranda rights. The appellant freely spoke to them but gave little useful information except that he maintained he was Boyington. The interrogation ended and the appellant was allowed to return to his cell to sleep. Several hours later, at 3:50 a.m., the detectives woke him and commenced a second interrogation without again informing him of his Miranda rights. The appellant, at the beginning and at various other points during the interview, either equivocally or unequivocally invoked his right to remain silent. The detectives disregarded his request to terminate the interrogation and continued questioning him, eventually eliciting a confession that the appellant was involved in the events leading up to Boyington's death.

A third interrogation occurred around 8:00 a.m. when detectives from Florida arrived. The Florida detectives re-Mirandized the appellant and he repeated the incriminating statements made during the second interrogation. At the appellant's trial for the murder of Boyington no detective who interviewed the appellant testified, but the tapes made of the three interrogations were played to the jury. The jury found him guilty of murder in the second degree and of robbery.

We find that during the first interrogation no error occurred because the appellant was properly informed of his rights and waived them. The problem in this case begins with the second interrogation and carries over to taint the third one as well. Inasmuch as the incriminating evidence was obtained during these latter two interrogations, the trial court erred in failing to suppress this evidence. When the appellant, undergoing a custodial interrogation, made his first equivocal invocation of his right to terminate the questioning during the second interrogation, the Georgia detectives continued the questioning without clarifying this equivocal invocation of his right to remain silent. The Florida detectives, although they properly informed the appellant of his rights before they began questioning him for the third interrogation, were the unwitting recipients of the Georgia detectives' violation of the appellant's rights.

The error committed during the second interrogation carried over into the third interrogation. As the Florida Supreme Court explained Gore v. State, 599 So.2d 978 (Fla.), cert. denied, 506 U.S. 1003, 113 S.Ct. 610, 121 L.Ed.2d 545 (1992), when a suspect exercises his right to remain silent, this does not create a per se proscription of indefinite duration upon any further questioning by any police officer on any subject. If the right to remain silent had been "scrupulously honored" when it was first invoked, then the statements subsequently made pass the first threshold of the test for voluntariness. In Gore, the first invocation of the right to remain silent had been "scrupulously honored" by the federal officials who first interrogated him. Therefore, when the Florida officials interrogated him seven days later and informed him of his Miranda rights, the statements Gore made after he waived those rights were properly admitted into evidence.

The scenario of Gore is not similar to the scenario in the instant case. The appellant's invocation of his right to remain silent at the beginning of the second interrogation was not "scrupulously honored" so the evidence obtained during the third interrogation must be considered involuntarily given as well, especially since the third interrogation took place on the heels of the second and under the circumstances here. The purpose of Miranda is to prevent repeated rounds of questioning to undermine the will of the person being questioned. We conclude that the appellant's will was seriously undermined during both the second and third interrogations by the continued questioning of the detectives disregarding his equivocal invocation of his right to remain silent. Thus, it was error to allow into evidence the appellant's statements obtained during the second and third interrogations.

Since the taped statements were the only evidence of the appellant's involvement in this crime, we further conclude that the state has not carried its burden to show the error was harmless. Accordingly, we reverse the judgment of guilt, vacate the sentence, and remand for a new trial with the incriminating evidence from the second and third interrogations suppressed.

REVIEW SECTION

READING COMPREHENSION

Detail the facts of the case leading to the confession.

When did problems begin with the interrogation and what were the effects on the outcome.

THINKING CRITICALLY

Elaborate why the test for voluntariness was not met in this case according to the court.

While no dissenting opinion was provided in this case, articulate the grounds that a dissent may entail.

SECTION 3: *MIRANDA V. ARIZONA* IN FLORIDA

OVERVIEW

Because suspects are confined to a strange location where psychological pressure and tricks are used in an attempt to secure a confession, the court created a measure to prevent involuntary confessions. In *Miranda v. Arizona* in 1966 the courts by a bare majority deemed interrogation inherently coercive and created the *Miranda* warning in an attempt to create a balance and overcome the pressures of interrogation. Keep in mind that this warning must be given only if officers intend to take the suspect into custody and interrogate the suspect. Thus, questioning of people at crime scenes, questioning of individuals prior to them being considered an official suspect, and questioning of people during Fourth Amendment stops do not require the *Miranda* warning. The *Miranda* warning includes four warnings that are now famous due to the proliferation of police shows on television:

(1)   Right to remain silent;

(2)   Anything you do say can and will be used against you in a court of law;

(3)   Right to an attorney; and

(4)   If you cannot afford an attorney, one will be appointed for you.

In addition to the standard *Miranda* warning, there are five more rules that the court has created to balance the coercion involved in interrogation, however the suspect does not have to be informed of these rules:

(1)   An individual can claim their right to silence at any time and the interrogation must stop immediately upon this request;

(2)   If an individual indicates they want an attorney present prior to the start of an interrogation, government officials may not begin interrogation. Further, if already begun, interrogation must cease once an individual requests and attorney;

(3)   If an individual gives a statement without an attorney present, the burden is on the state to prove that the right against self-incrimination and the right to an attorney were waived;

(4)   Any statement that is obtained in violation of these rules is inadmissible in a court of law; and

(5)   Should an individual employ the right against self-incrimination, s/he cannot be penalized through an inference of guilt.

As you read cases that address the *Miranda* warning, keep in mind the rights of the individual and at what point the burden shifts to the state if these rights are violated.

CASE

West v. State of Florida deals with an appellant convicted of first degree murder who contends that the trial court should have suppressed her confession because the Miranda warnings were inadequate.

WEST V. STATE OF FLORIDA
District Court of Appeal of Florida, Fourth District.
Case No. 4D03-2027 (2004)

In March 2001, appellant was arrested, and after being read what purported to be a Miranda warning, admitted her involvement in a plan which resulted in the victim being murdered. At a hearing on her motion to suppress, a detective testified that he read appellant her rights from a standard Broward County Sheriff's Office Miranda form. He did not inform appellant that she was entitled to have counsel present during questioning or that she could stop the interrogation at any time during questioning. The detective explained: I told her, you have the right to remain silent, that anything that you say can be used against you in a court of law. You have the right to talk to a lawyer and have a lawyer present before any questioning and if you cannot afford a lawyer, one will be appointed to represent you or for any questions if you wish. And I asked her, do you understand the rights that we just read and that is where she initialed, yes.

As to the first ground of appellant's motion to suppress, that she was not advised of her right to have an attorney present during questioning, Miranda v. Arizona, 384 U.S. 436, 471-72 (1966), held: An individual held for interrogation must be clearly informed that he has the right to consult with a lawyer and to have the lawyer with him during interrogation. With specific reference to the failure to advise a defendant of the right to have a lawyer present during interrogation, the Miranda court further stated: As with the warnings of the right to remain silent and that anything stated can be used in evidence against him, this warning is an absolute prerequisite to interrogation. No amount of circumstantial evidence that the person may have been aware of this right will suffice to stand in its stead. Only through such a warning is there ascertainable assurance that the accused was aware of this right.

There is authority supporting the view that a Miranda warning which fails to advise of the right to counsel during interrogation makes a confession inadmissible as a matter of law. In Miranda, with reference to a situation in which no warning was given, the Court stated: The Fifth Amendment privilege is so fundamental to our system . . . and the expedient of giving an adequate warning . . . so simple, that we will not pause to inquire in individual cases whether the defendant was aware of his rights without a warning being given.

At the hearing on the motion to suppress, in which the state had the burden of proving by a preponderance of the evidence that appellant waived her rights, the evidence centered on whether appellant was of sufficient intelligence to waive her rights. Appellant, who had never before been arrested, scored sixty-one on an IQ test, indicating that she was mildly retarded. Whether she had the intellectual capacity to intelligently waive her rights was disputed by experts. Without addressing the facial inadequacy of the warning, the trial court denied the motion to suppress, finding that under the totality of the circumstances appellant understood her rights and knowingly and intelligently waived them. The problem with the trial court's finding is that it overlooks that appellant was not informed that she was entitled to have counsel present during interrogation or that she could stop the interrogation at any time. Nor did the state produce evidence that appellant knew this and knowingly waived these rights. Her confession should accordingly have been suppressed. We therefore reverse for a new trial.

My reading of the case law is that the law is flexible in the form that Miranda warnings are given, but rigid as to their required content. It is unusual that a problem concerning the content of Miranda warnings has arisen in this day and age. Most law enforcement agencies comply with Miranda without incident, since Miranda has not proved to be a roadblock to effective law enforcement. The consensus of the first generation (1966-73) of empirical scholarship on the effect of Miranda, was that the Miranda rules had only a marginal effect on the ability of the police to elicit confessions and on the ability of prosecutors to win convictions, despite the fact that some detectives continued to perceive a substantial Miranda impact.

Beginning in 1996, the second generation of Miranda studies have generated considerable interpretive disagreement, debate, and commentary. Thomas and Leo observed that there appears to be relatively little dispute among second-generation researchers on several aspects of Miranda's real-world effects. First, police appear to issue and document Miranda warnings in virtually all cases. Second, police appear to have successfully "adapted" to the Miranda requirements. In practice, this means that police have developed strategies that are intended to induce Miranda waivers. Third, police appear to elicit waivers from suspects in 78-96 percent of their interrogations, though suspects with criminal records appear disproportionately likely to invoke their rights and terminate interrogation. Fourth, in some jurisdictions police are systematically trained to violate Miranda by questioning "outside Miranda" — that is, by continuing to question suspects who have invoked the right to counsel or the right to remain silent. Finally, some researchers have argued that Miranda eradicated the last vestiges of third-degree interrogation present in the mid-1960s, increased the level of professionalism among interrogators, and raised public awareness of constitutional rights.

The requirement of Miranda for the warning at issue in this case is not open to the wiggle room of creative interpretation. As Judge Klein writes in the majority opinion, Miranda explicitly holds that as "an absolute prerequisite to interrogation," a suspect in custody "must be clearly informed that he has the right to consult with a lawyer and to have the lawyer with him during interrogation" 384 U. S. at 471. Similar to the warning on the right to remain silent, the Supreme Court chose the requirement of a specific warning on the right to counsel as a "clearcut fact," to avoid assessments of the knowledge the defendant possessed, based on information as to his age, education, intelligence, or prior contact with authorities, which can never be more than speculation.

Most federal courts of appeals have recognized the importance of informing suspects that they have the right to have a lawyer present prior to and during interrogation. Nothing in any Supreme Court opinion suggests that it has relaxed the rigidity of Miranda regarding the content of the required warnings. At least three justices have expressed their concern about a Miranda warning identical to the one in this case. Because this Court may deny certiorari for many reasons, our denial expresses no view about the merits of petitioner's claim. And because the police apparently read the warnings from a standard-issue card, I write to make this point explicit. That is to say, if the problem purportedly present here proves to be a recurring one, I believe that it may well warrant this Court's attention. We therefore reverse for a new trial.

REVIEW SECTION

READING COMPREHENSION

What is the purpose of a *Miranda* warning?

Detail the logic of the court in *Miranda v. Arizona* (1966).

Did this case turn on the IQ of the appellant or on the fact that she was not advised she could have counsel present?

THINKING CRITICALLY

What role, if any, should a defendant's level of intelligence play in the voluntariness of a confession?

Do you believe *Miranda* has had a positive, negative, or neutral effect on law enforcement? Elaborate your rationale.

SECTION 4: THE WAIVER OF RIGHTS TO COUNSEL AND TO REMAIN SILENT

OVERVIEW

So, how do we decide if an individual has waived their right to remain silent and to have an attorney present? The court has adopted an implied waiver test which essentially means that the totality of the circumstances in each individual case must prove that the suspect was aware of their rights and gave those rights up voluntarily. A confession is thus considered involuntary if government officials engaged in coercion during interrogation and that this coercion caused the suspect to make incriminating statements. Interrogating officers are still permitted to make promises, false and misleading statements, or appeal to the defendant's emotions, without risking the voluntary nature of the confession. The essential element to remember is that *Miranda* was intended to remove coercion from the interrogation process, not to remove the element of pressure.

CASE

Henderson v. State of Florida is a case before the Court on appeal of judgments of conviction on three counts of first-degree murder. Henderson was sentenced to death for three capital offenses. After reviewing the record and considering appellant's arguments on appeal which involved his belief that he invoked his right to counsel and it was not considered, the court finds no reversible error and affirms the convictions and sentences of death. In the second *Henderson v. State of Florida,* the denial for a petition for a writ of certiorari to the Supreme Court of Florida is examined.

Henderson v. State of Florida
463 So.2d 196, 10 Fla. L. Weekly 43 (Fla., 1985)

Appellant's murder convictions are based upon the deaths of three hitchhikers in Hernando County, Florida. Henderson turned himself in to the sheriff's office in Charlotte County, Florida, on February 6, 1982. He confessed to murdering three hitchhikers in northern Florida and to several other unrelated murders. He then requested counsel and signed a "Notice of Defendant's Invocation of the Right to Counsel." On February 10, 1982, two Putnam County sheriff's deputies took custody of Henderson for an unrelated murder and were transporting him to Putnam County by automobile when Henderson volunteered to show them where the bodies of the three hitchhikers were. They advised him of his rights, after which he signed a waiver of rights form and led them to the field where the bodies were discovered. The following June, a Hernando County detective took custody of Henderson in Putnam County for the purpose of transporting him to Hernando County to be tried for the murders of the three hitchhikers. At first Henderson said he did not want to talk because he had already given his statement to the other deputies. Later during the ride Henderson changed his mind and, after executing a written waiver, talked about the details of the murders.

Henderson filed two pretrial motions to suppress the statements he made to the Putnam County deputies and to the Hernando County detective. The motions alleged that the statements were elicited from him after he had invoked his right to remain silent by requesting an attorney. After holding an evidentiary hearing, the trial court denied the motions.

At trial a deputy sheriff of Charlotte County testified that he was responding to a call reporting an automobile burglary when Henderson motioned to him. When the officer approached, Henderson said he wanted to give himself up for murder and that he was wanted in several states. The officer testified that Henderson surrendered a bag containing a .22 caliber revolver which Henderson said was the murder weapon. After the officer arrested Henderson and advised him of his constitutional rights, Henderson said that he had killed three hitchhikers in north Florida. Another Charlotte County deputy sheriff testified that he interviewed Henderson after advising him of his constitutional rights. According to this witness, Henderson said that he shot all three hitchhikers in the head and dumped their bodies in a remote area south of Perry, Florida. One of the Putnam County sheriff's deputies testified about Henderson's showing him the location of the bodies. The Hernando County detective testified that when he was transferring Henderson from Putnam to Hernando County, Henderson agreed to talk and gave details of the murders. A transcript of Henderson's confession was read to the jury. According to the transcript, Henderson said he picked up the hitchhikers, two male and one female, near Panama City and became concerned when he heard two of them talking about killing someone to get some money. Henderson was quoted as saying that he bound and gagged the three hitchhikers and shot them each in the head with a .22 caliber revolver.

There was substantial medical and scientific testimony corroborating Henderson's confessions. The medical examiner testified that the victims, two male and one female, had each died of a gunshot wound to the head. A firearms expert testified that the bullet fragments found in the victims had the same rifling characteristics as did bullets shot from the .22 caliber revolver found in Henderson's possession when he was arrested. Crime scene investigators testified that the victims' bodies were found bound and gagged with tape in the manner described in Henderson's statements.

The defense rested without presenting any evidence. The jury found Henderson guilty of three counts of first-degree murder. At the penalty phase of the trial, the state presented evidence of Henderson's prior convictions for two counts of first-degree murder. The state also called the Hernando County detective who testified that Henderson told him he had no regrets and that if he had his life to live over again, he would not change anything. The defense presented evidence that Henderson was abused as a child and that he showed the police the location of the victims' bodies so they could be buried.

The jury recommended that Henderson be sentenced to death. The trial judge adopted the jury's recommendation and found as aggravating circumstances that Henderson had previously been convicted of a violent felony; that the murders were especially heinous, atrocious, or cruel; and that they were committed in a cold, calculated and premeditated manner without any pretense of moral or legal justification. The judge found there was no evidence of any statutory mitigating circumstances and that the nonstatutory mitigating circumstances presented were of little if any weight.

Henderson's first point on appeal claims error in the denial of his pretrial motions to suppress the statements he made to the Putnam County deputy and the Hernando County detective. Henderson claims that these statements were improperly elicited from him after he had requested the assistance of counsel. It is true that when an accused asks to see counsel, interrogation must cease. However, there is nothing to prevent an accused from changing his mind and volunteering further information. In this case Henderson signed written waivers before making the statements in question. We therefore conclude that there is sufficient evidence to support the finding that he knowingly and intelligently waived his right to have counsel present when making these statements.

Next Henderson argues that the trial judge erred in denying in part his motion *in limine* to exclude references to unrelated crimes committed in other jurisdictions. In response to Henderson's motion, the state averred that the only evidence of collateral crimes it anticipated introducing was the statement Henderson made to the arresting officer that he was turning himself in for murder and that he was wanted in several states. The trial court ruled that this statement was admissible. We agree with Henderson's contention that the testimony concerning his admission to being wanted in other states bore no relevance to any material fact at issue in this case. Hence his motion to exclude all references to crimes committed in other jurisdictions should have been granted. However, we find that the error was harmless and could not possibly have affected the outcome of the case. The amount of evidence against Henderson is simply overwhelming. There were at least four confessions to four different police officers. There was also substantial circumstantial evidence linking him to the crime and corroborating his confessions. Given the magnitude of this evidence, we do not believe that the jury was unduly or improperly influenced by the evidence that Henderson admitted to being wanted in other states.

Next Henderson argues that the trial court erred by allowing into evidence gruesome photographs which he claims were irrelevant and repetitive. We find that the photographs, which were of the victims' partially decomposed bodies, were relevant. Persons accused of crimes can generally expect that any relevant evidence against them will be presented in court. The test of admissibility is relevancy. Those whose work products are murdered human beings should expect to be confronted by photographs of their accomplishments. The photographs were relevant to show the location of the victims' bodies, the amount of time that had passed from when the victims were murdered to when their bodies were found, and the manner in which they were clothed, bound and gagged. It is not to be presumed that gruesome photographs will so inflame the jury that they will find the accused guilty in the absence of evidence of guilt. Rather, we presume that jurors are guided by logic and thus are aware that pictures of the murdered victims do not alone prove the guilt of the accused. We therefore conclude there was no error in allowing the photographs into evidence.

Henderson argues that the trial judge erred when, in advising the jury of the probable duration of the trial, he suggested that there would be a second phase of the trial concerned with sentencing. Because a sentencing phase would only be required upon conviction of a capital offense, appellant argues that the statement indicated to the jury that the judge thought appellant would be found guilty of at least one of the charged first-degree murder counts. Upon the raising of an objection by the defense, the judge gave a curative instruction indicating that he only meant to estimate the maximum period of time to be set aside for the trial and had not made any judgment about what the evidence was likely to show. Defense counsel moved for a mistrial and now argues that the denial of the motion was reversible error. We find the argument to be completely without merit.

Henderson also argues that several of the provisions of section 40.013, Florida Statutes (1981), pertaining to permissible excusals from jury service, operated to deny him the right to be tried by a jury drawn from a venire representing a cross-section of the community. We find appellant's challenge to be without merit.

With respect to his sentence, Henderson argues that the trial judge erred in finding that the murders were especially heinous, atrocious or cruel. Henderson claims that the murders were not heinous, atrocious, or cruel because the victims died instantaneously from single gunshots to their heads. This argument overlooks the fact that the victims were previously bound and gagged. They could see what was happening and obviously experienced extreme fear and panic while anticipating their fate. We therefore conclude that this aggravating circumstance applies.

Appellant also argues that the court erred in finding that the murders were committed in a cold, calculated and premeditated manner without any pretense of moral or legal justification. We hold that there was sufficient evidence to support the trial judge's finding of this factor. Henderson rendered the victims helpless by binding their ankles with tape. He then coldly proceeded to shoot them one by one execution-style.

Finally Henderson argues that Florida's death penalty law is unconstitutional. However, all his arguments have previously been refuted by this Court on a number of occasions and therefore do not merit any further discussion.

In conclusion, the properly established aggravating circumstances are:
(1) Appellant had previously been convicted of two counts of first-degree murder.
(2) The murders were all heinous, atrocious, and cruel.
(3) The murders were all committed in a cold, calculated, and premeditated manner without pretense of moral or legal justification.
The trial court properly found that there were no mitigating circumstances sufficient to outweigh the aggravating circumstances found.

We therefore affirm the convictions on three counts of first-degree murder. Finding that the three sentences of death are appropriate under the law established in similar cases, we affirm them also. It is so ordered.

HENDERSON V. STATE OF FLORIDA
473 U.S. 916, 105 S.Ct. 3542, 87 L.Ed.2d 665 (1985)

Supreme Court of the United States On Petition for Writ of Certiorari to the Supreme Court of Florida. The petition for a writ of certiorari is denied.

Justice MARSHALL, with whom Justice BRENNAN joins, dissenting.

Petitioner, after contacting police and admitting involvement in a series of murders, unambiguously asserted his right to counsel and his desire to have no discussions with the police concerning his case outside the presence of counsel. The legal import of this assertion, made while in police custody, is clear; our cases establish a 'bright-line rule' that all questioning must cease after an accused requests counsel. In this case, petitioner contends that police violated this "bright-line rule" and through custodial interrogation did persuade him to incriminate himself further notwithstanding his earlier request for counsel's assistance during questioning; yet the Florida Supreme Court sustained the admission of the subsequently obtained evidence simply on the fact that petitioner was eventually persuaded and signed a waiver form. Such a rationale cannot be made to conform to this Court's precedents, which establish that as a precondition to a finding of waiver a court must find that the accused, rather than the police, reopened dialogue about the subject matter of the investigation.

This Court has not always found it easy to define exactly when and by whom dialogue was reopened, and perhaps the instant case can be explained as resulting from these difficulties. Here, however, the State argues that petitioner "initiated" further dialogue by minimally responding to an unrequested police explanation of the accused's fate and by "conveying" a willingness to talk through nonverbal expressions and unrelated "subtle comments." The valuable right to be free from police interrogations in the absence of counsel cannot be made to be so fragile as to crumble under the weight of elicited and subjective inconsequentials. I would grant the petition to make clear that waiver of this right is not so lightly to be assumed.

A few days after his assertion of the right to counsel and his consultation with an attorney, petitioner was transported from one jail to another in connection with an unrelated criminal investigation. The drive lasted almost five hours, and the police officers accompanying petitioner were informed that he had asserted his right to counsel and had been advised by his counsel not to talk with the police. The police officers had nevertheless equipped themselves for the trip by taking along specially prepared forms by which petitioner could waive his right to be free from police interrogation in spite of his previous assertion of that right. In particular, the form declared that the signatory desired to make a statement to the police, that he did not want a lawyer, and that he was aware of his constitutional rights to disregard the instruction of his attorney and to speak with the officers transporting him. During the course of the 5-hour drive, the police engaged in extended "casual conversation" with petitioner. Although the police officers asserted that none of this conversation concerned any aspect of the case, they also asserted that petitioner's general manner as well as various "subtle comments" conveyed to them that "his conscience was bothering him," and that "he wanted to discuss the [criminal] matter." Later, according to the officer, petitioner responded with a "look on his face" that made clear his willingness to talk with the police. The officer then directly asked petitioner if there was anything he would like to tell the police. When petitioner expressed a tentative willingness to give information about the location of his victims' bodies, the police confronted him with the previously prepared waiver forms, which he signed.

It is clear that the direct question by the police officer easily meets this Court's definition of interrogation. And the fact of the arrest, even without the 5-hour drive, makes the context clearly

140

custodial. Thus the issue is whether petitioner "initiated" a dialogue with the police concerning the subject matter of the investigation. By the police officer's own testimony, the only actual speech by petitioner that directly related to his case was the casual question of what would happen after the officer telephoned the "chief of detectives." The comment was a response to the police officer's unsolicited partial explanation of the police's intentions. If petitioner's question is deemed a general inquiry regarding the investigation, then the police officer's comment that elicited it must have been a similar reinitiation of dialogue. It is thus not surprising that the police insist that petitioner made clear his desire to talk through repeated, though "subtle," hints. But surely, the right to counsel cannot turn on a police officer's subjective evaluations of what must stand behind an accused's facial expressions, nervous behavior, and unrelated subtle comments made in casual conversation. If it were otherwise, the right would clearly be meaningless.

I dissent from the Court's denial of certiorari.

REVIEW SECTION

READING COMPREHENSION

What are the facts of this case?

Did the court have grounds to suppress the confession? Did the confession meet the test of voluntariness?

Do you agree with the aggravating circumstances as considered by the court?

THINKING CRITICALLY

Do you believe the exclusion of evidence regarding crimes in other states would have affected the outcomes of this case?

Do you believe Henderson's right to counsel was violated? Use the opinions of the court to support your response.

CONCLUSION

Three provisions in the U.S. Constitution, which are mirrored in the Florida Constitution, develop guidelines to oversee police interrogation and confession: the self-incrimination clause, the due process clause, and the right-to-counsel clause. This chapter examined police interrogation and confession through an elaboration of the interrogation and confession setting, the Constitution and self-incrimination, the application of *Miranda v. Arizona* in Florida case law, and the waiver of rights to counsel and to remain silent. This chapter made evident several of the court's 'bright-line' rules with respect to garnering of evidence by government officials.

Chapter Nine

Identification Procedures

For government officials to determine that a crime was committed is significantly less intensive than proving who committed such a crime. While recent technological advances such as DNA have improved the ability of the government to identify a suspect, eyewitness identification in the form of lineups, show-ups, and photo identification is debatable in its reliability, especially when the suspect is of another race than the person involved in identification.

This chapter will review:

(1)   The risks of mistaken eyewitness identification;

(2)   The Constitution and identification procedures; and

(3)   DNA profile identification.

SECTION 1: THE RISKS OF MISTAKEN EYEWITNESS IDENTIFICATION

OVERVIEW

If the goal of the American criminal justice system is punishment of those who are guilty and freedom for the innocent, then eyewitness identification throws a big wrench into this goal. As mentioned in your text, almost half of all wrongful convictions occurred due to mistaken identifications. These mistakes are a result of a myriad of elements such as perception, memory, suggestion, and recall. Both perception and attention influence how we see events and psychologists have determined that our brain does not record images exactly as we see them. When examining a crime committed by a stranger, our perception is influenced by how long we observed the stranger, any distractions that may have been occurring simultaneously, our focus of observation, any stress we may have been under at the time, and the race of both you and the stranger in question. As well, our memory fades during the first few hours after an event, however our confidence in our recollection increases. Finally, when presented with a lineup, shop-up or photo identification by police, most individuals feel they need to choose the best likeness of the perpetrator given the choices provided. All of these factors combine to form very shaky ground on which the criminal justice system relies in proving guilt beyond a reasonable doubt. The problem: given all these obstacles to observing an recalling an event involving a stranger, are eyewitness testimonies enough to prove guilt beyond a reasonable doubt?

CASE

McMullen v. State of Florida is a review of <u>McMullen v. State, 660 So.2d 340 (Fla. 4th DCA 1995)</u>, in which the district court affirmed petitioner's conviction, upholding the trial court's denial of McMullen's request to use an expert witness to testify regarding factors that affect the reliability of eyewitness identification. The question this raised for the court was: When the sole issue in a criminal prosecution is one of identity and the sole incriminating evidence is eyewitness testimony, should the court admit expert testimony upon the factors that affect the reliability of eyewitness identification?

MCMULLEN V. STATE OF FLORIDA
714 So.2d 368, 23 Fla. L. Weekly S207 (1998)

For the reasons expressed, we decline to answer the certified question as worded. We hold that the admission of such testimony is within the discretion of the trial judge and that, in this case, the trial judge did not abuse that discretionary authority by refusing to allow the introduction of the expert testimony. Thus the district court's affirmance of petitioner's conviction is hereby approved.

Scott McMullen was charged by a three-count information for shooting into a dwelling, aggravated assault with a firearm, and aggravated battery with a firearm. On the night of the offenses, an assailant allegedly approached Sheron Grewal while she was sweeping the parking lot outside of the beer store she owned with her husband, Mohinder. After grabbing Sheron by the shoulder, the assailant tried to push her inside the store. When she resisted, he brandished a gun and shoved it into her side. Hearing noises outside, Mohinder, who was inside the store attending the cash register, walked toward the doorway. As he approached the doorway, he caught a glimpse of the assailant, who shot him and then turned and fled. Both Mohinder and Sheron identified McMullen as the assailant. We also note that the assailant was of a different race than the witnesses and that McMullen was initially not among the police suspects. Further, the wife told the police detectives that she had never seen the assailant before the incident. Two months after the shooting, the witnesses' son called the police detectives and reported that his parents had seen the assailant in their drive-through window earlier that day. The police arranged a photographic lineup at the store. When the array of photographs was presented to the witnesses, the wife told the husband that McMullen was the one who had shot him. Contrary to her initial statement to the police after the incident, the wife testified at trial that she recognized the assailant as an occasional customer at the store. Both the husband and wife identified McMullen as the perpetrator. Alibi witnesses were presented by McMullen, and McMullen testified that he was not the person who accosted the wife and shot the husband.

Prior to trial, McMullen filed a motion to appoint an expert witness on eyewitness identification. The trial judge granted the motion, but the order did not address the admissibility of that expert's testimony. Subsequently, the State filed a motion *in limine* to exclude the defense expert on eyewitness identification. The State argued that the expert testimony should not be admitted because it was invading the province of the jury. McMullen's counsel proffered the testimony of Dr. John Brigham, a professor of psychology at Florida State University, regarding psychological factors believed to affect the reliability of eyewitness identification. According to Dr. Brigham, countless scientific studies have been conducted indicating that psychological factors, which are largely unknown to laypersons, can affect the accuracy of eyewitness identifications. Specifically, Dr. Brigham stated that he could testify about the following six issues at trial: (1) eyewitness identifications are incorrect much more often than the average person thinks; (2) a witness's confidence or certainty in an identification is unrelated to the accuracy of the identification; (3) cross-racial identifications are more difficult than same-race identifications; (4) "unconscious transference," i.e., it is easier for a person to remember a face than to remember the circumstances under which the person saw the face; (5) the accuracy of facial identifications decreases in stressful situations; and (6) the accuracy of identification decreases as the interval between the event and the time when the witness attempts to retrieve the memory increases.

The State objected to the introduction of Dr. Brigham's testimony, arguing that the substance of his testimony did not require any special knowledge or experience to assist the jurors in reaching their conclusions. During the argument on the motion *in limine*, the State argued that the admission of Dr. Brigham's testimony was within the discretion of the trial court. McMullen's counsel agreed. Relying on discretionary authority, the trial judge excluded the testimony, finding: This Court is of the opinion that the facts testified to by Dr. Brigham are not of such a nature as to require special knowledge in order for a jury to reach a decision. Subsequently, the jury found McMullen guilty of all charges. On appeal, the Fourth District Court of Appeal affirmed but certified the above question to this Court.

At the outset, it must be understood that there are three differing views as to the admissibility of an expert witness's testimony regarding the reliability of eyewitness identification. The first is the "discretionary" view, which provides that the admission of expert testimony regarding eyewitness identification is in the discretion of the trial judge. An overwhelming majority of both federal and state courts that have addressed this issue have adopted this view. The second view is the "prohibitory view," which expressly prohibits the use of this type of expert testimony. Finally, some jurisdictions have adopted the "limited admissibility" view, finding it to be an abuse of discretion to exclude this type of expert testimony in cases where there is no substantial corroborating evidence.

We have adopted the majority "discretionary" view in this state. Expert testimony should be excluded when the facts testified to are of such nature as not to require any special knowledge or experience in order for the jury to form its conclusions. A jury is fully capable of assessing a witness' ability to perceive and remember, given the assistance of cross-examination and cautionary instructions, without the aid of exert testimony. There is no abuse of discretion in the trial court's refusal to allow a witness to testify about the reliability of eyewitness identification.

Despite the overwhelming view to the contrary, McMullen has seized upon that confusion to urge us to follow what he asserts to be "the modern trend." According to McMullen, the modern trend advances the proposition that the admission of expert testimony on the reliability of eyewitness identification will enhance the jury's knowledge and help it resolve the issue presented, especially when eyewitness identification constitutes virtually the entire case against the defendant. We recognize that there are those who have written extensively in seeking the admission of expert testimony on this issue, arguing that the defendant should have the opportunity to present this type of expert testimony to challenge the credibility of eyewitnesses. As noted previously, however, only a minority of jurisdictions have accepted this view. We hereby affirm that the admissibility of expert testimony regarding the reliability of eyewitness testimony is left to the sound discretion of the trial judge. By so holding, we are continuing to align ourselves with a majority of other jurisdictions.

Upon review of the record here, which includes statements to the trial court by counsel for both McMullen and the State agreeing that the trial court had the discretion to admit or exclude the expert's testimony, we conclude that the trial court understood that the admission of the expert's testimony was discretionary. Further, we cannot find that the trial court abused its discretion in excluding the testimony. The trial court was in a far superior position to that of an appellate court to consider whether the testimony would have aided the jury in reaching its decision. We decline to address the other issues raised by McMullen, which are not within the scope of the certified question.

Accordingly, we decline to answer the certified question as worded, holding that the admission of such testimony is within the discretion of the trial judge and that, in this case, the trial judge did not abuse that discretionary authority by refusing to allow the introduction of the expert testimony. The decision of the district court of appeal is approved. It is so ordered.

ANSTEAD, Justice, concurring in part and dissenting in part.

While I concur in what appears to be a concession in the majority opinion that trial courts should have discretion to admit expert opinion evidence on eyewitness identifications, I must dissent from the majority's unwillingness to acknowledge and retreat from our categorical holding that such evidence should not be admitted, and from the majority's conclusion that the evidence was properly excluded in this case. Let us consider the important issues the majority opinion fails to address:

First, the certified question of great public importance. Presumably we accepted jurisdiction in this case because we agreed with the district court that the question certified was one of great public importance requiring resolution by this Court. However, having assumed jurisdiction we now cryptically announce that we are declining to address this important issue "for the reasons expressed." But look as I may, I cannot find any "reasons expressed" in the majority opinion for not answering the certified question. I would address the certified question and answer in the affirmative.

Second, how can our holding that jurors are fully capable of assessing eyewitness testimony without the assistance of expert evidence be reconciled with a rule vesting discretion in trial courts to admit such evidence? In other words, if jurors will never need or be aided by such evidence how can it be said that a court has "discretion" to admit it?

Third, how can it be said that the trial court here exercised its informed discretion when it announced on the record that its decision to exclude the evidence was predicated upon the holding that jurors do not need the assistance of experts to evaluate eyewitness testimony?

Fourth, if such expert testimony is not to be admitted in this case, where the district court points out compelling and unique circumstances supporting its admission, then under what circumstances should it be admitted?

I concur with the majority that appellant's conviction and sentence must be affirmed. However, I respectfully dissent from the question certified by the majority as a question of great public importance.

Section 90.702, Florida Statutes (1997), provides: If scientific, technical, or other specialized knowledge will assist the trier of fact in understanding the evidence or in determining a fact in issue, a witness qualified as an expert by knowledge, skill, experience, training, or education may testify about it in the form of an opinion; however, the opinion is admissible only if it can be applied to evidence at trial.

The fundamental problem is the premise that expert eyewitness testimony is within the common knowledge of the jury. Research indicates that the average juror actually knows little about factors affecting the accuracy of eyewitness identifications. The processes of perception and memory are complicated. While most people are satisfied in believing they have common sense, the memory process involves factors that are often counterintuitive. For example, Dr. Elizabeth Loftus points to four commonly held misconceptions about the reliability of eyewitness identifications:

1. Witnesses remember the details of a violent crime better than those of a nonviolent one. Research shows just the opposite.

2. Witnesses are as likely to underestimate the duration of a crime as to overestimate it. In fact, witnesses almost invariably think a crime took longer than it did.

3. The more confident a witness is, the more accurate the testimony is likely to be. Research suggests that there may be little relationship between confidence and accuracy, especially when viewing conditions are poor.

4. Police officers make better witnesses than ordinary citizens. Research shows that the testimony of law enforcement personnel is generally not more accurate than that of an ordinary citizen.

Research by psychologists aimed at determining the level of knowledge about eyewitness testimony among potential jurors produced consistent results: the participants had only around a fifty percent accuracy rate when answering questions about human perception. Thus, the rationale that expert testimony is within the common knowledge of the jury is not only unfounded, but it casts doubt on the seriousness with which these courts have addressed the problems associated with eyewitness identifications.

It is important that we note the unique circumstances of this case which are elaborated in Judge Farmer's concurrence in the district court: Here the principal--indeed only--evidence tying this defendant to the holdup of the store were the eyewitness identifications by the two owner-employees of the store, husband and wife, who were present during the holdup. The assailant, of a different race than the witnesses, immediately fled. The entire incident consumed mere seconds. Defendant was initially not among the police suspects.

Considering the unique facts of this case, I agree with Judge Farmer that the circumstances here present a "plausible cause for a trial judge to conclude that the admission of the expert testimony proffered might be of assistance to the jury." Further, I agree that, in combination, the weight of academic research and a significant body of well-reasoned case law should compel us to revisit our holding in Johnson that "a jury is fully capable of assessing a witness' ability to perceive and remember, given the assistance of cross-examination and cautionary instructions, without the aid of expert testimony." The primary test for the admission of expert testimony should be whether such evidence will assist the trier of fact in understanding the evidence or in determining a fact in issue. In accord with this, the trial judge should consider the particular circumstances of the case being tried and the age, life experience, or other relevant information about the jurors in determining if the expert testimony meets the "helpfulness" standard of section 90.702, Florida Statutes (1997). The trial judge may also consider the circumstances surrounding an eyewitness's testimony, including the age of the eyewitness; the presence of a weapon or violence at the scene where the eyewitness allegedly saw the defendant; the stress the eyewitness was under when allegedly making the initial identification; and any other relevant circumstances affecting the eyewitness' testimony.

In this case I would approve of the discretionary use of expert testimony about psychological factors that may affect eyewitness identification to give effect to the intent expressed in section 90.702. Further, while the question of admissibility of such expert testimony should be left to the sound discretion of the trial judge, the trial judge must exercise his or her discretion in furtherance of section 90.702's "helpfulness" standard. In considering a proffer of such evidence the trial court should be aware that it has the discretion to admit the evidence. It should be careful in assessing the qualifications of the expert presented as well as in making an evaluation of the helpfulness of the proffered testimony compared to the risk that it may cause juror confusion. None of that took place here.

I would answer the certified question in the affirmative and I would remand this case to the district court for reconsideration under a true discretionary standard.

REVIEW SECTION

READING COMPREHENSION

Detail the material facts of this case.

What are the problems with eyewitness identification as discussed by the two psychologists in this case?

THINKING CRITICALLY

When the sole issue in a criminal prosecution is one of identity and the sole incriminating evidence is eyewitness testimony, should the court admit expert testimony upon the factors that affect the reliability of eyewitness identification?

Should eyewitness identification alone be enough to establish proof beyond a reasonable doubt? What if the sentence is death?

Indicate your position in this case using arguments from the majority and dissenting opinions.

Did the majority address the important question? Why or why not?

Was Section 90.702 of the Florida Statutes violated in this case?

SECTION 2: THE CONSTITUTION AND IDENTIFICATION PROCEDURES

OVERVIEW

As you can probably imagine, the unreliable identification that often results from eyewitness testimony can violate the Fifth and Fourteenth Amendment rights to due process. The violation of course would be that misidentification could lead to deprivation of life, liberty, or property without due process of law. While the might-or-might-not-be-present instruction and blind administrators decrease somewhat the likelihood of a misidentification, courts rarely throw out such testimony regardless of how high the misidentification risk. The problem however, is that jurors usually believe this testimony.

CASE

In *State of Florida v. Kuntsman,* the court grants the state's petition for *writ of certiorari* and quashes the trial court's order which requires prosecution witnesses to view and be questioned about photographs during criminal depositions.

STATE OF FLORIDA V. KUNTSMAN
643 So.2d 1172, 19 Fla. L. Weekly D2161 (1994)

The State filed an information charging five defendants collectively, and as principals, with one count of armed robbery, two counts of burglary of a conveyance with assault, two counts of aggravated battery, and one count of criminal mischief. Attorneys for the defendants deposed one of the victims. Because four out of the five defendants had similar appearances, the victim distinguished them during the deposition based on their hair color and clothing. In an attempt to have the victim identify the criminal actions taken by each defendant, defense counsel requested the victim to view a photo array. This array consisted of thirty-eight black and white photographs, and included only four photos of the defendants. The State objected to the use of the photo array, and the victim refused to view or answer questions concerning the array. Defense counsel then certified the question. Following a hearing, the trial judge entered an order requiring all of the prosecution witnesses to view and respond to questions concerning the photo array. The state now petitions this court for a Writ of Certiorari to quash the trial court's order.

The criminal discovery process is governed by Florida Rule of Criminal Procedure 3.220. Furthermore, it is within the sound discretion of the trial judge to grant or limit criminal discovery. However, Rule 3.220 does not provide a trial judge with the authority to compel a witness to perform any type of involuntary physical examination. We hold that the trial judge in the instant case was not authorized to compel the prosecution witnesses to view the photo array, absent a showing by the defendants that strong or compelling reasons justified the order. The defendants herein did not demonstrate any strong or compelling circumstances which would justify the trial court's discovery order. The main reason asserted by the defendants in support of the order was their need to determine the specific allegations made by the prosecution's eyewitnesses against each defendant. That goal is achieved, however, by the taking of the deposition itself. Therefore, because the defendants did not present the trial court with a strong or compelling reason, the trial judge erred in ordering the prosecution witnesses to view the photo array.

The trial court's order also contravenes the purpose and intent of the criminal discovery rules. The purpose of criminal discovery is to avail the defense of evidence known to the state so that convictions will not be obtained by the suppression of evidence favorable to a defendant, or by surprise tactics in the courtroom. Thus, Rule 3.220 is not intended to provide defendants with an opportunity to build their cases during the discovery process by "creating" evidence, i.e. misidentifications. If the defendants in the instant case were only seeking to discover the extent of each defendant's involvement in the criminal incident, they would have exclusively formulated their questions solely around photographs of the defendants. Instead, they compiled a photo array containing thirty-eight black and white photographs, and including only four photos of the defendants. Surely, the defendants could have discovered the information they sought by conducting a proper deposition under the rules. Finally, the defendants attempt to elevate their argument to one of constitutional proportions by asserting that their due process rights will be violated if the trial court's order is quashed. That argument clearly lacks merit.

Consequently, for the foregoing reasons, we hold that the trial court departed from the essential requirements of the law by ordering the prosecution witnesses to view the photo array. We therefore grant the State's Petition for Certiorari and quash the trial court's order. Certiorari granted; order quashed.

REVIEW SECTION

READING COMPREHENSION

Detail the facts of this case.

Elaborate why the trial judge could not order prosecution witnesses to view and respond to questions about a photo array.

THINKING CRITICALLY

Does quashing of the trial judge's order impair the defendant's case? Should this be considered a violation of due process rights?

SECTION 3: DNA PROFILE IDENTIFICATION

OVERVIEW

DNA (deoxyribonucleic acid) testing has the power to potentially identify suspects or absolutely exclude an individual from consideration as a suspect. Courts have adopted a variety of standards for admission of DNA evidence at the trial stage and the *Florida Rules of Criminal Procedure 2004* Section 3.853 delineates the guidelines for a motion for postconviction DNA testing.

> (a) Purpose. This rule provides procedures for obtaining DNA (deoxyribonucleic acid) testing under section 925.11, Florida Statutes. (b) Contents of Motion. The motion for postconviction DNA testing must be under oath and must include the following: (1) a statement of the facts relied on in support of the motion, including a description of the physical evidence containing DNA to be tested and, if known, the present location or last known location of the evidence and how it originally was obtained; (2) a statement that the evidence was not tested previously for DNA, or a statement that the results of previous DNA testing were inconclusive and that subsequent scientific developments in DNA testing techniques likely would produce a definitive result; (3) a

statement that the movant is innocent and how the DNA testing requested by the motion will exonerate the movant of the crime for which the movant was sentenced, or a statement how the DNA testing will mitigate the sentence received by the movant for that crime; (4) a statement that identification of the movant is a genuinely disputed issue in the case and why it is an issue or an explanation of how the DNA evidence would either exonerate the defendant or mitigate the sentence that the movant received; (5) a statement of any other facts relevant to the motion; and (6) a certificate that a copy of the motion has been served on the prosecuting authority. (8) (d) Time Limitations. (1) The motion for postconviction DNA testing must be filed: (A) Within 2 years following the date that the judgment and sentence in the case became final if no direct appeal was taken; within 2 years following the date the conviction was affirmed on direct appeal if an appeal was taken; within 2 years following the date collateral counsel was appointed or retained subsequent to the conviction being affirmed on direct appeal in a capital case in which the death penalty was imposed; or by October 1, 2003, whichever occurs later; or (B) At any time, if the facts on which the petition is predicated were unknown to the petitioner or the movant's attorney and could not have been ascertained by the exercise of due diligence.

The goal of DNA testing should be to balance both the finality of litigation and protection of the rights of prisoners whose cases may need future review due to advances in the development of DNA technology.

CASE

Murray v. State of Florida reviews Murray's appeal from a judgment of conviction of first-degree murder and a sentence of death. The conviction in this case is reversed, the sentences are vacated, including the sentence of death, and the case is remanded for a new trial. One of the main issues addressed involves the use of DNA technology. Note this case involves a somewhat graphic description of the events resulting in the victim's death

MURRAY V. STATE OF FLORIDA
No. SC95470, Supreme Court of Florida
Case No. 92-3708 CFA (2002)

Appellant was initially convicted in 1994 for the September 1990 murder of fifty-nine-year-old Alice Vest. The jury found Murray guilty of first-degree murder, burglary of a dwelling with assault, and sexual battery and recommended death by a vote of eleven to one. The trial court followed the jury's recommendation and sentenced appellant to death. On appeal, this Court

reversed the convictions and sentences and remanded the case for a new trial. <u>Murray v. State,</u>
<u>692 So. 2d 157, 158 (Fla. 1997)</u>.

Murray was retried in February 1999. The evidence presented at trial revealed that on September 15, 1990, the victim (Alice Vest) arrived home around 11:30 p.m. after having dinner with a friend. Earlier that same evening, appellant and two friends, James "Bubba" Fisher and Steve Taylor, had played pool together; between 10:45 and 11:15 p.m., Fisher dropped appellant and Taylor about a mile from his home. Around 12:40 a.m., another witness, who lived approximately two miles from the victim's house, saw Murray and Taylor in her barn; the men ran away when she sent her dog to attack them. The victim's body was discovered the next morning (September 16, 1990) by a neighbor. The telephone lines leading into the house had been cut and a screen which covered the kitchen window had been removed. A shoeprint and some latent fingerprints were recovered from the scene of the crime, but none of the prints matched Taylor or Murray. In addition, several pieces of jewelry belonging to the victim were missing.

According to the medical examiner, the victim had been vaginally and anally raped and stabbed some twenty-four times. Most of the stab wounds were consistent with knife wounds, but some were consistent with infliction by a pair of scissors found near the victim's body. The victim also had a broken jaw and had been beaten about her head and face with several items, including a metal bar, a candle holder, and a glass bottle. The actual cause of death was ligature strangulation. The medical examiner asserted that the victim was probably stabbed first, then strangled with several ligatures, including a web belt and an electrical cord. Although he opined that the victim was alive during the stabbing, he could not say how long she remained conscious during the attack.

During the trial, the State admitted hair evidence found at the scene of the crime, which reflected that several hairs found on the victim's nightgown matched Murray's DNA profile. According to the State's DNA expert, Michael DeGuglielmo, the test results on those hairs also indicated the presence of a fainter, secondary DNA, consistent with the victim's DNA profile. This meant that while the fainter, secondary DNA could not be conclusively matched to the victim, the victim could not be excluded as a possible donor. The police also recovered hairs from the victim's body. DNA tests on these hairs indicated that one matched the DNA profile of the victim and one matched the DNA profile of Taylor. Although none of these hairs matched Murray's DNA profile, DeGuglielmo testified that the test results on the hair matching the victim's DNA also indicated the presence of a fainter, secondary DNA which was consistent with Murray's DNA profile. The hair evidence was also sent to an FBI lab in Washington, D.C., for comparison with known hair samples from three persons: Murray, Taylor, and the victim. According to Joseph DiZinno, a hair specialist with the FBI, some of the hairs found on the victim's nightgown were pubic hairs which had the same microscopic characteristics as Murray's hairs. As for the hairs found on the victim's body, the expert concluded that one of the hairs was a pubic hair which was consistent with Murray's hair. Taylor was excluded as a possible source of the hairs.

Additional evidence presented at trial revealed that approximately six months after his indictment for the murder of Alice Vest, Murray escaped from prison. While out, Murray confessed to the murder of Alice Vest to one of his co-escapees, Anthony Smith. According to Smith, Murray said that on the night of the murder Taylor came over to his house and wanted to go out. Murray initially refused, but Taylor was eventually able to convince him after the two consumed some beer. After drinking more beer, Taylor convinced Murray to rob a house, and together, the pair broke into what Murray thought was an unoccupied house. When Murray discovered the owner was home, he wanted to leave, but Taylor grabbed the female occupant, held a knife to her, and sexually assaulted her. Afterwards, Murray had the victim perform oral sex on him. Murray left Taylor alone with the victim and searched the house for things to steal. When he returned to the bedroom five or ten minutes later, Taylor had stabbed the victim. Together they found an extension cord and strangled her. On June 9, 1993, approximately seven months after his escape, Murray was captured in Las Vegas, Nevada. At the time of his arrest he was carrying two false identification cards.

The defense presented two witnesses: Dr. Howard Baum and Joseph Warren. Warren was the laboratory analyst who worked with DeGuglielmo and who actually performed the DNA tests. Warren testified that the DNA test results in this case were inconclusive and unreliable. He described several serious errors he committed during the test procedures and testified that, in addition, certain important controls were not maintained, thereby undermining the reliability of the test results. Dr. Baum, the Assistant Medical Examiner in New York City, criticized the DNA test procedures used in this case and expressed the opinion that the test results were both inconclusive and unreliable.

The jury convicted appellant of first-degree murder, burglary with assault, and sexual battery. During the penalty phase of the trial, the State presented evidence concerning appellant's three prior convictions for felonies in which he used violence or the threat of violence. The State also presented victim impact evidence from the victim's friend and daughter. The defense did not present any evidence or witnesses during the penalty phase. The jury recommended death by a vote of twelve to zero, and the trial court followed the recommendation in imposing a sentence of death. The trial court found four aggravating factors to which it attributed substantial weight, found no statutory mitigators, but found five non-statutory mitigating factors based on information presented in a PSI report.

Appellant raises nine issues for this Court's review, all of which pertain solely to the guilt/innocence phase of the trial. As Murray's fourth issue is dispositive, we treat it first. Murray challenges the admissibility of the DNA evidence introduced by the State on the ground that the procedure used in testing the DNA in this case did not comply with the accepted standards to ensure reliability and, therefore, the evidence should have been excluded. Specifically, he argues that the DNA evidence should have been ruled inadmissible because the laboratory's testing procedures did not meet the standards generally accepted within the scientific community and hence fell below the requirements for admissibility under Frye v. United States, 293 F. 1013 (D.C. Cir. 1923). We begin our analysis with the premise that the trial court's ruling on a Frye issue is subject to *de novo* review on appeal. Therefore, we must review the trial court's ruling as a matter of law rather than by an abuse of discretion standard. In Henyard v. State, 689 So. 2d 239 (Fla. 1996), we explained the applicable law when reviewing a claim that DNA testing procedures did not meet the necessary standards: In admitting the results of scientific tests and experiments, the reliability of the testing methods is at issue, and the proper predicate to establish that reliability must be laid. If the reliability of a test's results is recognized and accepted among scientists, admitting those results is within the trial court's discretion. When such reliable evidence is offered, any inquiry into its reliability for purposes of admissibility is only necessary when the opposing party makes a timely request for such an inquiry supported by authorities indicating that there may not be general scientific acceptance of the technique employed.

Subsequently in Hayes v. State, 660 So.2d 257, 264 (Fla. 1995), we took judicial notice that DNA test results are generally accepted as reliable in the scientific community, provided that the laboratory has followed accepted testing procedures that meet the Frye test to protect against false readings and contamination. Great emphasis was placed on the recommendations of the National Research Council (NRC) concerning the standards and methodology for DNA testing. The NRC explained that when courts apply the Frye test to DNA testing procedures, they should acknowledge that the reliability of DNA testing is based on the assumption that the analytical work comported with the proper procedures. This is an issue that can be resolved only case by case and is always open to question, even if the general reliability of DNA typing is fully accepted in the scientific community. The DNA evidence should not be admissible if the proper procedures were not followed. Moreover, even if a court finds DNA evidence admissible because proper procedures were followed, the probative force of the evidence will depend on the quality of the laboratory work. More control can be exercised by the court in deciding whether the general practices in the laboratory or the theories that a laboratory uses accord with acceptable scientific standards. Even if the general scientific principles and techniques are accepted by experts in the field, the same experts could testify that the work done in a particular case was so flawed that the court should decide that, under Frye, the jury should not hear the evidence. In making the determination as to whether the proper procedures were followed, however, courts are not confined only to the NRC's recommendations. Instead, the NRC recommendations are but one example of the testing procedures that meet the requirements of Frye for admissibility.

In the case at hand, the trial court permitted the DNA test results to be admitted, finding that it was for the jury to determine the weight which should be ascribed to the test results: The Court's function in considering the validity and reliability of the procedures performed by Mr. DeGuglielmo and his laboratory is essentially that of a gatekeeper. There can be no question that expert testimony will generally be of assistance to jurors in assessing DNA evidence. Defendant herein contends, however, that due to mistakes allegedly made during the testing in this case, the flaws in methodology and processes underlying the tests render their results so unreliable as to require exclusion from evidence. Defendant's objections can be divided into two principal categories: (1) allegations amounting to claims of inexact recordkeeping, and (2) challenges as to the potential causes and explanations of dual indications with respect to three of the polymarkers. As to the recording or clerical errors, the Court finds that, although certain errors in recording or memorializing portions of the data clearly occurred, these errors were in large part addressed and explained by the State's witnesses and were neither individually nor collectively significant enough to cast doubt upon the viability of the tests themselves, the reliability of the final results of the testing procedures, or the conclusions derived therefrom. The Court reaches this same conclusion with regard to defendant's objections regarding the DNA amplification, independent review, following of appropriate protocols, and potential for contamination of the evidence.

While defendant is certainly free to argue this point to a jury, the Court does not find that the errors which occurred are significant to the degree that they undermine the viability of the tests, the reliability of the test results, or the expert testimony to a degree requiring exclusion of the evidence.

As to the dispute regarding the significance of the "fainter" allele representations in various polymarkers, the Court finds the testimony of the State's expert to be persuasive. Though defense experts suggested that it was (at least theoretically) possible that the fainter allele was the result of a heterozygous donor or various other factors, both the submitted scientific data and the testimony of the State's experts demonstrate that the result is more likely than not the result of a mixture of DNA on the specimens resulting from the nature of the evidence at the scene; this is particularly true given the vast disparities in the strength of the indicators. In any event, though the experts may draw different conclusions from the test results, the testimony presented does not undermine the viability of the tests or the reliability of the results. Thus, these differing expert opinions pose no bar to the admissibility of the tests or results; the respective credibility of the experts, and the weight ultimately ascribed to their testimony, shall be determined by the jury.

Accordingly, the Court is persuaded that the scientific methods and procedures employed by Mr. DeGuglielmo, and the conclusions derived therefrom, are sufficiently reliable so as to meet the threshold requirements for admissibility under the Frye standard. Further, the Court is persuaded that the testimony of Dr. Tracy regarding population statistics and the probability results derived therefrom likewise satisfy these standards.

We disagree.

Because the State was seeking to introduce the DNA test results, it bore the burden of proving the general acceptance of both the underlying scientific principle and the testing procedures used to apply that principle to the facts of the case at hand. Numerous problems occurred, most of which concerned the significance of fainter alleles which appeared during the DNA testing. Even the State's expert, DeGuglielmo, testified that in order for DNA testing to be generally accepted as reliable within the scientific community, there must be an independent review by a second qualified analyst. In this case, Warren, a senior forensic scientist, conducted the tests and performed the initial review; he concluded that the test results were inconclusive because the faint alleles were too faint and ambiguous to be interpreted decisively. His supervisor, DeGuglielmo, reviewed Warren's report and disagreed, submitting a written DNA report which concluded that the tests were conclusive, that the hair sample was consistent with Murray's DNA, and that the faint alleles were consistent with the victim's DNA. DeGuglielmo never discussed with Warren the inconsistencies in the two reports or the possibility of another independent review. The State's argument that the two inconsistent reports meet the requirements of "a second independent review" is unavailing. If the purpose of the second review is to assure the reliability of the testing, this is hardly accomplished when the analyst conducting the initial testing and his supervisor conducting the "independent review" reach opposing conclusions. The results from the DNA testing become more uncertain, rather than more conclusive. This defeats the entire purpose of a second independent review and renders the initial review meaningless.

Accordingly, as the defense experts explained, one of the elements of a second independent review is to ensure that the results of the initial review were reliable, and should the two analysts disagree, the tests should be deemed inconclusive in the absence of further analysis.

Not only did the initial analyst and his supervisor disagree as to the results of the tests, but the analyst failed to properly document the required controls of the test-another step which the experts agree is required within the scientific community. Specifically, the analyst failed to take a picture of one of the control strips which would have shown whether the tests had been contaminated. This is particularly troubling in this case since there was expert testimony that the results normally should not have produced any fainter alleles and that contamination is a possible explanation for the presence of the fainter alleles. DeGuglielmo testified that normally hair follicles would not show fainter alleles of a different DNA because the hair root is the only portion of the hair which contains DNA. He contended, however, that fainter alleles could have occurred because the hair contacted some other substance like blood or semen, thus causing a mixture of DNA to appear. His explanation is troubling, particularly in light of Warren's testimony that when he performed the DNA testing, he washed the strands of hair in xylene and then washed the hair a second time in ethanol to remove the xylene; hence, there should have been no other substance on the hair. In addition, Warren admitted that he did not perform a hair shaft control-a control which would have shown whether the hair had any other DNA substance on it.

The unreliability of the testing procedures was compounded by the facts that (1) the State's expert used all of the DNA found in the hair, rendering it impossible for the defendant to conduct his own independent analysis; and (2) there was a general sloppiness in documenting the tests which even the analyst admitted was below the standards normally accepted. Because of the clerical errors and the below-standard documentation and paperwork, other experts who were retained by the defense were unable to adequately review the test results since necessary portions of the documentation were missing.

Based on the unique combination of errors and problems which occurred in the tests and the lack of documentation, we find that the State did not meet its burden in demonstrating the general acceptance of the testing procedures which were used in this case. Accordingly, we reverse the convictions, vacate the sentences, and remand for a new trial to be conducted in a manner consistent with this opinion. Although this issue is dispositive, we address other grounds raised on review that we deem worthy of comment.

In the next two issues raised by Murray, he argues that the trial court erred in admitting the test results from hairs recovered from the victim's body and from the victim's nightgown because the evidence had been tampered with. The trial court denied this claim, concluding that the defense failed to present proof to indicate "a probable likelihood of tampering." It reasoned that any objection to the admission of the evidence would be overruled until the defense showed something more than suspicions and conjectures. We disagree in part.

In reviewing these claims, we start with the basic legal principle that relevant physical evidence is admissible unless there is an indication of probable tampering. In seeking to exclude certain evidence, Murray bears the initial burden of demonstrating the probability of tampering. Once this burden has been met, the burden shifts to the proponent of the evidence to submit evidence that tampering did not occur. Murray contends that the evidence from the victim's body should have been excluded because it was tampered with or altered. The police claimed to have recovered only two hairs from the victim's body, whereas the expert with the FBI who conducted the tests stated that he received and tested several hairs. Murray challenges this apparent discrepancy. In support of his claim, Murray points to the portion of the record where Detective Chase testified that he collected two hairs from the victim's body, one from her chest and one from her leg. Chase testified that he placed the hairs in an envelope and then placed the envelope in the property room of the Jacksonville Sheriff's Office. That evidence was later sent to the FBI for comparison. Joseph DiZinno, the expert at the FBI, testified that he received debris from the victim's nightgown and hairs from the victim's body.

We find that Murray did not overcome his initial burden in demonstrating the probability of evidence tampering relative to the hairs collected from the body. Murray's allegations amount to mere speculation, and hence the trial court did not commit error in admitting the hairs into evidence.

Murray also argues that the test results on hairs recovered from the victim's nightgown should have been excluded because of questions concerning the bag in which the nightgown had been placed. According to the record on appeal, a bag of evidence initially contained a nightgown and a bottle of lotion when it was sealed, but when the bag was received by the FDLE, the lotion bottle was missing. Specifically, Officer Laforte testified that he collected a bottle of hand lotion and a nightgown from the same location and placed them both in the same bag in order to keep them together. The bag containing the nightgown and lotion was given to FDLE for processing. Despite the fact that the sealed bag had no indications that it previously had been opened, it did not contain the bottle of lotion. This discrepancy was never explained. In reviewing the testimony, we find that the defendant carried his burden in demonstrating the probability of evidence tampering, hence the burden shifted to the State to explain the discrepancy or to submit evidence that tampering did not occur. As the State failed to meet its burden, the trial court erred in finding the challenged evidence admissible.

In his third claim, appellant contends that the trial court erred in denying the defense's request that it be allowed to impeach DeGuglielmo with evidence that DeGuglielmo, the State's expert, had telephoned Warren, the defense's expert witness, in an attempt to influence the defense expert testimony. Murray argues that by denying the defense the opportunity to impeach the credibility of the State's expert witness, the trial court committed reversible error. The trial court sustained the State's request to preclude the defense from offering the evidence, finding that the testimony was not relevant and that there was no proof that DeGuglielmo acted on behalf of the State in calling Warren or that DeGuglielmo attempted to influence Warren's opinion. The trial court's ruling to exclude this testimony on this basis was error.

In issue five, Murray argues that the trial court committed reversible error by allowing the State to introduce evidence that Murray had escaped from prison and had used a false identification card and a false social security card. He contends that these crimes were not relevant to the crime charged because the escape occurred two years after the murder in this case while Murray was in prison on an unrelated charge and the use of false documents was unrelated to the murder. Thus, Murray contends that the State improperly used this evidence solely to show Murray's propensity to commit crimes. The State, on the other hand, argues that evidence of escape is relevant to show consciousness of guilt. We find no error in the trial court's decision permitting the State to present evidence of appellant's prison escape to show consciousness of guilt. Murray argues that due to the time delay between the murder and indictment for that crime and the date the escape occurred, the jury could not reasonably infer that Murray escaped from prison to avoid prosecution for the murder charges. Likewise, we find no error in the admission of evidence relating to Murray's use and possession of false identification cards at the time of his arrest. The use of false identification constituted additional evidence relevant to appellant's guilty knowledge at the time of his arrest. Accordingly, we affirm the trial court's ruling.

Murray argues that the trial court erred in not suppressing his statements to the police. He contends that Detective O'Steen told him that his DNA matched the DNA found at the murder scene. Murray then attempted to explain how that would be possible. However, the DNA evidence that Detective O'Steen referred to was later declared inadmissible, therefore Murray argues that because the DNA test results had been declared inadmissible, any responses to O'Steen's questions referring to the DNA evidence should also be declared inadmissible. The trial court overruled the objection, finding that Murray's response to the question was voluntary and therefore admissible. We find this claim to be without merit. We agree with the trial court that the sole issue concerning Murray's statements appears to be whether they were voluntarily made. The trial court ruled that Murray's statements to the police were voluntary and therefore admissible. Accordingly, we conclude that the trial court did not err in admitting Murray's statements to Detective O'Steen.

Finally, Murray contends that the evidence presented at trial was insufficient to support the trial court's denial of his motion for judgment of acquittal, and he should have been acquitted of the charges. In this case, the State submitted direct evidence that Murray confessed to a co-escapee. Based on our review of the record, there was competent, substantial evidence upon which the jury could return a first-degree murder verdict. Thus we find that the trial court properly rejected this motion.

Based on the foregoing analysis, we reverse Murray's convictions, vacate his sentences, and remand this case for a new trial. It is so ordered.

SHAW, PARIENTE, and QUINCE, JJ., concur. ANSTEAD, C.J., and LEWIS, J., concur in result only. WELLS, J., dissents with an opinion, in which HARDING, Senior Justice, concurs.

WELLS, J., dissenting.

I dissent because I believe the trial judge properly denied the objections to the DNA evidence. The Court's function in considering the validity and reliability of the procedures performed by Mr. Deguglielmo and his laboratory is essentially that of a gatekeeper. There can be no question that expert testimony will generally be of assistance to jurors in assessing DNA evidence. Defendant herein contends, however, that due to mistakes allegedly made during the testing in this case, the flaws in methodology and processes underlying the tests render their results so unreliable as to require exclusion from evidence. Further, I do not find that appellant's assertions in respect to the hair and lotion bottle support a claim of "probable tampering" so as to hold that the trial judge abused his discretion. There was simply no evidence presented at trial that the evidence containers which stored the various items had been altered in any way. The other errors found by the majority to have been made by the trial court, if error at all, were harmless beyond a reasonable doubt based upon this record. HARDING, Senior Justice, concurs.

REVIEW SECTION

READING COMPREHENSION

Elaborate the facts of this case.

Delineate Murray's claims and the finding of this court on each claim.

THINKING CRITICALLY

If, as defense witnesses asserted, DNA evidence was inconclusive, should it have been excluded? Or should the jury be free to assess varied interpretations of such evidence?

How would you decide this case? Use arguments from the majority and dissent to articulate your finding.

CONCLUSION

Proving who committed a crime is far more difficult than mere proof that a crime occurred. Recent developments in DNA technology have improved the ability of the government to identify a suspect. While this is a vast improvement on eyewitness identification in the form of lineups, show-ups, and photo identification all of which are debatable regarding reliability, DNA technology has difficulties of its own. This chapter examined the risks of mistaken eyewitness identification, the Constitution and identification procedures, and DNA profile identification. What you may want to give some thought to is the complicated nature of the presentation of DNA evidence in a court of law. Have we progressed to the point where scientists can adequately explain to everyday citizens the intricacies of this technology? Or are jurors merely left to sift through evidence that they do not fully comprehend in assessing an individual's guilt or innocence?

Chapter Ten

Constitutional Violations: Exclusionary Rule and Entrapment

During the trial stage there are two remedies that can affect the outcome of the state's criminal case and which are the subject of this chapter:

(1)   The exclusionary rule; and

(2)   The defense of entrapment.

These remedies are not mutually exclusive, but it is important to remember that while each is created by the U.S. Supreme Court with the intent to enforce constitutional rights, neither is backed by any constitutional right.

SECTION 1: THE EXCLUSIONARY RULE

OVERVIEW

The exclusionary rule is a frequently used remedy against state power which involves throwing out illegally obtained evidence against a defendant. The exclusion of such evidence was the rule in Florida long before the U.S. Supreme Court ruling <u>Mapp v. Ohio, 367 U.S. 643, 81 S.Ct. 1684, 6 L.Ed.2d 1081 (1961)</u> required state courts to follow the prohibition imposed on the federal courts through the <u>Weeks v. United States, 323 U.S. 383, 34 S.Ct. 341, 58 L.Ed. 652 (1914)</u> decision. Thus, Mapp had no real effect in Florida and the exclusionary rule is engrafted firmly into Florida law through Section Twelve of the Florida Constitution which states:

> Articles or information obtained in violation of this right shall not be admissible in evidence if such articles or information would be inadmissible under decisions of the United States Supreme Court construing the Fourth Amendment to the United States Constitution.

When the government obtains evidence that assists in determining the guilt of a defendant, the exclusionary rule allows this evidence to be excluded from trial if it was obtained in violation of any of the below amendments:

(1)   Fourth Amendment ban on unreasonable search and seizure;

(2)   Fifth Amendment ban on coerced statements that are incriminating;

(3)   Sixth Amendment right to counsel; or

(4)   Fifth and Fourteenth Amendment right of due process.

The exclusionary rule is used only in the United States and is an attempt to maintain police and judicial integrity, as well as to deter government officials from violating the law. In the dissenting words of Justice Brandeis in *Olmstead v. United States* (227 U.S. 438 1928), the effect of the exclusionary rule is that:

> The criminal goes free, if he must, but it is the law that sets him
> free. Nothing can destroy a government more quickly than its
> failure to observe its own laws, or worse, its disregard of the
> charter of its own existence.

Unlike the portrayal by mainstream media, the exclusionary rule affects a miniscule portion of cases, and has virtually no effect on violent crimes and serious property offenses. What the exclusionary does accomplish is a fundamental fairness of constitutional government for all citizens.

CASE

State of Florida v. Scarlet involves the application for review of the decision of the District Court of Appeal - Direct Conflict Third District - Case No. 3D99-3040 (Dade County). We have for review Scarlet v. State, 766 So. 2d 1110 (Fla. 3d DCA 2000), which expressly and directly conflicts with Johnston v. State, 768 So. 2d 504 (Fla. 4th DCA 2000).

STATE OF FLORIDA V. SCARLET
Supreme Court of Florida
Case No. SC00-2135 (2001)

The statement of the case and facts in the initial brief of Petitioner is accepted as a generally accurate account of the proceedings below, with the following addition: The trial court made the following finding regarding the search of the vehicle: The court finds that the search of the vehicle was without probable cause, without founded suspicion, without a warrant, and without consent. There are no lawful exceptions to the warrant requirement that apply to this case. Thus the search of the vehicle and the arrest of the Defendant were illegal under the Fourth Amendment to the United States Constitution and Article I, § 12 of the Florida Constitution. The court, however, admitted the tainted evidence at the probation violation hearing on the grounds that the exclusionary rule did not apply. Although the Court has concluded that the search and arrest of the Defendant were illegal and that the spontaneous statements were the fruit of those illegalities, the inquiry does not end there. These findings have resulted in the exclusion of the evidence and statements in the underlying felony trafficking in cocaine trial. However, because the Court finds that the exclusionary rule does not apply to probation violation hearings, the motion is denied in this matter. The trial court revoked the defendant's probation, based on the narcotics that were seized from his car, and sentenced him to a 54 months in state prison

The United States Supreme Court's decision in <u>Pennsylvania Board of Probation and Parole v. Scott, 524 U.S. 357 (1998)</u>, did not overturn well-established Florida precedents holding that illegally seized evidence must be excluded from probation revocation hearings. In Florida, the exclusionary rule is not a judicial creation, but a constitutionally mandated remedy and thus not subject to change based on evolving judicial policies. Under the rationale of <u>Soca v. State, 673 So. 2d 24 (Fla. 1996)</u>, unless the United States Supreme Court's interpretation of the Fourth Amendment is directly on point with respect to a specific issue, Florida must rely on its own decisional law. There are constitutionally meaningful differences between parole revocation hearings, which are non-adversarial administrative procedures where indigent parolees are not entitled to appointed counsel, and probation revocation hearings, which are judicial and adversarial in nature. Moreover, the instant case is factually distinguishable from *Scott*.

Florida's construction of the U.S. Supreme Courts decision in Scott is mandatorily limited to parole revocation proceedings, which are non-adversarial and administrative in nature and must not be extended to probation revocation hearings. The conformity clause of the 1982 constitutional amendment did not vitiate the principle of primacy of the Florida constitution. The rule of primacy requires that Florida follow the United States Supreme Court's Fourth Amendment decisional law when its holdings are specifically controlling; however, when the United States Supreme Court has not previously addressed a particular search and seizure issue which comes before the court for review, the court looks to precedent for guidance. The United States Supreme Court's holding in Scott is not binding on Florida with respect to the application of the exclusionary rule in probation revocation hearings for several reasons.

First, there are substantive conceptual differences between parole and probation for Fourth Amendment purposes. Florida draws a sharp legal distinction between parole and probation and thus they must be interpreted under different analytical frameworks. Revocation of parole is not part of a criminal prosecution, and thus the full panoply of rights due a defendant in such a proceeding does not apply to parole revocations. While there are similarities in probation and parole, there are also some significant differences. Probation is under the jurisdiction of the courts, and it was in the exercise of our authority over the court system that we determined that counsel must be furnished in all probation revocation hearings. Parole is administered by the Commission. Moreover, parole revocation proceedings are conducted by nonlawyers. Requiring that counsel be furnished in every case would inevitably lead to the use of counsel by the state. Finally, unlike probation revocation, parole revocation does not lead to a sentencing hearing which necessarily requires the appointment of counsel. Under section 947.23, Florida Statutes, a parole revocation is determined in an administrative, extra-judicial setting by non-lawyers. The hearing is not adversarial in nature, unlike probation revocation hearings. A commission, which usually consists of three or more commissioners, receive evidence and "if the hearing was conducted by three or more commissioners, a majority of them shall enter an order determining whether the charges of parole violation have been sustained, based on the findings of fact made by them" § 947.23(6)(a). In other words, a parole hearing is an administrative procedure presided over by commissioners, rather than a judge, the commissioners' verdicts need not be unanimous, an indigent parolee does not have the right to appointed counsel, and he will not be sentenced (he will, instead, serve the remainder of his pre-determined sentence). Probation is a sentencing alternative whereas parole is an early release mechanism (now archaic in Florida) whereby the

Department of Corrections ameliorates over-crowding through the grant of conditional, administrative release.

The Petitioner's argument is predicated on a misconception concerning the status of the exclusionary rule in Florida as opposed to the federal version. The Petitioner writes: The Scott opinion is based on the rationale that the State's use of evidence obtained in violation of the Fourth Amendment does not itself violate the Constitution. Rather, a Fourth Amendment violation is fully accomplished by the illegal search or seizure, and no exclusion of evidence from a judicial or administrative proceeding can cure the invasion of the defendant's rights which he has already suffered. The exclusionary rule is instead a judicially created means of deterring illegal searches and seizures. As such, the rule does not proscribe the introduction of illegally seized evidence in all proceedings or against all persons, but applies only in contexts where its remedial objectives are thought most efficaciously served. Moreover, because the rule is prudential rather than constitutionally mandated, the Court has held it to be applicable only where deterrence benefits outweigh its substantial social costs.

In a unanimous decision in Scarlet the Third District rejected the State's argument and explained: The Florida Supreme Court has held that in the absence of a controlling federal decision directly on point, evidence obtained through an unlawful search is inadmissible in a probation revocation hearing. State v. Cross, 487 So. 2d 1056 (Fla. 1986). Since then the United States Supreme Court has held that such evidence is admissible in parole revocation hearings. Pennsylvania Parole Bd. v. Scott, 524 U.S. 357, 118 S. Ct. 2014, 141 L. Ed.2d 344 (1998). Scott does not overturn Cross. Evidence discovered during an unlawful search is not admissible in a hearing to revoke probation. The State asked this court to certify this question to the Florida Supreme Court. We decline to do so, as the Florida Supreme Court has spoken so clearly on this matter. More recently, Williams v. State, 791 So. 2d 37 (Fla. 2d DCA 2001), the Second District followed Scarlet and held that the exclusionary rule is applicable in a probation revocation hearing, notwithstanding the Supreme Court's decision in Scott.

We have considered but decline to revisit our prior decisions State v. Cross, 487 So. 2d 1056 (Fla. 1986), and Grubbs v. State, 373 So. 2d 905 (Fla. 1979). Accordingly, we approve the Third District's decision in Scarlet concluding that Scott does not preclude the applicability of the exclusionary rule in probation revocation hearings. It is so ordered.

REVIEW SECTION

READING COMPREHENSION

Delineate the status of the exclusionary rule in Florida as opposed to its federal application.

For Fourth Amendment purposes, what are the differences between parole and probation?

CASE

Shadler v. State of Florida reviews State v. Shadler, 714 So. 2d 662 (Fla. 5th DCA 1998) which is in direct conflict with Bruno v. State, 704 So. 2d 134 (Fla. 1st DCA 1997). The Supreme Court of Florida quashes the decision in Shadler and finds that the exclusionary rule applies to an error committed by the Florida Department of Highway Safety and Motor Vehicles through its Division of Driver Licenses.

SHADLER V. STATE OF FLORIDA
Supreme Court of Florida
761 So.2d 279 (Fla. 1999)

On June 18, 1997, Deputy Gary Bowling received information from a fellow police officer that petitioner Stanley Shadler's license had been suspended. He subsequently verified this information through his dispatcher. About two hours later, Bowling stopped Shadler on the basis of the information received from the other officer and the dispatcher. At the stop, Bowling performed a computerized check through the Department of Highway Safety and Motor Vehicles, Division of Driver Licenses, which confirmed that Shadler's license had been suspended. In fact, however, as the parties agree, Shadler's license had not been suspended and the information relied upon by Bowling was in error. Relying upon the erroneous information, Bowling arrested Shadler for driving with a suspended license and searched him incident to that arrest. During the search, Bowling found contraband in a plastic bag inside Shadler's wallet. Bowling then charged Shadler with unlawful possession of the contraband.

After his arrest, Shadler went to the Motor Vehicle Bureau to inquire why his license was reported suspended. There, an examiner told him that the mistaken information was due to a computer error and that his license was not suspended. Before trial, Shadler filed a motion to suppress the fruits of the search, claiming that the arrest and search incident to that arrest were unlawful because they were predicated upon an erroneous belief that his license had been suspended. At the hearing, Shadler argued that the Division of Driver Licenses should be treated as a law enforcement entity because it is part of the Department of Highway Safety, which is also the parent department of the Florida Highway Patrol. Therefore the contraband should be excluded.

The trial court granted the motion, reasoning that the Department of Highway Safety's failure, through its driver's license division, to keep its records accurate and current was a mistake attributable to a law enforcement agency of the government. On appeal, the Fifth District reversed, and, focusing solely on the duties of the Division of Driver Licenses of the Department of Highway Safety, held that persons working for the Division should be treated as the court employees, and therefore the mistake should not be attributed to a law enforcement agency.

Shadler sought review in this Court based on conflict with Bruno v. State, 704 So. 2d 134 (Fla. 1st DCA 1997). In Bruno, an officer stopped the defendant, Bruno, for speeding and, upon verifying his license "over the radio," the officer was erroneously advised that the license had been suspended. As a result, the officer arrested Bruno. In a search incident to that arrest, the officer discovered contraband on Bruno's person. At trial, the judge denied Bruno's motion to suppress. The First District reversed.

Section 321.05 of the Florida Statutes (1997) gives broad law enforcement powers to "the highway patrol officers under the direction and supervision of the Department of Highway Safety and Motor Vehicles. Accordingly, because the Department of Highway Safety is charged with law enforcement both in fact and by law, we conclude that it is clearly a law enforcement agency. The Department of Highway Safety not only considers itself a major law enforcement agency, but it has specifically articulated as one of its three major goals the following: "Providing assistance to local, state, and federal agencies and highway safety organizations through a comprehensive records and management system which reflects driver and vehicle status information." The maintenance of records of revocations and suspensions clearly relate directly to the enforcement of the laws relating to driving privileges. More importantly however, as the State conceded, every law enforcement agency in the state relies on the division's records to verify driver's licenses and their current status in order to enforce the law. Accordingly, not only is the division an integral part of the Department of Highway Safety and its overall mission, but in terms of reliance upon the accuracy of its records, it is a vital part of the law enforcement infrastructure of the entire State of Florida. The United States Supreme Court has stated that the exclusionary rule is a "judicially created remedy designed to safeguard Fourth Amendment rights generally through its deterrent effect." Unites States v. Calandra, 414 U.S. 338, 348 (1974). Based upon our analysis of the duties and responsibilities of the Department of Highway Safety, we conclude that the Department is essentially a law enforcement agency.

We conclude that the exclusion of evidence in cases such as the one at bar will surely serve to encourage accurate record-keeping of driver's license information. The exclusionary rule is perhaps the only means by which the judiciary can help to ensure the accuracy of records and information compiled by the Department of Highway Safety and its divisions that routinely provide records to Florida's police and sheriffs' departments. Because the Department of Highway Safety is responsible for the related law enforcement functions of agency record-keeping and monitoring traffic offenses and crime on the state's highways, there is an institutional obligation as well as a direct mechanism for feedback from fellow employees to communicate the effect of the exclusionary rule. Surely, the Department of Highway Safety will consistently strive to see that no mistakes are made and that no citizen is wrongfully subjected to an arrest or search predicated upon a mistake. Accordingly, we quash the district court's decision and find that the trial court correctly excluded the evidence obtained during the unlawful search. It is so ordered. SHAW, PARIENTE and LEWIS, JJ., concur.

WELLS, J., dissents with the following opinion, in which HARDING, C.J., and QUINCE, J., concur. First, this Court has no jurisdiction. There is no conflict between the Fifth District's decision in this case and the First District's decision Bruno v. State, 704 So. 2d 134 (Fla. 1st DCA 1997). There is not one mention of the Florida Department of Highway Safety and Motor Vehicles or the Division of Driver Licenses in Bruno. If this Court does have conflict jurisdiction, it is Bruno which should be quashed for not expressly recognizing that the reach of State v. White, 660 So. 2d 664 (Fla. 1995), is limited to the law enforcement arresting agency. This is the only way that White can conform with the United States Supreme Court's decisions Arizona v. Evans, 514 U.S. 1 (1995), and United States v. Leon, 468 U.S. 897 (1984).

Second, though stating that it recognizes the directive of article I, section 12 of the Florida Constitution, the majority avoids the requirement that our search and seizure applications comply with the decisions of the United States Supreme Court. As Judge Sharpe correctly recognizes in the Fifth District opinion, the exclusionary rule in this context only excludes evidence which "stems from police or law enforcement employees" unless there is some showing of bad faith reliance by such law enforcement employees. The exclusionary rule operates as a judicially created remedy designed to safeguard against future violations of Fourth Amendment rights through the rule's general deterrent effect. Where "the exclusionary rule does not result in appreciable deterrence, then, clearly, its use . . . is unwarranted." United States v. Janis, 428 U.S. 433, 454 (1976). The exclusionary rule was historically designed as a means of deterring police misconduct, not mistakes by court employees and there is no evidence that court employees are inclined to ignore or subvert the Fourth Amendment. Finally, and most important, there is no basis for believing that application of the exclusionary rule in these circumstances will have a significant effect on court employees responsible for informing the police that a warrant has been quashed. It is patently erroneous to stretch the reach of the exclusionary rule to the Division of Driver Licenses.

REVIEW SECTION

READING COMPREHENSION

Elaborate the logic in defining, or not defining, the Division of Driver Licenses as a law enforcement agency.

What rules of law apply in this case?

THINKING CRITICALLY

Which opinion of the court do you agree with and why?

SECTION 2: THE DEFENSE OF ENTRAPMENT

OVERVIEW

What if you are going about your routine business and an undercover officer convinces you to commit a crime you would not have committed without his/her encouragement? Though attitudes have shifted remarkably, this is the purpose of the defense of entrapment. The logic behind this defense is to balance the need to cast a net for habitual criminals, while attempting not to capture otherwise law-abiding citizens. Historically, this practice arose to capture those involved in consensual crimes such as gambling and prostitution. This is known as an affirmative defense, not a constitutional right, and requires defendants have the burden of proving some evidence of entrapment. There is both a subjective and an objective test for entrapment.

The subjective test has been adopted by most states and the federal government, and requires the defendant to show that encouragement on the part of law enforcement crossed the line from acceptable to unacceptable. Defendants must demonstrate both that there existed no desire to commit the crime prior to the act of encouragement, and that the government's encouragement caused them to commit the crime in question. The question rests solely on intent. If intent was with the defendant, no entrapment occurred. If intent was with the government, entrapment did occur. Once a defendant has produced some evidence of persuasion, the government then must prove that indeed the defendant was predisposed to commit such a crime, thus shifting back the balance of intent.

The objective test of entrapment is also known as the hypothetical person test, and is adopted by a minority, but increasing number, of the courts. In this test, regardless of the defendant's past record or criminal inclination, the question is whether or not a reasonable, law-abiding citizen would have been induced to commit the crime with encouragement from law enforcement.

CASE

Herrera v. State of Florida is an examination of <u>Herrera v. State, 580 So.2d 653, 654 (Fla. 4th DCA 1991)</u>, wherein the district court found the following question to be of great public importance: Do Instruction 3.04(c)(2), Florida Standard Jury Instructions in Criminal Cases, and Section 777.201(2), Florida Statutes (1989), both applicable to offenses after 1987, unconstitutionally shift the burden to the defense to prove entrapment? The Supreme Court of Florida answers the question in the negative, and approves Herrera.

HERRERA V. STATE OF FLORIDA
Supreme Court of Florida
594 So.2d 275 (1992)

The State charged Herrera with trafficking in cocaine, conspiracy to traffic in cocaine, and obstructing an officer without violence. These charges resulted from a sting operation initiated by a confidential informant, and Herrera raised entrapment as an affirmative defense. Herrera asked the trial court to give the jury the former standard instruction on entrapment, the last paragraph of which stated: "On the issue of entrapment, the State must convince you beyond a reasonable doubt that the defendant was not entrapped." Instead, the court gave the jury the current standard instruction on entrapment, the final paragraph of which reads: "On the issue of entrapment, the defendant must prove to you by a preponderance of the evidence that his criminal conduct occurred as the result of entrapment." The jury convicted Herrera of the trafficking and obstruction charges, for which the trial court imposed consecutive fifteen and one-year sentences, respectively. The district court affirmed the convictions, but remanded for resentencing, and certified the question set out above.

The new paragraph in the entrapment instruction is based on section 777.201, Florida Statutes (1989), which reads as follows:

(1) A law enforcement officer, a person engaged in cooperation with a law enforcement officer, or a person acting as an agent of a law enforcement officer perpetrates an entrapment if, for the purpose of obtaining evidence of the commission of a crime, he induces or encourages and, as a

direct result, causes another person to engage in conduct constituting such crime by employing methods of persuasion or inducement which create a substantial risk that such crime will be committed by a person other than one who is ready to commit it.

(2) A person prosecuted for a crime shall be acquitted if he proves by a preponderance of the evidence that his criminal conduct occurred as a result of an entrapment. The issue of entrapment shall be tried by the trier of fact.

This section is derived from chapter 87-243, section 42, Laws of Florida, and codifies, for the first time, a general entrapment defense. This Court approved the new instruction for use in Florida's trial courts, but noted the instructions committee's concern over the constitutionality of the legislation and this Court's refusal to consider such an issue in nonadversarial proceedings.

Herrera argues that this Court's decisions on previous versions of the entrapment instruction demonstrate that the new instruction and subsection 777.201(2) violate the due process clauses of the United States and Florida Constitutions. The State, on the other hand, contends that the instruction and statute are constitutional because they shift only the burden of persuasion of an affirmative defense, not the burden of proving the elements of the crime charged and the defendant's guilt. The two district courts that have considered this issue have agreed with the State (Krajewski v. State, 587 So.2d 1175 (Fla. 4th DCA 1991); Gonzalez v. State, 571 So.2d 1346 (Fla. 3d DCA 1990). We do likewise.

Entrapment is a judicially created affirmative defense designed to prevent the government from contending a defendant is guilty of a crime where the government officials are the instigators of his conduct. To this end the predisposition and criminal design of the defendant are relevant. If the defendant is a person otherwise innocent whom the government is seeking to punish for an alleged offense which is the product of the creative activity of its own officials, common justice requires that the accused be permitted to prove it. Thus, we have defined the essential element of the defense of entrapment as the absence of a predisposition of the defendant to commit the offense. Subsection 777.201(1) now provides that lack of predisposition is an element of the defense.

Over the years Florida courts have gone back and forth on which side must produce evidence regarding the defendant's having been entrapped. Some cases hold that defendants must show entrapment by proving their lack of predisposition toward criminal activity (Priestly v. State, 450 So.2d 289 (Fla. 4th DCA 1984); Evenson v. State, 277 So.2d 587 (Fla. 4th DCA 1973); Koptyra v. State, 172 So.2d 628 (Fla. 2d DCA 1965). Other cases have held that the State must disprove entrapment by showing the defendant's predisposition to commit the offense (Moody v. State, 359 So.2d 557 (Fla. 4th DCA 1978). Subsection 777.201(2) evidences the legislature's intent that the defendant should prove entrapment instead of requiring the State to disprove it.

Entrapment is an affirmative defense and, as such, is in the nature of an avoidance of the charges. As this Court has previously stated: "An 'affirmative defense' is any defense that assumes the complaint or charges to be correct but raises other facts that, if true, would establish a valid excuse or justification or a right to engage in the conduct in question." State v. Cohen, 568 So.2d 49, 51 (Fla.1990). In considering affirmative defenses the United States Supreme Court has held that "it is normally 'within the power of the State to regulate procedures under which its laws are carried out, including the burden of producing evidence and the burden of persuasion,' and its decision in this regard is not subject to proscription under the Due Process Clause unless it offends some principle of justice so rooted in the traditions and conscience of our people as to be ranked as fundamental" Patterson v. New York, 432 U.S. 197, 201-02, 97 S.Ct. 2319, 2322, 53 L.Ed.2d 281 (1977). The burden of proving the elements of a crime cannot be shifted to a defendant. If "a State's method of allocating the burdens of proof does not lessen the State's burden to prove every element of the offense charged," however, "a defendant's constitutional rights are not violated." Walton v. Arizona, 497 U.S. 639, 110 S.Ct. 3047, 3055, 111 L.Ed.2d 511 (1990). Earlier Florida cases recognized the principles set out in these more recent Supreme Court cases.

For the first time the State, through the legislature, has decided that the burden is on defendants claiming entrapment to prove that they were entrapped. We hold that allocating this burden to a defendant is not unconstitutional. As stated earlier, the lack of predisposition to commit the crime charged is an essential element of the defense of entrapment. The predisposition to commit a crime, however, is not the same as the intent to commit that crime. As explained by the New Jersey Supreme Court in its consideration of this issue, "predisposition is not the same as *mens rea*. The former involves the defendant's character and criminal inclinations; the latter involves the defendant's state of mind while carrying out the allegedly criminal act" State v. Rockholt, 96 N.J. 570, 476 A.2d 1236, 1242 (1984). Requiring a defendant to show lack of predisposition does not relieve the State of its burden to prove that the defendant committed the crime charged. The standard instructions require the State to prove beyond a reasonable doubt all the elements of the crime, and we find no violation of due process in requiring defendants to bear the burden of persuading their juries that they were entrapped.

Therefore, we answer the certified question in the negative and approve the district court's decision in Herrera. It is so ordered.

REVIEW SECTION

READING COMPREHENSION

What are the facts of this case?

What does the Florida Statue read regarding entrapment?

THINKING CRITICALLY

This court noted: "The standard instructions require the State to prove beyond a reasonable doubt all the elements of the crime, and we find no violation of due process in requiring defendants to bear the burden of persuading their juries that they were entrapped." In your opinion, should the state or the defendant bear the burden of persuading a jury of entrapment?

CASE

Munoz v. State of Florida is a review of State v. Munoz, 586 So.2d 515 (Fla. 1st DCA 1991), wherein the district court determined that section 777.201, Florida Statutes (1987), abolished the objective entrapment test. The Supreme Court of Florida finds that in enacting section 777.201 the legislature did eliminate the objective test of entrapment, but also finds that the legislature cannot prohibit the judiciary from objectively reviewing the issue of entrapment to the extent such a review involves the due process clause of article I, section 9, of the Florida Constitution. As to the facts of this case, the court does not reach a due process objective evaluation of entrapment because, under the subjective test established by section 777.201, Manuel Munoz was entrapped as a matter of law.

MUNOZ V. STATE OF FLORIDA
Supreme Court of Florida
629 So.2d 90, 18 Fla. L. Weekly S537 (1993)

In order for this Court to properly evaluate the subjective test set forth in section 777.201 and determine whether section 777.201 abolished the objective entrapment test, it is necessary to examine the evolvement of the entrapment defense under both Florida law. In 1985, State v. Glosson, 462 So.2d 1082 (Fla.1985), this Court evaluated the issue of entrapment under the due process provision in article I, section 9 of the Florida Constitution. Subsequently, in Cruz v. State, 465 So.2d 516 (1985), we specifically rejected the subjective test for entrapment and adopted instead the basic principles of the objective standard of entrapment. In doing so, we articulated a threshold test for evaluating entrapment as a matter of law. Then, in 1987, the Legislature enacted section 777.201 establishing the subjective test for entrapment.

In reviewing the history of the entrapment defense in Florida, it is important to first examine the constitutional due process issue addressed by this Court in Glosson. In that case, Glosson was charged with trafficking in and conspiring to traffic in cannabis as the result of a reverse-sting operation. The sting was conducted through a paid informant. For the informant's services in assisting in this and other sting operations and subsequent prosecutions, the State agreed to pay the informant ten percent of all civil forfeiture proceedings resulting from any case the informant initiated. Asserting that the State's conduct violated his due process rights, Glosson moved to dismiss the charges. The trial court agreed that the State's conduct was improper as a matter of law and dismissed the charges. On appeal before this Court, the State argued that the due process defense was not available to a predisposed defendant. We disagreed. Under the facts of Glosson, we found the behavior of law enforcement officials in entering into a contingency contract to obtain convictions to be violative of due process under the Florida Constitution. Under that objective philosophy of entrapment, we determined that Glosson was entitled to a dismissal as a matter of law.

Shortly thereafter, we addressed the issue of entrapment in Cruz. In Cruz, law enforcement personnel positioned an officer, who appeared inebriated and who had money hanging visibly from his pocket, as a decoy in a high crime area. Cruz took the money from the decoy's pocket and was arrested as he walked from the scene. The police officers had not been seeking a particular individual nor were they aware of any prior criminal acts by Cruz. Focusing on Cruz's lack of predisposition, the trial court dismissed the charges, finding that Cruz was entrapped as a matter of law. In reviewing the trial court's decision in Cruz, we stated that the federal subjective test of entrapment generally involved a question of predisposition. However, we rejected the federal subjective standard, adopting instead the principles of the objective standard. Applying the objective threshold test to the facts in Cruz, we concluded that law enforcement agents had not targeted any specific activity. Consequently, we determined that Cruz had been entrapped as a matter of law.

In adopting this objective standard, we propounded a judicially formulated two-part objective threshold test for determining entrapment as a matter of law. Under that test, entrapment has not occurred as a matter of law where police activity (1) has as its end the interruption of a specific ongoing criminal activity; and (2) utilizes means reasonably tailored to apprehend those involved in the ongoing criminal activity. We did not, however, expressly find that such an evaluation was mandated by the due process clause contained in article I, section 9, of the Florida Constitution.

Subsequent to our decision in Cruz, the Florida Legislature, in 1987, enacted section 777.201. The legislative history of that statute clearly reflects that section 777.201 was enacted to reinstate the federal subjective test we rejected in Cruz. After the legislature adopted section 777.201, we again addressed the entrapment defense State v. Hunter, 586 So.2d 319 (Fla.1991). However, the offenses at issue in Hunter occurred before section 777.201's enactment. Consequently, section 777.201 was not at issue before this Court and was not discussed in the Hunter opinion. Nevertheless, Hunter is still important in the evolving development of entrapment law in Florida given its application of the Cruz entrapment test and related due process considerations.

In Hunter, Ron Diamond, a convicted drug-trafficker facing fifteen years in prison, sought a sentence reduction or suspension under section 893.135(3), Florida Statutes (1985), which allowed the prosecutor to request a sentence reduction for a defendant who provided substantial assistance in obtaining the conviction of others. In seeking to have his sentence reduced, Diamond arranged a deal between David Hunter and Kelly Conklin as follows: Diamond noticed that another resident of his apartment complex, Kelly Conklin, openly smoked marijuana. Conklin, a twenty-one-year-old recent graduate of an art school, had no prior criminal record. He lived with his pregnant girlfriend and worked for an advertising firm run by David Hunter. Approaching Conklin, Diamond asked for assistance in obtaining drugs, but Conklin could not provide any sources for the drugs that Diamond wanted. Diamond became more insistent and began telephoning Conklin almost daily. Eventually Conklin turned to Hunter, who agreed to help find drugs to sell to Diamond. Hunter sought out a former employee who provided the drugs, but, in doing so, insisted that Hunter, not Conklin, complete the transaction. When Hunter attempted to close the transaction with the police undercover buyers, both he and Conklin were arrested. At trial, both Conklin and Hunter presented the defense of entrapment to a jury, but the jury convicted them as charged. The district court of appeal, relying on our decision in Glosson, found a due process violation under article I, section 9, of the Florida Constitution, and directed that the charges against both Conklin and Hunter be dismissed. On review by this Court, we rejected the district court's determination that a due process violation had occurred. In Hunter, in applying our objective test from Cruz, we found that Conklin had established entrapment as a matter of law because the government knew of no ongoing drug-trafficking at the time Diamond approached Conklin. We rejected the application of the Cruz objective test to Hunter's case, however, because Hunter's involvement was voluntary and because Hunter was induced to commit the crime by Conklin rather than by the State or one of its agents.

Finally, we addressed section 777.201 in Herrera v. State, 594 So.2d 275 (Fla.1992). In that case, defendant Herrera, as a result of a sting operation, was charged with trafficking in cocaine, conspiracy to traffic in cocaine, and obstructing an officer without violence. The sting operation had been initiated by a confidential informant, and Herrera raised entrapment as an affirmative defense. At trial, Herrera requested that the pre-section 777.201 standard jury instruction be given to the jury rather than the jury instruction written to comply with section 777.201. Herrera requested the previous instruction on the grounds that the section 777.201 and the new instruction violated the due process clauses of both the federal and Florida Constitutions because they improperly placed the burden on a defendant to prove that the defendant was entrapped.

On review, we rejected Herrera's argument. We stated that it was not unconstitutional to shift the burden to defendants to prove they were entrapped. Additionally, we stated that lack of predisposition is an essential element of the defense of entrapment as a result of section 777.201's enactment. In rendering this decision, we did not discuss the subjective, two-step burden of proof test or a trial court's ability to rule as a matter of law on the issue of entrapment.

District court considerations of this Court's due process pronouncements under the Florida Constitution in Glosson, and this Court's adoption of the objective standard of entrapment in Cruz and our application of that standard, in conjunction with the legislative enactment of section 777.201 and our decision in Herrera, have created substantial uncertainty as to the status and application of the entrapment defense in Florida. Obviously, this uncertainty has caused the district courts of appeal to render conflicting decisions regarding the effect of section 777.201. By this opinion, we attempt to set forth specific principles of Florida's entrapment defense to harmonize the law and to ensure uniform application of the entrapment defense in Florida.

The legislature has the authority to statutorily establish entrapment as a defense in this state. However, the legislature cannot enact a statute that overrules a judicially established legal principle enforcing or protecting a federal or Florida constitutional right. Accordingly, section 777.201 cannot overrule a decision of this Court regarding entrapment in any case decided under the due process provision of article I, section 9, of the Florida Constitution. Although the United States Supreme Court has yet to determine in a case before it that the conduct of law enforcement agents in an entrapment case has violated federal due process rights, it has determined that law enforcement agents' conduct could, in fact, violate such rights. On the other hand, as noted above, we have determined, under the circumstances in Glosson, that the conduct of law enforcement agents violated the due process clause of the Florida Constitution.

Although the legislature may not enact a statute limiting the application of a constitutional right, it may overrule judicially established substantive principles that do not implicate established constitutional rights. Thus, to the extent the objective test for the entrapment defense adopted by this Court in Cruz was not based on due process, the legislature had the authority to overrule that judicially established standard and to establish entrapment as a defense to be evaluated under the subjective test. As we indicated in the Florida cases outlined above, it is the focus on the behavior of law enforcement officials rather than the objective test itself that implicates due process considerations. Consequently, the legislature had the authority to overrule the judicially established objective test set forth in Cruz to the extent that such objective test did not include due process concerns. As such, we find that the specific test set forth in Cruz has been eliminated by section 777.201. Additionally, we find that the subjective test set forth in section 777.201 is the test to be applied on the issue of entrapment in the absence of egregious law enforcement conduct. As noted above, however, in the presence of egregious law enforcement conduct, an entrapment defense is to be evaluated under the due process provision of article I, section 9, of the Florida Constitution as in Glosson and Williams.

Given the history of the entrapment defense, we find that the legislature, in establishing a legislatively-created entrapment defense through section 777.201, codified the subjective test delineated by the United States Supreme Court as the means for determining the application of that defense. Three principles arise under this test. The first two involve questions of fact and differing burdens of proof, and the third addresses whether the issue of entrapment must be submitted to the jury or whether the issue can be decided by the judge as a matter of law.

The first question to be addressed under the subjective test is whether an agent of the government induced the accused to commit the offense charged. On this issue, the accused has the burden of proof and, pursuant to section 777.201, must establish this factor by a preponderance of the evidence. If the first question is answered affirmatively, then a second question arises as to whether the accused was predisposed to commit the offense charged; that is, whether the accused was awaiting any propitious opportunity or was ready and willing, without persuasion, to commit the offense. On this second question, according to our decision in Herrera, the defendant initially has the burden to establish lack of predisposition. However, as soon as the defendant produces evidence of no predisposition, the burden then shifts to the prosecution to rebut this evidence beyond a reasonable doubt. In rebutting the defendant's evidence of lack of predisposition, the prosecution may make "an appropriate and searching inquiry" into the conduct of the accused and present evidence of the accused's prior criminal history, even though such evidence is normally inadmissible. However, admission of evidence of predisposition is limited to the extent it demonstrates predisposition on the part of the accused both prior to and independent of the government acts.

The third question under the subjective test is whether the entrapment evaluation should be submitted to a jury. Section 777.201 directs that the issue of entrapment be submitted to the trier of fact. Such direction is consistent with the subjective evaluation of entrapment because the two factual issues above ordinarily present questions of disputed facts to be submitted to the jury as the trier of fact. However, if the factual circumstances of a case are not in dispute, if the accused establishes that the government induced the accused to commit the offense charged, and if the State is unable to demonstrate sufficient evidence of predisposition prior to and independent of the government conduct at issue, then the trial judge has the authority to rule on the issue of predisposition as a matter of law because no factual "question of predisposition" is at issue. Such a ruling could be proper even when the government presents evidence of prior convictions. We reject any construction of section 777.201 that would require such an issue of law to be submitted to a jury. Under the constitution of this state, juries, as the finders of fact, decide factually disputed issues and judges apply the law to the facts as those facts are found by the jury. To construe section 777.201 as mandating that the issue of entrapment is to be submitted to a jury for determination as a matter of law would result in an unconstitutional construction that would violate article I, section 9, of the Florida Constitution. Consequently, we construe section 777.201 as requiring the question of predisposition to be submitted to a jury when factual issues are in dispute or when reasonable persons could draw different conclusions from the facts. In certain instances however, the trial judge and appellate courts clearly have the authority to rule on the issue as a matter of law. To hold otherwise would violate procedural due process.

Having thus determined the state of the entrapment defense in Florida under section 777.201, we turn to the facts of the instant case. Manuel Munoz, the owner of "Video Den," was charged with two counts of sale or distribution of harmful materials to a person under 18 years of age, in violation of section 847.012, Florida Statutes (1989). The record reflects that those charges stemmed from the following sequence of events. The Bay County Sheriff's Office received an anonymous complaint that minors were able to rent X-rated videotapes from a video store known as "Top Banana." In investigating whether minors were able to obtain X-rated videotapes from Top Banana, the sheriff's office decided to spread the investigation to other video stores in the Bay County area that rented X-rated movies. The names of the other video stores selling or renting X-rated videotapes were obtained by searching the Yellow Pages of the local phone book. Consequently, even though Video Den was totally unconnected to Top Banana and even though the sheriff's office had received no complaints regarding Video Den and had no independent knowledge as to whether Video Den was renting X-rated movies to minors, the sheriff's office decided to target Video Den in its investigation.

In conducting its investigation, the sheriff's office obtained a false membership card from Video Den under the fictitious name of Brian Jackson. The membership card reflected that Jackson was thirty-four years old. The sheriff's office also obtained the assistance of a sixteen-year-old girl who had recently been arrested for negotiating the purchase of a pound of marijuana. It is undisputed that the juvenile informant appeared to be at least eighteen years of age. The Sheriff's office gave the membership card to the juvenile informant and instructed her to rent an X-rated videotape from Video Den, to lie about her age, and to lie about her relationship with Jackson. She was instructed to indicate that she was either the sister or girlfriend of Jackson.

Video Den maintained its X-rated videotapes in a separate room and posted a sign explicitly stating that no person under the age of 18 was allowed to enter the room. On her first trip to Video Den, the juvenile informant obtained an X-rated video from the "adults only" room and presented the false membership card to Munoz at the cash register. In renting the X-rated video, she explained to Munoz that she was Jackson's girlfriend. Approximately two weeks later, she again rented two X-rated movies from Video Den. On the second trip, Munoz asked her age and she lied. She explained that she had walked to the store and had forgotten her driver's license. Additionally, she insisted that she had rented these movies before and again claimed to be either the girlfriend or sister of Jackson. After Munoz allowed the juvenile to rent the videotapes, he was charged with the sale or distribution of harmful materials to a minor.

The trial judge dismissed the charges against Munoz on the basis of entrapment as a matter of law based on the objective entrapment test set forth in Cruz. The district court reversed, holding that the legislature had abolished the objective entrapment test set forth in Cruz through the enactment of section 777.201.

Given the unrefuted facts in this case, we find that we need not address whether the conduct of law enforcement personnel constitutes a due process violation under article I, section 9, because we find that, under the subjective test set forth above, Munoz was the subject of entrapment as a matter of law. First, the undisputed facts clearly establish that law enforcement agents induced Munoz to rent the videotapes to the juvenile. Second, there was no evidence whatsoever of predisposition on Munoz's part prior to and independent of the government inducement. As such, we reject the State's contention that the issue of entrapment in this case should be submitted to a jury.

For the reasons expressed, we find that, through section 777.201, the Legislature established entrapment as a statutory defense to be evaluated under the federal subjective entrapment test and, by such action, eliminated the objective test. We additionally find that section 777.201 neither prohibits the judiciary from objectively reviewing the issue of entrapment to the extent such a review involves the due process clause of article I, section 9, of the Florida Constitution, nor prohibits the judiciary from determining under the subjective test that, in certain circumstances, entrapment has been established as a matter of law. In this case, we find that, under the subjective test, Manuel Munoz was entrapped as a matter of law. Although the district court in this case correctly noted that section 777.201 abolished the objective entrapment test set forth in Cruz, it did not reach the conclusion that Munoz was nevertheless entrapped as a matter of law. Consequently, we quash the decision of the district court and remand this case with the direction that the trial court's order of dismissal be reinstated. It is so ordered.

REVIEW SECTION

READING COMPREHENSION

Detail the history of the entrapment defense in Florida case law and the Florida legislature.

THINKING CRITICALLY

Speculate on the status and application of the entrapment defense in Florida. Support your position.

Elaborate the elements of the objective and subjective tests. Defend which test you believe should be used in the entrapment defense.

CONCLUSION

This chapter addressed in detail the exclusionary rule and the defense of entrapment. Though neither are backed directly by constitutional rights, each has been established by the U.S. Supreme Court with the intent to enforce constitutional rights. Both the exclusionary rule and the entrapment defense have been the subject of much debate in this country, both expressed in case law and in the legislature.

Chapter Eleven

Constitutional Violations: Other Remedies Against Government Misconduct

We have elaborated the exclusionary rule and the defense of entrapment which are remedies available to defendants in criminal trial cases, however there are also remedies an individual may pursue against an officer that are not available at the trial stage. Such remedies include prosecuting the officer through criminal law which rarely occurs as police misconduct is rarely viewed by the courts as a criminal action, suing a government official or entity through civil law in a state or federal court, or administrative discipline of an officer outside of the judicial system.

This chapter will review:

(1)   Remedies for official misconduct; and

(2)   Failure to protect by law enforcement.

SECTION 1: REMEDIES FOR OFFICIAL MISCONDUCT

OVERVIEW

Because criminal prosecution of an officer is rare, we will turn our attention to suing a government official or entity through the use of civil law at the state or federal level. Suing an individual law federal enforcement officer if a constitutional tort action or *Bivens* action named for the case decided in 1971 (*Bivens . Six Unnamed FBI Agents*). This case created a private right to sue federal officers who have violated a constitutional right of an individual. Plaintiffs are required to prove that officers were acting under color of authority and that the action of the officer did indeed deprive the individual of a constitutional right. Proof of these two elements however, does not automatically translate into a successful outcome of the case. Law enforcement personnel may employ the qualified immunity or 'good faith' defense wherein they demonstrate the action in question met the test of objective legal reasonableness which is measured by the legal rules established at the time of the officer's action. This defense was created as a balance to prevent frivolous lawsuits arising from actions that officers must use broad discretion in making in performance of job duties and protection of the public.

A lawsuit filed against the federal government for the constitutional torts of their officers is a Federal Tort Claims Act (FTCA) action. Under the held-over doctrine of sovereign immunity, a government cannot be sued without their consent, though laws that at least to some degree waive this immunity are employed by most states and U.S. governments.

If an individual wants to sue a state officer, they can use either a state tort lawsuits or a federal U.S. Civil Rights Act lawsuit. Keep in mind that when pursuing a state tort action, officers are afforded the defense of official immunity. A Civil Right Act action allows plaintiffs to use the federal court to sue state, county, and municipal officers for violations of federal constitutional rights. The standard of proof required is very similar to that in a *Bivens* action. Finally, to sue a state or local government, a suit can be brought as a state tort action or as a U.S. Civil Rights Action.

CASE

In *Hargrove v. Town of Cocoa Beach*, the plaintiff seeks reversal of an order of the trial judge sustaining a motion to dismiss her complaint against the Town in an action seeking damages for the alleged wrongful death of appellant's husband. This court determines whether a municipal corporation should continue to enjoy immunity from liability for the wrongful acts of police officers.

HARGROVE V. TOWN OF COCOA BEACH
96 So.2d 130 (Fla. 1957)

Appellant, as plaintiff, alleged that her husband was incarcerated in the town jail while in a helpless condition because of excessive intoxication. She alleged that the jailor locked all the doors and departed, leaving no guard or other attendant on duty; that during the night the cell became filled with smoke resulting in the fatal suffocation of appellant's husband. For the alleged negligence in leaving the jail unattended and the prisoner unprotected against the fire, thereby producing the death of her husband, Mrs. Hargrove sought damages from the City. The trial judge sustained a motion to dismiss the complaint on the theory that the municipality was immune to liability for this type of tort. Reversal of his order is now sought.

The appellant recognizes our prior decisions on the subject and frankly requests us to recede therefrom. The appellee, of course, cites our own precedents to support the ruling of the trial judge. We are here faced squarely with an appeal to recede from our previously announced rule which immunizes a municipal corporation against liability for torts committed by police officers. The rule against municipal liability for torts has been the subject of thousands of pages of learned dissertations. We are told that since 1900 well over two hundred law review articles alone have been written on the subject. Innumerable textbooks have made their dontribution, most of them adversely critical. Our own precedents reveal that this Court has many times had the matter under consideration. Because of these comprehensive discussions of the subject, there is very little that we can now add. Our own present study of the matter leads us to a consideration of the problem as one arising out of an historical recognition of a division of municipal functions into two categories, to wit, governmental and proprietary. It has been held that in the exercise of so-called governmental functions, the municipality is immune to liability. In the exercise of proprietary functions, the municipality has been held responsible for the torts of its agents.

Immunization in the exercise of governmental functions has been traditionally put on the theory that 'the king can do no wrong but his ministers may'. In applying this theory the courts have transposed into our democratic system the concept that the sovereign is divine and that divinity is beyond reproach. In preserving the theory they seem to have overlooked completely the wrongs that produced our Declaration of Independence and in the ultimate resulted in the Revolutionary

War. We, therefore, feel that the time has arrived to declare this doctrine anachoristic not only to our system of justice but to our traditional concepts of democratic government.

The immunity theory has been further supported with the idea that it is better for an individual to suffer a grievous wrong than to impose liability on the people vicariously through their government. If there is anything more than a sham to our constitutional guarantee that the courts shall always be open to redress wrongs and to our sense of justice that there shall be a remedy for every wrong committed, then certainly this basis for the rule cannot be supported. Tracing the rule to its ultimate progenitor we are led to the English case of Russel v. Men of Devon, 2 T.R. 667, 100 Eng.Rep.R. 359 (1788). The Men of Devon decision merely relieved the inhabitants of an unincorporated county from liability for damages resulting from a defective bridge. As early as 1850 City of Tallahassee v. Fortune, 3 Fla. 19, the Men of Devon decision was very clearly explained and distinguished. Our Court then pointed out that the leading English precedent turned on the proposition that it was an action against all of the people of an unincorporated community having no corporate fund or legal means of obtaining one. The law would not impose the burden on each individual citizen.

The appellee here contends that any recession from the rule of immunity should come about by legislation rather than judicial decree. It is insisted that the immunity rule is a part of the common law which we have adopted and that therefore its abolition should come about only by statute. We are here compelled to disagree. Assuming that the immunity rule had its inception in the Men of Devon case, and most legal historians agree that it did, it should be noted that this case was decided in 1788, some twelve years after our Declaration of Independence. Be that as it may, our own feeling is that the courts should be alive to the demands of justice. We can see no necessity for insisting on legislative action in a matter which the courts themselves originated.

The problem in Florida has become more confusing because of an effort to prune and pare the rule of immunity rather than to uproot it bodily and lay it aside as we should any other archaic and outmoded concept. This pruning approach has produced numerous strange and incongruous results. Lewis v. City of Miami, 127 Fla. 426, 173 So. 150 held the municipality liable to a prisoner who had contracted a communicable disease while in the city jail. Under the rule we have followed, if a police officer assaults and injures a prisoner, the municipality is immune but if the police officer is working the prisoner on the public streets and negligently permits his injury, the municipality can be held liable. If the police officer is driving an automobile and negligently injures a citizen, the municipality is liable but if the same police officer gets out of the same automobile and wrongfully assaults a citizen, the municipality is immune from responsibility.

We have mentioned these incongruities in the application of the immunization doctrine in Florida merely to justify the position, which we here take, that the time has arrived to face this matter squarely in the interest of justice and place the responsibility for wrongs where it should be. In doing this we are thoroughly cognizant that some may contend that we are failing to remain blindly loyal to the doctrine of *stare decisis*. However, we must recognize that the law is not static. The great body of our laws is the product of progressive thinking which attunes traditional concepts to the needs and demands of changing times. The modern city is in substantial measure a large business institution. While it enjoys many of the basic powers of government, it nonetheless is an incorporated organization which exercises those powers primarily for the benefit of the people within the municipal limits who enjoy the services rendered pursuant to the powers. To continue to endow this type of organization with sovereign divinity appears to us to predicate the law of the Twentieth Century upon an Eighteenth Century anachronism. Judicial consistency loses its virtue when it is degraded by the vice of injustice.

We therefore now recede from our prior decisions which hold that a municipal corporation is immune from liability for the torts of police officers. Affirmatively we hold that a municipal corporation may be held liable for the torts of police officers under the doctrine of respondent superior. We think it advisable to protect our conclusion against any interpretation that would impose liability on the municipality in the exercise of legislative or judicial, or quasi-legislative or quasi-judicial, functions. Subject to the limitations above announced, we here merely hold that when an individual suffers a direct, personal injury proximately caused by the negligence of a municipal employee while acting within the scope of his employment, the injured individual is entitled to redress for the wrong done. To support the rule we hearken back to our original Florida precedent, City of Tallahassee v. Fortune. Our judicial forebears there held that where an individual suffers a special personal damage not common to the community but proximately resulting from the negligence of the municipal corporation acting through its employees, such individual is entitled to redress. We think this general rule was sound when it was announced in 1850 and it should be reestablished as the law of Florida. Within the framework of the above announced limitations this is the rule of our present opinion. In this vein, we therefore point out that instead of disregarding the rule of *state decisis*, we now merely restore the original concepts of our jurisprudence to a position of priority in order to eradicate the deviations that have in our view detracted from the justice of the initial rule.

The further point is here made to the effect that our death by wrongful act statute (Section 768.01, Florida Statutes, F.S.A.) in imposing liability on corporations for wrongful death is not applicable to municipal corporations. We did hold in City of St. Petersburg v. Carter, Fla.1949, 39 So.2d 804, that in view of the subject matter regulated by the statute there under consideration, a municipal corporation could not have been within the contemplation of the legislature when it gave the Railroad Commission authority over certain corporations. On the other hand we have on several other occasions, directly or by necessary implication, considered municipal corporations as being within the contemplation of the legislature in enacting statutes with reference to 'corporations'. We hold that a municipal corporation was within the contemplation of the legislature when it adopted Section 768.01, Florida Statutes, F.S.A.

The conclusion here announced has not been hastily formulated. We add in absolute fairness to the trial judge who heard this case below that, in ruling as he did, he properly relied on our precedents. We here merely recede from the prior cases in order to establish a rule which we are convinced will be productive of results more nearly consonant with the demands of justice. The judgment appealed from is therefore reversed and the cause remanded for further proceedings consistent herewith.

REVIEW SECTION

READING COMPREHENSION

Detail the logic of the court in making its finding.

What is the immunity theory?

THINKING CRITICALLY

Does government liability for the actions of its officers negatively effect performance of duties or serve as a check against government abuse of power? Articulate your rationale.

CASE

City of Coral Gables v. Giblin involves a suit brought against the City of Coral Gables and one of its officers by an individual claiming false imprisonment and thus violation of due process rights.

CITY OF CORAL GABLES V. GIBLIN
District Court of Appeal of Florida, Third District.
127 So.2d 914 (1961)

The appellee, plaintiff below, instituted an action against the appellant City of Coral Gables, and Anderson, a police officer, for false imprisonment. The complaint alleged that Anderson, an employee of the City of Coral Gables, did, while acting within the scope and course of his employment, stop the appellee, who was proceeding in an automobile with her husband to the Dade County Courthouse, and thereupon proceeded to prepare a citation showing that the appellee had exceeded the lawful speed limits; that Anderson wrongfully and unlawfully delayed the preparation of the citation for an unreasonable length of time, depriving the appellee of her freedom and right to proceed and that thereafter, due to such delay, the appellee's husband drove her from the scene at a lawful rate of speed to a point approximately two and one-half miles away within the corporate limits of the City of Miami, where Anderson accosted them on his motorcycle and, by sounding his siren and reaching for his pistol, required the appellee's husband to stop their automobile; that upon stopping the automobile, Anderson, without cause or authority to do so, unlawfully, wrongfully and maliciously deprived appellee of her freedom and compelled the appellee to be driven to the municipal jail of the City of Coral Gables and did unlawfully, wrongfully and maliciously imprison her and deprive her of her freedom. There followed the charge that the appellee suffered loss of liberty, mental suffering, physical injury, humiliation and embarrassment as a result of the alleged wrongful acts. One paragraph of the complaint charged the appellant with negligent employment of Anderson as a police officer and his retention with knowledge of his incompetency. An answer was filed on behalf of the appellant which adopted the allegations of the answer filed on behalf of Anderson but denied the charge of negligent employment and retention of Anderson in the service of the city with knowledge of his incompetency.

Upon the issues made, the cause was tried before a jury and at the conclusion of the appellee's case, both the appellee and appellant moved for directed verdicts. At this time the appellee withdrew the charge against the appellant city that it was negligent in employing Anderson and retaining him in its employ. The trial judge denied the appellant's motion for directed verdict but granted the appellee's motion on the ground that appellee's arrest by Anderson was illegal. The cause went to the jury on the sole issue of damages, both compensatory and punitive, resulting in a verdict for the appellee in the sum of $34,000 against appellant and Anderson. Anderson has not appealed the judgment.

The testimony and evidence at trial developed that on the morning of January 23, 1959, the appellee, accompanied by her husband, was proceeding from their home, when their automobile, driven by the appellee, was stopped by Anderson, a police officer of the appellant city. The appellee's automobile was stopped within the municipal limits of the City of Coral Gables as a result of a radar check. The automobile operated by appellee was clocked at 36 miles per hour where the lawful posted rate of speed was 25 miles per hour. Upon stopping the appellee's car, Anderson took her driver's license, walked to the back of the automobile to obtain appellee's automobile license number, went to the right side of the appellee's car and obtained the inspection sticker number, and at that time, was allegedly apprised of the fact that appellee's husband, then one of the judges of the Circuit Court of the Eleventh Judicial Circuit of Dade County, Florida, had to be in court at 9:00 a. m. Other conversation ensued but resulted in the officer's walking to the rear of the automobile to speak to another officer some 30 feet away. While Anderson was conferring with the other police officer, appellee's husband took over the wheel of the automobile, called to Anderson, telling him that they were leaving and proceeded to drive away. At this point the testimony is in conflict as to whether or not Anderson, upon becoming aware that appellee's automobile was about to leave, informed appellee, her husband, or both, that they were under arrest and should not leave.

The appellee testified that Anderson's admonition was directed to her husband, while Anderson's testimony indicates that his command was addressed to the appellee. After they had driven approximately two and one-half miles, a motorcycle driven by Anderson was observed by appellee. The automobile was overtaken and they were ordered to stop by Anderson who had the motorcycle's siren and red light on. The appellee's husband at first refused to stop and did so only when Anderson 'went for his gun.' Thereupon, appellee's automobile was brought to a halt, after which Anderson opened the door, took the ignition keys and went to a private home and telephoned for help. As a result, two police patrol cars arrived on the scene, appellee's husband was personally searched by the police officers, and she and her husband were driven to the police station. The appellee's car was taken to the police station by police officers assisting Anderson. After one fruitless attempt to use the telephone, appellee was allowed to make a telephone call. The appellee and her husband remained in the booking room fifteen or twenty minutes and thereafter appellee accepted a traffic summons, signed it, pleading guilty to the charge of speeding, paid the fine and was released.

Four points have been posed and argued by the appellant under its assignments of error seeking reversal of the judgment. However, we deem it necessary to discuss only one aspect of the case, whether the trial judge erred in directing a verdict against the appellant city. At this point it should be observed that the trial judge, in directing a verdict of liability against the appellant city

181

and its police officer Anderson, did so upon the specific finding that the appellant's employee Anderson had illegally arrested the appellee in the City of Miami. The appellant argues that under the circumstances the arrest in the City of Miami was lawful and did not render the appellant liable for false arrest or false imprisonment. This point is urged upon the theory that when the appellant's employee Anderson stopped the appellee in the City of Coral Gables for the violation of a municipal ordinance, she was then under arrest; that the subsequent attempt by the appellee to flee the custody of the arresting officer permitted the arresting officer, without warrant, to retake the appellee into custody by immediate pursuit pursuant to § 901.22, Fla.Stat., F.S.A. Section 901.22.

Certainly if the arrest were lawful at its inception in the City of Coral Gables, it could be strenuously urged, due to the broad provisions of this statute, that the subsequent rescue or re-arrest in Miami was legal. However, if there were no arrest in Coral Gables, as the appellee contends, then, of course, the provisions of § 901.22 would not apply and in such event, the arrest in Miami would have been without legal authority. Therefore, the legality or illegality of the arrest in the City of Coral Gables becomes an immaterial issue.

Admittedly the appellee had committed no act which constituted a felony or misdemeanor under the law and obviously appellant's police office, absent a warrant, was without authority to arrest appellee for the violation of a municipal ordinance of the City of Coral Gables within the corporate limits of the City of Miami. It is generally conceded that the ordinances of a municipality are enforceable only within the territorial limits of the municipality. Neither City of Coral Gables, its city commission, nor any official thereof, had the authority, either real or apparent, to confer upon one of its police officers the power and authority to arrest a citizen without a warrant outside the territorial limits of the city for a violation of that municipality's traffic regulations. If the City of Coral Gables, as it must be conceded, had no jurisdiction to enforce its ordinances and such ordinances had no effect outside of its prescribed territorial limits, then it follows that no authority could have been conferred upon the appellant's police officer to have made the arrest which it is charged that he made.

Both parties to this appeal, in varying degrees, urge the applicability of the decision of the Supreme Court of Florida in Hargrove v. Town of Cocoa Beach, Fla.1957, 96 So.2d 130, 133, 60 A.L.R.2d 1193, but disagree as to the scope of such decision. The appellant contends that the Hargrove decision covers negligent acts and not intentional torts such as false imprisonment or false arrest, and that it was never intended by that decision to fix liability upon municipal corporations for the actions of their officers, servants or employees that were intentional in character or performed without any legal authority. On the other hand, the appellee just as strenuously argues that the language of the Hargrove decision leads to the inescapable conclusion that the import of that decision was to wipe away the archaic theory of sovereign immunity and thereby render municipalities liable for all acts both negligent and intentional committed by employees of a municipal corporation. Certainly some of the language of that decision supports the appellee's view.

In Hewitt v. Venable, Fla.App.1959, 109 So.2d 185, this court reiterated the rule established by the Hargrove decision. We recognized in the Hewitt case that liability of a municipality under the doctrine of respondeat superior was based upon the negligent act having been performed by the municipal employee while acting within the scope of his employment. If, as the appellee contends, vicarious liability is to be fixed upon a municipal corporation for the actions of its employee, then such liability, we feel, should stem from the negligent or unauthorized manner of the performance of a lawfully delegated duty, rather than from the commission of an unlawful, illegal or prohibited act. Certainly when the appellant's police officer was within the City of Coral Gables attempting to enforce the traffic regulations or police ordinances of that municipality, he was acting not only within the scope but the course of his employment. But when he ventured beyond the territorial limits of the municipality under the circumstances depicted by the record in this case, he possessed no more authority than an average citizen. His actions in this case amounted to no more or less than would any other *ultra vires* act attempted by an employee of a municipality.

It is true, as appellee argues, that the city by its answer conceded that its police officer was acting within the scope and course of his employment, but such admission could not carry with it the implication that the city had authorized or ratified an unlawful or illegal act. There was no admission that appellant's officer had performed an illegal act, as alleged in the complaint, as a part of or in the course of his employment. Although the doctrine of respondeat superior does not appear to have been the basis for fixing liability upon a sheriff for the actions of his deputies, nevertheless sheriffs appear to have been held liable for the negligent acts of their deputy sheriffs committed in the performance of the deputies' lawful duties. Conversely, sheriffs have been exonerated from liability for acts of deputies that were beyond or in excess of their duties prescribed by law.

The appellant, a municipal corporation, whose power and authority are circumscribed by charter or legislative act, could confer no more authority upon its police officers to make arrests than was authorized by law. The acts of appellant's police officer may have been committed 'under color of office' but certainly not 'by virtue of office.' The appellant has urged other points, including the contention that the verdict was excessive and improper because there was no differentiation in the verdict between compensatory and punitive damages. There is also injected into this contention the fact that punitive damages in a case of this type are not recoverable against a municipality because of the fact that malice on the part of a police officer in such circumstances could not be imputed to a municipality. In view of the conclusions reached, we deem it unnecessary to discuss these questions.

We conclude that the trial judge erred in directing a verdict against the appellant and, accordingly, the judgment as to this appellant is reversed and the cause remanded with directions to vacate the judgment as to appellant, grant appellant's motion for directed verdict and enter judgment thereon. Reversed and remanded with directions.

REVIEW SECTION

READING COMPREHENSION

Detail the facts of this case.

Elaborate the logic of this court in reversing and remanding the trial judge's order.

SECTION 2: FAILURE TO PROTECT BY LAW ENFORCEMENT

OVERVIEW

According to the U.S. Supreme Court's interpretation of the Fifth and Fourteenth Amendments, there is a no-affirmative-duty-to-protect rule. What this means in practice is that law enforcement has no affirmative duty to protect individuals from other individuals attempting to inflict injury. When however, the government imprisons individuals against their will, the special relationship exception prevails, indicating this is a violation of the Eighth Amendment as these individuals cannot protect themselves. As such, there exists a duty to protect in such situations.

So, what if your rights are violated and you decide to sue the government or its officers? Realistically, you should know you will be faced with many legal hurdles, and the citizen rarely prevails in such a suit. Such a lawsuit is both difficult and expensive to pursue, the U.S. Supreme Court has limited the ability of citizens to garner relief from police techniques even if they result in excessive force, and jurors are more likely to believe the testimony of an officer. In addition, qualified and absolute immunity protect most officials from successful lawsuits.

Where then does the average citizen seek accountability? The most common method by which officials are held accountable is through administrative review, including internal affairs units and external civilian reviews. While external civilian reviews would certainly appear to give the appearance of a fairer assessment, they were vehemently opposed during the 1960s when first suggested by liberal reformers. By the 1990s, most large cities had external civilian review procedures in place, though they are still opposed by government officials who believe the public cannot fully understand the complexities of the job and do not want the 'blue curtain' scrutinized.

CASE

Pollock v. Florida Department of Highway Patrol reviews <u>State Department of Highway Patrol v. Pollack, 745 So. 2d 446 (Fla. 3d DCA 1999)</u>. The Supreme Court of Florida has jurisdiction in review of this case, and you will remember from other case law that the Department of Highway Patrol is considered by the state of Florida to be an agency of law enforcement.

POLLOCK V. FLORIDA DEPARTMENT OF HIGHWAY PATROL
Supreme Court of Florida
No. SC99-8 (Fl, 2004)

The tragic facts of this unfortunate case were summarized by the Third District Court of Appeal in its opinion as follows: On September 5, 1993, at approximately 4:00 a.m., the decedents Suzanne Leeds and Elissa Pollack were instantly killed when the automobile that Suzanne was driving, and in which Elissa was a passenger, collided into the back of an unlit tractor-trailer which had stalled in the right-hand lane of the Palmetto Expressway. Earlier that morning, at approximately 3:00 a.m., Daniel Baregas had been driving this tractor-trailer when it stalled on the Palmetto Expressway, about 1000 feet away from a crescent in the highway. At or about the same time, Raul Pedrero was driving home on the Palmetto when he suddenly encountered the stalled tractor-trailer in the right-hand lane which had no markers, lights, or flares. Mr. Pedrero had to slam on his brakes and veer into the adjacent lane to avoid hitting the tractor-trailer. Moreover, the street lighting in the area was out, which made it all the more difficult to see the tractor trailer.

Mr. Pedrero exited the Palmetto, went to a gas station and telephoned 911. His call was transferred to FHP, where Mr. Pedrero informed the dispatcher that there was a stalled tractor-trailer on the Palmetto Expressway which had no lights and no warning signs. He also advised the FHP dispatcher that he had almost hit the truck. The dispatcher told Mr. Pedrero that he would "send a unit to check it out." Mr. Pedrero returned to the vicinity of the stalled tractor-trailer to await the arrival of FHP. He waited for twenty to twenty-five minutes, during which time he saw many vehicles take evasive action to avoid hitting the stalled tractor-trailer. When FHP did not show up after twenty-five minutes, Mr. Pedrero went home. Apparently, FHP's dispatcher had failed to enter Mr. Pedrero's call into the computer for assignment; consequently, no officer was dispatched to the scene. At the time, the FHP had internal operating rules requiring it to dispatch a trooper to the scene of stalled vehicles. The evidence at trial showed that officers were available to answer the call had it gone out.

The FHP Communication Policy/Procedures Manual, Policy 12.04.03 General Information provides in relevant part: All reports of vehicle crashes or incidents received in the communications center shall immediately be dispatched to the appropriate trooper. If the reported crash or incident is within a city limit, then it shall be reported to the local police department. If there is going to be a delay in dispatching a crash or incident report due to manpower shortage, then the appropriate FHP supervisor shall be notified. This notification shall be documented on the dispatch card. No matter how the information is received, a duty officer should learn how to quickly edit given information into the Official Standards, and then broadcast it.

In addition, Rule 12.00.00 entitled Crash Prevention, provides: Crash prevention and crash investigation are the primary functions of the Florida Highway Patrol and the duty officer's role in these endeavors are of major importance. Strict adherence to this chapter will enable every officer to handle these responsibilities in an efficient and professional manner.

In both cases, the trial court, consistent with the jury verdicts, entered judgments for the plaintiffs. On appeal, the district court reversed and directed that final judgments be entered in favor of the Florida Highway Patrol (FHP), because "there was nothing to indicate that FHP's actions or inactions were operational in nature and . . . FHP otherwise owed no special duty to the decedents, as a matter of law, so as to impose governmental tort liability." Furthermore, in response to the contention that FHP's duty toward the decedents arose from its own policies and procedures governing incident response, the district court held that "a governmental agency's policy or procedure manual cannot, standing alone, create an independent duty to individual citizens."

We begin by narrowing our focus to the issue squarely before us. We are not faced here with the question of whether, in a modern society led to rely upon the social compact with its protective network of safeguards against public harm, the public should not be entitled to rely upon that network, nor whether a governmental agency entrusted with implementation of one such safeguard should ever ignore its responsibility to respond when alerted to a potential crisis. The answers to these morally compelling questions are obvious. However, while our rule of law generally gives effect to its moral underpinnings, these are not the only concerns manifest in the area of the law we address today. There is also an august body of law which we must follow in determining those instances in which the sovereign will be liable for failings such as occurred here.

In the cases before us, FHP has successfully invoked sovereign immunity at the district court level in defending against the wrongful death actions filed by the Pollocks and the Leeds. In reviewing the district court decision, it is useful to restate the analytical framework applied to questions of governmental tort liability. The State of Florida has waived sovereign immunity from liability in tort actions "for any act for which a private person under similar circumstances would be held liable" Henderson v. Bowden, 737 So. 2d 532, 534-35 (Fla. 1999) (citing Art. X, § 13, Fla. Const.; § 768.28 Fla. Stat. (1995)). Thus, "there can be no governmental liability unless a common law or statutory duty of care existed that would have been applicable to an individual under similar circumstances."

If no duty of care is owed with respect to alleged negligent conduct, then there is no governmental liability, and the question of whether the sovereign should be immune from suit need not be reached. However, if a duty of care is owed, it must then be determined whether sovereign immunity bars an action for an alleged breach of that duty. In making this assessment, it is necessary to ascertain the character of the allegedly negligent governmental act or omission. As this Court has determined, basic judgmental or discretionary governmental functions are immune from legal action, whereas operational acts are not protected by sovereign immunity.

In the instant case, the petitioners contend that the duty of care owed by FHP to the decedents arose from two separate sources. First, the petitioners assert that as the governmental entity with the ultimate responsibility to patrol the state highways, and to control and regulate traffic, FHP had a common law duty to maintain the highway in a reasonably safe condition, to warn of known dangers on the roadway, and to correct any dangerous conditions. Second, the petitioners argue that FHP's policies and procedures governing incident response created a duty to dispatch an officer to the scene of the stalled tractor-trailer. After a careful review of these contentions and controlling caselaw, we conclude that FHP had no such duty of care.

The contention that FHP's common law duty to maintain the roadway and keep it free of obstructions is an outgrowth of its duty to patrol the state highways and control the movement of traffic misconstrues existing principles of duty and tort law. It is well settled that a public or private entity which owns, operates, or controls a property, including a roadway, owes a duty to maintain that property, and a corresponding duty to warn of and correct dangerous conditions thereon. Indeed, a review of the pertinent statutory provisions reveals that the responsibility for "the operation and maintenance of the roads" in this state falls to the Florida Department of Transportation and local governments for the roads within their respective jurisdictions. Nor does FHP have a duty to remove stalled or abandoned vehicles from the state highways. Florida law authorizes, but does not establish a legal duty, nor require, FHP officers to provide for the removal of stalled or abandoned vehicles. The statutory construct makes clear, however, that FHP's response to such disabled vehicles is permissive, rather than mandatory, and is in furtherance of its authority to enforce traffic laws, rather than pursuant to a duty to keep the highways free from obstructions.

Patrolling the state highways, controlling the flow of traffic, and enforcing the traffic laws are duties FHP owes to the general public, as opposed to an individual person. The responsibility to enforce the laws for the good of the public cannot engender a duty to act with care toward any one individual, unless an official assumes a special duty with regard to that person. A special tort duty does arise when law enforcement officers become directly involved in circumstances which place people within a "zone of risk" by creating or permitting dangers to exist, by taking persons into police custody, detaining them, or otherwise subjecting them to danger. The premise underlying this theory is that a police officer's decision to assume control over a particular situation or individual or group of individuals is accompanied by a corresponding duty to exercise reasonable care. Where police officers, such as FHP in the instant case, have not arrived on the scene or assumed any degree of control over the situation, the "zone of risk" analysis has no application.

Florida courts have also determined that a special duty is established when a police officer makes a direct representation to a plaintiff, or one so closely involved with the plaintiff that their interests cannot be separated, that he or she will take a specified law enforcement action. This principle does not extend to the instant case, where FHP made no representation to either the decedents or their close relatives that a unit would be dispatched to the scene of the stalled tractor-trailer. FHP did not, by word or deed, create a duty of care toward the decedents over and above its general duty to enforce the state's traffic laws. Thus, FHP owed no duty of care to the decedents to respond to the emergency call regarding the stalled tractor-trailer.

We further conclude that FHP's internal operating procedures and policies did not impose a duty to dispatch officers to the scene of the stalled tractor-trailer. On this issue, we approve the reasoned analysis of the district court which concludes that, in the context of governmental tort litigation, written agency protocols, procedures, and manuals do not create an independent duty of care. While a written policy or manual may be instructive in determining whether the alleged tortfeasor acted negligently in fulfilling an independently established duty of care, it does not itself establish such a legal duty vis-a-vis individual members of the public. This principle applies, unless, of course, the sovereign adopts such protocols and procedures as standards of conduct, in which case there would exist an independent duty of care.

Based on the foregoing, we determine that FHP had no special duty either to maintain the road on which this horrible accident occurred, or to dispatch officers in response to the emergency call. In determining whether internal policies and procedures create an independent duty of care is a fact question that must be taken as true in judging whether a trial court properly dismissed an action for failure to state a claim. Pursuant to our holding with regard to the legal force of internal operating policies, the assertion that such policies create an independent duty of care is legally erroneous, and cannot sustain an otherwise insufficient claim against a motion to dismiss.

While we conclude that the lack of a statutory or common law duty is determinative in this case, and renders a sovereign immunity analysis unnecessary, we address the topic to clarify confusion that might arise from the decision below. As reiterated throughout this opinion, a determination that a governmental actor owed a duty of care with regard to the allegedly negligent conduct is a prerequisite to proceeding with a sovereign immunity analysis and ultimately determining whether governmental tort liability exists. Therefore, characterizing a governmental action or omission as operational or discretionary in nature has no bearing on the initial duty analysis. We believe that this clarification is necessary because of the language in the district court's decision stating that "based upon the foregoing we find that FHP's actions or inactions were not operational in nature and that no special duty was owed to the decedents so as to constitute a waiver of sovereign immunity."

We believe the foregoing excerpt could be interpreted as conflating the duty and sovereign immunity analyses. The district court's opinion should not be interpreted as holding that governmental tort liability attaches as a matter of law in the absence of a statutory or common law duty if the activity in question is operational in nature. Such a conclusion would contravene fundamental and oft-repeated principles of duty and the law of sovereign immunity. Furthermore, we specifically refuse the petitioners' invitation to alter the law of sovereign immunity to provide that if a governmental act is operational in nature, then there automatically exists a duty of care to all persons injured by the act or omission.

We in no way condone FHP's failure to take prompt action when it was alerted to the potential danger caused by the stalled tractor-trailer. However, under settled principles of Florida law, having not responded to the scene to become directly involved in the roadway circumstances, FHP had no legally recognized particular tort duty which would generate or impose governmental tort liability with regard to responding to the scene, the issuance of warnings of the potential danger, or provision for the removal of the tractor-trailer under the circumstances presented in this case. We therefore approve the decision of the district court as clarified herein. It is so ordered. WELLS, LEWIS, CANTERO, and BELL, JJ., concur.

PARIENTE, J., dissents with an opinion, in which QUINCE, J., concurs.

I respectfully dissent. Under the circumstances of this case I conclude that FHP owed a duty of care to the decedents, Suzanne Leeds and Elissa Pollack, and that FHP's actions in this case were operational in nature, subjecting FHP to liability under Florida's waiver of sovereign immunity statute. Therefore, I would quash the Third District's decision in this case and remand with instructions to reinstate the jury's verdict in favor of the plaintiffs. The relevant facts are not in dispute. A jury returned a verdict in favor of the plaintiffs, finding FHP fifty percent negligent and the tractor-trailer driver fifty percent negligent.

I disagree with Chief Justice Anstead's conclusion that our case law allows the government "to provide emergency services without the government also assuming liability for the reasonableness of the response." As the majority recognizes, a duty arises when "a police officer makes a direct representation to a plaintiff, or one so closely involved with the plaintiff that their interest cannot be separated, that he or she will take specified law enforcement action." Thus, the basis on which the majority, including Chief Justice Anstead, concludes that there is no duty in this case cannot rest on the view that a governmental entity never assumes liability for the reasonableness of its response. Rather, the Court's decision rests on drawing what I consider to be an arbitrary line between a direct representation made to one "closely involved with the plaintiff" and a direct representation made to a third party.

In my view, the better approach in analyzing duty in governmental tort cases is to focus on conventional tort principles, and in particular foreseeability, which this Court has recognized as "crucial in defining the scope of the general duty placed on every person to avoid negligent acts or omissions." In this case, FHP was clearly authorized to respond to the stalled tractor-trailer under both section 321.05, Florida Statutes (1993), which requires FHP to patrol the state highways, regulating, controlling, and directing the flow of traffic, and section 316.194(3)(a), Florida Statutes (1993), which authorizes FHP to move a vehicle stopped on the main-traveled part of a highway. Nevertheless, the majority concludes that because FHP had not "arrived on the scene or assumed any degree of control over the situation, the `zone of risk' analysis has no application." This conclusion overlooks the fact that FHP assumed control over the situation when the dispatcher assured Mr. Pedrero that he would "send a unit to check it out." It was at this time that FHP assumed a common law duty of care to the decedents, who were a part of the small group of individuals that foreseeably could have been injured by the tractor-trailer's presence in the right-hand lane of the highway.

Having concluded that FHP owed a duty of care to the decedents, I further conclude that FHP is not shielded from liability in this case. The ministerial duty of logging 911 calls into FHP's computer for assignment does not fall within the category of governmental activity that involves planning. As noted in the majority opinion, FHP's Communication Policy/Procedure Manual states that "all reports of vehicle crashes or incidents received in the communication center shall immediately be dispatched." The manual's directive requiring the dispatch of officers to all reports of incidents represents the policy decision made by FHP. The act of logging the reports received by FHP is an operational-level activity that falls directly within the waiver of sovereign immunity contained in section 768.28.

In sum, I conclude that FHP assumed a duty to the decedents by assuring Mr. Pedrero that an officer would be dispatched to the area of the stalled tractor-trailer. I further conclude that the dispatcher's failure to log the call into the system is not a planning-level function protected by sovereign immunity. This case was therefore properly submitted to the jury, which considered the facts before it and found that FHP acted negligently. Accordingly, I would quash the Third District's decision in this case and remand with instructions to reinstate the jury's verdict in favor of the plaintiffs. QUINCE, J., Concurs.

REVIEW SECTION

READING COMPREHENSION

What are the facts of this case? Include in your discussion the findings of the lower courts.

Discuss the notion of sovereign immunity and its application in Florida.

THINKING CRITICALLY

Using opinion from the majority and dissent, discuss how you would decide this case.

CONCLUSION

We have now elaborated the exclusionary rule and the defense of entrapment which are remedies available to defendants in criminal trial cases, as well as remedies an individual may pursue against an officer that are not available at the trial stage, including prosecuting the officer through criminal law, suing a government official or entity through civil law, or administrative discipline of an officer outside of the judicial system. This chapter thoroughly reviewed these remedies for official misconduct, and discussed the issue of failure to protect by law enforcement and the conditions under which a duty to protect is assigned.

Chapter Twelve

Starting Court Proceedings

Once the police turn over a strong case to the prosecutor's office, it is the discretion of that office whether or not to charge the individual in question. Keep in mind that not all strong cases are prosecuted because it is the duty of the prosecutor's office not only to prosecute crime, but also do accomplish justice which may involve alternative criminal justice procedures such as diversion.

This chapter will review what happens after the start of court proceedings, including:

(1)   Probable cause;

(2)   First appearance and bail; and

(3)   Right to counsel.

SECTION 1: PROBABLE CAUSE

OVERVIEW

Once a defendant is arrested, the U.S. Constitution and Florida state law require a probable cause hearing within a reasonable length of time in order to avoid the deprivation of liberty that results from imprisonment. Accordingly, the Florida procedures challenged in the landmark case (*Gerstein v. Pugh 1974)* provided in this chapter, whereby a person arrested without a warrant and charged by information may be jailed pending trial without opportunity for a probable cause hearing are unconstitutional. The court has found that the prosecutor's assessment of probable cause, in and of itself, does not meet the requirements of the Fourth Amendment. The Constitution does not however, require judicial oversight of prosecutorial discretion and a conviction can not be vacated because the defendant was detained said hearing. As well, you may note that a probable cause determination is not considered part of the critical stage of prosecution and thus does not require appointed counsel. Further, Florida law denies preliminary hearing to persons confined under indictment (*Sangaree v. Hamlin 1970* and *Florida Rules of Criminal Procedure* 3.131(a)) and does not suggest that the issue of probable cause can be raised at arraignment (*Florida Rules of Criminal Procedure* 3.160).

Of particular note in this section is Section Fourteen of the Florida Constitution which reads:

Pretrial release and detention.--Unless charged with a capital offense or an offense punishable by life imprisonment and the proof of guilt is evident or the presumption is great, every person charged with a crime or violation of municipal or county ordinance shall be entitled to pretrial release on reasonable conditions. If no conditions of release can reasonably protect the community from risk of physical harm to persons, assure the presence of the accused at trial, or assure the integrity of the judicial process, the accused may be detained.

CASE

The issue in the landmark case *Gerstein v. Pugh* is whether a person arrested and held for trial under a prosecutor's information is constitutionally entitled to a judicial determination of probable cause for pretrial restraint of liberty. This case addresses Florida law and is heard by the U.S. Supreme Court, presenting two important issues: whether a person arrested and held for trial on an information is entitled to a judicial determination of probable cause for detention, and if so, whether the adversary hearing ordered by the District Court and approved by the Court of Appeals is required by the Constitution.

GERSTEIN V. PUGH
420 U.S. 103, 95 S.Ct. 854, 43 L.Ed.2d 54 (1974)

In March 1971 respondents Pugh and Henderson were arrested in Dade County, Fla. Each was charged with several offenses under a prosecutor's information. Pugh was denied bail because one of the charges against him carried a potential life sentence, and Henderson remained in custody because he was unable to post a $4,500 bond. In Florida, indictments are required only for prosecution of capital offenses. Prosecutors may charge all other crimes by information, without a prior preliminary hearing and without obtaining leave of court. At the time respondents were arrested, a Florida rule seemed to authorize adversary preliminary hearings to test probable cause for detention in all cases. But the Florida courts had held that the filling of an information foreclosed the suspect's right to a preliminary hearing. They had also held that habeas corpus could not be used, except perhaps in exceptional circumstances, to test the probable cause for detention under an information. The only possible methods for obtaining a judicial determination of probable cause were a special statute allowing a preliminary hearing after 30 days, Fla.Stat.Ann. § 907.045 (1973), and arraignment, which the District Court found was often delayed a month or more after arrest. As a result, a person charged by information could be detained for a substantial period solely on the decision of a prosecutor.

Respondents Pugh and Henderson filed a class action against Dade County officials in the Federal District Court, claiming a constitutional right to a judicial hearing on the issue of probable cause and requesting declaratory and injunctive relief. Petitioner Gerstein, the State Attorney for Dade County, was one of several defendants.

After an initial delay while the Florida Legislature considered a bill that would have afforded preliminary hearings to persons charged by information, the District Court granted the relief sought. The court certified the case as a class action and held that the Fourth and Fourteenth Amendments give all arrested persons charged by information a right to a judicial hearing on the question of probable cause. The District Court ordered the Dade County defendants to give the named plaintiffs an immediate preliminary hearing to determine probable cause for further detention. It also ordered them to submit a plan providing preliminary hearings in all cases instituted by information.

The defendants submitted a plan prepared by Sheriff E. Wilson Purdy, and the District Court adopted it with modifications. The final order prescribed a detailed post-arrest procedure. Upon arrest the accused would be taken before a magistrate for a 'first appearance hearing.' The magistrate would explain the charges, advise the accused of his rights, appoint counsel if he was indigent, and proceed with a probable cause determination unless either the prosecutor or the accused was unprepared. If either requested more time, the magistrate would set the date for a 'preliminary hearing,' to be held within four days if the accused was in custody and within 10 days if he had been released pending trial. The order provided sanctions for failure to hold the hearings at prescribed times. At the 'preliminary hearing' the accused would be entitled to counsel, and he would be allowed to confront and cross-examine adverse witnesses, to summon favorable witnesses, and to have a transcript made on request. If the magistrate found no probable cause, the accused would be discharged. He then could not be charged with the same offense by complaint or information, but only by indictment returned within 30 days.

The Court of Appeals for the Fifth Circuit stayed the District Court's order pending appeal, but while the case was awaiting decision, the Dade County judiciary voluntarily adopted a similar procedure of its own. Upon learning of this development, the Court of Appeals remanded the case for specific findings on the constitutionality of the new Dade County system. Before the District Court issued its findings, however, the Florida Supreme Court amended the procedural rules governing preliminary hearings statewide, and the parties agreed that the District Court should direct its inquiry to the new rules rather than the Dade County procedures.

Under the amended rules every arrested person must be taken before a judicial officer within 24 hours. Fla.Rule Crim.Proc. 3.130(b). This 'first appearance' is similar to the 'first appearance hearing' ordered by the District Court in all respects but the crucial one: the magistrate does not make a determination of probable cause. The rule amendments also changed the procedure for preliminary hearings, restricting them to felony charges and codifying the rule that no hearings are available to persons charged by information or indictment. In a supplemental opinion the District Court held that the amended rules had not answered the basic constitutional objection, since a defendant charged by information still could be detained pending trial without a judicial determination of probable cause. Reaffirming its original ruling, the District Court declared that the continuation of this practice was unconstitutional. The Court of Appeals affirmed, 483 F.2d 778 (1973), modifying the District Court's decree in minor particulars and suggesting that the form of preliminary hearing provided by the amended Florida rules would be acceptable, as long as it was provided to all defendants in custody pending trial.

State Attorney Gerstein petitioned for review, and we granted certiorari because of the importance of the issue. 414 U.S. 1062, 94 S.Ct. 567, 38 L.Ed.2d 467 (1973). We affirm in part and reverse in part.

Both the standards and procedures for arrest and detention have been derived from the Fourth Amendment and its common-law antecedents. The standard for arrest is probable cause, defined in terms of facts and circumstances 'sufficient to warrant a prudent man in believing that the (suspect) had committed or was committing an offense.' Beck v. Ohio, 379 U.S. 89, 91, 85 S.Ct. 223, 225, 13 L.Ed.2d 142 (1964). This standard, like those for searches and seizures, represents a necessary accommodation between the individual's right to liberty and the State's duty to control crime. To implement the Fourth Amendment's protection against unfounded invasions of liberty and privacy, the Court has required that the existence of probable cause be decided by a neutral and detached magistrate whenever possible. Maximum protection of individual rights could be assured by requiring a magistrate's review of the factual justification prior to any arrest, but such a requirement would constitute an intolerable handicap for legitimate law enforcement. Thus, while the Court has expressed a preference for the use of arrest warrants when feasible, it has never invalidated an arrest supported by probable cause solely because the officers failed to secure a warrant. Under this practical compromise, a policeman's on-the-scene assessment of probable cause provides legal justification for arresting a person suspected of crime, and for a brief period of detention to take the administrative steps incident to arrest.

Once the suspect is in custody, however, the reasons that justify dispensing with the magistrate's neutral judgment evaporate. There no longer is any danger that the suspect will escape or commit further crimes while the police submit their evidence to a magistrate. And, while the State's reasons for taking summary action subside, the suspect's need for a neutral determination of probable cause increases significantly. The consequences of prolonged detention may be more serious than the interference occasioned by arrest. Even pretrial release may be accompanied by burdensome conditions that effect a significant restraint of liberty. When the stakes are this high, the detached judgment of a neutral magistrate is essential if the Fourth Amendment is to furnish meaningful protection from unfounded interference with liberty. Accordingly, we hold that the Fourth Amendment requires a judicial determination of probable cause as a prerequisite to extended restraint of liberty following arrest.

This result has historical support in the common law that has guided interpretation of the Fourth Amendment. At common law it was customary, if not obligatory, for an arrested person to be brought before a justice of the peace shortly after arrest. This practice furnished the model for criminal procedure in America immediately following the adoption of the Fourth Amendment, and there are indications that the Framers of the Bill of Rights regarded it as a model for a 'reasonable' seizure.

Under the Florida procedures challenged here, a person arrested without a warrant and charged by information may be jailed or subjected to other restraints pending trial without any opportunity for a probable cause determination. Petitioner defends this practice on the ground that the prosecutor's decision to file an information is itself a determination of probable cause that furnishes sufficient reason to detain a defendant pending trial. Although a conscientious decision that the evidence warrants prosecution affords a measure of protection against unfounded detention, we do not think prosecutorial judgment standing alone meets the requirements of the Fourth Amendment. Indeed, we think the Court's previous decisions compel disapproval of the Florida procedure. In holding that the prosecutor's assessment of probable cause is not sufficient alone to justify restraint of liberty pending trial, we do not imply that the accused is entitled to judicial oversight or review of the decision to prosecute. Instead, we adhere to the Court's prior holding that a judicial hearing is not prerequisite to prosecution by information. Nor do we retreat from the established rule that illegal arrest or detention does not void a subsequent conviction. Thus, as the Court of Appeals noted below, although a suspect who is presently detained may challenge the probable cause for that confinement, a conviction will not be vacated on the ground that the defendant was detained pending trial without a determination of probable cause.

Both the District Court and the Court of Appeals held that the determination of probable cause must be accompanied by the full panoply of adversary safeguards—counsel, confrontation, cross-examination, and compulsory process for witnesses. A full preliminary hearing of this sort is modeled after the procedure used in many States to determine whether the evidence justifies going to trial under an information or presenting the case to a grand jury. The standard of proof required of the prosecution is usually referred to as 'probable cause,' but in some jurisdictions it may approach a prima facie case of guilt. These adversary safeguards are not essential for the probable cause determination required by the Fourth Amendment. The sole issue is whether there is probable cause for detaining the arrested person pending further proceedings. This issue can be determined reliably without an adversary hearing. The standard is the same as that for arrest. That standard—probable cause to believe the suspect has committed a crime—traditionally has been decided by a magistrate in a nonadversary proceeding on hearsay and written testimony, and the Court has approved these informal modes of proof. Whatever procedure a State may adopt, it must provide a fair and reliable determination of probable cause as a condition for any significant pretrial restraint of liberty, and this determination must be made by a judicial officer either before or promptly after arrest.

We agree with the Court of Appeals that the Fourth Amendment requires a timely judicial determination of probable cause as a prerequisite to detention, and we accordingly affirm that much of the judgment. As we do not agree that the Fourth Amendment requires the adversary hearing outlined in the District Court's decree, we reverse in part and remand to the Court of Appeals for further proceedings consistent with this opinion. It is so ordered.

REVIEW SECTION

READING COMPREHENSION

What are the Florida guidelines regarding a probable cause hearing?

Detail the history of this case.

SECTION 2: FIRST APPEARANCE AND BAIL

OVERVIEW

Section 3.131 of the *Florida Rules of Criminal Procedure* applies to first appearance and bail and will be quoted here at length:

> RULE 3.131. PRETRIAL RELEASE. (a) **Right to Pretrial Release.** Unless charged with a capital offense or an offense punishable by life imprisonment and the proof of guilt is evident or the presumption is great, every person charged with a crime or violation of municipal or county ordinance shall be entitled to pretrial release on reasonable conditions. If no conditions of release can reasonably protect the community from risk of physical harm to persons, assure the presence of the accused at trial, or assure the integrity of the judicial process, the accused may be detained. (b) **Hearing at First Appearance-Conditions of Release.** (1) Unless the state has filed a motion for pretrial detention pursuant to rule 3.132, the court shall conduct a hearing to determine pretrial release . . . (2) The judge shall at the defendant's first appearance consider all available relevant factors to determine what form of release is necessary to assure the defendant's appearance. If a monetary bail is required, the judge shall determine the amount. (3) In determining whether to release a defendant on bail or other conditions, and what that bail or those conditions may be, the court may consider the nature and circumstances of the offense charged and the penalty provided by law; the weight of the evidence against the defendant; the defendant's family ties, length of residence in the community, employment history, financial resources, and mental condition; the defendant's past and present conduct, including any record of convictions, previous flight to avoid prosecution, or failure to appear at court proceedings; the nature and probability of danger that the defendant's release poses to the community; the source of funds used to post bail; whether the defendant is already on release pending resolution of another criminal proceeding or is on probation, parole, or other release pending completion of sentence; and any other facts the court considers relevant.

Thus, when deciding matters of bail, the court must weight the constitutional rights of the defendant with community security. While there is no constitutional right to bail, there is a right against excessive bail and equal protection of the law requires all defendants be provided with the same opportunity for consideration for release without discrimination. So what happens if you are poor an cannot afford bail? Is this is violation of the equal protection clause?

CASE

The United States Court of Appeals for the Fifth Circuit in *Pugh v. Rainwater*, 557 F.2d 1189 (1977), held that the Florida bail system discriminated against indigent defendants because it did not give priority to release on personal recognizance. Although the statute made available alternatives, judges were left with discretion to set money bond. The court determined that while the state has an interest in assuring appearance at trial, money bail is not necessary to promote that interest and defendants must be provided with an opportunity to assist in their own defense.

PUGH V. RAINWATER
United States Court of Appeals, Fifth Circuit
557 F.2d 1189 (1977)

Since Florida's admission to the Union persons charged in the courts of that state with bailable offenses were entitled to obtain pretrial freedom by paying or having a surety pay to the court a sum of money refundable upon appearance at trial. Plaintiffs in the instant case, indigent pretrial detainees suing on behalf of themselves and others similarly situated, maintain that this traditional practice denies them equal protection of the law by conditioning their right to pretrial freedom on wealth-based criteria. We agree and hold that equal protection is not satisfied unless a judge is required to consider less financially onerous forms of pretrial release before he imposes money bail.

We preface our opinion by noting that we are asked to resolve a small part of a much larger problem. The practice of incarcerating indigent defendants prior to trial has sparked a flood of litigation in recent years. At first, advocates of bail reform brought their case before the state legislatures and Congress. Despite initial success, the movement became stalled. Perhaps as a result, vindication of the rights of pretrial detainees was increasingly sought in the federal courts. Almost without exception, the cases challenged the conditions, not the fact of pretrial detention. The guiding principle in each case has been that prior to trial a defendant is presumed innocent; his incarceration during that period is permissible only to assure his appearance at trial, not to inflict punishment. On this basis the courts have ordered sweeping changes in the character and administration of state prisons to assure that pretrial detainees, most often those with little or no resources, are not punished before they are found guilty.

Today we decide a narrow issue: whether the imprisonment of an indigent prior to trial solely because he cannot afford to pay money bail violates his right to equal protection under the Fourteenth Amendment. The issue before us boils down to whether an indigent, already denied the material comforts many of us take for granted, may be condemned to pretrial imprisonment under barbaric conditions for no other reason than his poverty.

It makes for clarity to delineate exactly what we are called upon to decide. First, this case does not involve the right to bail per se. Regardless of whether there is a federal constitutional right to bail, the plaintiffs here were entitled to bail by virtue of the Florida Constitution, Art. I, § 14. The State of Florida has chosen to guarantee bail to its citizens except in the case of crimes of the most serious nature. The issue before us is whether the state is invidiously discriminating in administering the right it has conferred.

Similarly, we are not called upon to decide whether any person is denied equal protection if he can make bail in some amount, but is unable to post the amount of bail set. We are confronted only with the question of the rights of indigents. As the Supreme Court has suggested in a different context, this distinction is not without constitutional significance: The individuals, or groups of individuals, who constituted the class discriminated against in our prior cases shared two distinguishing characteristics: because of their impecunity they were completely unable to pay for some desired benefit, and as a consequence they sustained an absolute deprivation of a meaningful opportunity to enjoy that benefit . . . Earlier cases do not touch on the question whether equal protection is denied to persons with relatively less money on whom designated fines impose heavier burdens. Sentencing judges may, and often do, consider the defendant's ability to pay, but in such circumstances they are guided by sound judicial discretion rather than by constitutional mandate (San Antonio Independent School District v. Rodriquez, 411 U.S. 1, 20-22, 93 S.Ct. 1278, 1290-91, 36 L.Ed.2d 16, 35-36 1973). Clearly, all but the most trifling money bail would be meaningless to the indigent who lacks funds even to pay a bail bondsman. "In the case of an indigent defendant, the fixing of bail in even a modest amount may have the practical effect of denying him release" (Bandy v. United States, 81 S.Ct. 197, 198, 5 L.Ed.2d 218, 219 1960). To continue to demand a substantial bond which the defendant is unable to secure raises considerable problems for the equal administration of the law . . . Can an indigent be denied freedom, where a wealthy man would not, because he does not happen to have enough property to pledge for his freedom?

Traditional equal protection analysis grants great deference to legislative classifications. If the distinctions drawn have some basis in practical experience, or if any state of facts reasonably may be conceived to justify them, and they are not drawn on the basis of criteria wholly unrelated to the objective of the statute, then the statute will withstand an equal protection challenge. "But the (Supreme) Court also has refined this traditional test and has said that a statutory classification based upon suspect criteria or affecting 'fundamental rights' will encounter equal protection difficulties unless justified by a 'compelling governmental interest'" (Schilb v. Kuebel, 404 U.S. 357, 365, 92 S.Ct. 479, 484, 30 L.Ed.2d 502, 511 1971). The Court has stressed that in such cases the State must demonstrate that the classification is necessary to promote a compelling governmental interest.

Accordingly, our analysis must focus on four questions:

(1) Does Florida's bail system create a classification?

(2) If so, is that classification "suspect" or does it affect "fundamental rights"?

(3) Is the State of Florida attempting to promote a compelling governmental interest by making the classification? and

(4) Are less restrictive means available to effectuate the desired end?

A. Does Florida's Bail System Create a Classification?

The plaintiffs do not allege that their bail was set solely on the basis of their lack of wealth. In contending that they are denied release solely because of their poverty, plaintiffs ignore other factors distinguishing them from released persons. The record shows that plaintiffs' confinement is not the result of a classification based solely upon wealth, consequently they have not been deprived of their right to equal protection of the law. We think, however, that the district judge misconstrued the nature of the plaintiff's complaint. The point is not whether the judge considers factors other than wealth in deciding whether money bail is necessary and, if so, the amount; rather, our concern is with the effect of the judge's decision. A judge may weigh all factors and decide, for example, that $5000 bail each is necessary to assure the appearance at trial of two defendants. One has a $10,000 savings account; the other is an indigent. Even though both have been assessed as presenting the same risk, the man of means can secure his pretrial freedom while the indigent has no choice but to remain in jail. A basic principle of equal protection is that "a law nondiscriminatory on its face may be grossly discriminatory in its operation." Thus, the lack of deliberate discrimination on the basis of poverty is not dispositive of plaintiffs' claim.

Since the ruling of the district court in 1971, the Florida Supreme Court has promulgated new rules governing pretrial release and bail. Under the latest system, "bail" is defined as six alternative forms of release. The judge is required to "consider all available relevant factors to determine what form of release is necessary to assure the defendant's appearance. If monetary bail is required, then the judge shall determine the amount." Fla.R.Crim.P. 3.130(b)(4)(ii). The new rules neither do away with money bail nor create a presumption in favor of release conditioned on non-financial factors. The result is that whenever a judge sets monetary bail he creates a de facto classification based on the defendant's ability to pay.

B. Does the Classification Involve "Suspect Criteria" or "Fundamental Rights"?

The Supreme Court has been extremely sensitive to classifications based on wealth in the context of criminal prosecutions. "In criminal trials a State can no more discriminate on account of poverty than on account of religion, race, or color" (Griffin v. Illinois, 351 U.S. 12, 17, 76 S.Ct. 585, 590, 100 L.Ed. 891, 898 1956). Griffin opened the door to equal protection attacks on procedures which, although nondiscriminatory on their face, in effect confront the indigent defendant with the "illusory choice" of paying a fee he cannot afford or forfeiting an opportunity available to those who can pay: "There can be no equal justice where the kind of trial a man gets depends on the amount of money he has." We conclude from these authorities that the wealth classification in the instant case warrants close judicial scrutiny.

Strict scrutiny is appropriate because the inability to raise money bail necessarily affects fundamental rights of the indigent defendant. Foremost among these rights is the presumption of innocence. Unless this right to bail before trial is preserved, the presumption of innocence, secured only after centuries of struggle, would lose its meaning. Because they have been convicted of no crime, pretrial detainees may not be punished. The sole permissible interest of the State is to assure their presence at trial. Furthermore, in a system that prides itself on a devotion to "equal justice under the law," it is difficult to maintain that conditions common in pretrial detention centers do not punish defendants presumed innocent but that the more wholesome conditions of minimum security prisons do punish convicted criminals.

Pretrial detention may also infringe upon an accused's right to a fair trial. Courts have long recognized that the right to freedom before conviction permits the unhampered preparation of a defense. If a defendant is locked up, he is hindered in his ability to gather evidence, contact witnesses, or otherwise prepare his defense. The factors of a wealth-based classification in the context of a criminal prosecution, combined with its effect on the fundamental right to be presumed innocent and to prepare an adequate defense, persuade us that the challenged bail practices require strict judicial scrutiny.

C. Does the Classification Serve a Compelling Governmental Interest?

The sole governmental interest served by bail is to assure the presence of the accused at trial. The State also has an interest in denying pretrial release to a defendant who presents an unreasonable danger to the community, however the State may not use bail to serve this end. Other means are available to Florida to secure pretrial detention of dangerous persons. Indeed, the Florida Constitution expressly withholds the right to bail in the case of certain serious crimes. We are not here asked to deprive the State of its power to protect the community from dangerous persons. Our inquiry is limited to those occasions where the State has set bail and has declared, in effect, that a person is free to reenter the community if he is willing to put up a sum of money.

D. Is Money Bail Necessary to Promote the State's Interest in Assuring Appearance?

Judicial condemnation of the modern system of commercial bail bondsmen has transcended political and ideological lines in emphasizing that monetary bail set by a judge has very little to do with assuring appearance at trial. The theory behind money bail is simple: It is assumed that the threat of forfeiture of one's goods will be an effective deterrent to the temptation to break the conditions of one's release. However, "under the professional bondsman system the only one who loses money for non-appearance is the professional bondsman, the money paid to obtain the bond being lost to the defendant in any event" (Pannell v. United States, 115 U.S.App.D.C. 379,

320 F.2d 698, 699 1963). The ultimate effect of such a system, "is that the professional bondsmen hold the keys to the jail in their pockets. They determine for whom they will act as surety who in their judgment is a good risk. The bad risks, in the bondsmen's judgment, and the ones who are unable to pay the bondsmen's fees, remain in jail. The court and the commissioner are relegated to the relatively unimportant chore of fixing the amount of bail."

These valid criticisms of the professional bondsman system persuade us to the view that, in the case of indigents, money bail is irrelevant in promoting the state's interest in assuring appearance. The indigent cannot on his own pay the amount of bail upon which his release has been conditioned. Unless a friend or relative qualifies as surety and is willing to post bond, the indigent must resort to the professional bondsman. Even if the bondsman deems him an acceptable risk, he is unable to pay the bondsman's fee.

The real assurance of appearance under the present system is the risk of forfeiture assumed by the bondsman. Because the bondsman does not want to lose money, he has a powerful incentive to make sure that the defendant for whom he is surety appears at trial. Thus, the bondsman has long enjoyed legal protection as a modern day bounty hunter, entitled to arrest his principal "even under extreme circumstances." In this sense, the accused pays the bondsman to perform a police function apprehension of a person who has jumped bail. An indigent defendant released on his own recognizance would face similar consequences. Presumably, then, the deterrence factor is comparable regardless of whether money bail has been posted.

Even though it is manifest to us that money bail is not always necessary to assure a defendant's appearance, it is necessary to consider whether other "less drastic" alternatives are available to the State. The Supreme Court of Florida, in amending its rule regarding pretrial release, has in effect conceded that many alternatives to money bail are available. It has adopted five additional forms of release, none of which is conditioned on a defendant's ability to pay. Because the new rule appears to be a significant departure from the former heavy emphasis on money bail, we must determine whether it vitiates plaintiffs' constitutional objections.

The new Florida rule is patterned after the Federal Bail Reform Act of 1966, 18 U.S.C. § 3146 (1970), which provides that a person charged with a bailable offense "shall . . . be ordered released pending trial on his personal recognizance or upon the execution of an unsecured appearance bond . . . unless the officer determines, in the exercise of his discretion, that such a release will not reasonably assure the appearance of the person as required." In that event, five alternative forms of release are prescribed in order of priority, with money bail third on the list. The statute thus creates a presumption in favor of release on recognizance, and requires consideration of three other forms of release before money bail. By contrast, while the Florida rule makes available the same release options as does the Federal Act, it omits both the presumption and the order of priority contained in its federal counterpart. Instead, it instructs the judge to "consider all available relevant factors to determine what form of release is necessary." We find nothing in the rule that requires a judge to give priority to forms of release that do not impose a financial burden on a defendant. In fact, the Florida Supreme Court has twice rejected a presumption favoring release on recognizance.

While the new Florida rule expands the options available for pretrial release, it does not provide that indigent defendants will be required to pay money bail only in the event that no other form of release will reasonably assure their appearance at trial. Because it gives the judge essentially unreviewable discretion to impose money bail, the rule retains the discriminatory vice of the former system: When a judge decides to set money bail, the indigent will be forced to remain in jail. We hold that equal protection standards are not satisfied unless the judge is required to consider less financially onerous forms of release before he imposes money bail. Requiring a presumption in favor of non-money bail accommodates the State's interest in assuring the defendant's appearance at trial as well as the defendant's right to be free pending trial, regardless of his financial status.

As a federal court we do not sit to write the rules of procedure of state courts. Plaintiffs in the instant case have not come to us with generalized complaints that the Florida rule concerning bail is unwise or not to their liking. Rather, they have presented a specific constitutional objection to the rule, that it violates an indigent's right to equal protection under the Fourteenth Amendment. We withheld decision of this issue for nearly two years on considerations of comity and out of respect for the responsibility of the Florida Supreme Court to prescribe rules for Florida courts to follow. That court has now promulgated a new rule on pretrial release which, for the reasons stated, has not in our judgment mooted the constitutional point raised by the plaintiffs.

We therefore remand with instructions to the district court to fashion a remedy not inconsistent with this opinion, either on the basis of the present or an augmented record, as that court shall determine.

We have been called upon to decide whether indigent pretrial detainees are deprived of Fourteenth Amendment equal protection of the law when they are imprisoned solely because they cannot afford money bail set under a system that does not require the judge first to consider less financially onerous conditions of release. In evaluating this problem, we have reached several conclusions: (1) When a judge sets money bail in Florida, he creates two de facto classes: non-indigents who presumptively can pay for their pretrial freedom and indigents who surely cannot; (2) This classification must be strictly scrutinized under the equal protection clause because it discriminates against indigent criminal defendants and directly affects their fundamental right to be presumed innocent and to prepare an adequate defense; (3) Although Florida has a compelling interest in assuring a defendant's appearance at trial, (4) money bail is not necessary to promote that interest because the bail bondsman system eliminates the basic premise behind such bail; (5) Florida may promote its compelling interest through alternative forms of release that do not discriminate on the basis of wealth. These factors lead inexorably to the conclusion that Florida's current bail system discriminates invidiously against indigents charged with crime. We hold that it violates the equal protection rights of such indigents.

Our holding is not that money bail may never be imposed on an indigent defendant. The record before us does not justify our telling the State of Florida that in no case will money bail be necessary to assure a defendant's appearance. We hold only that equal protection standards require a presumption against money bail and in favor of those forms of release which do not condition pretrial freedom on an ability to pay. The judgment appealed from is reversed, and this cause is remanded with instructions to the district court to fashion a remedy consistent with this opinion. REVERSED and REMANDED.

REVIEW SECTION

READING COMPREHENSION

Delineate what the court is called upon to decide in this case.

Discuss the court's view of applicable Florida law.

THINKING CRITICALLY

Discuss the impact of this case on varied classes of people.

Do you believe monetary bail is necessary to secure the appearance of a defendant?

SECTION 3: RIGHT TO COUNSEL

OVERVIEW

As mirrored in the Florida Constitution, the Sixth Amendment to the U.S. Constitution states:

> In all criminal prosecution, the accused shall enjoy the right . . . to
> have the assistance of counsel for his defense.

While the court has historically recognized the right to counsel, not until the 1900s did courts recognize the right for appointed counsel in cases where the defendant was unable to avoid such assistance. Such right to counsel attaches at the accusatory stage of the trial and involves the right to counsel that passes the reasonably competent attorney standard, historically referred to as the mockery of justice standard. Should a defendant claim ineffective counsel, s/he must prove that the attorney was no reasonably competent and that this was probably responsible for the conviction.

Section 3.111 of the *Florida Rules of Criminal Procedure* applies to the right to counsel in the case of indigents and will be quoted here at length:

RULE 3.111. PROVIDING COUNSEL TO INDIGENTS. (a) **When Counsel Provided.** A person entitled to appointment of counsel as provided herein shall have counsel appointed when the person is formally charged with an offense, or as soon as feasible after custodial restraint, or at the first appearance before a committing magistrate, whichever occurs earliest. (b) **Cases Applicable.** (1) Counsel shall be provided to indigent persons in all prosecutions for offenses punishable by incarceration including appeals from the conviction thereof. In the discretion of the court, counsel does not have to be provided to an indigent person in a prosecution for a misdemeanor or violation of a municipal ordinance if the judge, at least 15 days prior to trial, files in the cause a written order of no incarceration certifying that the defendant will not be incarcerated in the case pending trial or probation violation hearing, or as part of a sentence after trial, guilty or nolo contendere plea, or probation revocation. This 15-day requirement may be waived by the defendant or defense counsel. (2) Counsel may be provided to indigent persons in all proceedings arising from the initiation of a criminal action against a defendant, including postconviction proceedings and appeals therefrom, extradition proceedings, mental competency proceedings, and other proceedings that are adversary in nature, regardless of the designation of the court in which they occur or the classification of the proceedings as civil or criminal. (3) Counsel may be provided to a partially indigent person on request, provided that the person shall defray that portion of the cost of representation and the reasonable costs of investigation as he or she is able without substantial hardship to the person or the person's family, as directed by the court. (4) "Indigent" shall mean a person who is unable to pay for the services of an attorney, including costs of investigation, without substantial hardship to the person or the person's family; "partially indigent" shall mean a person unable to pay more than a portion of the fee charged by an attorney, including costs of investigation, without substantial hardship to the person or the person's family. (5) Before appointing a public defender, the court shall: (A) inform the accused that, if the public defender is appointed, a lien for the services rendered by the public defender may be imposed under section 27.56, Florida Statutes; (B) make inquiry into the financial status of the accused in a manner not inconsistent with the guidelines established by section 27.52, Florida Statutes. The accused shall respond to the inquiry under oath; (C) require the accused to execute an affidavit of insolvency in the format provided by section 27.52, Florida Statutes.

Section 3.111 of the *Florida Rules of Criminal Procedure* applies to waiver of counsel and will be quoted here at length:

> RULE 3.111. (d) **Waiver of Counsel.** (1) The failure of a defendant to request appointment of counsel or the announced intention of a defendant to plead guilty shall not, in itself, constitute a waiver of counsel at any stage of the proceedings. (2) A defendant shall not be considered to have waived the assistance of counsel until the entire process of offering counsel has been completed and a thorough inquiry has been made into both the accused's comprehension of that offer and the accused's capacity to make a knowing and intelligent waiver. Before determining whether the waiver is knowing and intelligent, the court shall advise the defendant of the disadvantages and dangers of self-representation. (3) Regardless of the defendant's legal skills or the complexity of the case, the court shall not deny a defendant's unequivocal request to represent himself or herself, if the court makes a determination of record that the defendant has made a knowing and intelligent waiver of the right to counsel. (4) A waiver of counsel made in court shall be of record; a waiver made out of court shall be in writing with not less than 2 attesting witnesses. The witnesses shall attest the voluntary execution thereof. (5) If a waiver is accepted at any stage of the proceedings, the offer of assistance of counsel shall be renewed by the court at each subsequent stage of the proceedings at which the defendant appears without counsel.

Of particular note in this section is Section Sixteen of the Florida Constitution which reads:

> In all criminal prosecutions the accused shall, upon demand, be informed of the nature and cause of the accusation, and shall be furnished a copy of the charges, and shall have the right to have compulsory process for witnesses, to confront at trial adverse witnesses, to be heard in person, by counsel or both, and to have a speedy and public trial by impartial jury in the county where the crime was committed.

CASE

Argersinger v. Hamlin examines the right of an indigent defendant in a criminal trial to the assistance of counsel, which is guaranteed by the Sixth Amendment as made applicable to the States by the Fourteenth. In this case, the Supreme Court of Florida erred in holding that the petitioner, an indigent who was tried for an offense punishable by imprisonment up to six months, a $1,000 fine, or both, and given a 90-day jail sentence, had no right to court-appointed counsel, on the ground that the right extends only to trials 'for non-petty offenses punishable by more than six months imprisonment.'

ARGERSINGER V. HAMLIN
407 U.S. 25, 92 S.Ct. 2006, 32 L.Ed.2d 530 (1971)

Petitioner, and indigent, was charged in Florida with carrying a concealed weapon, an offense punishable by imprisonment up to six months, a $1,000 fine, or both. The trial was to a judge, and petitioner was unrepresented by counsel. He was sentenced to serve 90 days in jail, and brought this *habeas corpus* action in the Florida Supreme Court, alleging that, being deprived of his right to counsel, he was unable as an indigent layman properly to raise and present to the trial court good and sufficient defenses to the charge for which he stands convicted. The Florida Supreme Court by a four-to-three decision, held that the right to court-appointed counsel extends only to trials 'for non-petty offenses punishable by more than six months imprisonment.' The case is here on a petition for certiorari, which we granted. We reverse.

The Sixth Amendment, which in enumerated situations has been made applicable to the States by reason of the Fourteenth Amendment provides specified standards for 'all criminal prosecutions.' One is the requirement of a public trial. Another guarantee is the right to be informed of the nature and cause of the accusation. Still another, the right of confrontation. And another, compulsory process for obtaining witnesses in one's favor. We have never limited these rights to felonies or to lesser but serious offenses.

While there is historical support for limiting the commitment to trial by jury to serious criminal cases, there is no such support for a similar limitation on the right to assistance of counsel. The Sixth Amendment extended the right to counsel beyond its common-law dimensions. But there is nothing in the language of the Amendment, its history, or in the decisions of this Court, to indicate that it was intended to embody a retraction of the right in petty offenses wherein the common law previously did require that counsel be provided. We reject, therefore, the premise that since prosecutions for crimes punishable by imprisonment for less than six months may be tried without a jury, they may also be tried without a lawyer. The assistance of counsel is often a requisite to the very existence of a fair trial.

In Gideon v. Wainwright, we dealt with a felony trial. But we did not so limit the need of the accused for a lawyer. We said: 'In our adversary system of criminal justice, any person haled into court, who is too poor to hire a lawyer, cannot be assured a fair trial unless counsel is provided for him. This seems to us to be an obvious truth. Governments, both state and federal, quite properly spend vast sums of money to establish machinery to try defendants accused of crime. Lawyers to prosecute are everywhere deemed essential to protect the public's interest in an orderly society. Similarly, there are few defendants charged with crime, few indeed, who fail to hire the best lawyers they can get to prepare and present their defenses. That government hires lawyers to prosecute and defendants who have the money hire lawyers to defend are the strongest indications of the widespread belief that lawyers in criminal courts are necessities, not luxuries. The right of one charged with crime to counsel may not be deemed fundamental and essential to fair trials in some countries, but it is in ours. From the very beginning, our state and national constitutions and laws have laid great emphasis on procedural and substantive safeguards designed to assure fair trials before impartial tribunals in which every defendant stands equal before the law. This noble ideal cannot be realized if the poor man charged with crime has to face his accusers without a lawyer to assist him' (372 U.S., at 344, 83 S.Ct., at 796).

The requirement of counsel may well be necessary for a fair trial even in a petty-offense prosecution. We are by no means convinced that legal and constitutional questions involved in a case that actually leads to imprisonment even for a brief period are any less complex than when a person can be sent off for six months or more. Beyond the problem of trials and appeals is that of the guilty plea, a problem which looms large in misdemeanor as well as in felony cases. Counsel is needed so that the accused may know precisely what he is doing, so that he is fully aware of the prospect of going to jail or prison, and so that he is treated fairly by the prosecution. In addition, the volume of misdemeanor cases, far greater in number than felony prosecutions, may create an obsession for speedy dispositions, regardless of the fairness of the result. The same picture is seen in almost every report: The misdemeanor trial is characterized by insufficient and frequently irresponsible preparation on the part of the defense, the prosecution, and the court. Everything is rush, rush. There is evidence of the prejudice which results to misdemeanor defendants from this 'assembly-line justice.' We must conclude, therefore, that the problems associated with misdemeanor and petty offenses often require the presence of counsel to insure the accused a fair trial.

We hold, therefore, that absent a knowing and intelligent waiver, no person may be imprisoned for any offense, whether classified as petty, misdemeanor, or felony, unless he was represented by counsel at his trial. We do not sit as an ombudsman to direct state courts how to manage their affairs but only to make clear the federal constitutional requirement. How crimes should be classified is largely a state matter. The fact that traffic charges technically fall within the category of 'criminal prosecutions' does not necessarily mean that many of them will be brought into the class where imprisonment actually occurs.

Under the rule we announce today, every judge will know when the trial of a misdemeanor starts that no imprisonment may be imposed, even though local law permits it, unless the accused is represented by counsel. He will have a measure of the seriousness and gravity of the offense and therefore know when to name a lawyer to represent the accused before the trial starts. The run of misdemeanors will not be affected by today's ruling. But in those that end up in the actual deprivation of a person's liberty, the accused will receive the benefit of the guiding hand of counsel so necessary when one's liberty is in jeopardy.

Reversed.

Mr. Chief Justice BURGER, concurring in the result.

I agree with much of the analysis in the opinion of the Court and with Mr. Justice POWELL's appraisal of the problems. Were I able to confine my focus solely to the burden that the States will have to bear in providing counsel, I would be inclined, at this stage of the development of the constitutional right to counsel, to conclude that there is much to commend drawing the line at penalties in excess of six months' confinement. Yet several cogent factors suggest the infirmities in any approach that allows confinement for any period without the aid of counsel at trial; any deprivation of liberty is a serious matter. The issues that must be dealt with in a trial for a petty offense or a misdemeanor may often be simpler than those involved in a felony trial and yet be beyond the capability of a layman, especially when he is opposed by a law-trained prosecutor. There is little ground, therefore, to assume that a defendant, unaided by counsel, will be any more able adequately to defend himself against the lesser charges that may involve confinement than more serious charges. Appeal from a conviction after an uncounseled trial is not likely to be of much help to a defendant since the die is usually case when judgment is entered on an uncounseled trial record.

Trial judges sitting in petty and misdemeanor cases—and prosecutors—should recognize exactly what will be required by today's decision. Because no individual can be imprisoned unless he is represented by counsel, the trial judge and the prosecutor will have to engage in a predictive evaluation of each case to determine whether there is a significant likelihood that, if the defendant is convicted, the trial judge will sentence him to a jail term. The judge can preserve the option of a jail sentence only by offering counsel to any defendant unable to retain counsel on his own. This need to predict will place a new load on courts already overburdened and already compelled to deal with far more cases in one day than is reasonable and proper. Yet the prediction is not one beyond the capacity of an experienced judge, aided as he should be by the prosecuting officer. As to jury cases, the latter should be prepared to inform the judge as to any prior record of the accused, the general nature of the case against the accused, including any use of violence, the severity of harm to the victim, the impact on the community, and the other factors relevant to the sentencing process. Since the judge ought to have some degree of such information after judgment of guilt is determined, ways can be found in the more serious misdemeanor cases when jury trial is not waived to make it available to the judge before trial.[*] This will not mean a full 'presentence' report on every defendant in every case before the jury passes on guilt, but a prosecutor should know before trial whether he intends to urge a jail sentence, and if he does he should be prepared to aid the court with the factual and legal basis for his view on that score.

This will mean not only that more defense counsel must be provided, but also additional prosecutors and better facilities for securing information about the accused as it bears on the probability of a decision to confine. The question before us today is whether an indigent defendant convicted of an offense carrying a maximum punishment of six months' imprisonment, a fine of $1,000, or both, and sentenced to 90 days in jail, is entitled as a matter of constitutional right to the assistance of appointed counsel. The broader question is whether the Due Process Clause requires that an indigent charged with a state petty offense be afforded the right to appointed counsel.

I am unable to agree with the Supreme Court of Florida that an indigent defendant, charged with a petty offense, may in every case be afforded a fair trial without the assistance of counsel. Nor can I agree with the new rule of due process, today enunciated by the Court, that 'absent a knowing and intelligent waiver, no person may be imprisoned . . . unless he was represented by counsel at his trial.' It seems to me that the line should not be drawn with such rigidity. There is a middle course, between the extremes of Florida's six-month rule and the Court's rule, which comports with the requirements of the Fourteenth Amendment. I would adhere to the principle of due process that requires fundamental fairness in criminal trials, a principle which I believe encompasses the right to counsel in petty cases whenever the assistance of counsel is necessary to assure a fair trial.

I am in accord with the Court that an indigent accused's need for the assistance of counsel does not mysteriously evaporate when he is charged with an offense punishable by six months or less. This is not to say that due process requires the appointment of counsel in all petty cases, or that assessment of the possible consequences of conviction is the sole test for the need for assistance of counsel. The flat six-month rule of the Florida court and the equally inflexible rule of the majority opinion apply to all cases within their defined areas regardless of circumstances. It is precisely because of this mechanistic application that I find these alternatives unsatisfactory. Due process, perhaps the most fundamental concept in our law, embodies principles of fairness rather than immutable line drawing as to every aspect of a criminal trial. While counsel is often essential to a fair trial, this is by no means a universal fact. Some petty offense cases are complex; others are exceedingly simple. Where the possibility of a jail sentence is remote and the probable fine seems small, or where the evidence of guilt is overwhelming, the costs of assistance of counsel may exceed the benefits. It is anomalous that the Court's opinion today will extend the right of appointed counsel to indigent defendants in cases where the right to counsel would rarely be exercised by nonindigent defendants.

Indeed, one of the effects of this ruling will be to favor defendants classified as indigents over those not so classified, yet who are in low-income groups where engaging counsel in a minor petty-offense case would be a luxury the family could not afford. The line between indigency and assumed capacity to pay for counsel is necessarily somewhat arbitrary, drawn differently from State to State and often resulting in serious inequities to accused persons. The Court's new rule will accent the disadvantage of being barely self-sufficient economically. Despite its overbreadth, the easiest solution would be a prophylactic rule that would require the appointment of counsel to indigents in all criminal cases. The simplicity of such a rule is appealing because it could be applied automatically in every case, but the price of pursuing this easy course could be high indeed in terms of its adverse impact on the administration of the criminal justice systems of 50 States. This is apparent when one reflects on the wide variety of petty or misdemeanor offenses, the varying definitions thereof, and the diversity of penalties prescribed. The potential impact on state court systems is also apparent in view of the variations in types of courts and their jurisdictions, ranging from justices of the peace and part-time judges in the small communities to the elaborately staffed police courts which operate 24 hours a day in the great metropolitan centers.

The rule adopted today does not go all the way. It is limited to petty-offense cases in which the sentence is some imprisonment. The thrust of the Court's position indicates, however, that when the decision must be made, the rule will be extended to all petty-offense cases except perhaps the most minor traffic violations. If the Court rejects on constitutional grounds, as it has today, the exercise of any judicial discretion as to need for counsel if a jail sentence is imposed, one must assume a similar rejection of discretion in other petty-offense cases. It would be illogical—and without discernible support in the Constitution—to hold that no discretion may ever be exercised where a nominal jail sentence is contemplated and at the same time endorse the legitimacy of discretion in 'non-jail' petty-offense cases which may result in far more serious consequences than a few hours or days of incarceration.

The Fifth and Fourteenth Amendments guarantee that property, as well as life and liberty, may not be taken from a person without affording him due process of law. The majority opinion suggests no constitutional basis for distinguishing between deprivations of liberty and property. In fact, the majority suggests no reason at all for drawing this distinction. The logic it advances for extending the right to counsel to all cases in which the penalty of any imprisonment is imposed applies equally well to cases in which other penalties may be imposed. Nor does the majority deny that some 'non-jail' penalties are more serious than brief jail sentences.

Thus, although the new rule is extended today only to the imprisonment category of cases, the Court's opinion foreshadows the adoption of a broad prophylactic rule applicable to all petty offenses. No one can foresee the consequences of such a drastic enlargement of the constitutional right to free counsel. But even today's decision could have a seriously adverse impact upon the day-to-day functioning of the criminal justice system. We should be slow to fashion a new constitutional rule with consequences of such unknown dimensions, especially since it is supported neither by history nor precedent.

The majority opinion concludes that, absent a valid waiver, a person may not be imprisoned even for lesser offenses unless he was represented by counsel at the trial. In simplest terms this means that under no circumstances, in any court in the land, may anyone be imprisoned—however briefly—unless he was represented by, or waived his right to, counsel. The opinion is disquietingly barren of details as to how this rule will be implemented. There are thousands of statutes and ordinances which authorize imprisonment for six months or less, usually as an alternative to a fine. These offenses include some of the most trivial of misdemeanors, ranging from spitting on the sidewalk to certain traffic offenses. They also include a variety of more serious misdemeanors. This broad spectrum of petty-offense cases daily floods the lower criminal courts. The rule laid down today will confront the judges of each of these courts with an awkward dilemma. If counsel is not appointed or knowingly waived, no sentence of imprisonment for any duration may be imposed. The judge will therefore be forced to decide in advance of trial—and without hearing the evidence—whether he will forgo entirely his judicial discretion to impose some sentence of imprisonment and abandon his responsibility to consider the full range of punishments established by the legislature. His alternatives, assuming the availability of counsel, will be to appoint counsel and retain the discretion vested in him by law, or to abandon this discretion in advance and proceed without counsel.

If the latter course is followed, the first victim of the new rule is likely to be the concept that justice requires a personalized decision both as to guilt and the sentence. The notion that sentencing should be tailored to fit the crime and the individual would have to be abandoned in many categories of offenses. In resolving the dilemma as to how to administer the new rule, judges will be tempted arbitrarily to divide petty offenses into two categories—those for which sentences of imprisonment may be imposed and those in which no such sentence will be given regardless of the statutory authorization. In creating categories of offenses which by law are imprisonable but for which he would not impose jail sentences, a judge will be overruling de facto the legislative determination as to the appropriate range of punishment for the particular offense. It is true, as the majority notes, that there are some classes of imprisonable offenses for which imprisonment is rarely imposed. But even in these, the occasional imposition of such a sentence may serve a valuable deterrent purpose. At least the legislatures, and until today the courts, have viewed the threat of imprisonment—even when rarely carried out—as serving a legitimate social function.

The new rule announced today also could result in equal protection problems. There may well be an unfair and unequal treatment of individual defendants, depending on whether the individual judge has determined in advance to leave open the option of imprisonment. Thus, an accused indigent would be entitled in some courts to counsel while in other courts in the same jurisdiction an indigent accused of the same offense would have no counsel. Since the services of counsel may be essential to a fair trial even in cases in which no jail sentence is imposed, the results of this type of pretrial judgment could be arbitrary and discriminatory. A different type of discrimination could result in the typical petty-offense case where judgment in the alternative is prescribed: for example, 'five days in jail or $100 fine.' If a judge has predetermined that no imprisonment will be imposed with respect to a particular category of cases, the indigent who is convicted will often receive no meaningful sentence. The defendant who can pay a $100 fine, and does so, will have responded to the sentence in accordance with law, whereas the indigent who commits the identical offense may pay no penalty. Nor would there be any deterrent against the repetition of similar offenses by indigents.

To avoid these equal protection problems and to preserve a range of sentencing options as prescribed by law, most judges are likely to appoint counsel for indigents in all but the most minor offenses where jail sentences are extremely rare. It is doubtful that the States possess the necessary resources to meet this sudden expansion of the right to counsel.

Perhaps the most serious potential impact of today's holding will be on our already overburdened local courts. The primary cause of 'assembly line' justice is a volume of cases far in excess of the capacity of the system to handle efficiently and fairly. The Court's rule may well exacerbate delay and congestion in these courts. We are familiar with the common tactic of counsel of exhausting every possible legal avenue, often without due regard to its probable payoff. In some cases this may be the lawyer's duty; in other cases it will be done for purposes of delay. The absence of direct economic impact on the client, plus the omnipresent ineffective-assistance-of-counsel claim, frequently produces a decision to litigate every issue. It is likely that young lawyers, fresh out of law school, will receive most of the appointments in petty-offense cases. The admirable zeal of these lawyers; their eagerness to make a reputation; the time their not yet crowded schedules permit them to devote to relatively minor legal problems; their desire for courtroom exposure; the availability in some cases of hourly fees, lucrative to the novice; and the recent constitutional explosion in procedural rights for the accused—all these factors are likely to result in the stretching out of the process with consequent increased costs to the public and added delay and congestion in the courts.

There is an additional problem. The ability of various States and localities to furnish counsel varies widely. Even if there were adequate resources on a national basis, the uneven distribution of these resources—of lawyers, of facilities, and available funding—presents the most acute problem. A number of state courts have considered the question before the Court in this case, and have been compelled to confront these realities. Many have concluded that the indigent's right to appointed counsel does not extend to all misdemeanor cases. In reaching this conclusion, the state courts have drawn the right-to-counsel line in different places, and most have acknowledged that they were moved to do so, at least in part, by the impracticality of going further. In other States, legislatures and courts through the enactment of laws or rules have drawn the line short of that adopted by the majority. These cases and statutes reflect the judgment of the courts and legislatures of many States, which understand the problems of local judicial systems better than this Court, that the rule announced by the Court today may seriously overtax capabilities.

I would hold that the right to counsel in petty-offense cases is not absolute but is one to be determined by the trial courts exercising a judicial discretion on a case-by-case basis. The determination should be made before the accused formally pleads; many petty cases are resolved by guilty pleas in which the assistance of counsel may be required. If the trial court should conclude that the assistance of counsel is not required in any case, it should state its reasons so that the issue could be preserved for review. The trial court would then become obligated to scrutinize carefully the subsequent proceedings for the protection of the defendant. If an unrepresented defendant sought to enter a plea of guilty, the Court should examine the case against him to insure that there is admissible evidence tending to support the elements of the offense. If a case went to trial without defense counsel, the court should intervene, when necessary, to insure that the defendant adequately brings out the facts in his favor and to prevent legal issues from being overlooked. Formal trial rules should not be applied strictly against unrepresented defendants. Finally, appellate courts should carefully scrutinize all decisions not to appoint counsel and the proceedings which follow.

It is impossible, as well as unwise, to create a precise and detailed set of guidelines for judges to follow in determining whether the appointment of counsel is necessary to assure a fair trial. Certainly three general factors should be weighed. First, the court should consider the complexity of the offense charged. For example, charges of traffic law infractions would rarely present complex legal or factual questions, but charges that contain difficult intent elements or which raise collateral legal questions, such as search-and-seizure problems, would usually be too complex for an unassisted layman. If the offense were one where the State is represented by counsel and where most defendants who can afford to do so obtain counsel there would be a strong indication that the indigent also needs the assistance of counsel. Second, the court should consider the probable sentence that will follow if a conviction is obtained. The more serious the likely consequences, the greater is the probability that a lawyer should be appointed. As noted in Part I above, imprisonment is not the only serious consequence the court should consider. Third, the court should consider the individual factors peculiar to each case. These, of course, would be the most difficult to anticipate. One relevant factor would be the competency of the individual defendant to present his own case. The attitude of the community toward a particular defendant or particular incident would be another consideration. But there might be other reasons why a defendant would have a peculiar need for a lawyer which would compel the appointment of counsel in a case where the court would normally think this unnecessary. Obviously, the sensitivity and diligence of individual judges would be crucial to the operation of a rule of fundamental fairness requiring the consideration of the varying factors in each case.

In concluding, I emphasize my longheld conviction that the adversary system functions best and most fairly only when all parties are represented by competent counsel. Before becoming a member of this Court, I participated in efforts to enlarge and extend the availability of counsel. The correct disposition of this case, therefore, has been a matter of considerable concern to me— as it has to the other members of the Court. We are all strongly drawn to the ideal of extending the right to counsel, but I differ as to two fundamentals: (i) what the Constitution requires, and (ii) the effect upon the criminal justice system, especially in the smaller cities and the thousands of police, municipal, and justice of the peace courts across the country. The view I have expressed in this opinion would accord considerable discretion to the courts, and would allow the flexibility and opportunity for adjustment which seems so necessary when we are imposing new doctrine on the lowest level of courts of 50 States. But the according of reviewable discretion to the courts in determining when counsel is necessary for a fair trial, rather than mandating a completely inflexible rule, would facilitate an orderly transition to a far wider availability and use of defense counsel.

In this process, the courts of first instance which decide these cases would have to recognize a duty to consider the need for counsel in every case where the defendant faces a significant penalty. The factors mentioned above, and such standards or guidelines to assure fairness as might be prescribed in each jurisdiction by legislation or rule of court, should be considered where relevant. The goal should be, in accord with the essence of the adversary system, to expand as rapidly as practicable the availability of counsel so that no person accused of crime must stand alone if counsel is needed. As the proceedings in the courts below were not in accord with the views expressed above, I concur in the result of the decision in this case.

REVIEW SECTION

READING COMPREHENSION

Elaborate the facts of this case.

What difficulties arise for "petty cases" that proceed without the benefit of counsel?

THINKING CRITICALLY

Defend your opinion regarding whether counsel should be required for any offense that may result in imprisonment. Discuss the potential burden on the criminal justice system.

CONCLUSION

At the discretion of the prosecutor's office, a defendant begins his/her journey through the start of court proceedings. In this chapter we addressed probable cause, first appearance and issues of bail, as well as the intricacies of the right to counsel – when this right attaches and under what conditions counsel is required. Especially with regard to the right to counsel, issues arise regarding the taxation on the criminal justice system and how this may or may not balance with the right of an individual to a fair proceeding.

Chapter Thirteen

Pretrial, Trial, and Conviction

After a decision to charge by the prosecutor's office, what follows are adversarial proceedings as well as informal negotiation. During the pretrial, trial, and conviction stages of the process, several formal rules govern criminal cases which are the subject of this section. Keep in mind Section Sixteen of the Florida Constitution which addresses information of charges filed, the right to counsel, the right to a speedy and public trial, rules regarding venue, and the rights of victims in such a proceeding:

> **Rights of accused and of victims.** (a) In all criminal prosecutions the accused shall, upon demand, be informed of the nature and cause of the accusation, and shall be furnished a copy of the charges, and shall have the right to have compulsory process for witnesses, to confront at trial adverse witnesses, to be heard in person, by counsel or both, and to have a speedy and public trial by impartial jury in the county where the crime was committed. If the county is not known, the indictment or information may charge venue in two or more counties conjunctively and proof that the crime was committed in that area shall be sufficient; but before pleading the accused may elect in which of those counties the trial will take place. Venue for prosecution of crimes committed beyond the boundaries of the state shall be fixed by law. (b) Victims of crime or their lawful representatives, including the next of kin of homicide victims, are entitled to the right to be informed, to be present, and to be heard when relevant, at all crucial stages of criminal proceedings, to the extent that these rights do not interfere with the constitutional rights of the accused.

This chapter will review:

(1)   Testing the government's case;

(2)   Pretrial motions; and

(3)   Conviction by jury trial.

SECTION 1: TESTING THE GOVERNMENT'S CASE

OVERVIEW

The government must engage in one of two procedures to test the case against a defendant. After a criminal information has been written, the case is tested in a preliminary hearing. This process is held in public and is an adversarial hearing wherein a judge presides and determines the facts of the case. If states provide a preliminary hearing, for which there is no constitutional right, the defendant does have the right to an attorney. Whether the judge decides to send the case to trial is based on either a *prima facie* case rule or a directed verdict rule, depending on the court. A *prima facie* case rule allows the judge to send the case to trial if evidence is presented that, if not rebutted by the defense, could convict the defendant. A directed verdict rule is one in which the judge views presentation of the evidence as if the hearing were a trial and makes a judgment accordingly. The *Florida Rules of Criminal Procedure* elaborate the elements of a preliminary hearing and its requirements and thus is quoted at length:

> **RULE 3.133. PRETRIAL PROBABLE CAUSE DETERMINATIONS AND ADVERSARY PRELIMINARY HEARINGS.** (a) **Nonadversary Probable Cause Determination.** (1) **Defendant in Custody.** In all cases in which the defendant is in custody, a nonadversary probable cause determination shall be held before a magistrate within 48 hours from the time of the defendant's arrest . . . (3) **Standard of Proof.** Upon presentation of proof, the magistrate shall determine whether there is probable cause for detaining the arrested person pending further proceedings. The defendant need not be present. In determining probable cause to detain the defendant, the magistrate shall apply the standard for issuance of an arrest warrant, and the finding may be based on sworn complaint, affidavit, deposition under oath, or, if necessary, on testimony under oath properly recorded. (4) **Action on Determination.** If probable cause is found, the defendant shall be held to answer the charges. If probable cause is not found or the specified time periods are not complied with, the defendant shall be released from custody unless an information or indictment has been filed, in which event the defendant shall be released on recognizance subject to the condition that he or she appear at all court proceedings or shall be released under a summons to appear before the appropriate court at a time certain. . . The magistrate shall order the release of the defendant after it is determined that the defendant is entitled to release and after the state has a reasonable period of time, not to exceed 24 hours, in which to establish probable cause. . . (b) **Adversary Preliminary Hearing.** (1) **When Applicable.** A defendant who is not charged in an information or indictment within 21 days from the date of arrest or service of the capias on him or her shall have a right to an

adversary preliminary hearing on any felony charge then pending against the defendant. The subsequent filing of an information or indictment shall not eliminate a defendant's entitlement to this proceeding.

Should the government seek an indictment, the case is presented to a grand jury for review. The Fifth Amendment to the U.S. Constitution provides:

> . . . no person shall be held to answer for a capital, or otherwise infamous crime, unless on presentment or indictment by a Grand Jury . . .

A grand jury review is a private proceeding in which only the government's case is presented, but which is intended to protect citizens from unwarranted intrusion by the state. A prosecutor presides over the review and the facts are determined by grand jurors. You should keep in mind that most grand juries follow the recommendation provided by the prosecutor.

SECTION 2: PRETRIAL MOTIONS

OVERVIEW

Pretrial motions are requests of the court to consider issues that do not need to be ruled on during the actual trial. These include speedy trial, double jeopardy, change of venue, and suppression of evidence.

While the Florida Constitution in Section Sixteen guarantees defendants the right to a speedy trial, it is important to remember that according to the U.S. Supreme Court, the clock does not begin until a suspect is formally charged. Prior to this time, defendants must rely on statutes that address specifically the length of time permitted between the commission of a crime and when the charge is filed. Also note that the right to a speedy trial only prevents against undue delays and in determination the court considers the length and reason for the delay and any prejudice the delay causes to the case. Delays that result from determining the competency of the defendant, trials of the defendant that may be occurring, hearings on pretrial motions, and interlocutory appeals are not considered.

The guidelines to a speedy trial are outlined in Rule 3.191 of the *Florida Rules of Criminal Procedure* which will be elaborated here in great detail:

> (a) **Speedy Trial without Demand.** Except as otherwise provided by this rule, and subject to the limitations imposed under subdivisions (e) and (f), every person charged with a crime by indictment or information shall be brought to trial within 90 days if

the crime charged is a misdemeanor, or within 175 days if the crime charged is a felony. If trial is not commenced within these time periods, the defendant shall be entitled to the appropriate remedy as set forth in subdivision (p). The time periods established by this subdivision shall commence when the person is taken into custody as defined under subdivision (d). A person charged with a crime is entitled to the benefits of this rule whether the person is in custody in a jail or correctional institution of this state or a political subdivision thereof or is at liberty on bail or recognizance or other pretrial release condition. This subdivision shall cease to apply whenever a person files a valid demand for speedy trial under subdivision (b). (c) **Commencement of Trial.** A person shall be considered to have been brought to trial if the trial commences within the time herein provided. The trial is considered to have commenced when the trial jury panel for that specific trial is sworn for *voir dire* examination or, on waiver of a jury trial, when the trial proceedings begin before the judge. (d) **Custody.** For purposes of this rule, a person is taken into custody (1) when the person is arrested as a result of the conduct or criminal episode that gave rise to the crime charged, or (2) when the person is served with a notice to appear in lieu of physical arrest. (f) **Consolidation of Felony and Misdemeanor.** When a felony and a misdemeanor are consolidated for disposition in circuit court, the misdemeanor shall be governed by the same time period applicable to the felony. (j) **Delay and Continuances; Effect on Motion.** If trial of the accused does not commence within the periods of time established by this rule, a pending motion for discharge shall be granted by the court unless it is shown that: (1) a time extension has been ordered under subdivision (i) and that extension has not expired; (2) the failure to hold trial is attributable to the accused, a codefendant in the same trial, or their counsel; (3) the accused was unavailable for trial under subdivision (k); or (4) the demand referred to in subdivision (g) is invalid. (*l*) **Exceptional Circumstances.** As permitted by subdivision (i) of this rule, the court may order an extension of the time periods provided under this rule when exceptional circumstances are shown to exist. Exceptional circumstances shall not include general congestion of the court's docket, lack of diligent preparation, failure to obtain available witnesses, or other avoidable or foreseeable delays. Exceptional circumstances are those that, as a matter of substantial justice to the accused or the state or both, require an order by the court.

Another pretrial motion is double jeopardy. The Fifth Amendment to the U.S. Constitution guarantees that a person will not be tried twice for the same offense. This means that after conviction a person may not be tried for the same offense, after acquittal a person may not be tried for the same offense, and multiple punishments for the same offense may not result. Keep in mind therefore, that if a trial ends prior to either conviction or acquittal, the prosecution reserves the right to re-file charges for the same offense. Also of relevance is that it is not considered double jeopardy to both prosecute and punish a defendant for the same offense in a separate jurisdiction, or to prosecute a defendant in multiple trials for separate offenses that arose out of the same incident.

The Sixteenth Amendment of the Florida Constitution guarantees a trial in the venue in which the crime was committed. Only the defense can move to change the venue of a trial, at which time the judge must consider the reasonable likelihood that the case was prejudiced in the initial venue. The final pretrial motion involves suppression of evidence using the exclusionary rule that has been discussed at length in a previous chapter.

CASE

Lippman v. State of Florida is a review of Lippman v. State, 595 So.2d 190, 194 (Fla. 3d DCA 1992). In that case, the Third District Court of Appeal raised the following questions: Whether an order modifying probation by prohibiting contact between probationer and victim or victim's minor siblings (for the purpose of protecting the victim and siblings) constitutes an additional punishment proscribed by the double jeopardy clause?; and Where a probationer is undergoing psychiatric treatment for a sexual offense as a condition of probation, does a probation modification order prohibiting contact between probationer and victim or victim's minor siblings constitute a modification of an existing probation condition or an additional punishment proscribed by the double jeopardy clause?

LIPPMAN V. STATE OF FLORIDA
Supreme Court of Florida
633 So.2d 1061, 19 Fla. L. Weekly S129 (1994)

For the reasons expressed in this opinion, we answer the first question in the affirmative and determine that the circumstances raised in the second question constitute an additional punishment proscribed by the Double Jeopardy Clause.

Timothy Lippman pled no contest to three counts of attempted capital sexual battery. The minor victim was one of Lippman's siblings. Pursuant to a plea agreement, the trial court sentenced Lippman to two years probation with the following special conditions: 1) that he "undergo psychiatric treatment until such time as the person in charge of such treatment and his Probation Supervisor determine that such treatment is no longer necessary"; and 2) as Lippman requested, that he would be permitted to transfer his probation to another state. Lippman began the psychiatric treatment, obtained a job as a security officer, and volunteered his services at the Florida City Police Department. During this time, Lippman lived in his parents' home with the victim and other minor siblings. Eight months into the probationary term, Lippman's probation officer filed an affidavit of violation. The affidavit stated that Lippman refused to comply with the probation officer's demands to resign from the volunteer job at the police department and to remove police department decals from his car. The affidavit also stated that Lippman had been charged with impersonating a police officer, the unlawful use of radio equipment, loitering, and prowling. When Lippman appeared in court pursuant to the affidavit, the trial judge noted that Lippman did not appear to be in violation of probation because the alleged violations seemed to arise from Lippman's job as a security officer. Accordingly, the court dismissed the affidavit because there was no evidence that Lippman had violated his probation.

Two days later the probation officer re-filed the same affidavit for violation of probation. However, the State withdrew the affidavit when the judge once again stated that Lippman had not violated any of his probationary conditions nor broken any laws. At the judge's suggestion, the State made an oral motion to modify probation in order to clarify the supervisory conditions. Prior to this hearing, the court received a letter from the therapist who was providing Lippman's court-ordered psychiatric treatment. Neither Lippman nor his attorney had seen this letter prior to the hearing. The therapist expressed concern over Lippman's arrest, his lack of progress in the psychiatric treatment program, and his irregular attendance at the program. The therapist asked the court to modify Lippman's probation by: 1) extending the term from two to seven years; 2) ordering Lippman to pay for and successfully complete the Mentally Disordered Sex Offender program; 3) prohibiting Lippman's participation in any job or activity where he would wear a police-type uniform or use police-type equipment; and 4) restricting Lippman's contact with his immediate family until the entire family entered a program for family members of mentally-disordered sex offenders and all therapists approved contact with the family.

Lippman and his family complained to the judge that the therapist's recommendation would be a great hardship as Lippman would have to move from his parent's residence but would have no income for rent because he would be required to quit his job. Although the trial judge agreed that it would be a great hardship, he entered the order modifying Lippman's probation as requested by the therapist, with the exception of the family contact provision. The judge only restricted Lippman's contact with the minor victim and the other minor siblings, not with his entire family. Lippman did not object to this modification as a violation of double jeopardy, nor did he appeal the enhanced probation order.

Seven months later the court revoked Lippman's probation for having contact with the minor siblings and sentenced him to twelve years in prison. Lippman appealed the revocation order on evidentiary grounds. The Third District Court of Appeal affirmed the judgment and sentence. Lippman then moved for post-conviction relief under Florida Rule of Criminal Procedure 3.850, arguing that the court order changing his probation conditions was imposed in violation of his constitutional right against double jeopardy, and thus his subsequent incarceration for violating the additional conditions also violated double jeopardy. The trial court denied Lippman relief under rule 3.850. On appeal, the Third District Court of Appeal ruled that the no-contact condition was "a modification of an existing probation condition rather than the imposition of a new condition" and did not violate double jeopardy. The district court also certified the questions to this Court.

Initially we determine that conditions described in the certified questions constitute enhancements of the original sentence rather than modifications. Even though the district court characterized the trial judge's order as a supervisory order entered for the protection of the victim and the victim's siblings rather than a sanction, the motivation for adding these conditions does not change their punitive effect. These "protective" measures required Lippman to leave his employment, move from his residence, and have absolutely no contact with his siblings. The trial judge even acknowledged that the new conditions would be an additional hardship. While such conditions could have been included in the initial probationary order had circumstances required, there is no question that the added conditions are more restrictive than those imposed by the initial order. Consequently, we find that the added conditions, including the no-contact condition, enhanced the terms of Lippman's original probationary sentence.

Both the United States Constitution and the Florida Constitution guarantee that no individual will be put in jeopardy more than once for the same offense. It is the protection against multiple punishments for the same offense that is implicated in this case. Probation is a sentence in Florida. Thus, the double jeopardy protection against multiple punishments includes the protection against enhancements or extensions of the conditions of probation. Before probation may be enhanced, a violation of probation must be formally charged and the probationer must be brought before the court and advised of the charge. Absent proof of a violation, the court cannot change an order of probation by enhancing the terms. In the instant case, the court specifically found no violation of probation, yet proceeded to enhance the terms of Lippman's probation. This violated the double jeopardy prohibition against multiple punishments for the same offense. Thus, the order modifying probation must be vacated. The consequences that resulted from Lippman's violation of that modified probation must be vacated as well, including the order revoking probation, the adjudication of guilt, and the sentence imposed.

The State argues that Lippman is procedurally barred from raising this matter in a rule 3.850 proceeding because it should have been raised on direct appeal from the trial court's modification order. We do not agree. The prohibition against double jeopardy is "fundamental." As this Court concluded State v. Johnson, 483 So.2d 420, 423 (Fla.1986), "the failure to timely raise a double jeopardy claim does not, in and of itself, serve as a waiver of the claim." Lippman appealed the judge's order, but failed to raise the double jeopardy claim. Although this Court cautioned that there may be limited instances in which a defendant may be found to have knowingly waived his double jeopardy rights, the circumstances of the instant case do not support such a finding. Lippman did not knowingly waive his double jeopardy protection. Thus, Lippman's double jeopardy claim is not procedurally barred.

Accordingly, we quash the decision of the district court below. We remand for further proceedings consistent with this opinion and with instructions that the order of modified probation, the order revoking probation, the adjudication of guilt, and the sentence of imprisonment be vacated. It is so ordered. BARKETT, C.J., and SHAW, GRIMES and KOGAN, JJ., concur.

McDONALD, J., dissents with an opinion, in which OVERTON, J., concurs.

I dissent. The original order of probation entered in this case preserved the right of the trial judge to modify the terms and conditions of probation. One of the responsibilities of a trial judge is to protect the public from the conduct of a probationer. It is thus important to allow a trial judge the authority to modify and, I believe, even to add new conditions to the terms of probation if, in the judgment of the trial judge, it is necessary to do so to assure successful completion of probation. Incidentally, the additional conditions were added at a probation revocation hearing and, even though the trial judge made no finding that Lippman had violated the terms of his original probation order, neither Lippman nor his attorney objected to the additional terms.

I recognize that in Clark v. State, 579 So.2d 109, 111 (Fla.1991), we stated, over my protest: "Absent proof of a violation, the court cannot change an order of probation or community control by enhancing the terms thereof...." That rule should have no application when a trial judge, in his or her own order, reserves the right to modify or change the conditions. Lippman is a sex offender. The trial judge, by adding the restriction that Lippman would have no contact with his minor siblings, was attempting to minimize the temptation to Lippman of repeating his offenses. This specific condition was added to protect the siblings and assist in the psychiatric management of Lippman after a report from the psychiatrist that Lippman was not making good progress in the court-mandated psychiatric treatment. Regrettably, my views have fallen on deaf ears with the majority. I reiterate, however, that the district court properly denied Lippman relief and, because I fervently believe it correct, republish what it said: As a preliminary matter, we need not reach the issue of whether the portion of the probation order which extended Lippman's probation from two to seven years was objectionable on double jeopardy grounds. That is so because Lippman's probation was revoked during the original two-year probationary term. Lippman never completed the initial two years and never began serving the five-year extended term. The probation has now been revoked and any question regarding the five-year extension is now moot.

We next consider the modification to the probation order for which Lippman's probation was revoked--the requirement that Lippman refrain from contact with his minor siblings. This requirement was not in the original probation order, but was added by the modification order. We conclude that the modification order did not violate the double jeopardy clause. To begin with, probation is "a form of community supervision requiring specified contacts with parole and probation officers and other terms and conditions as provided in s. 948.03." Sec. 948.001(2), Fla.Stat. (1987). Florida Statutes (1987) confer broad authority on the trial court to "determine the terms and conditions of probation...." The statute also provides: "The enumeration of specific kinds of terms and conditions shall not prevent the court from adding such other or others as it considers proper. The court may rescind or modify at any time the terms and conditions theretofore imposed...."

In the present case the trial court had the statutory authority to add the proscription against contact by the defendant with the minor victim and minor siblings. Lippman argues, however, that the no-victim-or-minor-sibling-contact prohibition constituted an additional punishment which violated the double jeopardy clause. We disagree. The double jeopardy clause does not impose a rule against modification of probation orders. Instead, the inquiry is whether there has been an impermissible increase in the penalty imposed. It is self-evident that the order prohibiting contact with the minor victim and minor victim's siblings is not a new, additional, or enhanced punishment within the meaning of the double jeopardy clause. It is a supervisory order entered for the protection of the victim and the victim's siblings. It was plainly not imposed as a sanction but on the contrary to safeguard those in need of protection. A provision of a modification order which protects a victim of crime from contact by a probationer is not a penalty for purposes of double jeopardy analysis and is not prohibited by the double jeopardy clause.

So far we have accepted for purposes of discussion Lippman's contention that the no-victim-or-minor-sibling-contact limitation was a new term of his probation, added by the modification order. It is our view, however, that the modification is also accurately characterized as a modification of an existing condition of probation. It is well settled that a court can modify a term or condition previously imposed. Lippman's original probation order included a requirement that he undergo psychiatric treatment. After a period of treatment, Lippman's therapists made four recommendations to the court. The trial court modified the recommendation so as to proscribe contact with the minors in the family, but not the parents. We conclude that the proscription against minor sibling contact is fairly viewed as a modification of an existing probation condition rather than the imposition of a new condition.

For the reasons stated, the provision of the modification order at issue here did not violate the double jeopardy clause of either the Florida or federal constitution. In our view, the analysis outlined here properly applies the teaching of the Florida Supreme Court and the United States Supreme Court.

REVIEW SECTION

READING COMPREHENSION

Detail the facts of this case.

THINKING CRITICALLY

Should a trial judge have the right to modify the terms and conditions of probation absent a violation?

How would you decide this case? Use the majority and dissenting opinion to formulate your argument. What role, if any, does the nature of the crime play in your decision?

CASE

State of Florida v. Naveira involves the speedy trial rule. The court must decide whether, when the State files a charging document on the last day of the speedy trial period and the defendant invokes his right to a speedy trial by filing a notice of expiration of the speedy trial period, but later moves for a continuance based on insufficient time to prepare for trial, the continuance should be charged to the State (thus discharging the defendant) or to the defendant. In the decision under review, the First District Court of Appeal held that the trial court properly discharged the defendant because he had been forced to request a continuance as the result of the State's delay in filing the information, and thus was not brought to trial within the speedy trial period. This holding conflicts with State v. Fraser, 426 So. 2d 46 (Fla. 5th DCA 1982), which held that the defendant was not entitled to discharge where he requested a continuance.

STATE OF FLORIDA V. NAVEIRA
Supreme Court of Florida
No. SC02-633 (Fla. 4/22/2004) (Fla., 2004)

For the reasons explained below, we quash the First District's decision and hold that the defendant's right to speedy trial under rule 3.191, Florida Rules of Criminal Procedure, was not violated in this case where trial was scheduled within the rule's deadlines and the defendant sought a continuance because he was not prepared for trial.

Respondent Juan Naveira was arrested for sexual battery and false imprisonment on February 25, 1999. On August 19, the 175th day after the arrest, the State filed an information charging Naveira with one count of sexual battery. Also on that day, the State responded to Naveira's previously filed demand for discovery. Five days later, Naveira filed a notice of expiration of speedy trial time under rule 3.191(p)(2), alleging that more than 175 days had elapsed since his arrest. Two days after that, the trial court held a hearing on Naveira's notice of expiration. The State explained that it had filed the information on the 175th day after arrest due to difficulty in contacting the victim, and that the delay was in no way attributable to Naveira. The State maintained, however, that the information was timely filed. The State then requested that trial be set for the following week. The defense argued that it could not be ready for trial the following week because the case involved a serious sexual battery charge and the defense had not had the opportunity to fully review the discovery. The trial court indicated that if the defense wished to move for a continuance, the continuance would probably be attributed to the State, but that the court would decide that issue the following week. The trial court then set the case for trial on August 30.

On August 27, Naveira filed a motion for continuance, arguing that it should be charged to the State. On September 9, Naveira filed a motion for discharge. The motion argued that more than fifteen days had elapsed since the filing of the notice of expiration. On October 21, the trial court granted Naveira's motion for continuance and ordered that it be charged to the State. On December 8, the trial court held a hearing on Naveira's motion for discharge. The State argued that Naveira was entitled to the continuance but not the discharge. The court granted Naveira's motion for discharge in a written order, ruling only that "Rule 3.191(a) requires the discharge of a defendant if the information is not even filed until the 176th day, as was done in this case." The State appealed. The First District reversed and remanded. The court found that the date of arrest is excluded when calculating the deadline under the speedy trial rule. Therefore, the court held that the information was filed on the 175th day, not the 176th day, after his arrest, and thus the information was filed within the speedy trial period. The court remanded for further proceedings, expressly not addressing whether there may be other grounds for discharging Naveira.

On remand, Naveira again moved for discharge. The trial court granted the motion, finding that, based on two cases from the First District, "even without a showing of misconduct on the State's part, discharge under the speedy trial rule is appropriate where a late-filed information implicates the ability to prepare a defense." The State again appealed. The First District upheld the discharge based on its precedent. The State now seeks review of that decision.

The State raises two issues. We first address the State's argument that once the appellate court ruled in Naveira and remanded the case to the trial court, the prior speedy trial deadlines no longer applied and under rule 3.191 the State automatically had another ninety days to bring Naveira to trial. We then address the State's argument that even if the prior speedy trial deadlines remained an issue, no speedy trial violation occurred because the State committed no misconduct and the only reason that Naveira was not tried within the speedy trial period was his own motion for continuance.

We first address what the State presents as its second issue because we believe it to be a threshold matter. The State claims that after its first appeal, it was automatically entitled to an additional ninety days to bring Naveira to trial under rule 3.191(m), Florida Rules of Criminal Procedure: Effect of Mistrial; Appeal; Order of New Trial. A person who is to be tried again or whose trial has been delayed by an appeal by the state or the defendant shall be brought to trial within 90 days from the declaration of a mistrial by the trial court, the date of an order by the trial court granting a new trial, the date of an order by the trial court granting a motion in arrest of judgment, or the date of receipt by the trial court of a mandate, order, or notice of whatever form from a reviewing court that makes possible a new trial for the defendant, whichever is last in time. If a defendant is not brought to trial within the prescribed time periods, the defendant shall be entitled to the appropriate remedy as set forth in subdivision (p).

In Naveira, the First District disagreed with the State's argument that rule 3.191(m) applied on remand. The court noted: The state argues that appellee waived his right to rely on remand on the alternative ground for discharge because he failed to raise that ground as an alternative basis for affirmance in the first appeal. Alternatively, it argues that the issue became moot following the first appeal because of rule 3.191(m), which extends the time within which a defendant must be brought to trial by 90 days following an appeal. We disagree. We are satisfied that the panel deciding the first appeal intended to permit the alternative ground for discharge to be considered on remand because the trial court had not previously addressed it. Therefore, appellee did not waive his right to raise that issue on remand, and the 90-day extension afforded by rule 3.191(m) would not come into play unless the trial court denied the motion for discharge (807 So. 2d).

We agree with the First District's resolution of this issue. The State's argument effectively ignores the procedural posture of this case. Naveira had effectively argued two grounds for discharge: (1) that the State did not file the information until the 176th day after arrest (in the notice of expiration and subsequent hearings); and (2) that he was not brought to trial within fifteen days of filing the notice of expiration (in the motion for discharge and subsequent hearings). The trial court granted Naveira's motion for discharge based on the first ground, without addressing the second. Thus, the sole issue in Naveira was "whether the day of arrest is counted in the calculation of the speedy-trial-rule time." The First District held it is not. The court did not address other possible grounds for discharge.

Therefore, when the First District remanded the case, the trial court had not yet ruled on Naveira's argument that he was not brought to trial within fifteen days under rule 3.191(p). Rule 3.191(m) does not apply in these circumstances. In other words, the automatic ninety-day extension after appeal in the rule does not apply where the appellate court has remanded a case in which the trial court has yet to rule on a defendant's motion for discharge alleging the speedy trial rule already had been violated before the appeal. Rule 3.191(m) grants the State 90 days after the appeal to bring the defendant to trial if the trial court finds no prior speedy trial violation.

We now consider whether the trial court properly discharged Naveira under rule 3.191. We initially note that, by its terms, rule 3.191 governs only the time for bringing a defendant to trial. It does not address the deadline for filing the charging document itself. Previously, however, we have held that the State cannot wait until after the speedy trial period to charge a defendant. The speedy trial period begins when a defendant is first taken into custody, not when charges are first filed. By holding that an information filed on the 175th day does not violate the speedy trial rule, the court implicitly held that the State may file the charging document on the last day for bringing the defendant to trial.

The First District also noted that the recapture provisions of rule 3.191(p) (allowing a defendant to be tried even after the speedy trial deadline) "presuppose that an information or indictment has been filed within the initial 175 day time period." We confirm that the State may file a charging document at any time within the applicable speedy trial period. The State cannot charge the defendant after that period expires. Essentially, then, the speedy trial deadline also acts as the deadline for charging the defendant.

We hold that the trial court erred in granting the motion for discharge. Naveira was not ready for trial on the date trial was scheduled and in fact requested a continuance; thus, he was unavailable for trial under subdivision (k) and was not entitled to be discharged. The speedy trial right at issue here is not one of constitutional dimension and clearly may be waived. Nor is the defendant's lack of fault, or even possible defense prejudice, a determining factor in deciding whether speedy trial was waived by the defense being unavailable for trial. In any event, Appellant is not prejudiced, as the defense at all times had available the 50 day speedy trial by demand remedy provided under rule 3.191, as well as speedy trial principles available under the state and U.S. constitutions. The Fourth District concluded that the defendant waived his right to speedy trial.

Naveira argues that our conclusion unlawfully forces him to choose between two rights, the right to speedy trial and the right to adequately prepare for trial. We disagree. Naveira had the right to invoke the speedy trial rule and go to trial within ten days. He also had the right to request a continuance because he was not prepared to go to trial in ten days. The State correctly did not oppose a continuance, and the trial court correctly granted it. In fact, denial of such a request may constitute an abuse of discretion in these circumstances. The mere fact that Naveira had to elect between a speedy trial under the rule and adequate preparation, did not violate his constitutional rights.

The right to speedy trial provided in rule 3.191 is not coextensive with the broader <u>constitutional</u> right to a speedy trial. No constitutional right exists to a trial within 175 days of arrest. Florida's speedy trial rule is a procedural protection and, except for the right to due process under the rule, does not reach constitutional dimension. When Naveira filed his notice of expiration, he was on notice that the trial court would hold a hearing within five days and a trial within ten days. Under the rule, he received the right to an immediate trial. He declined to exercise that right, as was his prerogative. But he cannot now protest that his right to a speedy trial was violated. Although we sympathize with the defendant's position in this case, the fact remains that under rule 3.191, Naveira's right to speedy trial existed until he declined to exercise it. Naveira was not <u>compelled</u>, as the dissent asserts, to abandon his right to a speedy trial.

The dissent argues that where the speedy trial period expires through no fault of the defendant, any continuance should be charged to the State. In this case, the dissent proposes that because the State did not file the information until the last day of the speedy trial period, and therefore the defendant was not ready for trial before the period expired, the defendant should be discharged. We disagree. Adopting such an interpretation would contradict the plain language of the applicable subdivisions of rule 3.191, as we have explained above. The flaw in the dissent's analysis is that in this case the State did not need, and therefore did not request, an extension of the speedy trial period. Following rule 3.191, it filed charges on the 175th day after arrest. It was then prepared to go to trial within the recapture period. Therefore, neither subdivision (i) (extensions of time) nor (*l*) (defining exceptional circumstances) applies. Rather, in this case both the State and the trial court followed all the rule's deadlines <u>without</u> any extensions.

The dissent's interpretation of the rule would replace a clear deadline with an amorphous one that depends on the circumstances of each case. According to the dissent, the State must file the information not only within the speedy trial period itself (175 days from arrest), but even before that—with sufficient time left in the period to give the defendant adequate time to prepare for trial. But whether the time remaining is adequate to prepare for trial will depend on many factors, including the seriousness of the charges filed, the crime allegedly committed, the facts of the case, the number of witnesses, and a host of other factors that determine trial preparation. Moreover, different judges will necessarily rule differently on whether, under the same circumstances, the State filed charges with sufficient time left in the period. Therefore, the State would not be able to predict, in any given case, whether the timing of its charging document complied with the rule. The speedy trial period would now include an implicit "speedy charging period" with a shifting and unknown deadline.

As we noted earlier, rule 3.191 does not by its terms impose any deadlines for charging a defendant; only for bringing the defendant to trial. Nevertheless, we have interpreted the rule also to require the State to <u>charge</u> the defendant within 175 days of arrest. The dissent's interpretation would require the State to charge the defendant even earlier, but at an unknown date that would depend on the circumstances. We decline to interpret the rule to impose such unclear deadlines, with Draconian results (dismissal) when the State fails to correctly predict them.

We approve in part and quash in part the First District's decision. We approve that part of the decision holding that upon remand, Naveira was entitled to raise the issue of whether the speedy trial period had expired. We quash the district court's decision on the merits, however. We hold that the defendant's right to speedy trial under 3.191 was not violated where Naveira invoked the speedy trial rule, trial was scheduled as provided in the rule's recapture provisions, and the only reason the trial was not held according to rule 3.191's recapture provision was Naveira's own motion for continuance. Thus, the trial court erred in discharging the defendant. We remand this case for proceedings consistent with this opinion. It is so ordered.

REVIEW SECTION

READING COMPREHENSION

What are the facts of this case? Detail the position of Naveira and the State.

Elaborate the Florida Rules of Criminal Procedure under examination.

SECTION 3: CONVICTION BY JURY TRIAL

OVERVIEW

While only ten percent of cases are decided in trial, the U.S. Supreme Court, the U.S. Constitution, and all state constitutions guarantee the right to trial by jury, the purpose being a check on government power by transference to a community-dominated body. The only exception to the right to trial by jury is the case of 'petty offenses,' those being ones with less than six months' imprisonment as the maximum penalty. There are however, exceptions to the exception, including deception of immigration officials, driving while under the influence, and shoplifting. These offenses give a defendant the right to trial by jury regardless of the state statute indicating length of prison term. According to Section Twenty-Two of the Florida Constitution,

> The right of trial by jury shall be secure to all and remain inviolate.
> The qualifications and the number of jurors, not fewer than six,
> shall be fixed by law.

The *Florida Rules of Criminal Procedure* further elaborate the right to trial by jury and the conditions attached as will be evident in the two rules listed below:

> **RULE 3.251. RIGHT TO TRIAL BY JURY.** In all criminal prosecutions the accused shall have the right to a speedy and public trial by an impartial jury in the county where the crime was committed.
>
> **RULE 3.260. WAIVER OF JURY TRIAL.** A defendant may in writing waive a jury trial with the consent of the state.

The constitution of the jury must represent a cross-section of the community in which the trial is held, including diversity of members based on race, gender, ethnicity, and religion. The Federal Jury Selection and Service Act outlines guidelines for selection of jurors and similar provisions are outlined in the *Florida Rules of Criminal Procedure* as quoted in depth below*:*

> **RULE 3.270. NUMBER OF JURORS**. Twelve persons shall constitute a jury to try all capital cases, and 6 persons shall constitute a jury to try all other criminal cases.
>
> **RULE 3.290. CHALLENGE TO PANEL.** The state or defendant may challenge the panel. A challenge to the panel may be made only on the ground that the prospective jurors were not selected or drawn according to law. Challenges to the panel shall be made and decided before any individual juror is examined, unless otherwise ordered by the court.
>
> **RULE 3.300. VOIR DIRE EXAMINATION, OATH, AND EXCUSING OF MEMBER.** (a) Oath. The prospective jurors shall be sworn collectively or individually, as the court may decide. The form of oath shall be as follows: "Do you solemnly swear (or affirm) that you will answer truthfully all questions asked of you as prospective jurors, so help you God?" If any prospective juror affirms, the clause "so help you God" shall be omitted. (b) Examination. The court may then examine each prospective juror individually or may examine the prospective jurors collectively. Counsel for both the state and defendant shall have the right to examine jurors orally on their voir dire. (c) Prospective Jurors Excused. If, after the examination of any prospective juror, the court is of the opinion that the juror is not qualified to serve as a trial juror, the court shall excuse the juror from the trial of the cause. If, however, the court does not excuse the juror, either party may then challenge the juror, as provided by law or by these rules.

The *Florida Rules of Criminal Procedure* also outline in detail the time and criterion for challenging a potential juror:

> **RULE 3.310. TIME FOR CHALLENGE.** The state or defendant may challenge an individual prospective juror before the juror is sworn to try the cause; except that the court may, for good cause, permit a challenge to be made after the juror is sworn, but before any evidence is presented.
>
> **RULE 3.350. PEREMPTORY CHALLENGES.** (a) Number. Each party shall be allowed the following number of peremptory challenges: (1) Felonies Punishable by Death or Imprisonment for Life. Ten, if the offense charged is punishable by death or imprisonment for life. (2) All Other Felonies. Six, if the offense charged is a felony not punishable by death or imprisonment for life. (3) Misdemeanors. Three, if the offense charged is a misdemeanor.

Once jurors are selected, they are required to take the following oath as documented in the *Florida Rules of Criminal Procedure* Rule 3.360:

> The following oath shall be administered to the jurors: "Do you solemnly swear (or affirm) that you will well and truly try the issues between the State of Florida and the defendant and render a true verdict according to the law and the evidence, so help you God?" If any juror affirms, the clause "so help you God" shall be omitted.

During the trial phase, prior to the deliberation by jurors, the judge instructs the members as outlined in the *Florida Rules of Criminal Procedure* Rule 3.390:

> (a) **Subject of Instructions.** The presiding judge shall charge the jury only on the law of the case at the conclusion of argument of counsel. Except in capital cases, the judge shall not instruct the jury on the sentence that may be imposed for the offense for which the accused is on trial. (b) **Form of Instructions.** Every charge to a jury shall be orally delivered, and charges in capital cases shall, and in the discretion of the court in noncapital cases may, also be in writing. All written charges shall be filed in the cause. Charges in other than capital cases shall be taken by the court reporter and, if the jury returns a verdict of guilty, transcribed by the court reporter and filed in the cause. (c) **Written Request.** At the close of the evidence, or at such earlier time during the trial as the court reasonably directs, any party may file written requests that the court instruct the jury on the law as set forth in the requests. The court shall inform counsel of its proposed action on the request and of the instructions that will be given prior to their argument to the

jury. (d) **Objections.** No party may raise on appeal the giving or
failure to give an instruction unless the party objects thereto before
the jury retires to consider its verdict, stating distinctly the matter
to which the party objects and the grounds of the objection.
Opportunity shall be given to make the objection out of the
presence of the jury.

What you may notice in the rule above is that in capital cases the judge does not instruct the jury
on the sentence that may be imposed. Is it fair to have the jury deliberate a defendant's guilt
while remaining unaware that the potential sentence is death?

CASE

Prior to his trial for robbery in the State of Florida, the petitioner in *Williams v. State of Florida*
filed a Motion for a Protective Order, seeking to be excused from the rule that requires a
defendant to give notice in advance of trial if the defendant intends to claim an alibi, and to
furnish the prosecuting attorney with information as to the place where he claims to have been
and with the names and addresses of the alibi witnesses he intends to use. In the motion, the
petitioner openly declared his intent to claim an alibi, but objected to the further disclosure
requirements on the ground that the rule compels the Defendant in a criminal case to be a witness
against himself in violation of his Fifth and Fourteenth Amendment rights. The motion was
denied. Petitioner also filed a pretrial motion to impanel a 12-man jury instead of the six-man
jury provided by Florida law in all but capital cases. That motion too was denied. Petitioner was
convicted as charged and was sentenced to life imprisonment. The District Court of Appeal
affirmed, rejecting petitioner's claims that his Fifth and Sixth Amendment rights had been
violated. The Supreme Court of Florida granted certiorari.

WILLIAMS V. STATE OF FLORIDA
Williams v. Florida, 399 U.S. 78, 90 S.Ct. 1893, 26 L.Ed.2d 446 (1970)

Florida's notice-of-alibi rule is in essence a requirement that a defendant submit to a limited form
of pretrial discovery by the State whenever he intends to rely at trial on the defense of alibi. In
exchange for the defendant's disclosure of the witnesses he proposes to use to establish that
defense, the State in turn is required to notify the defendant of any witnesses it proposes to offer
in rebuttal to that defense. Both sides are under a continuing duty promptly to disclose the names
and addresses of additional witnesses bearing on the alibi as they become available. The
threatened sanction for failure to comply is the exclusion at trial of the defendant's alibi
evidence—except for his own testimony—or, in the case of the State, the exclusion of the State's
evidence offered in rebuttal of the alibi.

In this case, following the denial of his Motion for a Protective Order, petitioner complied with
the alibi rule and gave the State the name and address of one Mary Scotty. Mrs. Scotty was
summoned to the office of the State Attorney on the morning of the trial, where she gave pretrial

testimony. At the trial itself, Mrs. Scotty, petitioner, and petitioner's wife all testified that the three of them had been in Mrs. Scotty's apartment during the time of the robbery. On two occasions during cross-examination of Mrs. Scotty, the prosecuting attorney confronted her with her earlier deposition in which she had given dates and times that in some respects did not correspond with the dates and times given at trial. Mrs. Scotty adhered to her trial story, insisting that she had been mistaken in her earlier testimony. The State also offered in rebuttal the testimony of one of the officers investigating the robbery who claimed that Mrs. Scotty had asked him for directions on the afternoon in question during the time when she claimed to have been in her apartment with petitioner and his wife.

We need not linger over the suggestion that the discovery permitted the State against petitioner in this case deprived him of 'due process' or a 'fair trial.' Florida law provides for liberal discovery by the defendant against the State, and the notice-of-alibi rule is itself carefully hedged with reciprocal duties requiring state disclosure to the defendant. Given the ease with which an alibi can be fabricated, the State's interest in protecting itself against an eleventh-hour defense is both obvious and legitimate. Reflecting this interest, notice-of-alibi provisions, dating at least from 1927, are now in existence in a substantial number of States. The adversary system of trial is hardly an end in itself; it is not yet a poker game in which players enjoy an absolute right always to conceal their cards until played. We find ample room in that system, at least as far as 'due process' is concerned, for the instant Florida rule, which is designed to enhance the search for truth in the criminal trial by insuring both the defendant and the State ample opportunity to investigate certain facts crucial to the determination of guilt or innocence.

Petitioner's major contention is that he was compelled to be a witness against himself contrary to the commands of the Fifth and Fourteenth Amendments because the notice-of-alibi rule required him to give the State the name and address of Mrs. Scotty in advance of trial and thus to furnish the State with information useful in convicting him. No pretrial statement of petitioner was introduced at trial; but armed with Mrs. Scotty's name and address and the knowledge that she was to be petitioner's alibi witness, the State was able to take her deposition in advance of trial and to find rebuttal testimony. Also, requiring him to reveal the elements of his defense is claimed to have interfered with his right to wait until after the State had presented its case to decide how to defend against it. We conclude, however, as has apparently every other court that has considered the issue, that the privilege against self-incrimination is not violated by a requirement that the defendant give notice of an alibi defense and disclose his alibi witnesses.

The defendant in a criminal trial is frequently forced to testify himself and to call other witnesses in an effort to reduce the risk of conviction. When he presents his witnesses, he must reveal their identity and submit them to cross-examination which in itself may prove incriminating or which may furnish the State with leads to incriminating rebuttal evidence. That the defendant faces such a dilemma demanding a choice between complete silence and presenting a defense has never been thought an invasion of the privilege against compelled self-incrimination. The pressures generated by the State's evidence may be severe but they do not vitiate the defendant's choice to present an alibi defense and witnesses to prove it, even though the attempted defense ends in catastrophe for the defendant. However 'testimonial' or 'incriminating' the alibi defense proves to be, it cannot be considered 'compelled' within the meaning of the Fifth and Fourteenth Amendments.

Very similar constraints operate on the defendant when the State requires pretrial notice of alibi and the naming of alibi witnesses. Nothing in such a rule requires the defendant to rely on an alibi or prevents him from abandoning the defense; these matters are left to his unfettered choice. That choice must be made, but the pressures that bear on his pretrial decision are of the same nature as those that would induce him to call alibi witnesses at the trial: the force of historical fact beyond both his and the State's control and the strength of the State's case built on these facts. Response to that kind of pressure by offering evidence or testimony is not compelled self-incrimination transgressing the Fifth and Fourteenth Amendments.

In the case before us, the notice-of-alibi rule by itself in no way affected petitioner's crucial decision to call alibi witnesses or added to the legitimate pressures leading to that course of action. At most, the rule only compelled petitioner to accelerate the timing of his disclosure, forcing him to divulge at an earlier date information that the petitioner from the beginning planned to divulge at trial. Nothing in the Fifth Amendment privilege entitles a defendant as a matter of constitutional right to await the end of the State's case before announcing the nature of his defense, any more than it entitles him to await the jury's verdict on the State's case-in-chief before deciding whether or not to take the stand himself. Petitioner concedes that absent the notice-of-alibi rule the Constitution would raise no bar to the court's granting the State a continuance at trial on the ground of surprise as soon as the alibi witness is called. Nor would there be self-incrimination problems if, during that continuance, the State was permitted to do precisely what it did here prior to trial: take the deposition of the witness and find rebuttal evidence. But if so utilizing a continuance is permissible under the Fifth and Fourteenth Amendments, then surely the same result may be accomplished through pretrial discovery, as it was here, avoiding the necessity of a disrupted trial. We decline to hold that the privilege against compulsory self-incrimination guarantees the defendant the right to surprise the State with an alibi defense.

Duncan v. Louisiana, 391 U.S. 145, 88 S.Ct. 1444, 20 L.Ed.2d 491 (1968), we held that the Fourteenth Amendment guarantees a right to trial by jury in all criminal cases that were they to be tried in a federal court—would come within the Sixth Amendment's guarantee. Petitioner's trial for robbery on July 3, 1968, clearly falls within the scope of that holding. The question in this case then is whether the constitutional guarantee of a trial by 'jury' necessarily requires trial by exactly 12 persons, rather than some lesser number—in this case six. We hold that the 12-man panel is not a necessary ingredient of 'trial by jury,' and that respondent's refusal to impanel more than the six members provided for by Florida law did not violate petitioner's Sixth Amendment rights as applied to the States through the Fourteenth. We had occasion in Duncan v. Louisiana to review briefly the oft-told history of the development of trial by jury in criminal cases. That history revealed a long tradition attaching great importance to the concept of relying on a body of one's peers to determine guilt or innocence as a safeguard against arbitrary law enforcement. That same history, however, affords little insight into the considerations that gradually led the size of that body to be generally fixed at 12. Some have suggested that the number 12 was fixed upon simply because that was the number of the presentment jury from the hundred, from which the petit jury developed. In short, while sometime in the 14th century the size of the jury at common law came to be fixed generally at 12, that particular feature of the jury system appears to have been a historical accident, unrelated to the great purposes which gave rise to the jury in the first place. The question before us is whether this accidental feature of the jury has been immutably codified into our Constitution.

This Court's earlier decisions have assumed an affirmative answer to this question. The leading case so construing the Sixth Amendment is Thompson v. Utah, 170 U.S. 343, 18 S.Ct. 620, 42 L.Ed. 1061 (1898). There the defendant had been tried and convicted by a 12-man jury for a crime committed in the Territory of Utah. A new trial was granted, but by that time Utah had been admitted as a State. The defendant's new trial proceeded under Utah's Constitution, providing for a jury of only eight members. This Court reversed the resulting conviction, holding that Utah's constitutional provision was an *ex post facto* law as applied to the defendant. In reaching its conclusion, the Court announced that the Sixth Amendment was applicable to the defendant's trial when Utah was a Territory, and that the jury referred to in the Amendment was a jury 'constituted, as it was at common law, of twelve persons, neither more nor less.' Arguably unnecessary for the result, this announcement was supported simply by referring to the Magna Carta, and by quoting passages from treatises which noted—what has already been seen—that at common law the jury did indeed consist of 12. Noticeably absent was any discussion of the essential step in the argument: namely, that every feature of the jury as it existed at common law—whether incidental or essential to that institution—was necessarily included in the Constitution wherever that document referred to a 'jury.' Subsequent decisions have reaffirmed the announcement in Thompson often in dictum and usually by relying where there was any discussion of the issue at all—solely on the fact that the common-law jury consisted of 12. While 'the intent of the Framers' is often an elusive quarry, the relevant constitutional history casts considerable doubt on the easy assumption in our past decisions that if a given feature existed in a jury at common law in 1789, then it was necessarily preserved in the Constitution.

Three significant features may be observed in the background of the Constitution's jury trial provisions. First, even though the vicinage requirement was as much a feature of the common-law jury as was the 12-man requirement, the mere reference to 'trial by jury' in Article III was not interpreted to include that feature. Indeed, as the subsequent debates over the Amendments indicate, disagreement arose over whether the feature should be included at all in its common-law sense, resulting in the compromise described above. Second, provisions that would have explicitly tied the 'jury' concept to the 'accustomed requisites' of the time were eliminated. Such action is concededly open to the explanation that the 'accustomed requisites' were thought to be already included in the concept of a 'jury.' But that explanation is no more plausible than the contrary one: that the deletion had some substantive effect. Indeed, given the clear expectation that a substantive change would be effected by the inclusion or deletion of an explicit 'vicinage' requirement, the latter explanation is, if anything, the more plausible. Finally, contemporary legislative and constitutional provisions indicate that where Congress wanted to leave no doubt that it was incorporating existing common-law features of the jury system, it knew how to use express language to that effect. Thus, the Judiciary bill, signed by the President on the same day that the House and Senate finally agreed on the form of the Amendments to be submitted to the States, provided in certain cases for the narrower 'vicinage' requirements that the House had wanted to include in the Amendments. And the Seventh Amendment, providing for jury trial in civil cases, explicitly added that 'no fact tried by a jury, shall be otherwise re-examined in any Court of the United States, than according to the rules of the common law.'

We do not pretend to be able to divine precisely what the word 'jury' imported to the Framers, the First Congress, or the States in 1789. It may well be that the usual expectation was that the jury would consist of 12, and that hence, the most likely conclusion to be drawn is simply that little thought was actually given to the specific question we face today. But there is absolutely no indication in 'the intent of the Framers' of an explicit decision to equate the constitutional and common-law characteristics of the jury. Nothing in this history suggests, then, that we do violence to the letter of the Constitution by turning to other than purely historical considerations to determine which features of the jury system, as it existed at common law, were preserved in the Constitution. The relevant inquiry, as we see it, must be the function that the particular feature performs and its relation to the purposes of the jury trial. Measured by this standard, the 12-man requirement cannot be regarded as an indispensable component of the Sixth Amendment.

The purpose of the jury trial is to prevent oppression by the Government. Given this purpose, the essential feature of a jury obviously lies in the interposition between the accused and his accuser of the commonsense judgment of a group of laymen, and in the community participation and shared responsibility that results from that group's determination of guilt or innocence. The performance of this role is not a function of the particular number of the body that makes up the jury. To be sure, the number should probably be large enough to promote group deliberation, free from outside attempts at intimidation, and to provide a fair possibility for obtaining a representatives cross-section of the community. But we find little reason to think that these goals are in any meaningful sense less likely to be achieved when the jury numbers six, than when it numbers 12—particularly if the requirement of unanimity is retained. And, certainly the reliability of the jury as a factfinder hardly seems likely to be a function of its size.

It might be suggested that the 12-man jury gives a defendant a greater advantage since he has more 'chances' of finding a juror who will insist on acquittal and thus prevent conviction. But the advantage might just as easily belong to the State, which also needs only one juror out of twelve insisting on guilt to prevent acquittal. What few experiments have occurred—usually in the civil area—indicate that there is no discernible difference between the results reached by the two different-sized juries. In short, neither currently available evidence nor theory suggests that the 12-man jury is necessarily more advantageous to the defendant than a jury composed of fewer members. Similarly, while in theory the number of viewpoints represented on a randomly selected jury ought to increase as the size of the jury increases, in practice the difference between the 12-man and the six-man jury in terms of the cross-section of the community represented seems likely to be negligible. Even the 12-man jury cannot insure representation of every distinct voice in the community, particularly given the use of the peremptory challenge. As long as arbitrary exclusions of a particular class from the jury rolls are forbidden, the concern that the cross-section will be significantly diminished if the jury is decreased in size from 12 to six seems an unrealistic one.

We conclude, in short, as we began: the fact that the jury at common law was composed of precisely 12 is a historical accident, unnecessary to effect the purposes of the jury system and wholly without significance 'except to mystics.' To read the Sixth Amendment as forever codifying a feature so incidental to the real purpose of the Amendment is to ascribe a blind formalism to the Framers which would require considerably more evidence than we have been able to discover in the history and language of the Constitution or in the reasoning of our past decisions. We do not mean to intimate that legislatures can never have good reasons for concluding that the 12-man jury is preferable to the smaller jury, or that such conclusions— reflected in the provisions of most States and in our federal system—are in any sense unwise. Legislatures may well have their own views about the relative value of the larger and smaller juries, and may conclude that, wholly apart from the jury's primary function, it is desirable to spread the collective responsibility for the determination of guilt among the larger group. In capital cases, for example, it appears that no State provides for less than 12 jurors—a fact that suggests implicit recognition of the value of the larger body as a means of legitimating society's decision to impose the death penalty. Our holding does no more than leave these considerations to Congress and the States, unrestrained by an interpretation of the Sixth Amendment that would forever dictate the precise number that can constitute a jury. Consistent with this holding, we conclude that petitioner's Sixth Amendment rights, as applied to the States through the Fourteenth Amendment, were not violated by Florida's decision to provide a six-man rather than a 12-man jury. The judgment of the Florida District Court of Appeal is Affirmed.

REVIEW SECTION

READING COMPREHENSION

Discuss the historical development of trial by jury in criminal cases.

Detail the facts of this case and the findings of lower courts.

THINKING CRITICALLY

Is it reasonable to require a defendant to give notice of an alibi in order to prevent an eleventh-hour defense?

Detail your opinion regarding the number of jurors. Considering most courts use a twelve-person jury in capital cases, does this imply any sort of advantage to a defendant with a twelve person as opposed to six person jury?

CONCLUSION

After a defendant is charged, both adversarial proceedings and informal negotiation follow that are dictated by several formal rules that prevail in criminal cases. These rules are informed by Section Sixteen of the Florida Constitution which addresses information of charges filed, the right to counsel, the right to a speedy and public trial, rules regarding venue, and the rights of victims in such a proceeding. This chapter explored the test of the government's case, the myriad of pretrial motions available, and rules governing trial by jury.

Chapter Fourteen

After Conviction

While offenders are entitled some rights after the conviction phase of the process, these rights are much more limited. Due process only minimally affects sentencing powers, there exists no constitutional right to appeal, and *habeus corpus* is limited.

This chapter will review the procedures that occur after conviction:

(1)   Sentencing;

(2)   Death sentences; and

(3)   Appeals and collateral attack.

SECTION 1: SENTENCING

OVERVIEW

From the 1600s to the late 1800s, fixed sentencing was the norm, wherein sentencing authority was in the hands of legislators. Following that a trend toward indeterminate sentencing emerged which tailored the punishment to suit the criminal with the power in the hands of judges and parole boards. Beginning in the 1970s the philosophy shifted again, this time to one of harsher penalties. While indeterminate sentencing remains, fixed sentences are beginning to gain ground in the form of sentencing guidelines and mandatory minimums. In theory, these sentences are to provide uniformity, provide certainty and truth, as well as meet the goals of retribution, deterrence, and incapacitation.

Major changes have occurred in Florida's criminal sentencing and punishment policies beginning in 1980 and continuing to present day. Florida has transformed the punishment of serious offenders and the indeterminate system has been replaced with the determinate methods. One example of such determinate sentencing is 'truth-in-sentencing' policy wherein all offenders are required to serve a minimum of 85% of their prison sentences.

Let us examine in detail the shift in sentencing policy in the state of Florida. As of October 1983, parole which has been in existence since 1941 was eliminated except in the case of capital crimes. In addition a deterministic sentencing guideline structure was created by the Supreme Court to be used for all felony conviction. As well, unearned gaintime served to reduce sentences by one-third and house arrest was implemented as a criminal justice policy.

In the late 1980s, a lack of adequate prison space resulted in passage of the Administrative Gaintime Law. This law enabled the Department of Corrections to reduce the overcrowding problem by increasing gaintime and inmate release. Eligibility for gaintime, later termed provisional credits was determined by the inmate's current and prior crimes. This period also resulted in the passage of Felony Habitual Offender and Violent Habitual Offenders laws wherein felony offenders with two prior convictions or one prior violent conviction could be sentenced to a longer prison term, without the benefit of early prison release due to less gaintime.

In 1991 there was a policy shift from the existing non-discretionary, statutorily mandated early release eligibility program that was managed by the Department of Corrections to a discretionary early release program under the authority of the Parole Commission. This shifted review to a case by case basis and replaced the program of provisional credits or gaintime previously used in Florida.

The mid-1990s saw many sentencing reforms in the state, beginning with the restructuring of the 1983 Sentencing Guidelines in an attempt to prioritize prison space. Gaintime which had previously been used to reduce sentences by one-third was effectively eliminated and power shifted from the Supreme Court to the Department of Corrections. Politically, the discontinuation of early release programs coincided with a massive and accelerated prison construction program throughout the state. In 1995 the legislature passed into law the Truth in Sentencing Law which requires all inmates to serve a minimum of 85% of the court imposed sentence regardless of mitigating factors, such as good behavior. As well, the Violent Career Criminal Act was passed which requires substantially longer prison terms for offenders who meet the following criterion: previous conviction of three or more forcible felonies and other crimes involving firearms or violence, and those who have previously been in prison but have not remained crime free for five years. The law requires such offenders to be sentenced under this Act unless exempted by the court.

The 1995 Sentencing Guidelines enhance punishment for a variety of current and prior crimes, with a focus on violent crimes. While these guidelines provided point level scores, recommended sentences for murder and sexual offenses were significantly enhanced and mandatory minimum sentences were implemented. In addition, the guidelines increased the value of aggravating factors such as prior record in determining an offender's sentence. These guidelines were enhanced further in 1997 when the Prison Releasee Reoffender Act was passed which required offenders who committed specified violent crimes within three years of prison release to be subjected to a mandatory maximum prison sentence and to serve 100% of this sentence.

In the late 1990s the Criminal Punishment Code was passed by the legislature which created a dramatic change in sentencing policy. Under this Code, any felony offender, regardless of their point level score according to the 1995 Sentencing Guidelines, can be sentenced up to the statutory maximum. Effectively, this Code lowers the sentencing threshold, making offenders more likely to receive longer prison terms.

As well, the 10-20-Life Mandates created mandatory minimum terms of imprisonment for the possession, discharge and causing death or injury with a firearm. Under this Mandate, mandatory minimums are as follows: possession of a firearm – 10 years; possession of a semi-automatic or machine gun – 15 years; discharge of any type of firearm – 20 years; and discharge with great bodily injury or death – 25 years to life. These are mandatory minimum sentencing requirements which removes all discretion from judges and fails to consider any type of mitigating circumstance. When an individual is convicted of an offense punishable by a mandatory minimum sentence, the judge must sentence the defendant to the mandatory minimum or to a higher sentence. Further, a prisoner serving a mandatory minimum sentence for a federal offense and for most state offenses is not be eligible for parole. Finally, 1999 saw the passage of the Three Strike Violent Felony Offender Act which mandates that offenders who have been convicted of specified violent offenses and have two prior conviction for any such offenses receive the maximum prison penalty for the offense in question. Discretion here lies at the hands of the state attorney and how the prosecutor's office decides to charge the individual. A third degree felony results in 5 years, a second degree felony results in 15 years, a first degree felony results in 30 years, and life felonies result in life imprisonment. As well, this Act created mandatory minimum terms of imprisonment for repeat offenders of sexual battery, drug trafficking, and some offenses committed against the elderly or law enforcement personnel.

Mandatory minimum sentencing is perhaps most pronounced when examining drug related issues, therefore we will devote some time to this discussion. All of these guidelines are adapted from the Florida Department of Corrections website and are current as of March 2003. First, let us look at possession offenses. The possession of drug paraphernalia is a misdemeanor, punishable by up to one year in jail and a fine of up to $1,000. Possession of 20 grams or less of marijuana is a misdemeanor, punishable by up to one year in jail and a fine of up to $1,000. Possession of greater than 20 grams of marijuana is a felony, punishable by up to five years in prison and a fine of up to $5,000. Next, let us look at sale or cultivation offenses. The delivery of 20 grams or less of marijuana for no consideration is a misdemeanor and is punishable by up to one year in jail and a fine of up to $1,000. Sale, delivery or cultivation of any other amount up to 25 pounds is a felony and punishable by up to five years in prison and a fine of up to $5,000. Sale, delivery or cultivation of greater than 25 pounds is considered trafficking, and all trafficking offenses have mandatory minimum sentences. For less than 2,000 pounds or less than 2,000 plants, there is a mandatory minimum sentence of three years and a fine of $25,000. For less than 10,000 pounds or less than 10,000 plants there is a mandatory minimum sentence of seven years and a fine of $50,000. For 10,000 pounds or 10,000 plants or greater, the mandatory minimum sentence is 15 years in prison and a fine of $200,000. In addition, any sale or delivery of drugs occurring within 200 feet of a college, public park or public housing, or occurring within 1,000 feet of a school, daycare center or church is punishable by up to 15 years in prison and a fine of $10,000. Furthermore, conviction on any of the above offenses requires by law the suspension of the offender's driver's license for at least six months but no longer than two years.

CASE

State of Florida v. Estevez is a review of Estevez v. State, 713 So. 2d 1039 (Fla. 3d DCA 1998), wherein the court posed the following question: Does the absence of a specific finding by the jury on the verdict form that the defendant is guilty of cocaine trafficking in an amount of 400 grams or more, in the face of uncontroverted evidence that the amount at issue exceeded 400 grams, preclude imposition of a minimum mandatory sentence under Section 893-135?

STATE OF FLORIDA V. ESTEVEZ
Supreme Court of Florida
753 So.2d 1 (Fla. 1999)

For the following reasons, we answer the certified question in the affirmative and approve the decision of the district court. Respondent, Luis Manuel Estevez, was charged by information with trafficking in cocaine in excess of 400 grams and with conspiracy to traffic in cocaine. Under the provisions of section 893.135, Florida Statutes (1995), the trafficking statute, it is unlawful to possess twenty-eight grams or more of cocaine. In addition, the mandatory minimum sentences to be imposed under the statute are dependent upon the amount of cocaine involved. The statute mandates a fifteen-year minimum sentence if the amount involved exceeds 400 grams.

At Estevez' trial, evidence was presented of his violation of section 893.135 and that the amount of cocaine involved exceeded 400 grams. Before the jury retired for deliberations, the court discussed the proposed verdict form with the parties and the jury. The proposed form contained a space for the jury to indicate that it found the defendant guilty of trafficking in cocaine as charged in the information, and alternatively, a space for the jury to indicate that it found the defendant not guilty of that charge. In addition, the form contained a line where the jury could indicate that "the defendant is guilty of cocaine trafficking," followed by several specific categories as to the amount of cocaine involved and a space next to each for the jury to indicate its finding as to the amount. After conferring with both parties, the trial judge crossed out "the defendant is guilty of cocaine trafficking" language, and explained to the jury that the form should now be easier to understand, while reminding the jurors that they still had to find the amount of cocaine involved by checking one of the choices provided.

Count one reads: We the jury find as follows: The defendant in this case, and check on one of two things. The defendant is guilty of Trafficking in Cocaine. That's Count One in the information. Or the defendant is not guilty. Those are the two choices here. And now if you believe that he is guilty of Trafficking in Cocaine as charged, then you will check A., more than four hundred grams, or B. more than two hundred grams, but less than four hundred grams, or C. more than twenty-eight grams but less than two hundred grams; or D.,less than twenty-eight grams, and then E., the defendant is found guilty of attempted trafficking in cocaine as a lesser included charge.

After deliberations, the jury returned a verdict finding Estevez guilty of trafficking in cocaine as charged in the information and not guilty of conspiracy to traffic. The verdict form reflects that although the jury checked off the space indicating "guilty of trafficking in cocaine as charged," it did not check on the verdict form the amount of cocaine involved. A different judge than the one who presided at trial received the jury's verdict. The substitute judge accepted the verdict and discharged the jury. Shortly thereafter, during sentencing discussions between the judge and the attorneys, defense counsel examined the verdict form and discovered that the jury had not indicated on the verdict form the amount of cocaine involved in the offense. However, over defense counsel's objection, and despite the lack of an express jury finding as to the amount of cocaine involved, the judge sentenced Estevez to serve a fifteen-year mandatory minimum term for trafficking in cocaine in excess of 400 grams.

On appeal, the Third District reversed and held that "before a defendant can be subject to a minimum mandatory sentence pursuant to section 893.135(1)(b), the verdict form must contain a finding that the defendant committed the crime prohibited by the minimum mandatory sentencing statute." Estevez, 713 So. 2d at 1040. Concluding that it could not determine whether the jury had exercised its inherent power to pardon the defendant by failing to make a specific finding as to the amount of cocaine, the court "reluctantly reversed" the mandatory minimum sentence and remanded for imposition of a guidelines sentence. However, concerned about the uncontroverted evidence of the amount of cocaine involved in the instant case, the Third District certified the aforementioned question of great public importance to this Court.

The defendant here was charged with violating section 893.135(1)(b)(1), Florida Statutes (1995). It provides: Any person who knowingly sells, purchases, manufactures, delivers, or brings into this state, or who is knowingly in actual or constructive possession of, 28 grams or more of cocaine, as described in s. 893.03(2)(a)(4)., or of any mixture containing cocaine, but less than 150 kilograms of cocaine or any such mixture, commits a felony of the first degree, which felony shall be known as "trafficking in cocaine." If the quantity involved:
a. Is 28 grams or more, but less than 200 grams, such person shall be sentenced pursuant to the sentencing guidelines and pay a fine of $50,000.
b. Is 200 grams or more, but less than 400 grams, such person shall be sentenced pursuant to the sentencing guidelines and pay a fine of $100,000.
c. Is 400 grams or more, but less than 150 kilograms, such person shall be sentenced to a mandatory minimum term of imprisonment of 15 calendar years and pay a fine of $250,000.

We begin our analysis by recognizing that this Court has expressly held that the jury is the fact finder charged with the obligation of determining the quantity of cocaine involved in cocaine trafficking under this statute. Thus, before the trial court can impose sentence on a defendant when enhancements of this type are authorized, the trial court must inform the jury that the minimum mandatory punishment for the offense is greater depending upon the quantity of the substance involved. The jury then must determine from the evidence adduced at trial the quantity of contraband involved in the commission of the offense, in effect advising the court as to the appropriate minimum penalty. Thus, the requested instructions on the amounts less than 400 grams should have been given so the appropriate minimum mandatory sentence could have been imposed, based on the jury's determination of the amount of cocaine involved. The trial court erred in determining otherwise.

In resolving this issue, the district court found it instructive to refer to this Court's line of cases interpreting section 775.087, Florida Statutes, dealing with the reclassification and minimum sentence imposition for crimes involving the possession or use of a weapon or firearm. Our cases interpreting section 775.087 have required a specific jury finding that a defendant used a firearm or weapon in the commission of an offense before a trial court may enhance the defendant's sentence or apply a mandatory minimum sentence for the defendant's use of a firearm or weapon in the commission of the offense. In this line of cases, we expressly rejected the proposition that a jury finding as to the presence of a firearm is not required where the evidence on that issue is not controverted at trial.

In the instant case, the State argues that when the evidence as to quantity is uncontroverted, the jury should not be allowed to "pardon" the defendant by failing to make a specific finding as to the amount of cocaine involved. The State points out that this Court acknowledged State v. Benitez, 395 So. 2d 514, 516-17 (Fla. 1981), the mandatory nature of section 893.135, which only allows the trial judge to deviate from the statute's mandatory minimum sentences under circumstances where the defendant is willing to cooperate with law enforcement authorities in apprehending other drug traffickers. Importantly, however, while section 893.135 limits a trial judge in sentencing once a specific conviction is secured, none of its provisions obviates the jury's inherent power to "pardon" a defendant by convicting the defendant of a lesser offense.

In the instant case, the jury was instructed that it could alternatively find Estevez guilty of a number of lesser included offenses, including: (1) possession of cocaine; (2) trafficking in the amount of 28 to 200 grams; (3) trafficking in the amount of 200 to 400 grams; and (4) attempted trafficking. To accept the State's position on this issue would, in essence, impair the jury's inherent power to pardon and, more precisely, its power to find the defendant guilty of one of these lesser offenses. More importantly, it would invade the jury's historical function as fact finder.

Here, it appears that the original trial judge and the parties involved intended for the jury to make an express finding as to the amount of cocaine involved. Unfortunately, the substitute judge, apparently misinterpreting the original trial judge's alteration of the verdict form, accepted the jury's incomplete verdict, which made no express reference to the amount of cocaine. Because the jury did not make an express finding that Estevez trafficked in cocaine in an amount of 400 grams or more, we agree with the district court that the trial judge improperly imposed the mandatory minimum sentence for cocaine trafficking under section 893.135. In short, trial judges are not free to "direct a verdict" as to the amount of cocaine involved in a trafficking offense, even where the evidence presented by the State as to the amount is not controverted.

Accordingly, we answer the certified question in the affirmative and hold that even in cases where the evidence is uncontroverted, the jury must still expressly determine the amount of cocaine involved before the relevant mandatory minimum sentence under the trafficking statute can be imposed. Accordingly, we approve the district court's decision and remand this matter for further proceedings consistent herewith. It is so ordered.

READING COMPREHENSION

What are the facts of this case and the role of mandatory minimum sentencing laws?

THINKING CRITICALLY

Should the jury have the power to 'pardon' a defendant by failing to make a finding as to the amount of drugs involved? What if the amount was uncontroverted at trial?

SECTION 2: DEATH SENTENCES

OVERVIEW

As you read this section on death sentences, keep in mind Section Seventeen of the Florida Constitution which deals with excessive punishments:

Excessive fines, cruel and unusual punishment, attainder, forfeiture of estate, indefinite imprisonment, and unreasonable detention of witnesses are forbidden. The death penalty is an authorized punishment for capital crimes designated by the legislature. The prohibition against cruel or unusual punishment, and the prohibition against cruel and unusual punishment, shall be construed in conformity with decisions of the United States Supreme Court which interpret the prohibition against cruel and unusual punishment provided in the Eighth Amendment to the United States Constitution. Any method of execution shall be allowed, unless prohibited by the United States Constitution. Methods of execution may be designated by the legislature, and a change in any method of execution may be applied retroactively. A sentence of death shall not be reduced on the basis that a method of execution is invalid. In any case in which an execution method is declared invalid, the death sentence shall remain in force until the sentence can be lawfully executed by any valid method. This section shall apply retroactively.

There are twelve states, in addition to the District of Columbia, that do not impose the death penalty. These states are Alaska, Maine, Minnesota, Vermont, Hawaii, Massachusetts, North Dakota, West Virginia, Iowa, Michigan, Rhode Island, and Wisconsin. In addition, there are several states which have carried out no executions since reforms in 1976. These states are New Hampshire, New Jersey, New York, South Dakota, Connecticut, and Kansas. You may notice from these lists, that Florida is not among either the states that do not pursue the death penalty, or the states that have not executed an offender since 1976. Indeed, as of June 21, 2004 there were 381 death row inmates in Florida.

There are several interesting facts surrounding the death penalty in Florida, so we will examine several of these prior to examination of case law. In January 2000, the Florida legislature passed a law allowing lethal injection as an alternative form of execution to the electric chair, which has been law since 1923. You may wonder who is the executioner? This is a private citizen paid $150 per execution and state allows for his/her identity to remain anonymous.

Historically, the first death sentence in the electric chair took place in 1924, and the first woman was executed in Florida in 1998. There was a period in Florida without executions, which included 1929 as well as the 15 year period from May 1964 through May 1979. Since revisions to death penalty legislation in 1976 however, there have been 59 executions in Florida.

There are many questions surrounding death row: who is on death row, how long do offenders stay on death row. The average age at time of offense of individuals on death row is 30 years, with 12 years being the average length of stay on death row prior to execution. Forty-three is both the average age of inmate on death row and the average age at time of execution. While there are currently no juveniles on death row, in the 1940s two sixteen year olds were executed for their crimes.

The issues of insanity and mental retardation spark further controversy when considering the death penalty. On June 20, 2002 in *Atkins v. Virginia* the U.S. Supreme Court held that execution of an offender who is mentally retarded is a violation of the ban on cruel and unusual punishment. Prior to this court ruling, eighteen states as well as the federal government prohibited such executions. Florida was among these states. The guidelines for insanity in a capital case is outlined in Rule 3.811 of the *Florida Rules of Criminal Procedure:*

> (a) **Insanity to Be Executed.** A person under sentence of death shall not be executed while insane. (b) **Insanity Defined.** A person under sentence of death is insane for purposes of execution if the person lacks the mental capacity to understand the fact of the impending execution and the reason for it. (c) **Stay of Execution.** No motion for a stay of execution pending hearing, based on grounds of the prisoner's insanity to be executed, shall be entertained by any court until such time as the Governor of Florida shall have held appropriate proceedings for determining the issue pursuant to the appropriate Florida Statutes. (d) **Motion for Stay after Governor's Determination of Sanity to Be Executed.** On determination of the Governor of Florida, subsequent to the signing of a death warrant for a prisoner under sentence of death and pursuant to the applicable Florida Statutes relating to insanity at time of execution, that the prisoner is sane to be executed, counsel for the prisoner may move for a stay of execution and a hearing based on the prisoner's insanity to be executed. (e) **Order Granting.** If the circuit judge, upon review of the motion and submissions, has reasonable grounds to believe that the prisoner is insane to be executed, the judge shall grant a stay of execution and may order further proceedings which may include a hearing pursuant to rule 3.812.

Let us now examine a capital case heard by the U.S. Supreme Court. As you read the case, keep in mind that it occurred during the 15 year period in which there were no executions in Florida.

CASE

In *Gardner v. Florida,* the petitioner was convicted of first-degree murder in a Florida court. After the required separate sentencing hearing, the jury advised the court to impose a life sentence on the ground that the statutory mitigating circumstances required to be taken into account in imposing a sentence outweighed the aggravating circumstances. The trial judge, relying in part on a pre-sentence investigation report, imposed the death sentence on the ground that a certain aggravating circumstance justified it and that there was no mitigating circumstance.

GARDNER V. FLORIDA
U.S. Supreme Court
430 U.S. 349 (1977)

The Florida Supreme Court affirmed the death sentence without expressly discussing petitioner's contention that the sentencing court had erred in considering the pre-sentence report, including the confidential portion, in deciding to impose the death penalty, and without reviewing such confidential portion. Held: The judgment is vacated and the case is remanded.

MR. JUSTICE STEVENS, joined by MR. JUSTICE STEWART and MR. JUSTICE POWELL, concluded that:

1. Petitioner was denied due process of law when the death sentence was imposed, at least in part, on the basis of information that he had no opportunity to deny or explain.

(a) In light of the constitutional developments whereby it is now recognized that death is a different kind of punishment from any other and that the sentencing process, as well as the trial itself, must satisfy due process, the capital-sentencing procedure followed here is not warranted by any of the following justifications offered by the State: (i) an assurance of confidentiality is necessary to enable investigators to obtain relevant but sensitive disclosures about a defendant's background or character; (ii) full disclosure of a pre-sentence report will unnecessarily delay the proceeding; (iii) such full disclosure, which often includes psychiatric and psychological evaluations, will occasionally disrupt the rehabilitation process; and (iv) trial judges can be trusted to exercise their sentencing discretion in a responsible manner, even though their decisions may be based on secret information.

(b) Even if it were permissible upon finding good cause to withhold a portion of a pre-sentence report from the defendant, and even from defense counsel, nevertheless the full report must be made a part of the record to be reviewed on appeal. Since the State must administer its capital-sentencing procedures with an even hand, that record must disclose to the reviewing court the considerations motivating the death sentence in every case in which it is imposed, since otherwise the capital-sentencing procedure would be subject to the defects that resulted in the holding of unconstitutionality in Furman v. Georgia, 408 U.S. 238 .

(c) Here defense counsel's failure to request access to the full pre-sentence report cannot justify the submission of a less complete record to the reviewing court than the record on which the trial judge based his decision to sentence petitioner to death, nor does such omission by counsel constitute an effective waiver of the constitutional error.

2. The proper disposition of the case is to vacate the death sentence and remand the case to the Florida Supreme Court with directions to order further proceedings at the trial court level not inconsistent with this opinion, rather than, as the State urges, merely remanding the case to the Florida Supreme Court with directions to have the entire pre-sentence report made a part of the record to enable that court to complete its reviewing function, since this latter procedure could not fully correct the error.

Petitioner was convicted of first-degree murder and sentenced to death. When the trial judge imposed the death sentence he stated that he was relying in part on information in a pre-sentence investigation report. Portions of the report were not disclosed to counsel for the parties. Without reviewing the confidential portion of the pre-sentence report, the Supreme Court of Florida, over the dissent of two justices, affirmed the death sentence. 313 So.2d 675 (1975). We conclude that this procedure does not satisfy the constitutional command that no person shall be deprived of life without due process of law.

On June 30, 1973, the petitioner assaulted his wife with a blunt instrument, causing her death. On January 10, 1974, after a trial in the Circuit Court of Citrus County, Florida., a jury found him guilty of first-degree murder. The separate sentencing hearing required by Florida law in capital cases was held later on the same day. The State merely introduced two photographs of the decedent, otherwise relying on the trial testimony. That testimony, if credited, was sufficient to support a finding of one of the statutory aggravating circumstances, that the felony committed by petitioner "was especially heinous, atrocious, or cruel." In mitigation petitioner testified that he had consumed a vast quantity of alcohol during a day-long drinking spree which preceded the crime, and professed to have almost no recollection of the assault itself. His testimony, if credited, was sufficient to support a finding of at least one of the statutory mitigating circumstances.

After hearing this evidence the jury was instructed to determine by a majority vote (1) whether the State had proved one of the aggravating circumstances defined by statute, (2) whether mitigating circumstances outweighed any such aggravating circumstance, and (3) based on that determination, whether the defendant should be sentenced to life or death. After the jury retired to deliberate, the judge announced that he was going to order a pre-sentence investigation of petitioner. Twenty-five minutes later the jury returned its advisory verdict. It expressly found that the mitigating circumstances outweighed the aggravating circumstances and advised the court to impose a life sentence.

The pre-sentence investigation report was completed by the Florida Parole and Probation Commission on January 28, 1974. On January 30, 1974, the trial judge entered findings of fact and a judgment sentencing petitioner to death. His ultimate finding was that the felony "was especially heinous, atrocious or cruel; and that such aggravating circumstances outweighs the

247

mitigating circumstance, to-wit: none." As a preface to that ultimate finding, he recited that his conclusion was based on the evidence presented at both stages of the bifurcated proceeding, the arguments of counsel, and his review of "the factual information contained in said pre-sentence investigation." There is no dispute about the fact that the pre-sentence investigation report contained a confidential portion which was not disclosed to defense counsel. Although the judge noted in his findings of fact that the State and petitioner's counsel had been given "a copy of that portion of the report to which they are entitled," counsel made no request to examine the full report or to be apprised of the contents of the confidential portion. The trial judge did not comment on the contents of the confidential portion. His findings do not indicate that there was anything of special importance in the undisclosed portion, or that there was any reason other than customary practice for not disclosing the entire report to the parties.

On appeal to the Florida Supreme Court, petitioner argued that the sentencing court had erred in considering the pre-sentence investigation report, including the confidential portion, in making the decision to impose the death penalty. The *per curiam* opinion of the Supreme Court did not specifically discuss this contention, but merely recited the trial judge's finding, stated that the record had been carefully reviewed, and concluded that the conviction and sentence should be affirmed. The record on appeal, however, did not include the confidential portion of the pre-sentence report. Justice Ervin and Justice Boyd dissented on several grounds. They regarded the evidence as sufficient to establish a mitigating circumstance as a matter of law, and also concluded that it was fundamental error for the trial judge to rely on confidential matter not provided to the parties.

Petitioner's execution was stayed pending determination of the constitutionality of the Florida capital-sentencing procedure. Following the decision in Proffitt v. Florida, 428 U.S. 242 , holding that the Florida procedure, on its face, avoids the constitutional deficiencies identified in Furman v. Georgia, 408 U.S. 238 , the Court granted certiorari in this case, 428 U.S. 908 , to consider the constitutionality of the trial judge's use of a confidential pre-sentence report in this capital case.

The State places its primary reliance on this Court's landmark decision in Williams v. New York, 337 U.S. 241 . In that case, as in this, the trial judge rejected the jury's recommendation of mercy and imposed the death sentence in reliance, at least in part, on material contained in a report prepared by the court's probation department. The New York Court of Appeals had affirmed the sentence, rejecting the contention that it was a denial of due process to rely on information supplied by witnesses whom the accused could neither confront nor cross-examine. The conviction and sentence were affirmed, over the dissent of two Justices.

In 1949, when the Williams case was decided, no significant constitutional difference between the death penalty and lesser punishments for crime had been expressly recognized by this Court. At that time the Court assumed that after a defendant was convicted of a capital offense, like any other offense, a trial judge had complete discretion to impose any sentence within the limits prescribed by the legislature. As long as the judge stayed within those limits, his sentencing discretion was essentially unreviewable and the possibility of error was remote, if, indeed, it existed at all. In the intervening years there have been two constitutional developments which require us to scrutinize a State's capital-sentencing procedures more closely than was necessary in 1949.

First, five Members of the Court have now expressly recognized that death is a different kind of punishment from any other which may be imposed in this country. From the point of view of the defendant, it is different in both its severity and its finality. From the point of view of society, the action of the sovereign in taking the life of one of its citizens also differs dramatically from any other legitimate state action. It is of vital importance to the defendant and to the community that any decision to impose the death sentence be, and appear to be, based on reason rather than caprice or emotion.

Second, it is now clear that the sentencing process, as well as the trial itself, must satisfy the requirements of the Due Process Clause. Even though the defendant has no substantive right to a particular sentence within the range authorized by statute, the sentencing is a critical stage of the criminal proceeding at which he is entitled to the effective assistance of counsel. The defendant has a legitimate interest in the character of the procedure which leads to the imposition of sentence even if he may have no right to object to a particular result of the sentencing process.

In the light of these developments we consider the justifications offered by the State for a capital-sentencing procedure which permits a trial judge to impose the death sentence on the basis of confidential information which is not disclosed to the defendant or his counsel.

The State first argues that an assurance of confidentiality to potential sources of information is essential to enable investigators to obtain relevant but sensitive disclosures from persons unwilling to comment publicly about a defendant's background or character. The availability of such information, it is argued, provides the person who prepares the report with greater detail on which to base a sentencing recommendation and, in turn, provides the judge with a better basis for his sentencing decision. But consideration must be given to the quality, as well as the quantity, of the information on which the sentencing judge may rely. Assurances of secrecy are conducive to the transmission of confidences which may bear no closer relation to fact than the average rumor or item of gossip, and may imply a pledge not to attempt independent verification of the information received. The risk that some of the information accepted in confidence may be erroneous, or may be misinterpreted, by the investigator or by the sentencing judge, is manifest.

If, as the State argues, it is important to use such information in the sentencing process, we must assume that in some cases it will be decisive in the judge's choice between a life sentence and a death sentence. If it tends to tip the scales in favor of life, presumably the information would be favorable and there would be no reason why it should not be disclosed. On the other hand, if it is the basis for a death sentence, the interest in reliability plainly outweighs the State's interest in preserving the availability of comparable information in other cases. The State also suggests that full disclosure of the pre-sentence report will unnecessarily delay the proceeding. We think the likelihood of significant delay is overstated because we must presume that reports prepared by professional probation officers, as the Florida procedure requires, are generally reliable. In those cases in which the accuracy of a report is contested, the trial judge can avoid delay by disregarding the disputed material. Or if the disputed matter is of critical importance, the time invested in ascertaining the truth would surely be well spent if it makes the difference between life and death.

The State further urges that full disclosure of pre-sentence reports, which often include psychiatric and psychological evaluations, will occasionally disrupt the process of rehabilitation. The argument, if valid, would hardly justify withholding the report from defense counsel. Moreover, whatever force that argument may have in noncapital cases, it has absolutely no merit in a case in which the judge has decided to sentence the defendant to death. Indeed, the extinction of all possibility of rehabilitation is one of the aspects of the death sentence that makes it different in kind from any other sentence a State may legitimately impose.

Finally, Florida argues that trial judges can be trusted to exercise their discretion in a responsible manner, even though they may base their decisions on secret information. However acceptable that argument might have been before Furman v. Georgia, it is now clearly foreclosed. Moreover, the argument rests on the erroneous premise that the participation of counsel is superfluous to the process of evaluating the relevance and significance of aggravating and mitigating facts. Our belief that debate between adversaries is often essential to the truth-seeking function of trials requires us also to recognize the importance of giving counsel an opportunity to comment on facts which may influence the sentencing decision in capital cases.

Even if it were permissible to withhold a portion of the report from a defendant, and even from defense counsel, pursuant to an express finding of good cause for nondisclosure, it would nevertheless be necessary to make the full report a part of the record to be reviewed on appeal. Since the State must administer its capital-sentencing procedures with an even hand, it is important that the record on appeal disclose to the reviewing court the considerations which motivated the death sentence in every case in which it is imposed. Without full disclosure of the basis for the death sentence, the Florida capital-sentencing procedure would be subject to the defects which resulted in the holding of unconstitutionality in Furman v. Georgia. In this particular case, the only explanation for the lack of disclosure is the failure of defense counsel to request access to the full report. That failure cannot justify the submission of a less complete record to the reviewing court than the record on which the trial judge based his decision to sentence petitioner to death.

Nor do we regard this omission by counsel as an effective waiver of the constitutional error in the record. There are five reasons for this conclusion. First, the State does not urge that the objection has been waived. Second, the Florida Supreme Court has held that it has a duty to consider "the total record" when it reviews a death sentence. Third, since two members of that court expressly considered this point on the appeal in this case, we presume that the entire court passed on the question. Fourth, there is no basis for presuming that the defendant himself made a knowing and intelligent waiver, or that counsel could possibly have made a tactical decision not to examine the full report. Fifth, since the judge found, in disagreement with the jury, that the evidence did not establish any mitigating circumstance, and since the pre-sentence report was the only item considered by the judge but not by the jury, the full review of the factual basis for the judge's rejection of the advisory verdict is plainly required. For if the jury, rather than the judge, correctly assessed the petitioner's veracity, the death sentence rests on an erroneous factual predicate. We conclude that petitioner was denied due process of law when the death sentence was imposed, at least in part, on the basis of information which he had no opportunity to deny or explain.

There remains only the question of what disposition is now proper. Petitioner's conviction, of course, is not tainted by the error in the sentencing procedure. The State argues that we should merely remand the case to the Florida Supreme Court with directions to have the entire pre-sentence report made a part of the record to enable that court to complete its reviewing function. That procedure, however, could not fully correct the error. For it is possible that full disclosure, followed by explanation or argument by defense counsel, would have caused the trial judge to accept the jury's advisory verdict. Accordingly, the death sentence is vacated, and the case is remanded to the Florida Supreme Court with directions to order further proceedings at the trial court level not inconsistent with this opinion. Vacated and remanded.

MR. JUSTICE MARSHALL dissenting.

Last Term, this Court carefully scrutinized the Florida procedures for imposing the death penalty and concluded that there were sufficient safeguards to insure that the death sentence would not be "wantonly" and "freakishly" imposed (Proffitt v. Florida, 428 U.S. 242 1976). This case, however, belies that hope. While I continue to believe that the death penalty is unconstitutional in all circumstances, and therefore would remand this case for re-sentencing to a term of life, nevertheless, now that Florida may legally take a life, we must insist that it be in accordance with the standards enunciated by this Court. In this case I am appalled at the extent to which Florida has deviated from the procedures upon which this Court expressly relied. It is not simply that the trial judge, in overriding the jury's recommendation of life imprisonment, relied on undisclosed portions of the pre-sentence report. Nor is it merely that the Florida Supreme Court affirmed the sentence without discussing the omission and without concern that it did not even have the entire report before it. Obviously that alone is enough to deny due process and require that the death sentence be vacated as the Court now holds. But the blatant disregard exhibited by the courts below for the standards devised to regulate imposition of the death penalty calls into question the very basis for this Court's approval of that system in Proffitt.

In Proffitt v. Florida, this Court gave its approval to the new death penalty statute of Florida, but very carefully spelled out its reasons for doing so. The court noted in particular that "the Florida Supreme Court has stated . . . that in order to sustain a sentence of death following a jury recommendation of life, the facts suggesting a sentence of death should be so clear and convincing that virtually no reasonable person could differ, and that the Florida "statute requires that if the trial court imposes a sentence of death, it shall set forth in writing its findings upon which the sentence of death is based as to the facts: (a) that sufficient statutory aggravating circumstances exist . . . and (b) that there are insufficient statutory mitigating circumstances . . . to outweigh the aggravating circumstances. In addition, the opinion, concerned that Florida provided no "specific form of review," found assurance in the fact that "since, however, the trial judge must justify the imposition of death sentence with written findings, meaningful appellate review of each such sentence is made possible, and the Supreme Court of Florida, like its Georgia counterpart, considers its function to be to guarantee that the aggravating and mitigating reasons present in one case will reach a similar result to that reached under similar circumstances in another case. . . . If a defendant is sentenced to die, this Court can review that case in light of the other decisions and determine whether or not the punishment is too great.

After studying the performance of the Florida Supreme Court in reviewing death cases, this Court satisfied itself that these guarantees were genuine and that "the Florida court has undertaken [430 U.S. 349, 367] responsibility to perform its function of death sentence review with a maximum of rationality and consistency," and "has in effect adopted the type of proportionality review mandated by the Georgia statute" upheld in Gregg v. Georgia. The opinion placed great emphasis on this factor, reasoning that because of its statewide jurisdiction, the Florida Supreme Court can assure consistency, fairness, and rationality in the evenhanded operation of the state law.

In the present case, however, the Florida Supreme Court engaged in precisely the "cursory or rubber-stamp review" that the opinion in Proffitt trusted would not occur. The jury, after considering the evidence, recommended a life sentence: "We, the Jury, have heard evidence, under the sentencing procedure in the above cause, as to whether aggravating circumstances which were so defined in the Court's charge, existed in the capital offense here involved, and whether sufficient mitigating circumstances are defined in the Court's charge to outweigh such aggravating circumstances, do find and advise that the mitigating circumstances do outweigh the aggravating circumstances. We therefore advise the Court that a life sentence should be imposed herein upon the defendant by the Court."

The judge, however, ignored the jury's findings. The Florida Supreme Court affirmed with two justices dissenting. The *per curiam* consisted of a statement of the facts of the murder, a verbatim copy of the trial judge's "findings," a conclusion that no new trial was warranted, and the following "analysis": "Upon considering all the mitigating and aggravating circumstances and careful review of the entire record in the cause, the trial court imposed the death penalty for the commission of the afore-described atrocious and heinous crime. Accordingly, the judgment and sentence of the Circuit Court are hereby affirmed. It is so ordered." 313 So.2d 675 (1975).

From this quotation, which includes the entire legal analysis of the opinion, it is apparent that the State Supreme Court undertook none of the analysis it had previously proclaimed to be its duty. The opinion does not say that the Supreme Court evaluated the propriety of the death sentence. It merely says the trial judge did so. Despite its professed obligation to do so, the Supreme Court thus failed "to determine independently" whether death was the appropriate penalty. The Supreme Court also appears to have done nothing "to guarantee" consistency with other death sentences. Its opinion makes no comparison with the facts in other similar cases. Nor did it consider whether the trial judge was correct in overriding the jury's recommendation. There was no attempt to ascertain whether the evidence sustaining death was "so clear and convincing that virtually no [430 U.S. 349, 369] reasonable person could differ." Indeed, it is impossible for me to believe that that standard can be met in this case.

As the plurality notes, there are two mitigating factors that could apply to this case and apparently were found applicable by the jury: "The capital felony was committed while the defendant was under the influence of extreme mental or emotional disturbance" and "the capacity of the defendant to appreciate the criminality of his conduct or to conform his conduct to the requirements of law was substantially impaired." The purpose of these two categories is to protect that person who, while legally answerable for his actions, may be deserving of some mitigation of sentence because of his mental state.

It is undisputed that the petitioner had been drinking virtually the entire day and night prior to the killing. Both court-appointed psychiatrists found that petitioner was an alcoholic and that "had he not been under the influence of alcohol at the time of the alleged crime, he would have been competent, knowing right from wrong and being capable of adhering to the right." Furthermore, his actions after the murder - falling asleep with his wife's dead body, seeking his mother-in-law's help the next morning because his wife did not appear to be breathing properly, weeping when he realized she might be dead, and waiting for the police to come with no attempt to escape - are consistent with his being temporarily mentally impaired at the time of the crime. In light of these facts, it is not surprising that the jury found that the mitigating circumstances outweighed the aggravating. Clearly, this is not a case where the evidence suggesting death is "so clear and convincing that virtually no reasonable person could differ." Had the Florida Supreme Court examined [430 U.S. 349, 370] the evidence in the manner this Court trusted it would, I have no doubt that the jury recommendation of life imprisonment would have been reinstated.

In Proffitt, a majority of this Court was led to believe that Florida had established capital-sentencing procedures that would "assure that the death penalty will not be imposed in an arbitrary or capricious manner." 428 U.S., at 253 . This case belies that promise and suggests the need to reconsider that assessment.

REVIEW SECTION

READING COMPREHENSION

Discuss the prevailing logic of the majority and the dissent.

Detail the fact of this case and the role of the pre-sentence report.

THINKING CRITICALLY

Should a trial judge have the discretion to sentence using secret information unavailable to the defense?

Should a judge have the power to ignore the sentencing recommendation of the jury? Should a judge be able to turn a death sentence into a life sentence? A life sentence into a death sentence?

SECTION 3: APPEALS AND COLLATERAL ATTACK

OVERVIEW

It has been mentioned earlier that while there is no constitutional right to appeal, every jurisdiction in the United States has created a statutory right to appeal which applies to the intermediate appellate courts and in capital cases to the supreme courts. Other appeals to the supreme courts are discretionary. Appeals are considered direct attacks because the purpose is to attack the decision made by the trial court and/or the guilt verdict.

Conversely, *habeus corpus* proceedings are termed collateral attacks because the intent is to indirectly attack the judgment in a noncriminal forum. *Habeus corpus* is a civil action used to determine if the offender is being unlawfully detained and is extremely limited. Most *habeus corpus* proceedings begin only after all direct attacks have been exhausted, and then such a proceeding starts in the U.S. District Court, followed by the U.S. Court of Appeals, and can even reach the U.S. Supreme Court for a final review.

Habeus corpus guidelines regarding custody during this process are outlined in Rule 3.820 of the *Florida Rules of Criminal Procedure:*

> (a) **Custody Pending Appeal of Order of Denial.** When a defendant has been sentenced, and is actually serving the sentence, and has not appealed from the judgment or sentence, but seeks a release from imprisonment by habeas corpus proceedings, and the writ has been discharged after it has been issued, the custody of the prisoner shall not be disturbed, pending review by the appellate court. (b) **Custody Pending Appeal of Order Granting.** Pending review of a decision discharging a prisoner on habeas corpus, the prisoner shall be discharged on bail, with sureties to be approved as other bail bonds are approved for the prisoner's appearance to answer and abide by the judgment of the appellate court.

CASE

In *Cole v. State of Florida* Loran Cole, an inmate under sentence of death, appeals an order of the circuit court denying his motion for post-conviction relief under Florida Rule of Criminal Procedure 3.850. He also petitions the Court for a writ of habeas corpus. The Supreme Court of Florida affirms the trial court's order denying relief under rule 3.850, and denies the petition for writ of habeas corpus.

COLE V. STATE OF FLORIDA
Supreme Court of Florida, Nos. SC00-1388 & SC01-192 (2003)

The facts briefly stated are that on Friday, February 18, 1994, Florida State University freshman John Edwards met his sister, Pam Edwards, then a senior at Eckerd College in St. Petersburg, for a weekend of camping in the Ocala National Forest. On the Friday evening of their arrival, the Edwardses were discovered by Cole and his companion, William Paul. During the course of the evening and during the following day John Edwards was brutally beaten and murdered, and Pam Edwards was sexually battered. Police arrested Cole and Paul on Monday, February 21, 1994. A jury convicted Cole of first-degree murder, two counts of sexual battery, two counts of kidnapping with a weapon, and two counts of robbery with a weapon. The trial court followed the jury's unanimous death recommendation, finding four aggravators, no statutory mitigators, and two non-statutory mitigators. We affirmed the convictions and death sentence on direct appeal.

Cole timely filed an initial Florida Rule of Criminal Procedure 3.850 motion and thereafter an amended rule 3.850 motion. The trial court held a hearing after which the trial court summarily denied several of Cole's claims and scheduled an evidentiary hearing on the remaining claims. Following the evidentiary hearing, the trial court entered a final order denying all relief. Cole raises numerous claims and subclaims in his rule 3.850 appeal and in his habeas petition. We have rearranged the order of the claims presented by Cole and will initially discuss the guilt phase claims and then discuss the penalty phase claims.

In Florida, claims of ineffective assistance of trial counsel are cognizable in a rule 3.850 motion. In his claim, Cole raises numerous arguments that trial counsel was ineffective during the guilt phase. After an evidentiary hearing, the trial court denied Cole's rule 3.850 motion as to each of these subclaims. Cole first argues that trial counsel should have questioned each prospective juror individually, and counsel's failure to do so constitutes deficient performance. Cole maintains that he was prejudiced because two of the five non-individually questioned venire members ultimately became members of the jury that convicted Cole. The trial court found that every prospective juror was questioned individually by the trial court, by the State, or by trial counsel, and that trial counsel was an active participant throughout *voir dire*, even though trial counsel did not question each juror individually. There is competent, substantial evidence to support the trial court's findings. We find no error with the trial court's determination that, on the basis of this record, Cole has failed to demonstrate his trial counsel's ineffectiveness. Therefore, this subclaim is without merit.

Cole next argues that trial counsel should have exercised a peremptory challenge to remove juror Cutts, an employee of the Department of Corrections. The record reflects that trial counsel unsuccessfully attempted to remove Cutts for cause. During *voir dire*, trial counsel concluded and advised Cole that a peremptory challenge should be exercised to remove Cutts; however, Cole stated to counsel that he wanted to retain Cutts. Trial counsel's conclusion as to juror Cutts was not sufficiently strong that counsel interfered with what Cole wanted to be done. We find no error in the trial court's determination that, under these circumstances, trial counsel's decision not to peremptorily challenge juror Cutts did not constitute deficient performance.

Cole alleges that trial counsel should have presented co-defendant Paul's testimony because the evidence of Cole's guilt was mainly circumstantial. The trial court found after the evidentiary hearing that:

1. William Paul testified at deposition-wherein he was actively questioned by Defendant's trial counsel-that Defendant was the individual who killed John Edwards and raped Pam Edwards. William Paul's deposition testimony was consistent with his statement to law enforcement immediately after his arrest.

2. Pam Edwards testified at trial that the Defendant-not William Paul-killed John Edwards and raped her. Pam Edwards' trial testimony was consistent with William Paul's deposition testimony and his statement to law enforcement.

3. William Paul wrote a letter to both Defendant's trial counsel and counsel for the State and informed them that he would not willingly testify for either party.

4. Defendant's trial counsel had no reason to believe that William Paul's testimony would be helpful to his client. Therefore, he made a tactical decision not to call William Paul as a witness. Defendant, who had been supplied with a copy of Paul's deposition by his trial counsel, concurred with counsel's decision.

We find that there is competent, substantial evidence supporting the trial court's finding that trial counsel's decision was tactical. Trial counsel testified at the evidentiary hearing that he had taken Paul's deposition, that he was aware of the substance of Paul's statement to Marion County deputies, and that he was familiar with the physical evidence in the case. Prior to trial, trial counsel and Cole extensively discussed whether Paul should testify. Trial counsel testified that Cole reviewed Paul's statement and letter. Trial counsel concluded that having Paul testify would not help Cole, and counsel discussed with Cole the advantages and disadvantages of having Paul testify. At that time, Cole agreed with counsel not to have Paul testify. Thus, we find no error in the trial court's conclusion that Cole failed to demonstrate that trial counsel performed deficiently.

Cole's fourth subclaim asserts trial counsel's failure to contemporaneously object to the prosecutor's opening statement during the guilt phase. Trial counsel did not immediately object. Instead, at the conclusion of the prosecutor's opening statement, counsel moved for a mistrial, citing the prosecutor's "mankind at its worst" statement made during the opening statement. The trial court denied the motion but offered a curative instruction, which trial counsel declined. Cole argues that counsel's failure to immediately object to the "mankind at its worst" comment and counsel's failure to accept the curative instruction constituted ineffective assistance. Cole's claim must rely on counsel's decision not to contemporaneously object and not on a failure to object because counsel moved for a mistrial at the conclusion of the prosecutor's statement. Thus, Cole must demonstrate that his counsel performed deficiently and that he was prejudiced by counsel's decision to wait until the conclusion of the prosecutor's opening statement before moving for a mistrial on the basis of the prosecutor's argument.

Trial counsel testified at the evidentiary hearing that he decided to wait until after the opening statement so that the comment would not be emphasized and also testified that the curative instruction in this case would have had the effect of repeating the offensive comment. We find that competent, substantial evidence supports the trial court's conclusions that trial counsel's decision to wait until the conclusion of the prosecutor's opening statement before moving for mistrial was tactical as well as counsel's decision to decline the curative instruction. We conclude that Cole has failed to demonstrate that he was prejudiced.

Next, Cole asserts that trial counsel was ineffective for calling John Thompson as Cole's only witness during Cole's case-in-chief, thereby losing the right to the rebuttal argument. While the specific claim relates to witness John Thompson, an examination of this claim also involves witness Mary Gamble. Both Thompson and Gamble, who did not previously know each other, met each other and Cole months prior to the murder and rape while they and others jointly lived at the Salvation Army in Marion County. Gamble and Cole formed a friendship and engaged in sexual relations, and after Cole's arrest, Gamble visited Cole at the jail. Gamble testified during the State's case-in-chief that while she visited Cole in jail, he confessed to her that he raped Pam Edwards and slit John Edwards' throat. Thompson had driven Gamble to the jail to visit Cole. Counsel called Thompson during Cole's case-in-chief to have Thompson testify that Gamble never told him that Cole confessed to the murder, even though he drove Gamble to the jail.

The record establishes that Thompson was the State's fifteenth trial witness, and Gamble was the State's eighteenth witness. Thompson testified, when called by the State, that he drove Gamble to the jail to see Cole while Cole was awaiting trial. When Thompson testified for the State, the State did not elicit any testimony concerning any conversation Gamble had with Cole at the jail. When Gamble later testified, she testified that Cole confessed to committing these crimes. Thus, trial counsel called Thompson as a witness for the defense so that Thompson could testify that Gamble never told him that Cole confessed. Cole contends that trial counsel should have elicited the testimony impeaching Gamble during Thompson's cross-examination, when Thompson was a State's witness and prior to Gamble's testimony. We do not agree because the record shows that at the time Thompson testified there was no predicate in the record upon which Gamble could be impeached.

At the evidentiary hearing, trial counsel testified that he knew by calling Thompson trial counsel was losing the right to a rebuttal closing but thought that the benefit of having Thompson refute Gamble, the only person who testified that Cole confessed, outweighed the benefits of giving the rebuttal argument. We find there to be competent, substantial evidence supporting the trial court's finding that counsel's decision to call Thompson was tactical. We find no error in the trial court's conclusion that Cole failed to demonstrate how his trial counsel performed deficiently and therefore is not entitled to relief on this claim.

Cole's last subclaim to this issue is that cumulative error occurred during the guilt phase. Because all of Cole's guilt phase issues are either meritless or procedurally barred, there is no cumulative error to consider.

Cole claimed that trial counsel failed to object to hearsay statements made by Dan Jackson and Deputy Tammy Jicha. Dan Jackson was the motorist that Pam Edwards flagged down when fleeing the national forest. He testified that while driving Pam out of the forest to call the police that "she said that she had been tied up and raped." Tammy Jicha was a deputy with the Lake County Sheriff's office and responded to Pam's telephone call. Deputy Jicha testified that even though she determined that the alleged crimes occurred in Marion County and not in Lake County, she continued talking with Ms. Edwards to determine whether Ms. Edwards was reporting real events or making a false crime report. Deputy Jicha further testified, "I felt like she was telling the truth, because everything just added up, right down the line." Counsel did not object to these statements. Cole contended in his rule 3.850 motion that the failure to object to these statements allowed the State to improperly bolster Ms. Edwards' credibility and that the prejudice was the extra weight the jury likely gave her testimony. The trial court ruled that the rule 3.850 motion contained insufficient allegations as to prejudice and that the allegations made were entirely speculative. On the basis of the evidence in the trial record, we find no error in the trial court's denial of this claim for lack of prejudice.

Cole raises a Brady v. Maryland, 373 U.S. 83 (1963) argument. The trial court conducted an evidentiary hearing on this claim. Eleanor Simpson testified at the evidentiary hearing that at the conclusion of the oral argument in the direct appeal of Cole's conviction and sentence, she talked with Brad King, the elected state attorney who prosecuted Cole. She maintains that she asked King why he did not call Paul to testify and that King replied that he was afraid that Paul would attempt to take blame for the entire incident. King testified at the evidentiary hearing that he briefly spoke with Simpson. In response to Simpson's question as to why King did not put Paul on the stand, King testified that he said, "I didn't need to, that we had a good case without him; he was there and could have been called, but I chose not to call him because I could never tell for a certainty what he would say if he testified." King further testified that he never had an indication that Paul slit John Edwards' throat and that King had always been convinced it was Cole who actually killed John. In its final order denying Cole's rule 3.850 motion, the trial court also found that the State provided the defense with all statements made by Paul and that trial counsel deposed Paul, knew that Paul would not willingly testify for either the State or Cole, and knew that Paul pled guilty to murder in exchange for a life sentence. Competent, substantial evidence exists in the record supporting the trial court's findings. Thus, we find no error in the trial court's denial of this claim.

In another claim on appeal, Cole seeks a DNA test. Cole did not include this claim in his rule 3.850 motion; instead, Cole made an oral request for the DNA testing at the Huff hearing. The trial court summarily denied Cole's request without explanation. We note that the trial court's denial of Cole's DNA request came prior to the effective date of section 925.11, Florida Statutes (2001), and Florida Rule of Criminal Procedure 3.853 (DNA testing). We do not address Cole's request for relief at this time except to state that our decision should not be read to prohibit Cole from seeking such testing pursuant to the mandates of section 925.11 and rule 3.853.

We find Cole's claim that he should be allowed to contact the jurors in an attempt to determine juror misconduct and that the ethical prohibition preventing Cole from contacting the jurors is unconstitutional, to be procedurally barred. Having considered all of Cole's guilt phase issues, we affirm the trial court's denial of the 3.850 motion in respect to the guilt phase of Cole's trial.

In his claim, Cole argues that his trial counsel was ineffective during the penalty phase for failing to request and argue the statutory mental mitigators: (1) the capital felony was committed while the defendant was under the influence of extreme mental or emotional disturbance; and (2) the capacity of the defendant to appreciate the criminality of his or her conduct or to conform his or her conduct to the requirements of law was substantially impaired. Cole maintains that there was some evidence adduced during the guilt and penalty phases which supported both mitigators. After an evidentiary hearing on this claim, the trial court denied relief, finding that Cole had failed to establish prejudice. We find no error in the trial court's conclusion that Cole had failed to demonstrate prejudice in respect to the ineffectiveness claim.

The State initially argues that this issue is procedurally barred because trial counsel conceded the nonexistence of the two statutory mental mitigators and that jury instruction issues must be raised on direct appeal. Alternatively, the State contends that Dr. Berland's testimony did not establish that these mitigators existed, and even if it did, Cole suffered no prejudice given the enormity of the aggravating circumstances. We reject the State's argument that this issue is procedurally barred. The failure to request jury instructions is properly evaluated in a rule 3.850 motion for ineffective assistance of trial counsel. This claim is not procedurally barred by the direct appeal because the trial court was never requested to make a ruling on the instructions at trial. Thus, we proceed to the merits of this claim. The trial record reveals that Dr. Robert Berland, a board certified forensic psychologist, performed a mental health examination of Cole. A careful reading of Dr. Berland's testimony shows that Dr. Berland did not testify as to his opinion of whether the two statutory mitigators applied to Cole's murder of John Edwards. The trial court in its sentencing order specifically rejected the existence of either statutory mental mitigator. Thus, the trial court when sentencing Cole concluded that these two statutory mental mitigators did not exist. The trial court in the same sentencing order then evaluated this evidence as non-statutory mental mitigation. Upon evaluating the testimony, the Court finds that the Defendant has established the mitigating factors of organic brain damage and mental illness by the greater weight of the evidence. However, the testimony has failed to establish that such affected the Defendant's judgment in any significant manner. Dr. Berland was unable to definitively connect any psychotic influence on the Defendant's criminal acts. Therefore, the Court can only attach slight to moderate weight to this mitigating factor. At the evidentiary hearing no expert evidence was presented that counsel was deficient on the basis of the trial record for not requesting jury instructions on these two statutory mental mitigators. Based upon Dr. Berland's testimony, the trial court's sentencing order, and the rule 3.850 evidentiary hearing record, we find no error in the trial court not granting relief on this claim.

Cole next argues that he did not receive effective mental health assistance as required by Ake v. Oklahoma, 470 U.S. 68 (1985). This claim was not presented in this form to the trial judge; however, on the basis of the record, we conclude there is no basis for relief.

In the penalty phase, Cole raises numerous arguments, alleging trial counsel's ineffectiveness, which the trial court summarily denied without an evidentiary hearing. In his first subclaim, Cole posits that trial counsel should have presented evidence of Cole's long-term history of drug and alcohol abuse. Cole argues that even though counsel presented evidence of marijuana abuse, counsel should have presented evidence of additional drug use. Upon review of the record, it is clear that trial counsel presented extensive evidence of Defendant's history of alcohol and drug use during the penalty phase. Defendant's allegation that his counsel was ineffective for failing to present evidence of alcohol and drug use is amply refuted by the record. Any additional evidence of drug and alcohol use would have been cumulative of that actually presented. We find no error in the trial court's conclusion that Cole was not entitled to an evidentiary hearing to present what the trial court found would have been cumulative evidence.

Cole next contends that trial counsel failed to present evidence of child abuse. Trial counsel presented extensive evidence of Defendant's childhood abuse and poor upbringing during the sentencing phase of this case. Defendant's allegations that his counsel was ineffective for failing to present evidence of childhood abuse and poor upbringing is amply refuted by the record. Any additional evidence of childhood abuse would have been cumulative of that actually presented. We find no error in the trial court's determination that Cole's claim is refuted by the trial record and that the evidence which Cole now asserts should have been presented would have been cumulative.

Cole claims that trial counsel failed to object to prosecutorial misconduct during penalty phase closing argument. Cole argues that the prosecutor told the jury that William Paul could not have cut John Edwards with a knife, as Paul's hand was "broken," and that the statement was inaccurate because Paul's left hand was hurt but was not broken. We find no error in the trial court's determination in respect to this subclaim that Cole is not entitled to any relief.

Cole asserts that trial counsel should have requested a limiting instruction for the heinous, atrocious, or cruel (HAC) aggravator. Cole contended in his rule 3.850 motion that actions taken after a victim becomes unconscious or after the victim dies cannot support the HAC aggravator. Cole maintains in the instant case that, although trial counsel raised the issue that John Edwards could likely have been unconscious when his throat was cut, counsel was ineffective to the extent that trial counsel did not present the trial court with case law that entitled Cole to an instruction that the jury could not consider actions after the victim was unconscious. Cole is correct that we have held that events occurring after the victim's loss of consciousness or death are not relevant to the HAC aggravator determination. The record reflects that trial counsel requested and the trial court instructed the jury that events occurring after the victim's death were not relevant for the HAC aggravator. Thus, Cole's ineffective counsel claim can only rest upon trial counsel's alleged failure to request a further limiting instruction that would have advised the jury that events occurring after the victim's loss of consciousness are not relevant for the HAC aggravator. However, as indicated by the trial court in denying this rule 3.850 claim, the trial court in its sentencing order found there to be sufficient acts that occurred while the victim was conscious for the HAC aggravator to be established beyond a reasonable doubt. This Court on direct appeal affirmed the finding of HAC beyond a reasonable doubt. Thus, again, we find no error in the trial court's granting no relief on this claim.

Cole next claims that trial counsel was ineffective for failing to introduce into evidence co-defendant Paul's life sentence. Cole submits that the jury would have probably sentenced Cole to life had the jury known of the disparate sentence. We agree with the State that this issue is procedurally barred, as we addressed the disparate treatment argument on direct appeal and found it to be without merit. Moreover, it is clear from the on-the-record statements by Cole and his counsel during trial that the decision not to put on this evidence was influenced by the fact that presenting such evidence would have opened the door to other, harmful evidence. In view of the present record, Cole has no basis upon which to claim this decision was a result of an error by his trial counsel.

Cole's next claim is that trial counsel should have hired co- counsel to assist with the penalty phase. We find that this subclaim is legally insufficient because Cole has alleged neither deficient performance nor resulting prejudice for the trial court's failure to secure co-counsel. The only prejudice alleged by Cole with any specificity concerns the presentation of Paul's life sentence. However, as noted above, Cole is not entitled to relief on that claim. The general allegation that mitigating evidence could have been better presented is an insufficient allegation of prejudice. As Cole makes no further allegation of prejudice relating to this subclaim, Cole has failed to demonstrate that his counsel was ineffective for failing to request co-counsel.

Cole asserts that the trial court impermissibly relied upon non-statutory aggravating factors when sentencing Cole and that Cole is therefore entitled to a new sentencing proceeding. Cole points to the trial court's final order denying the rule 3.850 motion. On direct appeal, Cole raised numerous challenges to aggravating and mitigating circumstances, which we rejected. Cole did not contend on direct appeal that the trial court considered non-statutory aggravating circumstances in its imposition of the death penalty, and we clearly identified that the trial court only considered four statutory aggravating circumstances in its evaluation of the imposition of the death penalty. We agree with the State that Cole's current argument is procedurally barred as the issue could have and should have been raised on direct appeal.

Cole's eleventh claim is that he is entitled to an evidentiary hearing to explore trial counsel's failure to litigate the unconstitutional nature of the aggravating circumstances. He maintains that because of his robbery conviction, he was automatically eligible for the death penalty, that the jury instructions improperly shifted the burden to Cole to prove mitigating circumstances, that section 921.141(5), Florida Statutes (1993), is unconstitutionally vague, and that the jury instructions precluded the jurors from considering the totality of the circumstances. We agree with the State's position that these issues are procedurally barred, as they could have and should have been raised on direct appeal.

Lastly, Cole argues that cumulative error requires reversal of the death sentence and a new sentencing proceeding. We disagree and find that Cole is not entitled to relief.

This Court's habeas corpus standard of review for ineffective assistance of appellate counsel claims mirrors the Strickland standard for trial counsel's ineffectiveness. Initially, Cole argues that his appellate counsel was ineffective for counsel's failure to argue that Florida's death sentencing statute is unconstitutional as applied to him. Cole contends that a death sentence is not the maximum penalty under Florida's sentencing statute. Relatedly, Cole asserts that his counsel was ineffective for failing to raise the trial court's denial of Cole's motion for a statement of particulars, which sought a listing of those aggravating circumstances upon which the State would rely. Cole's second habeas argument centers on the prosecutor's penalty phase closing argument, which Cole maintains constitutes fundamental error. Cole again raises the argument that the "broken hand" argument was improper and further argues that the prosecutor impermissibly argued to the jury that it should show the same amount of mercy that Cole showed his victim. We addressed the merits of the "broken hand" argument in that portion of the opinion rejecting Cole's 3.850 motion in which we agreed with the trial court's conclusion that no prejudice was demonstrated as to that unobjected-to comment. For the same reasons, we conclude that the habeas claim based on this same argument lacks merit.

Cole's third habeas claim is that he may be incompetent to be executed, but he concedes that the claim is premature under Florida Rules of Criminal Procedure 3.811 and 3.812. Cole asserts that he makes this argument to preserve his ability to pursue a similar claim in the federal system. We agree with Cole's concession that this issue is not yet ripe, and we therefore find it to be without merit. Finally, in habeas claim four, Cole raises an ex post facto challenge to his death sentence and argues that electrocution remains the mandated form of execution. Moreover, Cole contends that electrocution is cruel punishment or unusual punishment or both. Alternatively, in habeas claim five, Cole argues that, if lethal injection is a valid manner of execution, lethal injection is cruel or unusual or both. We summarily reject these arguments, as we previously have found similar arguments to be without merit.

Accordingly, we affirm the trial court's denial of Cole's rule 3.850 motion and deny Cole's petition for writ of habeas corpus. Our decision to deny Cole's request for a DNA test, however, is without prejudice to allow him to seek such a test consistent with the provisions of section 925.11, Florida Statutes (2001), and Florida Rule of Criminal Procedure 3.853. It is so ordered.

REVIEW SECTION

READING COMPREHENSION

Detail the facts of this case.

Elaborate Cole's claims with regard to ineffective counsel.

CONCLUSION

This chapter should have illustrated that after the conviction phase, rights of offenders are much more limited than prior to conviction. While states have provided the right to appeal, there is no constitutional right as such. A review of sentencing, death sentences, and appeals and collateral attack should have provided an in-depth examination of proceedings after conviction.

Chapter Fifteen

Criminal Procedure in Crisis Times

During times of emergency, such as war, there is a recalibration of the balance between government power and individual liberties with the result being an expansion of governmental power. Because this occurs at the federal level, application at the state level is weak at best, therefore analysis in this final chapter will be primarily federal in nature. Such emergency extension of power is permitted when and to the extent it is necessary and must be temporary in nature.

This chapter will review:

(1)   Balancing rights and security during emergencies;

(2)   Surveillance and terrorism; and

(3)   Terrorist trials by military courts after 9/11.

SECTION 1: BALANCING RIGHTS AND SECURITY DURING EMERGENCIES

OVERVIEW

On September 11th, 2001 Executive Order Number 01-262 detailed emergency management in the state of Florida in response to the destruction of the World Trade Center. This occurred in conjunction with federal mandates aimed at preventing terrorism. Governor Jeb Bush by the authority granted in Article IV, Section 1(a) of the Florida Constitution and by the Florida Emergency Management Act asserted that the following would take effect immediately:

> Section 1. I hereby declare that a state of emergency exists in the State of Florida. I further find that the precautions needed to protect the State from a recurrence of such terrorist acts require a coordination of efforts by a number of agencies, and that central authority over these activities will be needed to ensure such coordination. Section 2. I hereby delegate to the Department of Law Enforcement the operational authority to coordinate and direct the law enforcement resources and other resources of any and all state, regional and local governmental agencies that the Department may designate to take the precautions needed to protect the State of Florida from terrorist acts. I hereby place all law enforcement resources under the operational authority of the Department of Law Enforcement while this Executive Order remains in effect, and I hereby designate the Commissioner of the

Department of Law Enforcement as Incident Commander for this emergency. Section 3. I hereby designate the Interim Director of the Division of Emergency Management as the State Coordinating Officer for the duration of this emergency, and as my Authorized Representative. Section 5. In accordance with Sections 252.36(5)(a) and 252.46(2), Florida Statutes, all statutes, rules and orders are hereby suspended for the duration of this emergency to the extent that literal compliance with such statutes, rules, and orders may be inconsistent with the timely performance of emergency response functions.

In line with Sections 252.36(1)(a) and 252.36(5) of the Florida Statutes, Bush delegated the State Coordinating Officer with the following powers in Executive Order Number 01-262:

The authority to activate the Comprehensive Emergency Management Plan; The authority to invoke and administer the Statewide Mutual Aid Agreement, and the further authority to coordinate the allocation of resources under that Agreement so as best to meet this emergency; The authority to invoke and administer the Emergency Management Assistance Compact and other Compacts and Agreements existing between the State of Florida and other States, and the further authority to coordinate the allocation of resources from such other States that are made available to the State of Florida under such Compacts and Agreements so as best to meet this emergency; The authority to distribute any and all supplies stockpiled to meet the emergency; The authority to suspend the effect of any statute or rule governing the conduct of state business, and the further authority to suspend the effect of any order or rule of any governmental entity, to include, without limiting the generality of the foregoing, any and all statutes and rules which affect budgeting, printing, purchasing, leasing, procurement, and the conditions of employment and the compensation of employees; provided, however, that the State Coordinating Officer shall have authority to suspend the effect of any statute, rule or order only to the extent necessary to ensure the timely performance of vital emergency response functions; The authority to relieve any and all state agencies responsible for processing applications or petitions for any order, rule, or other final action subject to the Administrative Procedure Act, as amended, from the deadlines specified in that Act and in other applicable laws for the duration of this emergency, if the State Coordinating Officer finds that such deadlines cannot be met because of this emergency; The authority to direct all state, regional and local governmental agencies, including law enforcement agencies, to identify personnel needed from those agencies to assist in meeting the needs created by this emergency, and to place all such personnel under the direct command of the State Coordinating Officer to meet this emergency; The authority to seize and utilize any and all real or personal property as needed to meet this emergency, subject always to the duty of the State to compensate the owner; The authority to order the evacuation of any or all persons from any location in the State of Florida, and the authority to regulate the movement of any or all persons to or from any location in the State; The authority to regulate the return of the evacuees to their home communities; and The authority to designate such Deputy State Coordinating Officers as the State Coordinating Officer may deem necessary to cope with the emergency.

Of special note should be Section Five of this Executive Order which dictates that all statutes, rules and orders of Florida are suspended for the duration of this emergency.

SECTION 2: SURVEILLANCE AND TERRORISM

OVERVIEW

While much of the material in this chapter was relevant only at the federal level, an interesting case has arisen in Florida which is potentially precedent-setting. Former University of South Florida professor Sami Al-Arian was arrested in 2003 on terrorist charges. Al-Arian and seven other men have been indicted on 50 counts related to support, promotion and fundraising for Palestinian Islamic Jihad, considered a terrorist group by the U.S. government. This case presents several legal and unusual challenges.

First, taped conversations spanning more than a decade would take 2.5 years to listen to in a court of law provided the tapes were played without a break. The tapes are a result of 152 warrants made by a panel of judges who comprise the Foreign Intelligence Surveillance Court. Further, the Department of Justice obtained this intelligence under the belief that it would not be used for prosecution, only for intelligence gathering. This however changed under the guidelines of the US Patriot Act.

Second, Al-Arian is being confined in a federal prison until the start of the trial in January 2005. Third, several document from the case were inadvertently shredded by court employees, potentially allowing Al-Arian's attorneys to challenge the lawfulness of the searches under which the tapes in question were obtained. Many more issues are likely to arise such as the audibility of recordings, disputes over Arabic translation of the tapes, as well as the constitutionality of the US Patriot Act.

CASE

While this case is somewhat outside of the scope of what has been discussed thus far, the details below provide a background that will prove useful in following this case which begins in January 2005. The case is a criminal action against alleged members of the Palestinian Islamic Jihad-Shiqaqi Faction (the "PIJ") who purportedly operated and directed fundraising and other organizational activities in the United States for almost twenty years. The PIJ is a foreign organization that uses violence, principally suicide bombings, and threats of violence to pressure Israel to cede territory to the Palestinian people. On February 19, 2003, the government indicted the Defendants in a 50 count indictment that included counts for: (1) conspiracy to commit racketeering; (2) conspiracy to commit murder, maim, or injure persons outside the United States; (3) conspiracy to provide material support to or for the benefit of foreign terrorists; (4) violations of the Travel Act; (5) violation of the immigration laws of the United States; (6) obstruction of justice; and (7) perjury.

UNITED STATES OF AMERICA v. SAMI AMIN AL-ARIAN, SAMEEH HAMMOUDEH, GHASSAN ZAYED BALLUT, HATIM NAJI FARIZ
308 F. Supp. 2d 1322; 2004 U.S. Dist. LEXIS 4227; 17 Fla. L. Weekly Fed. D 419 (2004)

Count 1 of the Indictment alleges a wide ranging pattern of racketeering activity beginning in 1984 lasting through February 2003, including murder, extortion, and money laundering. The Indictment details some 256 overt acts, ranging from soliciting and raising funds to providing management, organizational, and logistical support for the PIJ. The overt act section of the Indictment details numerous suicide bombings and attacks by PIJ members causing the deaths of over 100 people, including 2 American citizens, and injuries to over 350 people, including 7 American citizens. These same overt acts (or parts of them) support the remaining counts of the Indictment.

Each of the Defendants filed numerous pretrial motions primarily seeking the dismissal of Counts 1 through 4 of the Indictment and the striking of various overt acts or parts of overt acts as surplusage. The government opposed each motion.

Center stage in the motions are two statutes: (1) the Antiterrorism and Effective Death Penalty Act of 1996, Pub. L. No. 104-132 ("AEDPA"); and (2) the International Emergency Economic [*1329] Powers Act, 50 U.S.C. § 1701, et seq. ("IEEPA").

AEDPA authorizes the Secretary of State (the "Secretary"), in consultation with the Attorney General and the Secretary of the Treasury, to designate an organization as a Foreign Terrorist Organization ("FTO"). Designation as a FTO has severe consequences to an organization, its members, and its supporters. For example, after designation, the Secretary of the Treasury may freeze all assets of a FTO in or controlled by a United States financial institution. Additionally, representatives and certain members of FTOs may be barred from entry into the United States. More relevant to this case, the designation of an organization as a FTO has potential criminal ramifications on a FTO's supporters.

266

In order to designate an organization a FTO under AEDPA, the Secretary must find that the: (a) organization is foreign; (b) organization engages in "terrorist activity," "terrorism," or has the capability and intent to engage in terrorist activity or terrorism; and (c) the terrorism or terrorist activity threatens either the security of United States nationals or national security. AEDPA provides no pre-designation notice to a potential FTO. A designation takes effect upon publication. A designation lasts for two years unless revoked by Congress or the Secretary. The Secretary may renew a FTO designation every two years. Note here that terrorism is defined as "premeditated, politically motivated violence perpetrated against noncombatant targets by subnational groups or clandestine agents." 22 U.S.C. § 2656f(d)(2). Further, AEDPA precludes a criminal defendant's right to "raise any question concerning the validity of the issuance of such designation as a defense or objection at any trial or hearing." On October 8, 1997, the Secretary designated PIJ as a FTO under AEDPA. The Secretary's designation of PIJ as a FTO was renewed in 1999, 2001, and 2003. Neither Congress nor the Secretary revoked the PIJ's designation at any time, and the PIJ has not sought judicial review of its designations as a FTO.

The second statute central to these motions is IEEPA. Under IEEPA, the President is granted the authority "to deal with any unusual and extraordinary threat ... to the national security, foreign policy, or economy of the United States, if the President declares a national emergency with respect to such threat." 50 U.S.C. § 1701(a). The President's authority includes the power to investigate, regulate, or prohibit financial transactions. Section 1705(b) makes it unlawful to willfully violate or attempt to violate any executive order or regulation issued pursuant to IEEPA and provides for imprisonment of up to 10 years for such a violation. On January 23, 1995, pursuant to IEEPA, President Clinton issued Executive Order 12947 (the "Executive Order"). The Executive Order declared a national emergency with respect to the Middle East peace process that threatened the United States' national security, foreign policy, and economy. The Executive Order prohibited financial transactions with any specially designated terrorist ("SDT"). The President also authorized the Secretary, in coordination with the Attorney General and Secretary of the Treasury, to promulgate regulations to carry out the Executive Order. The annex to the Executive Order designates the PIJ as a SDT.

The Secretary of the Treasury promulgated regulations that are contained in Title 31 C.F.R. part 595. Most relevant to this case, Section 595.204 makes it unlawful to "deal in property or interests in property of a ... [SDT], including the making or receiving of any contribution of funds, goods, or services to or for the benefit of a [SDT] ...." (31 C.F.R. § 595.204). The regulations interpret this prohibition to include charitable contributions or "donation[s] of funds, goods, services, or technology to relieve human suffering, such as food, clothing, or medicine." The regulations interpret the prohibition against financial transactions to extend to conspiracies and attempts.

Not all transactions with a SDT are banned or are criminal. For example, the regulations make clear that there is no liability for a charitable contribution if the contribution is made "without knowledge or reason to know that the donation or contribution is destined to or for the benefit of a [SDT] ...." In addition, the regulations exempt certain transactions from the ban, including transactions that: (a) are licensed or authorized; (b) involve personal communications that do not transfer anything of value; (c) involve some types of information and informational materials; or (d) are incidental to travel. IEEPA itself does not explicitly or implicitly provide for judicial

267

review of an executive order, but it does provide a procedure for court review of classified information. The regulations provide a process for administrative review of a designation of an organization as an SDT. Courts have held that judicial review of a designation under IEEPA or its regulations exists and that the Administrative Procedures Act governs that review.

Federal Rules of Criminal Procedure Rule 12(b) allows a defendant to "raise by pretrial motion any defense, objection, or request that the court can determine without a trial of the general issue." Moreover, Rule 12(b)(3) of the Federal Rules of Criminal Procedure requires certain motions be made prior to trial including motions alleging a defect in the indictment. In addition, this Court may strike surplusage from an indictment. The standard for striking surplusage is "exacting." The standard requires it to be clear that the allegedly surplus language is irrelevant to the charge and is also inflammatory and prejudicial. The Court may reserve ruling on a motion to strike surplusage until hearing the evidence and determining its relevance at trial. The motions pending before this Court can be segregated into three categories. First, Defendants' motions raise a host of statutory construction and constitutional issues purportedly on which this Court should dismiss or strike Counts 1 through 4 (or parts of Counts 1 through 4). Second, Defendants raise a variety of technical or procedural arguments to some of the Counts and acts contained in the Indictment. Third, Defendants Ballut and Fariz have appealed the Magistrate's order on the bill of particulars (Dkt. # 428). This Court will examine each category in turn.

Before reaching the statutory construction issues, it is helpful, if not necessary, to understand certain constitutional arguments raised by the parties that affect this Court's construction of AEDPA and IEEPA. Defendants have moved to dismiss Counts 1 through 4 of the Indictment, arguing that the Indictment attempts to criminalize their First Amendment rights of speech in support of and association with the PIJ. Defendants assert that Counts 1 through 4 are unconstitutional because they do not require either: (a) a specific intent to further the unlawful activities of the PIJ; or (b) an intent to incite and a likelihood of imminent disorder. Alternatively, Defendants argue that Counts 1 through 4 are not content neutral and are subject to analysis under strict scrutiny, which is rarely, if ever, met and is not met in this case.

As a corollary to their First Amendment argument, Defendants also claim that the doctrines of overbreadth and vagueness invalidate AEDPA or IEEPA in whole or in part. Defendants assert that the statutes sweep so broadly that they include substantial amounts of constitutionally protected advocacy within their prohibitions. Similarly, Defendants argue that the material terms of each statute are so broadly defined that a person is incapable of knowing when otherwise protected activity becomes criminal. In support of Defendants' position, Defendants cite to two Ninth Circuit opinions where that court twice concluded that portions of AEDPA are unconstitutionally vague as applied to the plaintiffs in that case. Defendants argue that the same hypothetical utilized by the Ninth Circuit indicates that other sections of AEDPA and IEEPA are similarly vague and unconstitutional.

The government responds that the Indictment alleges that Defendants engaged in criminal conduct and activities, not protected speech or association. The government asserts that the Indictment alleges that Defendants conspired with the PIJ and assisted the PIJ in the accomplishment of unlawful activities, including, but not limited to, murder, extortion, and money laundering. According to the government, speech is utilized in the Indictment to show

Defendants' agreement to participate in the conspiracy, and their role, motive, and intent, all of which is allowable under the First Amendment. The government argues that AEDPA and IEEPA need not contain a specific intent to further unlawful activities or be limited to situations where a defendant intends to incite and a likelihood of imminent disorder, because the statutes and the Indictment are aimed at conduct and not speech or association. Similarly, the government asserts that AEDPA and IEEPA need not meet strict scrutiny, but only need meet the intermediate scrutiny standard of United States v. O'Brien, which is far easier to meet and, according to the government, is met by AEDPA and IEEPA. The government also cites to the Ninth Circuit's Humanitarian cases, where the Ninth Circuit twice applied this analysis and concluded that AEDPA did not violate the First Amendment rights of the plaintiffs in those cases.

The government also opposes the Defendants' contentions that AEDPA and IEEPA are overbroad or vague. The government relies on the presence of "knowingly" or "willfully" mens rea requirements in the statutes to remove protected speech from the prohibited conduct covered under both statutes. Similarly, the government argues that the statutes in the vast number of applications cover only unprotected conduct and only in remote hypothetical situations do AEDPA and IEEPA even come close to impinging upon protected speech. The government cites to a line of Supreme Court cases, which have held in such circumstances that courts should not use the overbreadth and vagueness doctrines to invalidate statutes.

While it may not be apparent from either parties' arguments, the dispute between the parties on what analysis applies and the constitutionality of Counts 3 and 4 of the Indictment actually turns on how this Court interprets AEDPA and IEEPA. The broader this Court interprets AEDPA and IEEPA, the more likely that the statutes receive a higher standard of review and are unconstitutional. For example, if this Court interprets AEDPA and IEEPA as requiring a specific intent to further the illegal activities of the FTO or SDT, then no constitutional problems exist. Similarly, if this Court interprets AEDPA's and IEEPA's prohibitions broadly and does not impose a specific intent mens rea requirement, it will likely be forced to perform a vagueness analysis and find portions of AEDPA and IEEPA unconstitutional, as did the Ninth Circuit in the Humanitarian cases.

Turning to AEDPA, Section 2339B(a)(1) makes it unlawful for a person to "knowingly provide material support or resources to a foreign terrorist organization, or attempts or conspires to do so ...." (18 U.S.C. § 2339B(a)(1)). The Ninth Circuit has twice in a single case interpreted Section 2339B and found portions to be unconstitutionally vague as applied to the plaintiffs in that case. This Court agrees with the Ninth Circuit in Humanitarian I that a purely grammatical reading of the plain language of Section 2339B(a)(1) makes it unlawful for any person to knowingly furnish any item contained in the material support categories to an organization that has been designated a FTO. And like Humanitarian II, this Court agrees that this construction renders odd results and raises serious constitutional concerns. For example under Humanitarian I, a donor could be convicted for giving money to a FTO without knowledge that an organization was a FTO or that it committed unlawful activities, and without an intent that the money be used to commit future unlawful activities. This Court does not believe this burden is that great in the typical case. Often, such an intent will be easily inferred. For example, a jury could infer a specific intent to further the illegal activities of a FTO when a defendant knowingly provides weapons, explosives, or lethal substances to an organization that he knows is a FTO because of the nature of the support. Likewise, a jury could infer a specific intent when a defendant knows that the organization continues to commit illegal acts and the defendant provides funds to that organization knowing that money is fungible and, once received, the donee can use the funds for any purpose it chooses. That is, by its nature, money carries an inherent danger for furthering the illegal aims of an organization. Congress said as much when it found that FTOs were "so tainted by their criminal conduct that any contribution to such an organization facilitates that conduct."

This opinion in no way creates a safe harbor for terrorists or their supporters to try and avoid prosecution through utilization of shell "charitable organizations" or by directing money through the memo line of a check towards lawful activities. This Court believes that a jury can quickly peer through such facades when appropriate. This is especially true if other facts indicate a defendant's true intent, like where defendants or conspirators utilize codes or unusual transaction practices to transfer funds. Instead, this Court's holding works to avoid potential constitutional problems and fully accomplish congressional intent.

While no court has construed the criminal prohibition contained in IEEPA, this Court concludes that a conviction under IEEPA in these circumstances requires similar proof of intent similar to that required under AEDPA. In other words, this Court concludes that to criminally convict a defendant for violating IEEPA the government must prove a defendant: (a) knew either that an organization was a SDT or committed unlawful activities that caused it to be designated as a SDT; and (b) had a specific intent that the contribution be used to further the unlawful activities of the SDT. This Court's conclusion is based on the plain language of Section 1705(b), which criminalizes only "willfully" committed violations of the Executive Order and the regulations interpreting the Executive Order.

Before reaching the constitutional issues, this Court has one additional statutory construction issue to determine: whether 8 U.S.C. § 1189(a)(8) precludes judicial review of a constitutional challenge to AEDPA. Section 1189(a)(8) provides that a criminal defendant may not "raise any question concerning the validity of the issuance of such designation as a defense or objection at any trial or hearing." Defendants argue that Section 1189(a)(8) only precludes review of the Secretary's designation of an organization as a FTO and not a criminal defendant's ability to raise a constitutional challenge. This Court agrees.

In addition to the general rules of statutory construction discussed above, the Supreme Court requires a clear and convincing showing of congressional intent before a court construes a statute to prohibit judicial review because of the serious constitutional concerns that such a prohibition causes. The most natural reading of Section 1189(a)(8) prohibits a criminal defendant from challenging the designation of an organization as a FTO, but does not prohibit a criminal defendant from challenging AEDPA's constitutionality. Neither the language, the structure, nor the legislative history of AEDPA suggests that Congress intended to preclude a criminal defendant from asserting that AEDPA is unconstitutional. Moreover, this Court's construction of Section 1189(a)(8) is reinforced by the Supreme Court's decision and construction of a similarly worded clause in Johnson. Therefore, this Court concludes that this Court may review the constitutionality of AEDPA.

This Court will address two points raised by Defendants as to the Indictment in general. First, this Court agrees with the government that the Indictment does not criminalize "pure speech." Instead, the overt acts section of the Indictment utilizes the speech of Defendants to show the existence of the conspiracies, the Defendants' agreement to participate in them, their level of participation or role in them, and the Defendants' criminal intent. It is well established that the government can use speech to prove elements of crimes such as motive or intent. The fact that Defendants' speech is contained in the overt act section of the Indictment is of little consequence. As the Eleventh Circuit stated in United States v. Lanier, "an overt act need not be criminal, and may indeed be otherwise innocent ...." (920 F.2d 887, 893 11th Cir. 1991). In support of that proposition, the Eleventh Circuit cited to and relied on a Seventh Circuit case that held constitutionally protected speech can constitute an overt act. The reason that an overt act can include even protected speech is that it is the agreement that is punishable in a conspiracy charge and not the overt act itself. Therefore, this Court denies Defendants' motion to dismiss on "pure speech" grounds.

Second, this Court declines Defendants' invitation to heighten the level of First Amendment protection given to seeking and donating funds. The Supreme Court has repeatedly considered the issue and determined that such activities are more like expressive conduct than pure speech. The Supreme Court has termed the protection of the foreign policy interests of the United States to be of great importance. Likewise, other courts have concluded that the government's interest in stopping the spread of global terrorism is "paramount" or "substantial." This Court agrees and would conclude that stopping the spread of terrorism is not just a sufficiently important governmental interest, but is a compelling governmental interest.

Similarly, a congressional decision to stop the spread of global terrorism by preventing fundraising and prohibiting support is closely drawn to further this interest. This Court's construction of AEDPA and IEEPA (requiring proof of a specific intent to further the unlawful activities of a SDT or FTO) reinforces this Court's conclusion that the prohibitions in AEDPA and IEEPA are closely drawn to further the governmental interest. Therefore, this Court denies Defendants' motion to dismiss on First Amendment grounds.

Finally, Defendants argue that Counts 1 through 4 attempt to punish the Defendants for conduct that was not criminal when it took place in violation of the ex post facto clause of the Constitution. Defendants argue that this Court should strike any overt act or reference to an act that occurred prior to PIJ's designation as a FTO (October 8, 1997) or prior to PIJ's designation as a SDT (January 23, 1995). Alternatively, Defendants argue that this Court should strike any act prior to the respective designation date from Counts 3 and 4. The government responds that the Defendants' conduct in this case has always been unlawful and that the PIJ's designation as a SDT and a FTO provided additional bases for criminal liability. The government also responds that conduct prior to either designation date is relevant to Counts 3 and 4 because Defendants are charged with being in conspiracies that continued after the conduct was criminalized and acts prior to the designation dates go to the existence of a conspiracy, the parties' agreement, and Defendants' purpose, motive, and intent.

Neither of Defendants' arguments are well taken. Defendants are correct only to the extent that the ex post facto clause prohibits the enactment by Congress of a statute that punishes an act which was innocent when committed. However, Counts 1 and 2 of the Indictment seek to punish Defendants for violating 18 U.S.C. §§ 1962(d) and 956(a)(1). Both statutes were enacted (1970 and 1948 respectively) well prior to any act alleged in the Indictment. As to Counts 3 and 4, the Eleventh Circuit has held that the ex post facto clause was not violated when a conspiracy continues after the effective date of a statute making that action illegal. The Indictment alleges overt acts in furtherance of the conspiracy after 1995 and 1997. Therefore, this Court denies Defendants' motions to dismiss or strike on ex post facto grounds.

Defendants also argue that the Indictment violates their Fifth and Sixth Amendment rights by giving them insufficient notice of the crimes with which they are charged such that Defendants cannot prepare an adequate defense. For example, Defendants claim Count 1 provides insufficient notice of what two predicate acts Defendants knowingly or intentionally agreed would be committed by the conspiracy. Defendants also argue that these infirmities cause a second due process violation because they do not give Defendants notice of the potential penalty. Finally, Defendants argue that certain counts and allegations contained in the Indictment should be dismissed or stricken because the government has admitted that it misidentified the speaker or its identification of the speaker is suspect. This Court concludes that Defendants' motions challenging the sufficiency of the Indictment should be denied.

Defendants move to strike the words "terrorism," "terrorist" and "terrorist activity" from the Indictment. The standard for striking surplusage is "exacting" and requires it to be clear that the allegedly surplus language is irrelevant to the charge and is also inflammatory and prejudicial. This Court cannot conclude that the use of the words "terrorism," "terrorist," and "terrorist activity" are irrelevant. First and foremost, an essential element of two of the charges against Defendants is that they supported and conducted prohibited transactions with groups designated by the United States as terrorists. Second, the government can prove Defendants' participation, intent, and the existence of the four conspiracies alleged in the Indictment in part by showing the acts of the groups with which he was affiliated with and aided committed terrorist acts.

Second, Defendants move to strike all phrases that indicate animus towards the United States. Defendants argue that such phrases are irrelevant to the charges against them and are also highly prejudicial. The government argues that such phrases are relevant to the nature and goals of the PIJ enterprise and show Defendants' motive and intent. At this stage, this Court will reserve ruling on Defendants' motion to strike these phrases until determining the language's relevance at trial.

After reviewing the motions, this Court concludes that the motions for reconsideration should be denied.

It is therefore ORDERED AND ADJUDGED that:

1. Defendant Ballut's Motion to Dismiss or Strike Counts 1 through 4, 19, 36 through 38, and 40 through 42 (Dkt. # 200) is DENIED in part and DEFERRED in part.

2. Defendant Ballut shall file within FIVE (5) DAYS from the date of this Order a legal

memorandum of no more than FIVE (5) PAGES addressing the applicability of the statute of limitations to Count 19. The government shall file a response FIVE (5) DAYS after the date of service of no more than FIVE (5) PAGES.

3. Defendant Al-Arian's Motion to Dismiss Counts 1, 2, 3 and 4 of the Indictment (Dkt. # 245) is DENIED.

4. Defendant Fariz's Motion to Dismiss Count 44 of the Indictment (Dkt. # 250) is DENIED.

5. Defendant's Fariz's Motion to Strike Surplusage (Dkt. # 251) is DENIED in part and DEFERRED in part.

6. Defendant Fariz's Motion to Dismiss Count 1 of the Indictment (Dkt. # 255) is DENIED.

7. Defendant Fariz's Motion to Strike as Surplusage Paragraphs 43(236), (240), (247), and (253) of the Indictment, and to Dismiss Counts 35, 37, 41, and 43 of the Indictment (Dkt. # 256) is DENIED without prejudice.

8. Defendant Al-Arian's Amended Motion to Dismiss Counts 1, 2, 3 and 4 of the Indictment (Dkt. # 273) is DENIED.

9. Defendant Fariz's Motion to Dismiss Counts 3 and 4 of the Indictment (Dkt. # 301) is DENIED.

10. Defendant Fariz's Motion to Quash Section (b) of Paragraph 26 of the Indictment for Failure to State a Legal Basis for Relief (Dkt. # 302) is GRANTED.

11. Defendant Fariz's Request for Oral Argument on Defendant's Pretrial Motions (Dkt. # 303) is DENIED as moot.

12. Defendant Hammoudeh's Motion to Dismiss Count 1 of the Indictment (Dkt. # 313) is DENIED.

13. Defendant Hammoudeh's Amended Motion to Dismiss Count 1 of the Indictment (Dkt. # 330) is DENIED.

14. Defendant Fariz's Motion for Reconsideration of Magistrate Judge's Order Denying in Part Fariz's Motion for Bill of Particulars (Dkt. # 440) is DENIED.

15. Defendant Ballut's Motion for Reconsideration of Motion for Bill of Particulars (Dkt. # 441) is DENIED.

SECTION 3: TERRORIST TRIALS BY MILITARY COURTS AFTER 9/11

OVERVIEW

Individuals who are suspected of committing terrorist acts can be tried in Article III courts or for war crimes in special military courts. Trials that occur in Article III courts follow all the same procedures discussed in chapters ten through fourteen. In military courts however, there are relaxed rules of procedure and proof, as well as diminished rights for the defendants. The President can establish a military commission, which is a panel of military officers that act under military authority to try war crimes, under three sources of authority: Article II, Section 2 of the U.S. Constitution which makes him commander in chief of the armed forces; Article II, Section 2 of the U.S. Constitution which gives the President the power to ensure laws are executed; and the joint resolution which gives the President the power to use all necessary force against persons considered terrorists. Keep in mind that the power of the military commission extends only to noncitizen who do not benefit from the same constitutional rights as American citizens, even if the individual is in the U.S. legally. Further, such individuals are removed from the jurisdiction of all courts in and outside the U.S. Finally, no constitutional provisions apply which means the defendant has no right to a speedy trial, no right to trial by jury, no right to counsel, no right to remain silent, and there exists no requirement of proof beyond a reasonable doubt. If found guilty by the military commission panel, any sentence, including that of death, may be imposed.

In November 2001, President Bush declared an emergency in response to 9/11 which empowered him to order military trials for any individual suspected of being or collaborating with a terrorist. This results in the bypass of the American criminal justice system and all the rules of evidence and constitutional guarantees that we have discussed throughout this text. There is no judicial review and the President himself decides which defendants will face such trials. While this measure is unusual, it is not unprecedented and occurred under President Franklin D. Roosevelt during World War II. Under Roosevelt, eight suspected Nazis were tried by military commission and executed while the U.S. Supreme Court maintained that the trial was unconstitutional. The rationale used to support such commissions is "the interest of national security." An important sidenote is that some scholars and activists favor creation of international tribunals under the authority of the United Nations which would not authorize the death penalty.

CONCLUSION

This chapter elaborated what can result during times of emergency, and what has resulted since 9/11. In such a period, there is a temporary recalibration of the balance between government power and individual liberties with the result being an expansion of governmental power, especially for noncitizens. Most of this occurs at the federal level, making application at the state level weak, though this chapter did examine an upcoming case of a former University of South Florida professor.

CONSTITUTION OF THE STATE OF FLORIDA

AS REVISED IN 1968 AND SUBSEQUENTLY AMENDED

The Constitution of the State of Florida as revised in 1968 consisted of certain revised articles as proposed by three joint resolutions which were adopted during the special session of June 24-July 3, 1968, and ratified by the electorate on November 5, 1968, together with one article carried forward from the Constitution of 1885, as amended. The articles proposed in House Joint Resolution 1-2X constituted the entire revised constitution with the exception of Articles V, VI, and VIII. Senate Joint Resolution 4-2X proposed Article VI, relating to suffrage and elections. Senate Joint Resolution 5-2X proposed a new Article VIII, relating to local government. Article V, relating to the judiciary, was carried forward from the Constitution of 1885, as amended.

Sections composing the 1968 revision have no history notes. Subsequent changes are indicated by notes appended to the affected sections. The indexes appearing at the beginning of each article, notes appearing at the end of various sections, and section and subsection headings are added editorially and are not to be considered as part of the constitution.

PREAMBLE

We, the people of the State of Florida, being grateful to Almighty God for our constitutional liberty, in order to secure its benefits, perfect our government, insure domestic tranquility, maintain public order, and guarantee equal civil and political rights to all, do ordain and establish this constitution.

ARTICLE I

DECLARATION OF RIGHTS

SECTION 1. **Political power.**--All political power is inherent in the people. The enunciation herein of certain rights shall not be construed to deny or impair others retained by the people.

SECTION 2. **Basic rights.**--All natural persons, female and male alike, are equal before the law and have inalienable rights, among which are the right to enjoy and defend life and liberty, to pursue happiness, to be rewarded for industry, and to acquire, possess and protect property; except that the ownership, inheritance, disposition and possession of real property by aliens ineligible for citizenship may be regulated or prohibited by law. No person shall be deprived of any right because of race, religion, national origin, or physical disability.

History.--Am. S.J.R. 917, 1974; adopted 1974; Am. proposed by Constitution Revision Commission, Revision No. 9, 1998, filed with the Secretary of State May 5, 1998; adopted 1998.

SECTION 3. **Religious freedom.**--There shall be no law respecting the establishment of religion or prohibiting or penalizing the free exercise thereof. Religious freedom shall not justify practices inconsistent with public morals, peace or safety. No revenue of the state or any political subdivision or agency thereof shall ever be taken from the public treasury directly or indirectly in aid of any church, sect, or religious denomination or in aid of any sectarian institution.

SECTION 4. **Freedom of speech and press.**--Every person may speak, write and publish sentiments on all subjects but shall be responsible for the abuse of that right. No law shall be passed to restrain or abridge the liberty of speech or of the press. In all criminal prosecutions and civil actions for defamation the truth may be given in evidence. If the matter charged as defamatory is true and was published with good motives, the party shall be acquitted or exonerated.

History.--Am. proposed by Constitution Revision Commission, Revision No. 13, 1998, filed with the Secretary of State May 5, 1998; adopted 1998.

SECTION 5. **Right to assemble.**--The people shall have the right peaceably to assemble, to instruct their representatives, and to petition for redress of grievances.

SECTION 6. **Right to work.**--The right of persons to work shall not be denied or abridged on account of membership or non-membership in any labor union or labor organization. The right of employees, by and through a labor organization, to bargain collectively shall not be denied or abridged. Public employees shall not have the right to strike.

SECTION 7. **Military power.**--The military power shall be subordinate to the civil.

SECTION 8. **Right to bear arms.**--

(a) The right of the people to keep and bear arms in defense of themselves and of the lawful authority of the state shall not be infringed, except that the manner of bearing arms may be regulated by law.

(b) There shall be a mandatory period of three days, excluding weekends and legal holidays, between the purchase and delivery at retail of any handgun. For the purposes of this section, "purchase" means the transfer of money or other valuable consideration to the retailer, and "handgun" means a firearm capable of being carried and used by one hand, such as a pistol or revolver. Holders of a concealed weapon permit as prescribed in Florida law shall not be subject to the provisions of this paragraph.

(c) The legislature shall enact legislation implementing subsection (b) of this section, effective no later than December 31, 1991, which shall provide that anyone violating the provisions of subsection (b) shall be guilty of a felony.

(d) This restriction shall not apply to a trade in of another handgun.

History.--Am. C.S. for S.J.R. 43, 1989; adopted 1990.

SECTION 9. **Due process.**--No person shall be deprived of life, liberty or property without due process of law, or be twice put in jeopardy for the same offense, or be compelled in any criminal matter to be a witness against oneself.

History.--Am. proposed by Constitution Revision Commission, Revision No. 13, 1998, filed with the Secretary of State May 5, 1998; adopted 1998.

SECTION 10. **Prohibited laws.**--No bill of attainder, ex post facto law or law impairing the obligation of contracts shall be passed.

SECTION 11. **Imprisonment for debt.**--No person shall be imprisoned for debt, except in cases of fraud.

SECTION 12. **Searches and seizures.**--The right of the people to be secure in their persons, houses, papers and effects against unreasonable searches and seizures, and against the unreasonable interception of private communications by any means, shall not be violated. No warrant shall be issued except upon probable cause, supported by affidavit, particularly describing the place or places to be searched, the person or persons, thing or things to be seized, the communication to be intercepted, and the nature of evidence to be obtained. This right shall be construed in conformity with the 4th Amendment to the United States Constitution, as interpreted by the United States Supreme Court. Articles or information obtained in violation of this right shall not be admissible in evidence if such articles or information would be inadmissible under decisions of the United States Supreme Court construing the 4th Amendment to the United States Constitution.

History.--Am. H.J.R. 31-H, 1982; adopted 1982.

SECTION 13. **Habeas corpus.**--The writ of habeas corpus shall be grantable of right, freely and without cost. It shall be returnable without delay, and shall never be suspended unless, in case of rebellion or invasion, suspension is essential to the public safety.

SECTION 14. **Pretrial release and detention.**--Unless charged with a capital offense or an offense punishable by life imprisonment and the proof of guilt is evident or the presumption is great, every person charged with a crime or violation of municipal or county ordinance shall be entitled to pretrial release on reasonable conditions. If no conditions of release can reasonably protect the community from risk of physical harm to persons, assure the presence of the accused at trial, or assure the integrity of the judicial process, the accused may be detained.

History.--Am. H.J.R. 43-H, 1982; adopted 1982.

SECTION 15. **Prosecution for crime; offenses committed by children.**--

(a) No person shall be tried for capital crime without presentment or indictment by a grand jury, or for other felony without such presentment or indictment or an information under oath filed by the prosecuting officer of the court, except persons on active duty in the militia when tried by courts martial.

(b) When authorized by law, a child as therein defined may be charged with a violation of law as an act of delinquency instead of crime and tried without a jury or other requirements applicable to criminal cases. Any child so charged shall, upon demand made as provided by law before a trial in a juvenile proceeding, be tried in an appropriate court as an adult. A child found delinquent shall be disciplined as provided by law.

SECTION 16. **Rights of accused and of victims.**--

(a) In all criminal prosecutions the accused shall, upon demand, be informed of the nature and cause of the accusation, and shall be furnished a copy of the charges, and shall have the right to have compulsory process for witnesses, to confront at trial adverse witnesses, to be heard in person, by counsel or both, and to have a speedy and public trial by impartial jury in the county where the crime was committed. If the county is not known, the indictment or information may charge venue in two or more counties conjunctively and proof that the crime was committed in that area shall be sufficient; but before pleading the accused may elect in which of those counties the trial will take place. Venue for prosecution of crimes committed beyond the boundaries of the state shall be fixed by law.

(b) Victims of crime or their lawful representatives, including the next of kin of homicide victims, are entitled to the right to be informed, to be present, and to be heard when relevant, at all crucial stages of criminal proceedings, to the extent that these rights do not interfere with the constitutional rights of the accused.

History.--Am. S.J.R. 135, 1987; adopted 1988; Am. proposed by Constitution Revision Commission, Revision No. 13, 1998, filed with the Secretary of State May 5, 1998; adopted 1998.

SECTION 17. **Excessive punishments.**--Excessive fines, cruel and unusual punishment, attainder, forfeiture of estate, indefinite imprisonment, and unreasonable detention of witnesses are forbidden. The death penalty is an authorized punishment for capital crimes designated by the legislature. The prohibition against cruel or unusual punishment, and the prohibition against cruel and unusual punishment, shall be construed in conformity with decisions of the United States Supreme Court which interpret the prohibition against cruel and unusual punishment provided in the Eighth Amendment to the United States Constitution. Any method of execution shall be allowed, unless prohibited by the United States Constitution. Methods of execution may be designated by the legislature, and a change in any method of execution may be applied retroactively. A sentence of death shall not be reduced on the basis that a method of execution is invalid. In any case in which an execution method is declared invalid, the death sentence shall remain in force until the sentence can be lawfully executed by any valid method. This section shall apply retroactively.

History.--Am. H.J.R. 3505, 1998; adopted 1998; Am. H.J.R. 951, 2001; adopted 2002.

SECTION 18. **Administrative penalties.**--No administrative agency, except the Department of Military Affairs in an appropriately convened court-martial action as provided by law, shall

278

impose a sentence of imprisonment, nor shall it impose any other penalty except as provided by law.

History.--Am. proposed by Constitution Revision Commission, Revision No. 13, 1998, filed with the Secretary of State May 5, 1998; adopted 1998.

SECTION 19. **Costs.**--No person charged with crime shall be compelled to pay costs before a judgment of conviction has become final.

SECTION 20. **Treason.**--Treason against the state shall consist only in levying war against it, adhering to its enemies, or giving them aid and comfort, and no person shall be convicted of treason except on the testimony of two witnesses to the same overt act or on confession in open court.

SECTION 21. **Access to courts.**--The courts shall be open to every person for redress of any injury, and justice shall be administered without sale, denial or delay.

SECTION 22. **Trial by jury.**--The right of trial by jury shall be secure to all and remain inviolate. The qualifications and the number of jurors, not fewer than six, shall be fixed by law.

SECTION 23. **Right of privacy.**--Every natural person has the right to be let alone and free from governmental intrusion into the person's private life except as otherwise provided herein. This section shall not be construed to limit the public's right of access to public records and meetings as provided by law.

History.--Added, C.S. for H.J.R. 387, 1980; adopted 1980; Am. proposed by Constitution Revision Commission, Revision No. 13, 1998, filed with the Secretary of State May 5, 1998; adopted 1998.

SECTION 24. **Access to public records and meetings.**--

(a) Every person has the right to inspect or copy any public record made or received in connection with the official business of any public body, officer, or employee of the state, or persons acting on their behalf, except with respect to records exempted pursuant to this section or specifically made confidential by this Constitution. This section specifically includes the legislative, executive, and judicial branches of government and each agency or department created thereunder; counties, municipalities, and districts; and each constitutional officer, board, and commission, or entity created pursuant to law or this Constitution.

(b) All meetings of any collegial public body of the executive branch of state government or of any collegial public body of a county, municipality, school district, or special district, at which official acts are to be taken or at which public business of such body is to be transacted or discussed, shall be open and noticed to the public and meetings of the legislature shall be open and noticed as provided in Article III, Section 4(e), except with respect to meetings exempted pursuant to this section or specifically closed by this Constitution.

(c) This section shall be self-executing. The legislature, however, may provide by general law passed by a two-thirds vote of each house for the exemption of records from the requirements of subsection (a) and the exemption of meetings from the requirements of subsection (b), provided that such law shall state with specificity the public necessity justifying the exemption and shall be no broader than necessary to accomplish the stated purpose of the law. The legislature shall enact laws governing the enforcement of this section, including the maintenance, control, destruction, disposal, and disposition of records made public by this section, except that each house of the legislature may adopt rules governing the enforcement of this section in relation to records of the legislative branch. Laws enacted pursuant to this subsection shall contain only exemptions from the requirements of subsections (a) or (b) and provisions governing the enforcement of this section, and shall relate to one subject.

(d) All laws that are in effect on July 1, 1993 that limit public access to records or meetings shall remain in force, and such laws apply to records of the legislative and judicial branches, until they are repealed. Rules of court that are in effect on the date of adoption of this section that limit access to records shall remain in effect until they are repealed.

History.--Added, C.S. for C.S. for H.J.R.'s 1727, 863, 2035, 1992; adopted 1992; Am. S.J.R. 1284, 2002; adopted 2002.

[1]SECTION 25. **Taxpayers' Bill of Rights.**--By general law the legislature shall prescribe and adopt a Taxpayers' Bill of Rights that, in clear and concise language, sets forth taxpayers' rights and responsibilities and government's responsibilities to deal fairly with taxpayers under the laws of this state. This section shall be effective July 1, 1993.